1987

Computer
Graphics
in Application

Computer Graphics in Application

GEORGE R. MARSHALL

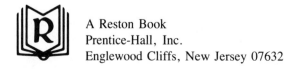

A Reston Book
Prentice-Hall, Inc.
Englewood Cliffs, New Jersey 07632

Library of Congress Cataloging-in-Publication Data

Marshall, George R.
  Computer graphics in application.

  1. Computer graphics.   I. Title.
T385.M366 1987   006.6   86-9337
ISBN 0-8359-0997-2

Editorial/production supervision: *Joan McCulley*
Cover design: *Photo Plus Art*
Manufacturing buyer: *Ed O'Dougherty*

A Reston Book
Published by Prentice-Hall, Inc.
A Division of Simon & Schuster
Englewood Cliffs, New Jersey 07632

Printed in the United States of America

10   9   8   7   6   5   4   3   2   1

ISBN   0-8359-0997-2   025

Prentice-Hall International (UK) Limited, *London*
Prentice-Hall of Australia Pty. Limited, *Sydney*
Prentice-Hall Canada Inc., *Toronto*
Prentice-Hall Hispanoamericana, S.A., *Mexico*
Prentice-Hall of India Private Limited, *New Delhi*
Prentice-Hall of Japan, Inc., *Tokyo*
Prentice-Hall of southeast Asia Pte. Ltd., *Singapore*
Editora Prentice-Hall do Brasil, Ltda., *Rio de Janeiro*

This text is dedicated
to my teacher and brother, Ösel Tendzin,
for his profound and brilliant insight and inspiration,
to my mother, Anne Lee Marshall,
for her unfailing friendship,
and to both for their kindness and love.

CONTENTS

PREFACE

• PURPOSE OF THIS TEXT

The purpose of this text is to show what people are doing with computer graphics and, therefore, what the reader can do. The applications for computer graphics are vast and profound. We are in the midst of a great transition and revolution, where the individual is being provided with powerful tools of communication and connection: the graphics-based personal computer workstation, custom configured to individual needs, networked together and supported by big computers.

The approach used in the text is the description of computer graphics systems and applications in many areas, supported by illustrated examples that the reader can explore directly. That is, in large measure, the graphics systems and software used as vehicles of instruction in the text are generally available. Further, the reader is provided with all the necessary technical information on hardware and software required to understand the applications being discussed. The reader is also introduced to computer graphics programming using BASIC, LOGO, and Pascal, and to new emerging approaches to programming.

We are in a period of transition from the industrial to the information age. "We are drowning in information and starved for knowledge," writes John Naisbitt in *Megatrends*. If a picture is worth a thousand words (or ten thousand bytes), then computer graphics may be a "lifebelt" to help us stop drowning.

Computer graphics is both a new language and a new medium; not until very recently was it generally available. Computer graphics belonged to the high priests of computer technology, requiring esoteric skills in programming performed on very expensive computers, or computers designed by pioneer explorers, to create images. Now it belongs to all of us.

But will we take advantage of our new inheritance? Unless we are familiar with it, the answer is no. It has been estimated that of 30 million people who will have the opportunity to use computer graphics in the next decade, only 5 percent, or 1.5 million, will do so.

We need to learn about computer graphics because it is powerful; computer-generated imagery defies us to distinguish between reality and illusion. We need to know what it can do to us and what we can do with it. We need to learn the *know-how* in order to understand the *know-why*. The new medium moves us from *passive receivers to active producers* and promises to counteract the effect of *non*interactive media, identified by Marshall McLuhan as "perceptual numbing" in which only the most extreme experiences have any impact.

• THE IBM PC AND THE APPLE MACINTOSH

A large proportion of the graphics applications in this text are based on graphics systems and software available for the IBM PC and the Apple Macintosh. Many other systems are discussed, however, and an extensive list of graphics systems classified by application (presentation graphics, analytic graphics, computer-aided design, paint systems, graphics workstations), is included in Appendix C.

• WHO SHOULD READ THIS TEXT

Students in business, management, commerce, economics, education, government, social science, applied social science, communication, media, art, design, the humanities, liberal arts, or those studying for entry into a profession (law, medicine) will benefit from this text, especially if there is an interest in the communication, education, training, or management aspects of their disciplines or professions. Computer science students requiring a survey of graphics applications will also benefit from this text.

• COURSES SUPPORTED

Courses supported include *Introduction to Computers; Computer Literacy; Computers in Application;* and *Computers in Business,* especially if the instructor wishes to emphasize a graphics approach (graphics is becoming the interface or connection of choice between man and machine); *Introduction to Computer Graphics; Computer Graphics in Business, Management, and Marketing; Computer Graphics in Application, Communication and Media;* and courses for teacher education and training.

The text is also suitable as a *supplementary text for a computer graphics course for computer science students*, when the intent of the course is to introduce students to graphics applications, prior to or in parallel with graphics programming. Computer science students are often unaware of the computers' capabilities in relation to real-life problems. Such information is *not* readily acquired during summer employment, or soon after graduation.

• BACKGROUND

No knowledge of computer operation or functioning is required as background for this text. Chapter 2 provides an overview of what a computer is and how it works. Interest and some sense of confidence, however, are required. Many of us are afraid of technical language and subjects, incorrectly relating the use of technology to an understanding of mathematics or science. We simply assume we cannot understand such matters; we do not have the mind for it. No special mind is required. There is no such thing.

Technical discussions in the text that relate to an understanding of the internal functioning of computer graphics systems are minimal but complete. People prefer to read and scan more for the purpose of clarity, than to read and scan less in the service of obscurity. People prefer being treated as if they were intelligent. Einstein believed that any subject, no matter how technical, could be explained in understandable terms to the interested person.

Sometimes a number of images have been used to illustrate the same point. A professor of mine believed that he had to repeat every lecture three times since as he said "at any given time one third of you are asleep." This, as you might imagine, led to some extremely boring lectures. I hope multiple images will not lead to the same comatose state, but rather enrich understanding.

• WHAT THE READER CAN EXPECT TO GAIN FROM THIS TEXT

The reader will learn *how* to use computer graphics to communicate, influence, analyze, organize, design, model, simulate, animate, signal, control, monitor, program, and evaluate. The learning will *not* be abstract, but will relate to the use of tools that exist *now*, and that are, in large measure, readily available.

In order to arouse the reader's *exploration of creative possibilities* in his or her own field, examples from many disciplines have been described. They include applications in management, business, operations research, economics, design, architecture, art, education, anthropology, and others. Fields of study are not mutually exclusive. Discoveries in one arouse insights into others. An application of computer graphics in anthropology, for example, may arouse a creative solution to a business or management problem. Artists are business people, designers are researchers, and managers are philosophers. Interesting things are more likely to happen at the edge or border of things, not in the middle.

Computer graphics has its roots in the *evolution* of computation, computers, communication, and media. In Chapter 1 a chart is used to show the historical development of those roots up until the present day, and to provide the reader with some perspective. Not everything important started in 1950.

The emphasis is on applications, not programming. However, this text attempts to *open the doors to programming* by introducing the reader to BASIC, Pascal, and LOGO, and by presenting recently developed languages in which graphics itself is used to program. Since we learn by imitating, I have taken the approach of presenting small graphics programs in these three languages that the reader can enter, modify, and expand using whatever computer facilities are available. Sometimes the programs in the different languages produce the same or similar output, thus allowing for comparison. Elsewhere in the text, graphics command languages are discussed as used in various professions such as architecture, engineering, product design, and publishing.

• ORGANIZATION OF THE TEXT

The text is organized into four broad parts: *introduction, applications, programming,* and *needs*. The table of contents shows the obvious emphasis on applications. The reader may choose to study Chapter 2 and the other background chapters in the introduction in digestible doses, and read the applications chapters in parallel.

In order to make sense of the plethora of technical terms and relations, *taxonomies* have been developed of computer hardware and software in various contexts throughout the text. Many disciplines use taxonomies to help make sense of data, for example, Zoology, and we need to develop similar organizing structures for all the "species" of computer hardware and software.

A conscious effort was made throughout the text to *define terms* accurately but simply. Specialized languages are necessary, but if new terms are not defined precisely they can add to the confusion and create an unnecessary "mystique."

For each chapter a set of *questions, problems,* and *field exercises* is provided.

• A NOTE TO INSTRUCTORS

Although the text uses IBM PC and Apple Macintosh, and software for these systems as the prime vehicles for discussing computer graphics, *any* graphics computer system may be used along with this text. It is the *principles* discussed, *not* products, that constitute the heart of the book.

Color plates have *not* been used in this text. Color raises cost. It is suggested that a set of slides be used in the course to demonstrate color computer graphics. Slides for presentation graphics, analytic graphics, art, and design are often available from publishers and producers of graphics software and hardware.

The text will support either a half year or a full year program of study. The materials in the text, and the questions and exercises in Appendix A, have been designed to support the *three-pronged educational approach* discussed briefly in the conclusion to the last chapter of this text, namely: *lecture, experiment,* and *experience in practical application.* The instructor will find support for all three of these approaches in each chapter.

The appendices involve different kinds of activities including assigning tests, exercises, and field projects; reviewing product descriptions and the products themselves, and evaluating and comparing computer graphics software and hardware.

A course of study that includes the hands-on use of graphics computer systems is necessary for students to experience the synergy that comes from interactive use. It is suggested that a *tutorial workshop* be offered introducing students to computer operation. In this manner, students will progress rapidly to application, and not spend too much time getting to know the system and learning how to push buttons and move mice.

The author is interested in hearing from instructors with suggestions for improvements and information on where and how the text is being used:

Dr. George R. Marshall, Associate Professor   Dr. George R. Marshall, President
Department of Finance and Management Science   G. R. Marshall & Associates, Consultants
St. Mary's University   2112 Bauer Street
Halifax, Nova Scotia, B3H 3C3   Halifax, Nova Scotia, B3K 3W3

ACKNOWLEDGMENTS

Many people and companies helped write and produce this text. However, the author wishes to extend a special word of thanks to the following people for their continued and unflagging support: Al Atkinson of Mensa Computers, Dartmouth, Nova Scotia; my good friend, Christine Anthony; Wayne Brehaut of the Jodrey School of Computer Science, Acadia University, Wolfville, Nova Scotia, who always had time to listen and offer valuable advice; and Jeff Jordan, a graduate of Kings Regional Vocational School, Kentville, Nova Scotia, who gave unstintingly of his time far beyond the call of duty. Also my thanks to the people at Prentice-Hall; they tried to keep me away from dangerous paths, but sometimes I strayed. They include the executive editor of computer science texts, Jim Fegen, and Joan McCulley, the production editor for the text.

This text was produced on an *Apple Macintosh* computer and *LaserWriter* printer using primarily *1st Base*, *Factfinder*, and *ThinkTank*, to organize information, and *MacWrite*, *MacPaint*, and *MacDraw*, to produce text and images. *PageMaker* was used to layout all pages. My many thanks to all of the creative inventors and producers of these innovative products. Surely, without these tools I could not have produced this entire book.

The following products are registered trademarks ® of the companies indicated:

Product	Company
Apple	Apple Computer, Inc.
Atari	Atari, Inc.
Apple IIe	Apple Computer, Inc.
ATT 6300	AT&T Bell Laboratories
ATT PC	AT&T Bell Laboratories
ATT UNIX	AT&T Bell Laboratories
Business Filevision	Telos Software Products
CP/M	Digital Research Inc.
CP/M 80	Digital Research Inc.
CP/M 86	Digital Research Inc.
ClickArt Personal Publisher	T/Maker Company
DEC VAX	Digital Equipment Corporation
Do-It	Studio Software Corporation
Filevision	Telos Software Products
IBM	IBM Corporation
IBM Quietwriter	IBM Corporation
IBM 3270 PC/G	IBM Corporation
IBM PC	IBM Corporation
IBM PC AT	IBM Corporation
IBM PC XT	IBM Corporation
IBM PC/GX	IBM Corporation
IBM System/360	IBM Corporation
Jazz	Lotus Development Corporation
Lotus 1-2-3	Lotus Development Corporation
Macintosh is licensed to	Apple Computer, Inc.
MicroSoft	MicroSoft Corporation
MS-DOS	MicroSoft Corporation
Multiplan	MicroSoft Corporation
Omnis 3	Blyth Software Inc.
PFS:File	Software Publishing Corporation
PFS:Graph	Software Publishing Corporation
Prime	Prime Computer, Inc.
Sci-Mate	Institute for Scientific Information
Softstrip	Cauzin
Sun-2/50 Workstation	Sun Microsystems, Inc.
Sun-3/160 Workstation	Sun Microsystems, Inc.
Sun Workstation	Sun Microsystems, Inc.
Symphony	Lotus Development Corporation
VisiCalc	Lotus Development Corporation
WordStar	Micropro International Corporation
Xerox 5700 electronic printer	Xerox Corporation
dBase II and dBase III	Ashton-Tate
smARTWORK	Wintek Corporation

The following products are trademarks ™ of the companies indicated:

Product	Company
1st Base	Desktop Software, Inc.
1st Merge	Desktop Software, Inc.
520ST	Atari, Inc
Advanced PRO-ject 6	Softcraft, Inc.
Amiga	Commodore-Amiga, Inc.
AppleTalk	Apple Computer, Inc.
Applesoft BASIC	Apple Computer, Inc.
Aria Standalone Color Workstation	Applicon Canada
Artwork	West End Film Inc.
Atlas	Starategic Locations Planning
AutoCAD	Autodesk Inc.
AutoMac	Genesis Micro Software
Automentor	Software Recording Corporation
BRS	BRS
Barriers & Bridges	G. R. Marshall & Assoc., Consultants
Business Filevision	Telos Software

Canon Laser Printer	Canon U.S.A. Corporation
Chameleon	Seequa Computer Corporation
Chart-Master	Decision Resources
Cheap Paint	Hayden Software Company Inc.
Compaq	Compaq Computer Corporation
Comtec DS-300	Daiken/Comtec
daVinci Building Blocks	Hayden Software Company Inc.
DEC and Rainbow 100	Digital Equipment Corporation
DFD Draw	McDonnell Douglas Automation Corporation
Data General/One	Data General Corporation
Datacopy Model 90	Datacopy Corporation
DecisionMap	SoftStyle, Inc.
Demo Program	Software Garden, Inc.
Diagraph	Computer Support Corporation
Draft Math	DM Systems
E-Chart	G. R. Marshall & Assoc., Consultants
EXECADD	Tritek Vision Systems
Easylan	Server Technology
Energraphics	Enertronics Research, Inc.
Engineering Toolkit	Sof-Tools
Entrepreneur	Microsoft Corporation
Ethermac	3Com
Ethernet	Xerox Corporation
Excelerator	Index Technology Corporation
Exec*U*Stat	Exec*U*Stat, Inc.
Executive Picture Show	PCsoftware
ExperLogo	ExperTelligence, Inc.
FONTagenix	Devonian International Software Company
Factfinder	Forethought Inc.
Filemaker	Forethought Inc.
Filevision	Telos Software
Fontrix	Data Transforms, Inc.
Framework	Ashton-Tate
Freelance	Graphics Communications, Inc.
Fugitsu Micro 16	Fujitsu America Inc.
GDSS	Data Business Vision, Inc.
Graphic Decision Support System	Data Business Vision, Inc.
GEM	Digital Research Inc.
Graftalk	Redding Group Inc.
Graphwriter	Graphics Communications, Inc.
HP 7470 personal computer plotter	Hewlett-Packard
HP 7475 personal computer plotter	Hewlett-Packard
Halographics	Media Cybernetics Inc.
Hayden:Speller	Hayden Software Company Inc.
Hewlett Packard Desk Plotter	Hewlett-Packard
Hotview	Lotus Development Corporation
Hypernet	General Computer
ImageWriter	Apple Computer, Inc.
Imagen's Software	Imagen Inc.
Imigit	Chorus Data Systems
Integral PC	Hewlett-Packard
Integrated Profit Planning Systems	Softouch Software Inc.
Interleaf Electronic Publishing System	Interleaf, Inc.
Kaypro 2,4,10	Kaypro, Inc.
Kurzweil 4000	Kurzweil Computer Products
Lanpac	Racore
LaserWriter	Apple Computer, Inc.
LightSource	Computer Learning Systems
MacAtlas	Micro;Maps
MacDraft	Innovative Data Design, Inc.
MacDraw	Apple Computer, Inc.
MacMap	Strategic Locations Planning
MacPaint	Apple Computer, Inc.
MacPlot	Microspot
MacProject	Apple Computer, Inc.
MacPublisher II	Boston Software Publishers Inc.
MacSpin	D2 Software
MacSurf	Graphic Magic
MacVision	Koala Technologies, Inc.
MacWrite	Apple Computer, Inc.

McPic! Volume 2	Magnum Software
Micro D-Cam	The Micromint, Inc.
MicroCAD	Diehl Graphsoft Inc.
Minicad 3D-Designer	Diehl Graphsoft Inc.
Morrow MDII	Morrow, Inc.
Mouse Artist	Village Computer Resources
MSFile	MicroSoft Corporation
Multidraw	Cymbol Cybernetics Corporation
Norton Utilities	Peter Norton Computing Inc.
ORCA	Orcatech
Odesta Helix	Odesta Corporation
OverVUE	Provue Development Corporation
PageMaker	Aldus Corporation
PC eye	Chorus Data Systems
PC/IT	Sperry Corporation
PERQ	Three Rivers Computer Corporation
Perceptor	Micro Control Systems, Inc.
Picture Perfect	Computer Support Corporation
PictureBase	Symmetry Corporation
PLATO	Control Data, Institute for Advanced Technology
Polycad/10	Cubicomp, Inc.
Princeton graphic systems	Princeton Graphics Systems
Pro-Search	Personal Bibliographic Software, Inc.
ProKey	Rosesoft
Professional Bibliographic System	Personal Bibliographic Software, Inc.
Profit Projections/Breakeven Analysis	Harris Technical Systems
Project Scheduler Network	Scitor Corporation
QuickWord	Enterset, Inc.
ReadySetGo	Manhattan Graphics
Reflex For The Mac	Borland International
SIGHT	Image Resource Corporation
Sage IV	Sage Systems Inc.
Samurai Image Processor	Image Resource Corporation
Sidekick	Borland International
Sign-Master	Decision Resources
Space Tablet	Micro Control Systems, Inc.
StatView	Brainpower, Inc.
Statmap	Ganesa Group International, Inc.
Super Project	Computer Associates International, Inc.
Switcher	Apple Computer, Inc.
Systemizer	Applied Creative Technology
Tekalike	Mesa Graphics
The Finder	Apple Computer, Inc.
ThinkTank	Living Videotext, Inc.
ThunderScan	Thunderware, Inc.
TopView	IBM Corporation
Turbo-graphix	Borland International
Type Processor One	Bestinfo, Inc.
UNIX	AT&T Bell Laboratories
VCN Concorde	Visual Communication Network, Inc.
Vetrix Midas Color Card	Vetrix Corporation
Videoshow 150	General Parametrics Corporation
VideoWorks	Hayden Software Company Inc.
WIPS (Word Image Processing System)	Datacopy Corporation
Windows	Microsoft Corporation
XTAR Graphics Micro processor	Xtar Electronics
ZyINDEX	Zylab Corporation

The following is a service mark of the company indicated:

Product	Company
Dialog	Dialog Information Services Inc.

The following are product names of the companies indicated:

Product	Company
GKS (Graphical Kernel System)	IBM Corporation
Graphics Development Toolkit	IBM Corporation
QuickDraw	Apple Computer, Inc.

Computer Graphics in Application

1

A Scenario, an Overview, and a History

1.1 IMAGES AND INFLUENCE: A SCENARIO

Let us imagine that we are involved in the establishment of a new venture: a library of applications software and computer systems that provides a place for people to evaluate, compare, and "test drive" many different computer system configurations prior to selection and purchase.* Further, the library supports consulting work, education and training, and a monthly newsletter distributed to subscribers. We are interested in raising venture capital, establishing one or two test locations, and then, if things prove worthwhile, we will consider opening other locations.

Before we embark on our venture, we call in a group of close and knowledgeable associates and ask them to listen to a presentation on this new venture. Knowing that the way we present the information is important, we decide to conduct the presentation under rather strict conditions. With one small group, we present *a supporting view of the venture with the aid of graphics*: summary statements, key words, graphs, and so forth. With another group we present *a critical view of the venture with the aid of graphics*. With a third small group, *no graphics are used* at all.

Our extremely cooperative colleagues are asked to respond to the venture proposal with a go or no-go response, and also to tell us what they think of the presentation itself.

1.2 SOME FINDINGS

The responses are enlightening. With the use of graphics our colleagues are swayed in the direction of the view being presented: 67 percent in agreement and 33 percent not in agreement. With no graphics it is a tossup: 50 percent for and 50 percent against. These results are diagrammed in Exhibit 1.1.

Further, presenters who use graphics are able to obtain closure on a decision in 28 percent less time and are perceived to be more professional, persuasive, credible, and interesting.

We seem to have discovered something about the impact of graphics. Our colleagues have not helped us make a decision about our new venture, but they have helped us discover a powerful tool. We decide that, in all our future work in creating, nurturing, and operating our enterprise, we will pay close attention to the analytic, communication, and persuasion effects of graphics.

1.3 THE WHARTON STUDY

The above findings are based on an actual study conducted at the Wharton Applied Research Center of the Wharton School at the University of Pennsylvania. In the Wharton study, a fictitious beer was used, rather than a fictitious library service. In the actual study, small groups of students were asked to respond to graphics and nongraphics presentations exactly as we describe in our scenario. The study continued over a six-month period, and Exhibit 1.1 portrays part of the Wharton findings.

The medium of presentation and the graphics used in the actual study were very simple: overheads on an overhead machine. But the impact was still there. Using more sophisticated and

---

* Applications software are computer programs that perform specific end tasks (word processors that produce text documents). A program is a stored set of instructions to the computer.

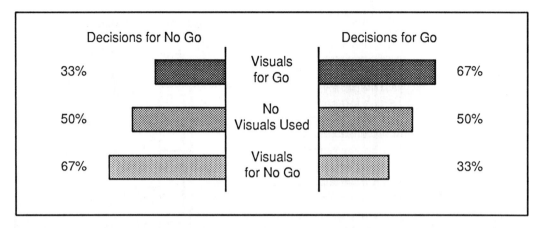

Exhibit 1.1: Influence of graphics on group decisions
(Reprinted with permission of Integrated Software Systems Corp. Copyright, 1982)

higher impact graphics involving simulation and animation, capabilities now available on desktop computers, might produce greater influence. Let us continue with the scenario and see the many uses to which we put computer graphics.

1.4 THE SCENARIO CONTINUED

As the principals involved in establishing the enterprise, we are responsible for the overall organization and direction of the business, the finances and accounting, the marketing and public relations, the inventory control and liaison with manufacturers—in fact, all of the functional areas and activities within those areas, as diagrammed in Exhibit 1.2.

Exhibit 1.2 also shows the computer graphics applications discussed in the text and their relation to the functional areas of the enterprise. In order to not clutter the exhibit with too many lines, the computer graphics applications that are useful to all functional areas are labeled *all*. They include presentation graphics, analytic graphics, project management, computer aided publishing—sometimes called in-house or personal publishing—and systems analysis. Those applicable to many areas are labeled *many*. They include visual database and visual programming.

All of the terms and applications are defined and explained throughout the text. The purpose of Exhibit 1.2 is to provide a comprehensive picture which the reader can scan in one glance to obtain a map of where we are heading and to provide an additional guide in following the scenario.

1.5 AN OVERVIEW OF APPLICATIONS

How will we use graphics to establish and run our business? We will assume that we have access to a variety of computer graphics capabilities.

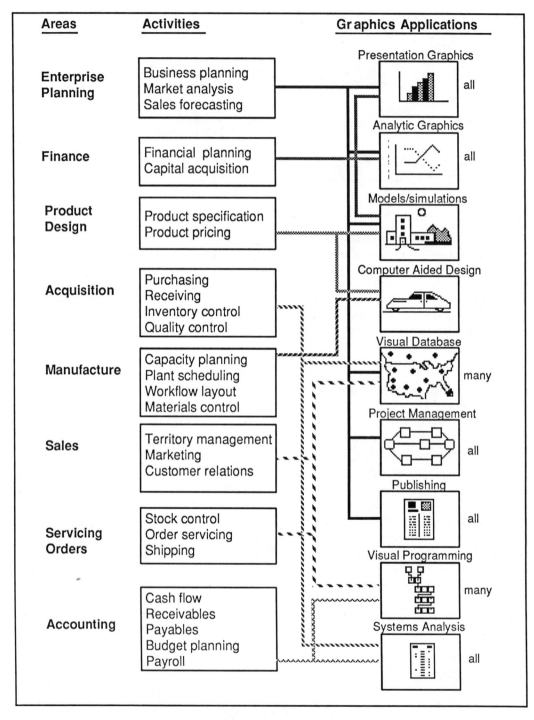

Exhibit 1.2: Enterprise functions and computer applications

1.5-1 Presentation graphics

We use presentation graphics to influence investors, show market analyses and forecast sales, and show the effects of product costs on product prices. All areas of our enterprise will use presentation graphics continuously to communicate better to colleagues, suppliers, and clients. Chapter 6 surveys this form of computer use.

1.5-2 Analytic graphics

We are concerned that the right decisions be made. We want to make some projections based on estimates of first year costs and income over a period of six years. Realizing the communication impact of graphics in comparison to numbers, we use one of the many systems available for translating spreadsheet data into a graph.

Further, based on data obtained concerning similar operations, we perform some projected break-even analyses in relation to the fees that need to be charged, and the income realized on a weekly basis in relation to expected expenses. Chapter 7 discusses the above and other methods involving analytic graphics.

1.5-3 Models and simulations

We need to raise capital funds for the total venture and for establishing the two library locations. We want to simulate the two locations using computer graphics to allow potential investors to "walk" through the library and experience how the library feels as well as what it does. We know that it is possible, using the techniques of visual simulation (called *Computer Generated Imagery—CGI*) and animation, to simulate reality. Rather than showing a physical model—or in addition to—we are going to walk our potential investors through and around the proposed library building, showing the appearance of the interior when it is raining outside and when the sun is shining, zooming in for detail when it is requested, portraying the interior or exterior from any angle on the computer screen.

We are also planning to develop a series of *Computer Aided Learning (CAL)* materials to teach people how to use the systems and the software in the library. We will show through animation on the screen the proper sequence of key strokes, or mouse movements, required to perform a task in a given application.* We are well aware of the paucity of well-designed documentation, of the difficulty in producing good user manuals, and we suspect that the computer could be a better trainer. The problem, of course, is that it takes a lot of effort to develop good computer aided learning programs. We are working on a system that will allow our clients to write their own learning materials. Simulation, modeling and computer aided learning are described in Chapter 8. Input and the human-computer interface are discussed in Chapter 4. Output and display are discussed in Chapter 5.

---

* A mouse is a hand-held device, about the size of a pack of cigarettes, used to interact with and command the computer.

1.5-4 Computer aided design (CAD)

We decide to use a computer aided design system to draft layouts of the floor plans of the library, to show the location of computer work stations, and also to show the electrical and computer cabling and outlets we would like installed interior to walls or ceilings in support of the work-stations and any possible future networking.

If we were in the business of manufacturing, we could use the same CAD system to view, review, test, change, and approve products and possibly avoid the cost of building prototypes. Further, following design, we might have the option of sending the specifications on a product to various machines which then, under computer control, produce the product or parts in the product. This latter stage is known as *Computer Aided Manufacturing (CAM)*. We discuss computer aided design in Chapter 9.

1.5-5 Visual database

In order to handle product acquisition and management, we decide to establish a database in the library for keeping track of all systems, software, peripherals, and their suppliers. We discover a unique approach: a visual filing system on computer. We map the location of all suppliers in the United States and Canada and, by pointing to a supplier's map location, we are able to retrieve data on that supplier. Plans of the office locations and drawings of all library shelves and cabinets at each office location are on computer. By pointing to any given shelf location or cabinet, we can display its contents. Items in stock may be retrieved and highlighted visually (all suppliers of a given class of software, and all locations in all stores of that class of software). Chapter 10 provides a description and examples of visual databases.

1.5-6 Project management

We use a project management system on a microcomputer to establish enterprise tasks—who will do them, by when—and the "milestones" we will use to evaluate progress. We use the project management system on the enterprise planning level and also on each sublevel of the enterprise. We discover that there is an advantage in taking a hierarchical approach to the use of project management systems. In Chapter 11 we show the graphics methods used to plan and monitor projects.

1.5-7 Computer aided publishing (CAP)

All divisions of our enterprise will be able to use an in-house, interactive, microcomputer-based publishing system that allows for documents to be produced rapidly at low cost and by a wide variety of personnel. We will produce documents using word processors, idea processing software, page layout systems, and a variety of graphics programs including CAD and free form paint programs. The final copy will be produced on a laser printer ready for reproduction. Chapter 12 discusses the steps, systems, and software involved in computer aided publishing.*

1.5-8 Visual programming

A number of principals and staff have expressed an interest in programming. They are aware of the fourth generation languages that allow nonprogrammers to program applications, but are not aware that databases and languages are being created that provide the user with graphics or icon tools to produce applications. This makes the abstract processes and logic of software concrete and visible, and facilitates the understanding and the learning of programming. Programming using graphics, or visual programming, is discussed in Chapter 14.

1.5-9 Systems analysis and evaluation

We need to obtain a number of computer systems for the library. We will need to represent the major small systems available, such as the *IBM PC* and the *Apple Macintosh*, but other systems that compare favorably should be appropriately represented. How will we know what systems are superior and for what tasks or applications? Tools must always fit jobs. We do not think of a hammer as being superior to a screwdriver, and therefore we would not use a screwdriver to drive a nail. We know that one computer system may be very suitable for some tasks and completely unsuitable for others. The answer lies in systems analysis of needs and the acquisition of systems that fit needs. We find that systems analysis uses a wide variety of graphics approaches.

Further, we have developed a decision support system (DSS) for our clients to use to evaluate and compare computer products. The system uses a database of ratings made by experts on computers and software (the tools), and experts on different industry or enterprise needs (the jobs). One of the reports produced is a simple graph showing the ratings of systems when they are compared to each other.

Chapter 15 provides an overview of systems analysis approaches, the use of graphics in analysis, the criteria we would use to evaluate computer graphics systems, and the decision support system (in paper form) described briefly here. Chapter 2 explains that a computer system is much more than a computer, and Chapter 3 surveys the classes of graphics systems available today.

1.6 SOME KEY EVENTS

Many users now have access to low cost professional quality computer graphics, formerly available only to those with access to expensive systems. Certain key developments allowed this

---

* Personal publishing is a term often used to reference this application of computers. However, computer-based publishing systems can be extensive, going far beyond the personal level. The author has rarely seen the term Computer Aided Publishing (CAP) used, but it seems to be appropriate and clear, especially since we use terms like Computer Aided Design (CAD), Computer Aided Manufacturing (CAM), Computer Aided Engineering (CAE), Computer Aided Instruction (CAI), and Computer Aided Learning (CAL). Therefore, CAP would refer to all forms of computer supported publishing, and Personal Publishing to those supported by a personal computer. CAP should also be contrasted to Electronic Publishing (EP), or the publication of materials in electronic rather than in paper form.

to happen. The developments, with a continuing increase in performance obtainable at decreasing cost, include:

- the microprocessor
- memory and storage
- dot addressable raster graphics monitors
- device-independent graphics software
- interactive graphics

All of these developments took place in the seventies and eighties. The microprocessor provides more processing power at lower cost. Manipulating graphics requires a lot of processing, memory, and storage. Solid state technology developed in the seventies provides the stepping stone to lower processing and storage costs and allows for superior graphics on small computers.

In the mid-seventies low cost graphics displays with low to medium resolutions became available. The different types of graphics displays are discussed in Chapter 5. Now high quality and relatively low cost displays are becoming available.

Device-independent software allows for operation on different systems with different output devices. This trend promotes the acceptance of graphics standards.*

In the early days of computing, when the interface with a computer was the remote key punch machine and the production of punched IBM cards for batch processing, computer graphics was not interactive; it was remote and often required many cycles of corrections to punched cards in order for the machine to produce the graphics correctly on a printer or plotter. In the meantime, the user sat passively by, possibly the reason for the name given to this form of graphics production, *Passive Graphics*.

Passive Graphics may be contrasted with *Interactive Graphics*, where the user is in direct interaction with the system and is able to control graphics display, correction, and production immediately. The user can produce a correct image on the screen, going through many repeat cycles to do so, before producing a hard copy on paper, video tape, or film. This is the modern form of graphics.

1.7 A PICTURE IS WORTH . . .

If an image is worth many words, then the two images provided in Exhibits 1.3 and 1.4 should speak for themselves.

The image in Exhibit 1.3 represents the "list of basic requirements" for producing professional business charts given in a 1962 text (Francis, 1962), *Using Charts to Improve Profits*. However, the image is from a text on *Engineering Graphics*, published in 1985.

Drafting has not left engineering but it may have been replaced in management and business graphics production by the computer graphics system shown in Exhibit 1.4 (and others like it) which, in the short span of two decades, replaces all that is shown in Exhibit 1.3. Further, the graphics computer allows more of us to explore good graphics design and production, without having to learn the fine visual motor skills required to be a good drafter (see Exhibit 1.5.).

---

* Graphics standards are discussed in Appendix D. Standards are important but may be of less interest to the user and of more interest to the computer specialist.

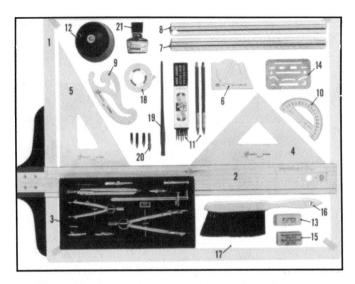

Exhibit 1.3: Minimal equipment required for manual drafting and design
(Reprinted with permission of Macmillan Publishing Company from *Engineering Graphics with Computer Graphics* (3rd ed.) by F. E. Giesecke, A. Mitchell, H. C. Spencer, I. L. Hill, R. O. Loving, and J. T. Dygdon. Copyright © 1985 by Macmillan Publishing Company)

Exhibit 1.4: An executive producing presentation graphics
(Courtesy of Hercules Computer Technology)

Producers of graphics systems are aware of this advantage, as shown by the advertisement for a computer graphics system in Exhibit 1.6.

Melvin L. Prueitt (1984) discovered, in relation to another discipline (art), that he was able to express his artistry by using the computer as his paintbrush. In similar fashion, the manager and business person can express his or her ability to communicate by using graphics without having to learn all the *production* skills of the graphics designer or drafter. The need for good design remains, and powerful tools like computer graphics can lead to the proliferation of very poor as

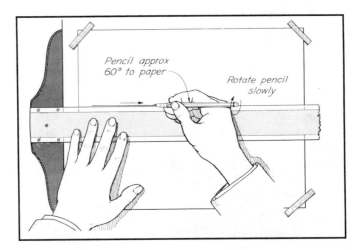

Exhibit 1.5: Manual drafting requires fine motor skills (Reprinted with permission of Macmillan Publishing Company from *Engineering Graphics with Computer Graphics* (3rd ed.) by F. E. Giesecke, A. Mitchell, H. C. Spencer, I. L. Hill, R. O. Loving, and J. T. Dygdon. Copyright © 1985 by Macmillan Publishing Company)

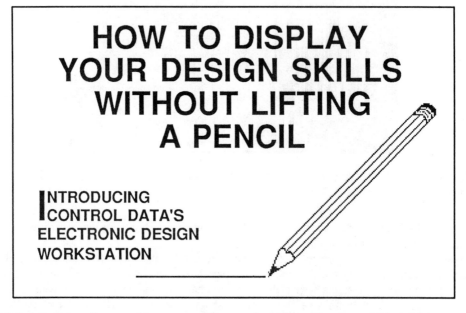

Exhibit 1.6: Advertisement for a graphics workstation (Courtesy of Control Data)

well as very good graphics; the computer does not care. We discuss some of the principles of good design in Chapter 6.

1.8 THE EVOLUTION OF COMPUTER GRAPHICS

Before humans could write they drew pictures. Early humans recorded their experiences and dreams in finger paintings in ochre on cave walls, spear point and arrow head scratchings on stone, and charcoal and soot impressions (Prueitt, 1984). Later, people used fingers on clay, chisels in wood, weaving in cloth, fireworks in the sky, quill pens on papyrus, and printing presses on paper. Later still they used air brushes, drafting equipment, cameras, and television.

Now we record our experiences, dreams, and visions with engravings on electronic and magnetic media in the simplest language possible—zeros and ones—produced by, and accessed through, computers. We awake to the tools we create. The awakening takes time, often occurring long after the tool's creation.

Exhibits 1.7 charts the evolution of computer graphics tracing the two main roots: computing and computers, and communication and media. These two roots merged in the middle of the twentieth century and became indistinguishable. Other people and events *not* listed in the chart made contributions to the present state of computer graphics. The reader is challenged to add some notations to the diagram. Further, blank spaces have been provided for adding people and events for the rest of the years left in this decade. The reader may note that the history of computing is quite extensive, that of communications less so, of computers less still, and that computer graphics began only 30 years ago. We can truthfully say that computer graphics is an infant discipline, and we have only recently progressed beyond the crawling stage.

Exhibit 1.7: Evolution of Computer Graphics*

COMPUTING & COMPUTERS		COMMUNICATION & MEDIA
B.C.		
3500	Earliest known numerals in Egypt	
3000	Dust abacus of Southwest Asia	
2000	Egyptians use knotted rope triangle with Pythagorean numbers	
2000	Decimal system in Crete	
500		Stonehenge astronomical calendar
		Sunrise at Summer Solstice / Sunrise at Winter Solstice / Sunset at Summer Solstice / Sunset at Winter Solstice
200	Hipparchus of Nicea invents trigonometry	
1st to 11th century A.D.		
100		Paper introduced in China
200	·Abacus/soroban used in China and Japan	
814	Arabs take over Indian numerals including zero to multiply by ten	
942		First postal and news service developed by the Arabs
975	Arabs introduce arithmetical notation to Europe	
978		First encyclopedia—1000 volumes in China
1000	Sridhara, Indian mathematician, recognizes importance of zero	

* The texts used as the basis for the history chart are listed separately in the bibliography. Sometimes the assignment of a particular event to either of the two broad categories used was not obvious. All images were produced using *ThunderScan*, a unique digitizer for the *Apple Macintosh* described in Chapter 4.

Exhibit 1.7: Evolution of Computer Graphics (Continued)

COMPUTING & COMPUTERS	COMMUNICATION & MEDIA
14th to 17th Century	
1396	Gutenberg invents movable type, based on the combining of the wine press and the striking of metal coins
1452	Metal plates used for engraving and printing
1500 Checkered tablecloth with buttons is basis for British Exchequer	
1500 Leonardo da Vinci designs calculator on paper	
1569	Mercator creates map of the world for navigational use
1591 Viete uses letters for algebraic quantities	
1600 Blaise Pascal builds first mechanical calculator called the Pascaline	
Blaise Pascal	
1614 Napier discovers logarithms, basis for lengthy calculations	
1637 Descartes invents analytic geometry	
1653	First mailboxes used in Paris, France
1654 Blaise Pascal and Pierre de Fermat state "Theory of Probability"	
1657 Liebnitz invents differential and integral calculus	

Exhibit 1.7: Evolution of Computer Graphics (Continued)

COMPUTING & COMPUTERS	COMMUNICATION & MEDIA
18th and 19th Century	
1795 Mahone's Arithmetic Machine, basis of Babbage's Calculating Engine	
1798	German inventor, Aloys Senefelder, invents lithography, a method of printing from smooth stone or metal
1800 Volta produces electricity from a battery	
1820	Paris invents first animation device, the Thaumatrope
1827	Joseph Niepce produces photographs on metal plates; the age of photography is born
1829	The first patent on a typewriter is issued to Willima Burt of Detroit, Michigan
1833 Babbage invents Analytical Engine, incorporating similar concepts to the modern computer	
1837 Scheultz builds tabulating machine based on Babbage's work	
1840 Lady Lovelace, considered the "first programmer," describes loops, subroutines, and jumps, part of the basis of modern programming; brilliant young mathematician who appreciated work of Babbage and cooperated with him	
 Ada Lovelace	
1841	Viennese mathematician, Joseph Petzval, produces photographic portrait lens with a speed of f/3.6

Exhibit 1.7: Evolution of Computer Graphics (Continued)

COMPUTING & COMPUTERS		COMMUNICATION & MEDIA
1844		S. F. B. Morse's telegraph used for the first time between Baltimore, Maryland and Washington, D.C.
1847	George Boole publishes "Mathematical Analysis of Logic"; inventor of Boolean algebra, basis for logic describing modern computer functioning and binary arithmetic	
	George Boole	
1854		German watchmaker, Heinrich Goebel, invents first form of electric light bulb
1855		David E. Hughes invents printing telegraph
1873		The gunsmith firm of E. Remington and Sons begin to produce typewriters
1873		Color photographs first produced
1876		Alexander Graham Bell invents the telephone
1877		Thomas Edison invents the phonograph
1880		Thomas Edison and J. W. Swan independently devise the first practical electric lights
1885		George Eastman manufactures coated photographic paper
1888		Eastman perfects Kodak, the box camera

Exhibit 1.7: Evolution of Computer Graphics (Continued)

	COMPUTING & COMPUTERS	COMMUNICATION & MEDIA
1889	Hollerith creates punch card system, basis for IBM punched card; founding partner in International Business Machines	

Hollerith Card Punch

	COMPUTING & COMPUTERS	COMMUNICATION & MEDIA
1890	Burroughs invents adding and listing machine	
1894		Louis Lumiere invents cinematography
1895		Marconi invents radio telegraphy
1897		William Thompson (Lord Kelvin) studies cathode rays, basis for television
1898		Photographs first taken using artificial light
1899		First magnetic recordings of sound

20th Century

1901	Following a "century of steam," the "century of electricity" begins	
1904		First telegraphic transmission of photographs; Aurthur Korn, Munich to Nurenburg
1907		Louis Lumiere develops a process for color photography using a three-color screen
1921		Encoding and transmission of digital pictures, via a transatlantic cable using a digital system and teletype machines simulating halftones
1925		Phototypesetting begins to appear

Exhibit 1.7: Evolution of Computer Graphics (Continued)

COMPUTING & COMPUTERS	COMMUNICATION & MEDIA
1925	First Leica camera built by Oskar Barnack
1925	Transmission of recognizable features via television demonstrated by J. L. Baird
1926	Kodak produces first 16mm movie camera and film
1927	R. Buckminster Fuller designs the Dymaxion map of the world; a map with minimal surface distortion
1928	First color motion pictures exhibited by George Eastman of Kodak in Rochester, New York
1928	Teleprinters and teletypewriters come into restricted use in the U.S., Britain, and Germany
1928	Color TV demonstrated by J. L. Baird
1930	Picture telegraphy service begins between Britain and Germany
1930	Shannon models electrical switching circuits using Boolean algebra and establishes the foundation for Information Theory	

Claude Shannon

1933	Farnsworth develops TV
1936	Brilliant mathematician, Alan Turing, at the age of 24, proves that it is possible to perform computations in	

Exhibit 1.7: Evolution of Computer Graphics (Continued)

COMPUTING & COMPUTERS	COMMUNICATION & MEDIA
number theory using a machine that embodies the rules of a formal system; that is, a computer. The universal machine Turing described underlies *all* of the applications— virtual machines — computers may become through programming	

Alan Turing

1938	Lajos Biro of Hungary invents ballpoint pen
1939 Shannon receives Nobel prize for work in 1930	
1940 John Atanasoff and Clifford Berry design computer with vacuum tube switching units	
1942	Magnetic recording tape invented
1943-46 First all electronic digital computer built, called the ENIAC, by John Mauchley Jr., Presper Eckert, and John Von Neumann, the latter being one of the most brilliant and influential scientists in this era. In this same period Norbert Weiner and colleagues orginated the concepts of Cybernetics, that is, the importance of feedback on both human and computer functioning	
1946	Xerography process invented by Chester Carlson

Exhibit 1.7: Evolution of Computer Graphics (Continued)

	COMPUTING & COMPUTERS	COMMUNICATION & MEDIA
1947	Transistor invented at Bell Telephone Laboratories	
1949	One of the first stored program computers, the EDSAC, built at Cambridge University, England	
1950	Captain Grace Hopper USN, the "Mother of COBOL," works on the language's development	
1950		Simple plots appear using hard copy devices, teletype, or line printers
1951		Color television first introduced (in U.S.)
1950	John Whitney Sr. pioneers computer graphics and experimental computer animation	
1951	Vacuum tubes developed by IBM	
1952	Whirlwind I computer installed at the Massachusetts Institute of Technology (MIT) with cathode ray tube specifically for plotting	
1955	Vacuum tubes developed by IBM	
1955	$14.54: cost for large systems to perform a fixed amount of data processing consisting of 1700 typical processing operations involving millions of computer instructions including payroll, file maintenance, and report preparation. Not adjusted for inflation but in dollars of the period in question (figures also reported for 1960, 1965, 1975, 1983)*	
1956	Bardeen, Brattain, and Shockley share Nobel prize in physics for transistor	
1956		Bell Telephone Company begins to develop the "visual telephone," a device that never caught on
1958	SAGE air defense system becomes operational; early example of a system relying on use of computer graphics; used light pen as an input device	

* Based on a chart by IBM and reported in Canadian Datasystems, October, 1983, and reproduced with permission.

Exhibit 1.7: Evolution of Computer Graphics (Continued)

COMPUTING, COMPUTERS, COMMUNICATION, and MEDIA*	
1960	J. C. R. Licklider, psychologist at MIT, sets forth the concepts of interactive processing; also originates concept of time sharing and interactive processing with a large computer, a step from batch processing to personal computing
1960	$2.48: cost for large systems to perform a fixed amount of data processing
1960	Zajec and Knowlton develop the first computer animations at Bell Telephone Labs
1960	New York Institute of Technology (NYIT) establishes one of the first computer graphics laboratories; develops first computer painting program; possesses one of the most extensive computer graphics environments in the world
1960	MAC, acronym for *Machine-Aided Cognition,* or *Multi-Access Computing,* or *Maniacs and Clowns,* first temple of hackers—brilliant, unorthodox, young, and addicted programmers—at MIT; established by Licklider and at different times administered by the famous including Minsky (early explorer of artificial intelligence), and Papert (originator of LOGO); site of first defeat of human chess player by computer
1962	Ivan Sutherland, protegé of Claude Shannon and father of real-time interactive computer graphics, completes Ph.D. thesis at MIT entitled "Sketchpad: a man-machine graphical communication system."
1963	Douglas Engelbart reports on conception of word processing as example of augmenting human capabilities through computers; inventor of the mouse
1964	Kemeny and Kurtz originate BASIC at Dartmouth College
1965	47 cents: cost for large systems to perform a fixed amount of data processing
1965	Control Data Corporation (CDC) supplies one of the first computer aided design and manufacturing (CAD/CAM) systems to GM. Term "User-friendly" coined here
1965	Edward A. Feigenbaum and colleagues start to design first expert system, DENDRAL, for determining molecular structure of chemical compounds
1967	Alan Kay develops early desktop system called FLEX; originator of *Small Talk,* a graphic programming language of objects that communicate with each other
1969	Intel builds first microprocessor, the 4004
1970	Xerox's Palo Alto Research Center (PARC) begins research on the visual interface using the mouse, icons, and pull-down menus
1971	Intel develops the 8008 microprocessor
1972	Nolan Bushnell invents PONG, the first video game, marketed by Atari
1972	Early turnkey CAD/CAM minicomputer-based systems appear
1974	Intel develops the 8080 microprocessor, destined to be the CPU for many micros
1974	Xerox releases the Alto, the first computer to use graphics interface, icons, windows, mouse; predecessor of the Apple Lisa and Macintosh of a decade later
1975	20 cents: cost for large systems to perform a fixed amount of data processing
1975	Gates of Microsoft writes BASIC for early microcomputer, the Altair
1975	Low cost raster graphics displays become available
1976	Gary Kildall founds Digital Research, originators of CP/M, the first OS for micros
1976	The first issue of BYTE magazine

* By the sixties, computing, computers, communication, and media cannot be subdivided — they are becoming a part of each other. Earlier pioneer work integrating computers and media includes Whitney's studies of computer graphics, the Whirlwind computer at MIT, and the SAGE air defense system.

Exhibit 1.7: Evolution of Computer Graphics (Continued)

COMPUTING, COMPUTERS, COMMUNICATION, and MEDIA	
1976	Stephen Wozniack, one of the founders of Apple Computer, demonstrates the Apple I at the Homebrew Computer Club, the first computer club
1977	Apple Computer begins operation and introduces the Apple II; started in a garage by Steve Jobs and Steve Wozniack
1978	Apple Computer initiates Lisa research and development
1979	Micropro releases *WordStar*
1979	Dan Bricklin and Robert Frankston program and introduce the first electronic spread sheet (ESS), *VisiCalc*
1981	*dBASE II* introduced by Ashton-Tate; to become leading database for micros
1981	First portable computer introduced by Adam Osborne
1981	There are over a half million microcomputer owners
1982	IBM announces the personal computer
1983	7 cents: cost for large systems to perform a fixed amount of data processing
1983	Apple announces the Lisa
1983	There are nearly 3 million microcomputer owners, close to 150 microcomputer manufacturers, and close to 70 computer periodicals
1983	Mitch Kapor, founder of Lotus Corporation, announces *Lotus 1-2-3*, first integrated software package
1983	High capacity silicon chips technology introduced by IBM
1984	Apple introduces the Macintosh
1984	Telos releases *Filevision,* a graphics-oriented data manager
1985	Aldus Corporation introduces *PageMaker,* page layout on the Macintosh
1985	Odesta releases *Helix ,* an icon driven database and programming language
1985	Large expansion in graphics applications and graphics user interfaces
1986	_____
1986	_____
1986	_____
1987	_____
1987	_____
1987	_____
1988	_____
1988	_____
1988	_____
1990	_____
1990	_____
1990	_____

2

A Computer System Is More Than a Computer

2.1 INTRODUCTION

In this chapter we provide an overview of computer systems and how they function. The purpose is to answer the following questions:

- What is a computer?
- What is a computer system?
- What is a graphics computer system?
- What systems contain computer systems?
- What systems form computer systems?
- How do computers work?
- What makes one computer system different from another?

We do not need to know a lot of technical information to operate a computer. But technical knowledge is required when we wish to understand product specifications, evaluate and select systems, and feel comfortable with the specialized language of computers. Consider the product description for a presentation graphics program shown in Exhibit 2.1.

Memory Size:
Minimum 192K (256K required for printer graphics or for the Polaroid Palette; 320K recommended for color printers).
Disk Drives:
2 double-sided floppy disk drives **or** 1 double-sided floppy disk drive and a hard disk drive.
Display Screens:
Color Display and Color Graphics Adapter (board) required for on-screen color graphics.
Operating Systems:
DOS 1.1 or higher. Also supports 100% IBM-compatibles such as the Compaq.
Printers:
Data South DS 180, Epson FX80, IBM Graphics Printer (many other printers supported).
Polaroid Palette Recording System:
For 35mm slides and 4.25 x 3.25 photos. A minimum of 256K memory and a color graphics adapter are required.
Plotters:
Amdek Amplot II, Hewlett-Packard 7720 B, C, S, or T (many other plotters supported).

Exhibit 2.1: Hardware requirements for CHARTMASTER, and SIGN-MASTER, for the IBM PC, IBM PC/XT, and IBM PC AT
(Note: The above is an abbreviation of the actual specification sheet. Courtesy of Decision Resource, Inc.)

We need to know what product descriptions mean. This is not too different from reading vehicle specifications when purchasing an automobile. In time, the language in Exhibit 2.1 will be equally familiar. Many of the concepts of computer operation are simple in principle and can be readily understood. Often it is specialized languages that make different disciplines appear obtuse and difficult.

The background provided in this chapter on *how* computers function should facilitate our understanding of *what* graphics systems are available (Chapter 3). Further, we are introduced in this chapter to the *process* of data capture and information display, while Chapters 4 and 5 describe *methods* or *media* for entering data into the system, and for getting information out.

2.2 SOME BASICS

A computer is a machine for turning raw *data* into useful *information and knowledge*. A diagram of *any* computer is given in Exhibit 2.2.

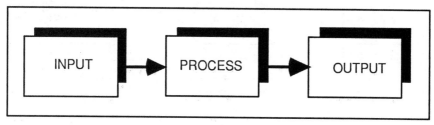

Exhibit 2.2: Diagram of any computer

The raw data (input) can be letters, numbers, graphic symbols, sounds, sightings—anything we can enter into the computer; the information (output) can be reports, documents, tables, lists, pictures, art, music, braille—anything we can get out of the computer. Exhibit 2.3 illustrates this point with several examples.

A *graphics* computer system functions in a manner similar to a *non*graphics system, except it has one additional and important type of data it can manipulate: images. The graphics system, as we shall see, can accept images as input, and can produce images as output.

Our *needs, problems,* and *goals* determine the computer system required. The computer system selected should help us meet, solve, or reach our needs, problems, and goals. If this relationship appears obvious, then we might wonder why it is so often overlooked. We expand upon the process of analysis and selection in Chapter 15.

More specifically, our needs determine the *applications software required*, which in turn determines everything else. Applications software are programs that do specific jobs and can be used directly by nonprogramming staff (word processing, business graphics). All of the examples in Exhibit 2.3 are applications programs.*

---

* The operating environment—how the system allows the user to function and do things—is as important as applications software. This is due to the greater variability in operating environments in small systems initiated by the introduction of the Apple Macintosh. Obviously, if the required applications are not available, then the machine is totally useless. However, if applications are available and are rendered difficult to use by a poorly conceived operating environment, the availability of applications is immaterial.

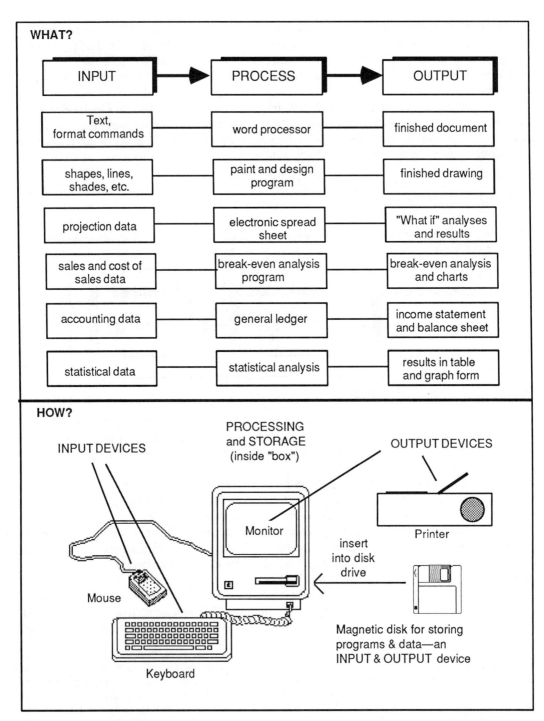

Exhibit 2.3: From data to information and knowledge

Knowledge of new technology changes perception. An example from an older technology will make this point clear. Exhibit 2.4 shows a very large boulder in a farmer's best growing field.

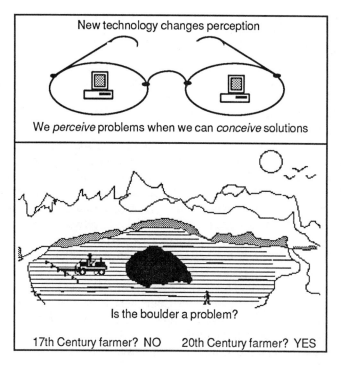

Exhibit 2.4: Technology changes how we see and influence our world

Is the boulder "a problem"? For a 17th century farmer, no, but for a 20th century farmer, yes. The difference is that *we do not perceive problems unless we can conceive solutions.* For the 17th century farmer the boulder is something to live with. For the 20th century farmer it is something to dynamite and bulldoze out of his best growing field. Interactive graphics, where we are in direct control of images and imaging, goes even further; it changes our brain, arouses the perceptual mind, and allows us to see and work with patterns.

2.3 SYSTEMS WITHIN SYSTEMS

The diagram of any computer in Exhibit 2.2 provides us with a starting point for taking an *outside view*, that is, what are the systems that provide a context for computers; and an *inside view*, what are the systems that are a part of the computer itself. In order to understand computer design, application, and impact, we must remain aware of four major areas: *People, Machines, Interface* between people and machines, and *Context.* Exhibit 2.2 diagrams the machine only. If we take the traditional approach of expanding upon the diagram in Exhibit 2.2 in the direction of an inside view only, we may well overlook important considerations provided by the larger picture, or an outside view, and the other major areas listed above.

2.3-1 Context: an outside view

Exhibit 2.5 is a map; a bird's-eye image of the computer industry. Like an aerial map, Exhibit 2.5 shows the large "land and water formations" of the computer field.

The *Research and Evolution* of computer systems in relation to graphics has diverse roots, as shown in the history chart in Exhibit 1.7.

Systems Analysis and Design constitute the evolution of a *single* computer system, and the tools of analysis, design, and system development are discussed in Chapter 15.

Exhibit 2.5 shows the three major forms of processing: *batch processing, interactive processing, and process control.* Batch processing involves the entry of large amounts of data, which are then processed as a group or in a batch and a report or some other output obtained. It is the older form of processing and still has its uses. In graphics it may involve the entry and manipulation under program control of many coordinate image points and the subsequent display of many images. This may be the better choice with certain graphics problems than an interactive mode, for example, the continuous generation of designs or patterns based on certain criteria.

The interactive mode of processing is the constant dialogue between person and machine. The person presses keys or moves a light pen, and the computer responds immediately with a change in the display. The interactive mode is the basis for interactive graphics and the highly creative synergy that can take place between person and machine.

Process control is the relationship between the computer and other machines: punches, lathes, welders, drill presses, factories, rockets, and more. Computers, rather than humans, are used to control the machine's operation. Graphics come into play when displays are used to show the process occurring in real time. Complex control operations in oil pipe lines, energy production, or a factory operation may all be displayed using flow diagrams in different colors. Graphics also come into play in the design of products, and the computer may then be involved in the manufacture of the product it helped design. This is the field of *Computer Aided Design and Computer Aided Manufacturing (CAD/CAM).*

When the computer is used by one person at a time, it is a *single-user* system; when used by many at one time, a *multi-user* system; also referred to as a *timeshare* system. It may be a *super-mainframe* suitable for rapidly processing many numbers (weather and atmospheric research); a *mainframe* for a large business (bank); a *mini-computer* for smaller applications (a graphics design workstation dedicated to one task: architectural design); or a *micro- or personal computer* (productivity tool for the manager).

When the computer is not connected to any other computer, the system is functioning in a *stand-alone* mode. Computers may be connected to other computers locally (in a complex of buildings) by a *network* (called *Local Area Networks,* or *LANS*) through physical cabling in some type of configuration (computers connected in a ring, a star, or all in a row), or via phone or satellite in a *telecommunications* mode. The computer is attached to the phone via a device called a *modem* (for mo̲dulate and de̲modulate). Text and/or images can be transmitted, depending upon the physical setup. Thus, teams of people separated geographically may each, from their respective graphics workstations or graphics personal computers, cooperate on design and development.

The three major forms of processing (batch, interactive, and process control), in these three major forms of configurations (stand-alone, network, or temporary connect via telecommunications), provide the basis for *all* the computer *applications* and *impacts* we experience.

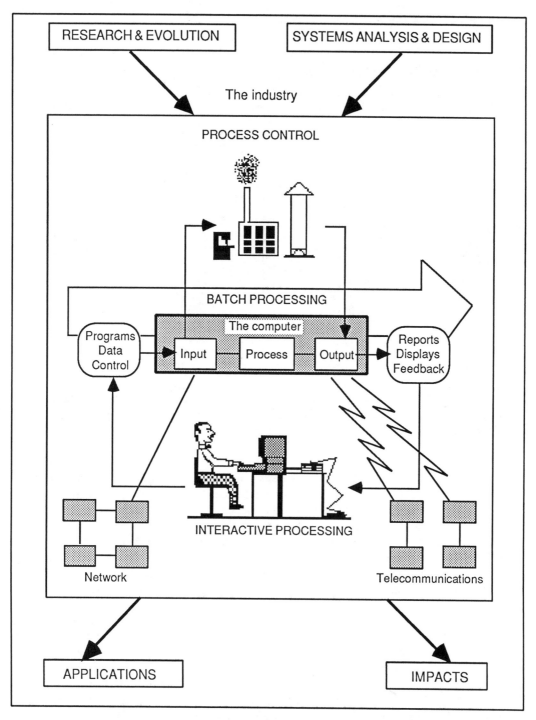

Exhibit 2.5: A bird's-eye view of the computer industry

2.3-2 Interface: person-machine connection

Exhibit 2.6 shows the relationship between person and machine in interactive processing, based on a diagram in Kantowitz and Sorkin (1983).

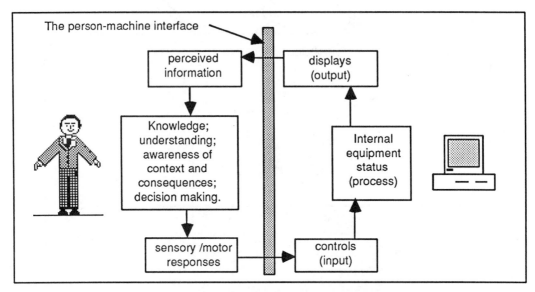

Exhibit 2.6: The person-machine interface in interactive processing
(Based on a diagram in B. H. Kantowitz and R. D. Sorkin, *Human Factors: Understanding People-System Relationships*, copyright © John Wiley & Sons, 1983. Reprinted by permission of John Wiley & Sons)

Our familiar "input-process-output" appears on the machine side. The person-machine interface looks like a barrier separating person and machine. Computer graphics is playing a major role in transcending this barrier through its use in the design of links and paths from the human perspective; machines to fit humans, not humans to fit machines. For example, the design of displays from the viewpoint of human perception is critical. Screen design depends on a knowledge of human visual acuity and discrimination, movement perception (flicker-fusion), color sensitivity, pattern recognition, perception of form, eye movements and attention, and visual fatigue. Similarly, the design of input devices requires a knowledge of motor skills and eye-hand coordination.

The human side in Exhibit 2.6 appears to be a replay of the input-process-output of the machine side. But the similarity is misleading. A person is more than an information processing machine. That is, we might be tempted to view the human "component" of the total system as contributing only information processing followed by decision making. However, this does not take into consideration human awareness of context and consequences. Information is *transformed* as it moves through a system, especially on the human side, not simply *transported*. Therefore, we have identified the human involvement in Exhibit 2.6 in broader terms.

2.3-3 Component systems: an inside view

Exhibit 2.7 opens the first layer of the computer box.

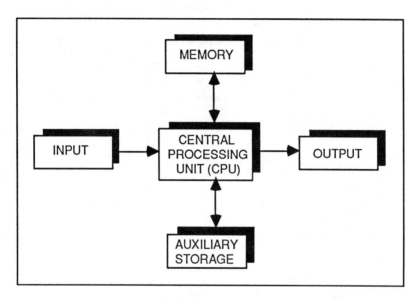

Exhibit 2.7: Diagram of any computer expanded

Processing involves three major subsystems; a *Central Processing Unit (CPU)*, *memory*, and *auxiliary storage*. The CPU processes data according to instructions, the memory temporarily holds instructions and data during processing, and auxiliary storage keeps information and data permanently. What do the arrows in Exhibit 2.7 mean? We enter instructions and data (input), the CPU works with the instructions and data while in memory and when complete, the new information is stored in auxiliary storage. If a report or image is needed, we can obtain it on a screen or print it (output). This highly simplified description is expanded later in this chapter.

2.3-4 Forms of input and output

Exhibit 2.8 provides an overview of the different forms or mediums of input and output available. Input and output are particularly important for computer graphics work. They are expanded on in Chapters 4 and 5.

2.4 NONGRAPHIC AND GRAPHIC SYSTEMS

Exhibit 2.9 provides a list of the required components for a minimal, *nonprofessional* (home, game) computer system, a *nongraphic professional* level system, and a *graphic professional* level system. Exhibit 2.9 clearly shows that a computer system is much more than a computer.

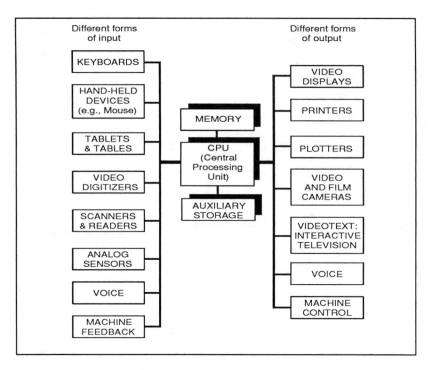

Exhibit 2.8: An overview of input and output

(A variety of storage devices—disks, tapes, punched cards—could have been legitimately added to both input and output in the exhibit. The emphasis in the exhibit is on interactive processing.)

2.5 BITS AND BYTES

We do *not* need to know about bits and bytes to operate a computer, graphic or otherwise. But, to understand computer systems specifications; to evaluate, compare, and select computer systems; to communicate with computer technologists; and to be computer-literate and not feel dumb; we do need to know what they mean. They are not difficult concepts; they are merely unfamiliar.

Bits and bytes are units of measure. They are used to

- Identify computers (8-, 16-, or 32- bit)
- Indicate the size of main memory
- Indicate the size of auxiliary storage
- Act as the base for agreed-upon codes to represent
  letters, numbers, and special characters
- Define screen resolution
- Define rates of data transmission

Some basic definitions and relations are given in Exhibit 2.10. Binary, according to Webster's dictionary, is a system of numbers having two as its base. We are more familiar with base ten,

Exhibit 2.9: A computer system is more than a computer

Component	Minimal	Nongraphics	Graphics
Software			
Application Software		•	•
Systems Software			
Operating System	•	•	•
Utilities	•	•	•
Windows/shells/add-ons		Δ	Δ
Programming languages		•	•
Application Generators and DBMS		•	•
Hardware			
The Computer			
Central Processing Unit	•	•	•
Memory	•	•	•
Storage		•	•
Graphics Controller board(s)			•
Monitor			
B&W or Color	•	•	•
Character addressable	•	•	
Dot addressable			•
Input Devices			
Keyboard	•	•	•
Mouse, roll ball, joy stick			Δ
Graphics Tablet			Δ
Light pen			Δ
Video digitizer			Δ
Output devices			
Printer			
Dot matrix		Δ	Δ
Impact		Δ	Δ
Ink jet			Δ
Laser			Δ
Plotter			Δ
Communications			
Modems		•	•
Ports			
Parallel		•	•
Serial		•	•
Adjunct			
Operator Manuals	•	•	•
System's Documentation	•	•	•
Service and Support	•	•	•
Installation		Δ	Δ
Materials: disks, paper, ribbons, etc.		•	•

• Required   Δ At least one in a given category is likely to be present, for example, graphics systems with optional input devices.

Bit is short for <u>B</u>inary Dig<u>it</u>
Binary = Two things
Digit = Any whole number from 0 through 9*
Binary digit = The first two whole numbers
Bit = 0 or 1
Byte = 8 bits (usually; some computers use a variable size byte)

Exhibit 2.10: Some basic definitions

(*Not quite true. The above definition applies only to the decimal system, or base ten. Actually defined as N-ary digit = any whole number from 0 to N-1. For Bi-nary, N=2 and N-1=1. Therefore, there are only two numbers in the binary system: 0 and 1.)

undoubtedly due to our familiar number of fingers (if our forefathers had known the future ubiquity of computers, they might have chosen two arms, legs, eyes, or ears as the basis for the number base). If we had six fingers we would most likely use a numbering system to the base six. In any case, the binary number system is particularly useful when discussing and describing digital computers because they use only two signals. Further, our forefathers did not make a mistake; counting and calculating in binary may be suitable for computers, but it is unsuitable for humans.

The 0 and the 1 of the binary system are used to represent an inactive or active wire or device. With enough electronic wires or devices, we can store or transmit all the unique codes, or signals required to represent all the letters, numbers, and so forth. Exhibit 2.11 demonstrates this point.

A wire is either active or inactive, represented by 0 and 1
One wire can transmit *two* different *one*-bit messages
     ----- 0   ----- 1
Two wires can transmit *four* different *two*-bit messages
----- 0   ----- 0   ----- 1   ----- 1
----- 0   ----- 1   ----- 0   ----- 1
Three wires can transmit *eight* different *three*-bit messages
----- 0   ----- 0   ----- 0   ----- 0
----- 0   ----- 1   ----- 0   ----- 1
----- 0   ----- 0   ----- 1   ----- 1

----- 1   ----- 1   ----- 1   ----- 1
----- 0   ----- 1   ----- 0   ----- 1
----- 0   ----- 0   ----- 1   ----- 1
And, as we keep adding wires: 4 wires, 16 4-bit messages, etc.

Exhibit 2.11: Wires and messages

In Exhibit 2.11, the assumption is that data are being transmitted in *parallel* across a number of wires. However, the computer is capable of transmitting "packets" of signals—or sets of zeros and ones—in sequence or in *serial* transmission across one wire. Serial transmission is slower than parallel transmission. The connection between the various major components of a computer system—the computer, the printer, the keyboard, and so forth—are either parallel or serial.

2.5-1 The keyboard

When depressed, each key on the computer keyboard generates an 8-bit code. An agreed-upon sequence of zeros and ones represents each upper- and lower-case letter, each number, each special character, and each special command (sound bell). These agreed-upon signals are called the American Standard Code for Information Interchange (ASCII). A sample is shown in Exhibit 2.12.*

Character	ASCII
0	01010000
1	01010001
2	01010010
3	01010011
4	01010100
A	10100001
B	10100010
C	10100011

Exhibit 2.12: Some ASCII codes

Exhibit 2.13 shows the code transmitted when the letter "B" on the keyboard is pressed.

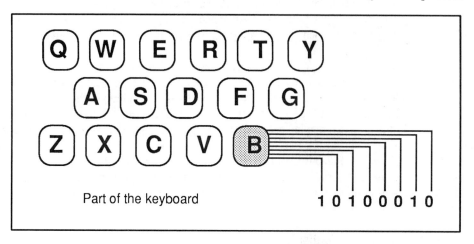

Part of the keyboard   1 0 1 0 0 0 1 0

Exhibit 2.13: The binary sequence representing the letter "B"

---

* Another common standard similar to ASCII used on most IBM computers other than the IBM PC is the Extended Binary Coded Decimal Interchange Code (EBCDIC).

2.5-2 External data transmission

For most communication between computers across telephone lines or in local area networks, 8-bit codes are transmitted. Sometimes longer codes may be used; additional bits to check for the accuracy of transmission, and an address code for the message code's destination.

One of the bits *not* used to code a letter or number, but to act as a check that the proper code is transmitted, is called a *parity bit*. A simple rule is followed of adding or not adding a "1" to the rest of the bits in the message to make the *number* of ones odd or even. Then all messages can be checked to see if they stay odd or even in transmission. The form of parity chosen, odd or even, is inconsequential. Internal data transmission between different subparts of the computer is discussed later in this chapter.

2.6 GRAPHICS DISPLAYS

2.6-1 Dot addressable displays

The images on all computer screens are made up of dots. Each dot is called a *pixel* (short for picture element). In a computer graphics screen each pixel is stored and represented in memory by a sequence of bits. When the screen is represented in memory in this manner, the screen is called *bit-mapped*. The location of the corresponding bits in memory is called a *frame buffer*. A *display controller* passes the contents of the frame buffer to the screen at least once every 30 seconds to maintain a steady picture and avoid flicker. Bit-mapped displays are necessary for graphics. The more dots or pixels per square inch on the computer screen, the higher the *resolution* or visual clarity of the image.

Exhibit 2.14 shows the exact correspondence between an image on the screen (set for demonstration purposes to a ridiculous 16 pixels by 16 pixels, or a total of 256 dots) and the sequence of zeros and ones in the 32 eight-bit bytes (or a total of 256 bits) in the frame buffer. A real display screen could easily have over 256,000 dots and, therefore, 256,000 bits in the frame buffer. Changes in the graphics display require that changes be made to the contents of the frame buffer.

When a signal can be transmitted to each dot to turn on or off, or (in more sophisticated systems) display a shade of gray, or (in color systems) a given color tint, the monitor is *dot-addressable*. It may be contrasted to the *character-addressable* screen.

2.6-2 Character addressable displays

Simple and very primitive graphics are possible with character addressable systems. Letters, after all, are graphics. It is possible to have a set of fixed graphic characters of various kinds (squares, rectangles, lines). Monitors that do not allow each dot to be addressed and thus changed, but allow only for changes by characters, are suitable for displaying text only. In this case, the smallest addressable unit is some subset or matrix of dots as shown in Exhibit 2.15.

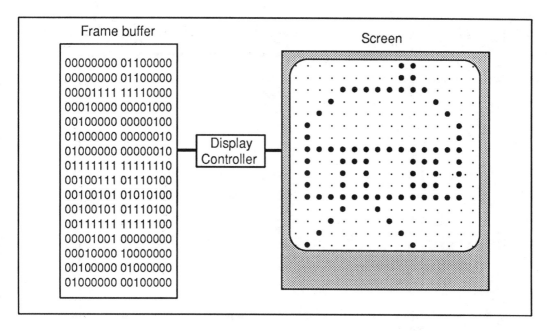

Exhibit 2.14: The bits in the frame buffer determine the on-off pixels on the screen (Note the shape of the house represented in the 1s in the buffer.)

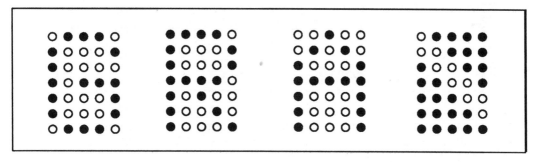

Exhibit 2.15: With a character-addressable system a matrix of dots can be changed, not each dot

2.6-3 A Demonstration

The images in Exhibits 2.16 and 2.17 are taken from the screen of the Macintosh based on an image from McPic Volume 2, a library of graphics images available commercially.

Exhibit 2.17 shows the *"fat bits"* option in *MacPaint*, a menu selection that blows up a section of a drawing, allowing the user to make fine changes. It shows the square pixels used on the Apple Macintosh. In the Macintosh, the pixels can only be on or off, or black and white. Shades of gray are formed by different arrangements of on and off pixels. There is no color.

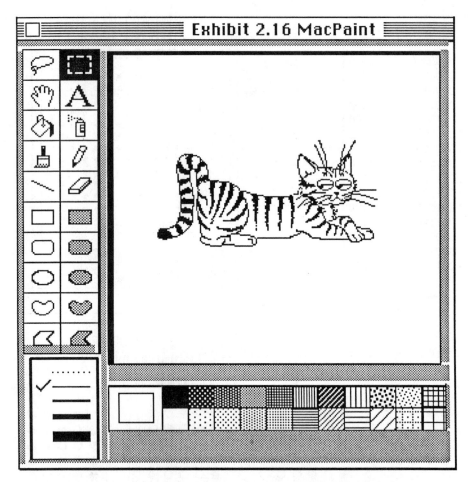

**Exhibit 2.16: A drawing made with *MacPaint* on the *Apple Macintosh*
using the various drawing "tools" shown on the borders of the screen**
(The above exhibit is not a completely accurate rendition of the *MacPaint* screen because it was
reduced to fit the page and it was drawn using *MacDraw*.)

On the Macintosh, the bit mapping takes up about 22,000 bytes of memory. The screen size
is 4-3/4 inches by 7 inches (12 by 18 cm) with a resolution of 512 by 342, or 175,104 pixels or
dots. Since there are 8 bits in a byte, then the bit mapping in the frame buffer needed to represent
this level of resolution on the screen consumes approximately 176,000 bits, or, dividing by 8,
22,000 bytes. The 512 by 342 in this size screen is a very good resolution for a micro computer
and suitable for business graphics, but not suitable for more sophisticated applications requiring
finer resolution or color.

When gray tones or color are added, the number of bits required to represent the additional
data and the demands made on memory and processing increase considerably. The color displays on
microcomputers in many cases are not of very high quality because of the great demands being
made on a system with limited memory and processing resources, and something has to be given

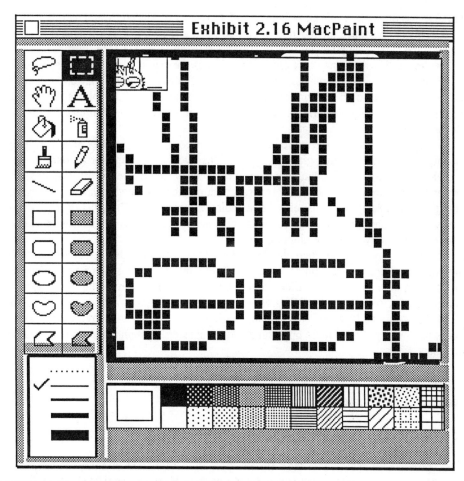

Exhibit 2.17: A part of the drawing in Exhibit 2.16 "blown up" and showing each individual pixel or picture element

up as color is added; usually resolution. That is, fewer dots are used but color is added; in general, a poor choice. Or, the resolution is acceptable, and color has been added, but the screen flickers in an annoying manner since the processor cannot keep up with the demand for screen refresh of all the dots and all the colors once every thirty seconds. Graphics places a much greater demand on a system's engineering, integration, and design, in comparison to a system that needs to handle text and numeric information only.

2.6-4 System expansions and graphic display improvement

When a system has an *open architecture* it can be more readily expanded by adding other hardware components. This defines open architecture; it can be good and bad. The positive side is the flexibility; the negative side is the potential lack of system's integration and cohesiveness.

Some system expansions may cost two or three times the original cost of the basic computer system. They make the computer into a different machine. For example, one may add a specialized graphics microprocessor board which provides very rapid generation of complex and high quality color images. Applications include flight simulation, architectural drawings, animated story boards for the development of TV commercials, and so forth.

Once a system has been converted for a dedicated purpose, it may not be convenient to use it for other purposes, including other graphics applications, word processing, or accounting. It may still be capable of these functions, but awkward in use. For example, special function keys on the keyboard can be programmed to mean different sets of commands initiated with a single key stroke. Once set to perform special functions related to a dedicated application, the function keys will need to be reset when switching to other applications. This is not particularly difficult technically, but from a user's point of view it can be nightmarish.

Closed architecture systems, like the Macintosh, give rise to *modeless operation*; that is, when moving from one application to another all commands remain consistent. This makes operation of the system, and a wide variety of applications, easier to learn and to remember. Open architecture systems, like the IBM PC, give rise to different modes of operation. This makes operation of the system and a wide variety of applications hard to learn and to remember. The open architecture, however, provides more opportunity for expansion. System expansions are discussed further in Chapter 3.

2.7 MEMORY AND STORAGE

2.7-1 Forms of memory and storage

Exhibit 2.18 provides an overview of the different types of memory and auxiliary storage. Memory is basically of two types; *ROM* which stands for *Read Only Memory*, and *RAM* which stands for *Random Access Memory*.

2.7-2 ROM

We cannot change the contents of ROM. The instructions in ROM are placed there by the manufacturer of the computer. ROM provides the computer with enough intelligence in the form of hard-wired instructions so that when the machine is turned on, the screen displays a message instructing the user what to do, such as "Insert disk." We insert the disk and then through commands entered through the keyboard we can load programs from the disk into RAM.

ROM may contain more than the above. For example, the ROM on the IBM PC contains a BASIC interpreter. The Apple Macintosh computer has a portion of its operating system and an extensive library of graphics routines in ROM.

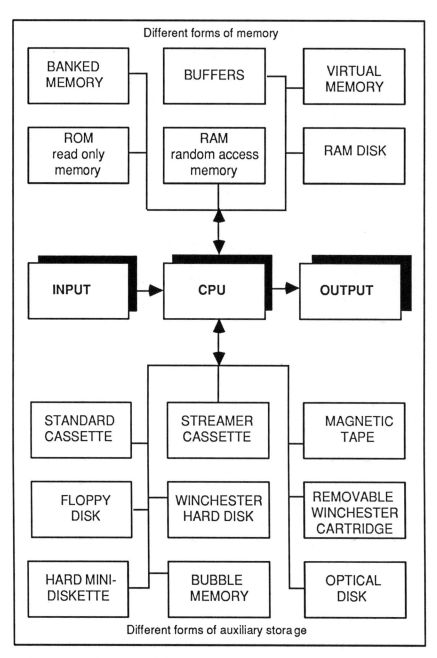

Exhibit 2.18: An overview of memory and storage

2.7-3 RAM

RAM is where our programs and data must reside when we are working with them. The larger the RAM memory, the more programs and data it can contain at any one time. Information in RAM can be accessed much faster than information on disk. Having more of the program and data you are working with in RAM can make for a dramatic improvement in the speed of operation.

It is possible, in fact quite usual, to have only part of an applications program in RAM memory, that part of the program in use at any given time. When another part of the application is required, it is loaded in to RAM from the disk. This is called *swapping*, or *overlaying*, and it is the way large programs are squeezed into small memories.

But, a price is paid when too much squeezing takes place. When we need a part of the program not in memory, then the system must retrieve that part from the disk. This is a relatively slow process. We may find ourselves with fingers poised over the keyboard as the system makes us wait while it loads the part of the program we need. When this happens the application program is said to be *disk bound*.

The *Winchester disk drive*, an auxiliary magnetic storage device, possesses faster access times than *floppy disks* (another storage device), and this can alleviate delays.* The only way to find out if an operation is irritatingly slow is to run a given application on some given computer system.

The trend today is toward integrating different applications so that they work together in some cohesive manner; for example, word processing, graphics, database, and spreadsheet. Another trend is to provide more user support and training in the applications software. This means larger and more programs are required to be in memory at the same time, which means larger memories are needed.

2.7-4 Measuring memory

Memory is measured in *bytes*. One byte (8 bits) identifies one character: a single letter, a number, or a special symbol. Therefore, a RAM memory of 512K (K=1000) can hold 512,000 characters of programs and data at any one time (actually 512 times 1,024, or 524,288 characters). We are working with a binary, not a decimal number system. The number 1,000 does not exist in a binary system.

For many years 64K memory was considered the minimum necessary for a professional system; this is no longer true. Graphics programs, integrated programs, programs with more user support, all require larger memories. Now 256K to 1 megabyte (mega=1 million)—or 1 MB—of memory is not at all unusual on microcomputer systems.

However, it is not the size of *total* memory but the size of RAM that determines memory available for application programs and related data. When memory size is listed in a specification sheet, it is necessary to check and see how much of it is RAM, and how much of it is taken up by ROM, the operating system, and other functions.

---

* The Winchester drive derives its name from the Winchester 30-30 rifle. The first Winchester developed by IBM consisted of two drives, each capable of storing thirty million bytes (30 megabytes)—thus, a thirty-thirty—which then led to association with the Winchester rifle. Storage is discussed later in this chapter.

2.7-5 RAM disk*

Another use for memory is as a *simulated* disk called a RAM Disk. A RAM disk is electronic, not magnetic like an ordinary disk. When a program or related data are on a magnetic disk in the disk drive it takes time for the read/write head—like the phonograph arm on a record player—to get to the proper location, or address, on the disk (called the *seek and search time*). Mechanical operations are always slow compared to electronic operations.

RAM disk is electronic memory, and is often created by a software utility that allows the user to partition off part of RAM and "fool" the computer into treating it as an auxiliary disk drive. Programs can then be placed in a RAM disk, just as they can a regular disk, but the program then operates very quickly because it is in RAM.

A major advantage is that programs do not have to be rewritten to take advantage of the RAM disk as they do when banked memory (discussed later) is involved. Is there a disadvantage? Yes. Most RAM memory is volatile. When the electric power is interrupted, *everything in RAM disappears instantly.* Nothing in a RAM disk is stored in the usual sense. This is not a problem if we transfer our work often to more permanent storage on magnetic disk. During operation we should periodically transfer work from RAM to storage in order to ensure against loss of data due to power loss or surges, and other possible system's failures. Some programs will perform this operation automatically, but it is unwise to depend on anything but our own well-established operating procedures and good work habits. Only the loss of some important work drives this point home.

2.7-6 Buffers

Buffer is another term for memory, a term used in relation to the memory needed for a peripheral. A peripheral is any device, such as a printer, plotter, or modem, connected to a computer. Printers need buffers, or a place to store data during printing received from the computer. In fact, it is wise to obtain a large buffer, or box of memory, so that a document for printing may be stored in the buffer while printing takes place. Printers are relatively slow. They are mechanical devices connected to electronic devices. When the computer is tied up printing, no other functions can take place.

Keyboards need buffers. If we type on the keyboard while the computer is doing something else and it does not have a keyboard buffer, or it has one that is too small, we may out-type the computer or the too small buffer and lose characters we typed. What we typed will simply not register. Very irritating.

---

* The reader may wish to study Section 2.7-7 Auxiliary Storage, on the use of magnetic disks, before reading the discussion here, on the use of memory as a simulated disk.

2.7-7 Auxiliary storage

Computer auxiliary storage is usually a magnetic medium (analogous to the cassette tape or phonograph record). The most common form of storage is disks and consists of three types as follows:

- Floppy disks
- Winchester disks
- Minidiskettes or microdisks

A floppy disk or diskette is a thin, circular, pliable, removable, random access (defined in the next section of this chapter) device that resembles the old 45 rpm records. Floppy disks are contained in flexible protective plastic jackets with small openings to allow the *read/write head* access to the surface of the floppy disk. The read/write head is analogous to the head of the record player, but they are called read/write heads because they can perform two functions; read the disk and record on the disk. When programs and data stored on a disk need to be used, the disk is inserted into a floppy disk drive located inside the same case as, or in a separate box connected to, the computer. Floppy disks hold from 200 kilobytes to 1.2 megabytes of data, stored on one or both sides of the disk (recent technology is pushing this limit up to 10 megabytes). For disks recorded on two sides, we require a disk drive that possesses two read/write heads (analogous to having a record player with two playing arms).

A Winchester disk may be used in place of a floppy disk drive and floppy disks. A Winchester disk is a rigid, nonremovable, random access, magnetic disk concealed inside the computer or located in an attached box. Hard disks have much larger storage capacities; 5 to 380 megabytes. Winchester disks are suitable for use with single computer systems, or in a network configuration to provide shared storage for a number of systems. Since graphics require high storage capacities, they are a good choice in this regard.

Minidiskettes or microdisks, and minidisk drives function in the same manner as floppy disks. A minidiskette or microdisk is an inflexible, removable, random access disk, 3-1/4" in diameter and holding 400 to 800 kilobytes of data. The minidiskette is encased in a permanent rigid plastic casing with a small metal slide window that opens when inserted into the computer to allow the read/write head access to the disk. The slide window provides superior protection against dust and scratches on the disk, in comparison to the floppy disk and its permanently open window. However, the Winchester drive, which is never opened mechanically, provides superior protection still. The Macintosh uses minidiskettes. They are particularly suitable for portable units. Minidiskettes may become an industry standard for small computers because of their size and convenience.

With floppies and minidiskettes we can store an unlimited amount of data by simply using more disks. However, separate disks cannot be in the same disk drive with data available (on-line) at the same time. With large data storage requirements, continuously exchanging floppies in and out of a disk drive is inconvenient and can make summary reports, based on all the data, difficult or clumsy to obtain.

2.7-8 Basic operation

Data are located on the disk by *tracks* and by *sectors*. Exhibit 2.19 provides a schematic.

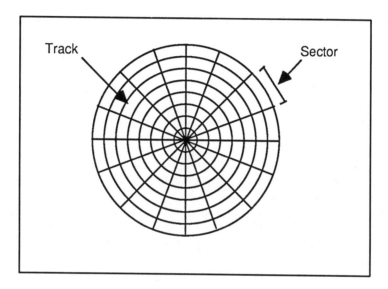

Exhibit 2.19: Schematic of a disk

The tracks are channels on the disk with data recorded in them. The tracks are divided into sectors, like a pie sliced up for eating. The disk does not contain a continuous track like a phonograph record.

All data are tagged automatically as to their location on the disk; that is, a specific address on a given track in a given sector. The operating system automatically takes care of this important item of housekeeping. When an item on the disk is required—the item could be part of a program or related data—the read/write head moves rapidly to the relevant sector and track. Then the disk spins to place the required data beneath the read/write head. This is called *seek and search*.

If one experimented and placed a small light on top of the read/write head and took a time lapse photograph of its movement for a few minutes of operation, it would look like the head was moving randomly all over the place as it sought different disk locations. Thus the name *random access* for disk storage, and *sequential access* for tape storage. Obviously, tape storage must be sequential. You can readily guess which one is more efficient and convenient.

2.8 THE CENTRAL PROCESSING UNIT (CPU)

The CPU is "the brain" of the computer. The program, to continue the analogy, is "the mind." The CPU processes data according to instructions in the software. Different computers have different CPUs. A computer should not be chosen on the basis of its CPU. Other criteria are more important, for example:

- Availability of applications software
- User interface and ease of use
- Reliability
- Expandability
- Cost effectiveness

The computer and the CPU finally obtained may indeed influence the above, but the CPU obtained should follow, not lead, a choice.

There are a few dominant CPUs used with small computers, and there are some strong trend setters. The IBM PC uses an Intel 8088. Some of the IBM PC look-alikes use the more powerful 8086 processor, with its "true" 16-bit capability, as opposed to the "pseudo" 16-bit design of the 8088. The meaning of this statement is explained later in this section.

The popular Apple IIe computer and all the Apple IIe look-alikes use the 6502, a slow processor by today's standards. But the cost effectiveness of the APPLE IIe, the plethora of software for this machine, and its open architecture may outweigh in importance its processor speed. Open architecture means the machine can be added to and expanded. The disadvantage is a lack of consistency in operation—different system configurations and software will function differently; for example, the same keys on the keyboard—or key sequences—will mean different things when using different applications. That is, the system possesses different modes. Other machines possess a closed architecture and expansion is more difficult, but operation is modeless or consistent. Presently the Macintosh has a closed architecture.

Then there are a large number of computers by various manufacturers that use a CPU called a Z80, or the faster Z80A or Z80B. Examples are the Kaypro 2, 4, and 10, and the Morrow MD 11. These CPUs support an operating system, CP/M, that is receiving little software development these days. But, systems based on the Z80 and the CP/M often provide a very good cost/performance ratio, and a large base of applications software.

There is another dominant CPU, the M68000 by Motorola. The M68000 is the fastest, the biggest, and the most powerful of all of the above. The Apple Macintosh and the Sage IV are two computers that use the MC68000. Highly graphic interfaces, windowing, integrated applications, and acceptable speeds of operation place heavy demands upon a system and require powerful CPUs to support them.

Recently, Commodore announced the Amiga computer, a system that also uses the powerful M68000, but, in addition, uses three custom processors for controlling graphics, sound, and input and output. This is comparable to having adjunct "brains" that take the load off the main CPU. Different systems are discussed in Chapter 3.

2.8-1 CPU capabilities

One important capability of a CPU is the amount of memory it can address. An analogy commonly used for memory and storage are postal boxes. Postal boxes have numbers, that is, addresses, and they contain letters, that is, information. Each computer memory location has an address and also contains letters, but of the alphabet variety, or numbers, or special characters. In small computers the memory "postal box" size is quite small—one byte, or character. These characters make up the programs and data used. You cannot get to the contents of memory, the programs and data, unless the contents are addressable.

Another factor, to be discussed in the next section, that affects the efficiency of processing is the amount of data that can be transmitted and processed at any one time. If a CPU can address more locations in memory, transmit more, and process more, then it is a more powerful CPU. The speed of the CPU will obviously affect the efficiency of these processes.

2.8-2 CPU speed

A computer runs by a clock; it has to, otherwise nothing would be coordinated. The clock runs faster in some CPUs than in others. The speed of the CPU is expressed in Megahertz (MHz). MHz is 1,000,000 cycles per second (mega meaning million, and hertz meaning cycle per second). Obviously, if a machine is executing a program instruction at 5 MHz it will execute it twice as fast as if it were running at 2.5 MHz.

The same CPU may function at different speeds on different machines. Further, upgrade kits that can be rapidly installed by a technician that will double CPU speed for some systems are available at low cost—less than $100.

Although a faster CPU is better, speed may have little to do with the efficiency of final operation. Other factors that affect the speed of operation are disk seek and search time and how well the operating system and the applications have been written. The CPU might be the "horsepower," but the software and the user are the "drivers" of the vehicle—the software acting as an automatic "co-pilot"—and determine how well the machine finally functions. If we want to know how fast and how well a particular application runs doing some given operation on some given computer, and how easy it is to use, we need to go "drive" it!

2.8-3 Memory and the CPU

Let us describe an imaginary "simple" computer. It has only 3 wires in the address bus (a bus is a number of wires like a cable) connecting the CPU and the RAM memory. The CPU executes program instructions using related data, and RAM stores the program and data when in use.

As we know, with 3 wires we may send a total of only 8 messages. That is, with 3 wires we can address only 8 RAM locations. Exhibit 2.20 shows a diagram of our simple computer with the CPU, the RAM memory and the 8 memory locations (or cells) in it, a data bus that carries data from RAM to the CPU, and an address bus that allows the CPU to access or address the data.

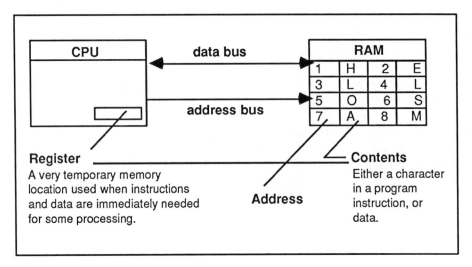

Exhibit 2.20: A simple computer

Here are some facts that our simple computer should help make apparent:

√ More memory than can be addressed is useless memory.
√ The number of addressable memory locations is limited
   by the number of wires in the address bus (but as we shall
   see there are ways of getting around this).
√ The number of bits of data that can be sent at any one time
   is dependent on the number of wires in the data bus.
√ A larger register means that more data can be processed
   at any one time. (The *register* size is what identifies a computer
   as being 8-, 16-, or 32-bit. It is only *one* factor that affects
   the efficiency of operation.)

The means by which CPUs can be compared are

√ Size of Register
√ Size of Data Bus
√ Size of Address Bus
√ Speed of CPU
√ Speed of Memory

The speed of memory is often overlooked or not mentioned, possibly because there is very little one can do about it after selecting a system. In fact, selection is wisely based on factors (availability of desired software, interface, compatibility with existing equipment—unless it deserves to be scrapped) that should take precedence over *any* of the variables named above. That is, selecting a system *because* of its register size, a 16-bit over an 8-bit, or a 32-bit over a 16-bit, is not very consequential even though hyped in the marketplace. People do not buy Apple

Macintosh, for example, because it is a 32-bit machine. Engineers at APPLE chose a 32-bit CPU and that helps Macintosh function the way it does.

Exhibits 2.21 and 2.22 provide schematics for the 8-bit and the 16-bit computers.

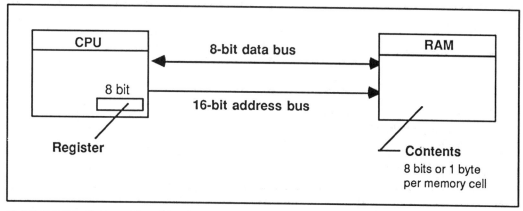

Exhibit 2.21: Schematic of typical 8-bit computers

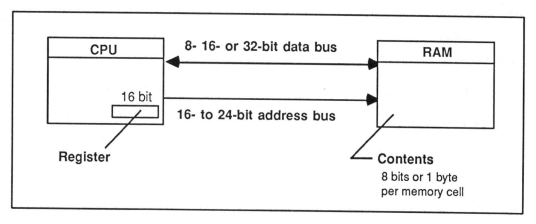

Exhibit 2.22: Schematic of typical 16-bit computers

The reader may compute for him- or herself the different number of memory locations that can be addressed, and other differences that can exist between different computers. In that regard, in Exhibit 2.23, selected systems are listed in the far left column followed by the name of the CPU they use and related data.

Some listed CPUs have different letters following them or end in different numbers. This refers to different generations of the same CPU. Register size (sometimes called the word size or bit width) identifies a CPU as 8-, 16-, or 32-bit. But, this is only one aspect of a CPU that affects operation. Note, for example, that the CPU, the 8088, in the IBM PC computer is a *quasi* 16-bit chip. It differs only in the size of the register and somewhat in CPU speed to the 8-bit Z80A. Space is provided to add data on other CPUs.

System	CPU	Speed in MHz	Register Size	Address Bus	Data Bus
Apple IIe+*	6502	2.0	8	16	8
Kaypro II*	Z80	2.5	8	16	8
Morrow Design*	Z80A	4.0	8	16	8
IBM PC	8088	5.0	16	16	8
Sage	M68000	8.0	32	24	16
Macintosh	M68000	12.0	32	24	16
ATT UNIX**	M68010	10.0	32	24	32
Sun Workstation**	M68010	10.0	32	24	32
Onyx	Z8000	12.0	32	32	16
—	—	—	—	—	—
—	—	—	—	—	—

Exhibit 2.23: Comparing CPUs
* Will accept 8088 chip making it a dual processor unit.
** Uses the UNIX Operating System; powerful, but not easy to use. Designers of total systems using UNIX must create a shell or an interface for the user.

2.8-4 Getting around limits

With 8-bit CPUs there are 16 wires from the CPU to RAM. RAM is made up of memory locations. Each memory location holds one byte. Each memory location has an address, and for data to be used they must be accessed through some address. Therefore, the maximum size RAM possible with 8-bit computers is 65,536; invariably referenced as *64K RAM* memory.

• Memory Banks

Clever engineers who dislike limits have found ways to expand addressable memory. They will organize memory into *banks* of 64K each. But the application software or the operating system must be rewritten to take advantage of the extra bank(s) of memory. The rewritten software must be able to address by bank, and then by memory location in that bank. If not, the memory is just like the gray matter we do not use. Useless.

• Ram Disk Revisited

Another way around the limit is to use extra RAM memory to *emulate* a disk drive as discussed earlier. In essense, when using a RAM disk, the computer is "fooled" into responding as if the RAM memory was a disk. It will store programs and data on that disk. The only problem, of course, is that RAM is volatile and once the power is turned off, all the contents of the RAM disk will disappear. However, programs in RAM disk will function very quickly, just as they would in "regular" RAM.

2.9 MULTIPLE CPUs

Some computers contain multiple CPUs. The DEC Rainbow 100 system contains the Z80 and 8088. The Operating Systems, or OSs (OSs are discussed in the next section), for the Rainbow are CP/M 80 for the Z80 and CP/M 86 for the 8088. However, and this is important, DEC made it so that when one loads in a program the computer "knows" what OS and CPU the application runs under and automatically sends it to the right CPU. Further, all software can communicate with all other software since the two OSs are basically the same.

Unless a manufacturer has provided for this type of compatibility and ease of use, multiple CPUs and multiple OSs are *not* particularly positive. They simply confuse the issue. More software may run on a multiple CPU system, but it is not more we want; it is better, easier, and more integrated. Other multiple CPU units are the Chameleon and the Fugitsu Micro 16.

Multiple CPUs in the same microcomputer should not be confused with the use of multiple CPUs with each performing different aspects of some task or application. This is an entirely different architecture related to parallel- or multiprocessing, fifth generation computers, and the future; possibly the near future.

Nor should the above be confused with multiuser network systems where all the CPUs for each station may be located in one box, called a "network in a box"; or a true network system where all the CPUs are located at the station, or node, along with auxiliary storage. In fact, in a true network, each node is a complete computer system capable of functioning independently.

2.10 GRAPHICS SOFTWARE

In earlier days, the production of graphics required a knowledge of programming. Further, it was a lengthy and tedious task specifying how one wanted an image to appear. Today children "paint" using computers. When computers were simple on the inside, they were complex to use on the outside. Today the initial learning of the tools of presentation, art, and design computer graphics is easy and enjoyable.* We are left to concentrate on design rather than learning to communicate with the computer. By contrast, the demands on the programmer are much greater; applications must be easier, better integrated, and more sophisticated. As computers become more powerful and simpler to use on the outside, they become more complex on the inside.

There are times when programming a graphics application is the superior choice to using some end application like a paint or computer aided design program. For example, if we wanted to generate many patterns for weaving, based on certain criteria or algorithms, it would obviously be much easier to let the computer do the processing and repeat pattern regeneration, rather than the human redrawing patterns in interactive mode.

The task of programming has been eased by the creation of *graphics toolboxes*; sets of programming routines that draw pictures or help draw pictures. These routines may be called by a program written in one of the standard languages, such as BASIC or Pascal.

---

* I say "initial" because small computers today are very powerful tools that can perform many sophisticated tasks, sometimes requiring extensive experience in order to take advantage of the many capabilities present.

On the Apple Macintosh, the toolbox is called *Quickdraw*, and it is installed permanently in ROM. Further, the ROM contains all the programs that make for the highly visual "face" of the Macintosh, and that also monitor that increasingly ubiquitous desktop tool for communicating with computers, the mouse. Lu (1984) describes the Macintosh environment in further detail.

On the IBM PC a number of graphics toolboxes are available, including *Halographics,* the *Graphics Kernel System (GKS),* and the *Graphics Development Toolkit;* the latter two are available from IBM.

2.11 THE OPERATING SYSTEM (OS)

The OS is the general manager of the computer. The analogy is a good one. In an office we have to go through the office manager to get anyone else to do anything. Further, the best office managers remain invisible—an iron hand in a velvet glove. It is the same with operating systems. It is this master program that we use to access all other programs, including applications, and the best OSs provide support for easy application use and development.

The OS tracks, directs, organizes, and manages all the resources of the system, largely automatically. The OS resides in memory; sometimes in RAM, sometimes in ROM. The functions performed by the OS:

- coordinating program compiling and interpreting—source
  to object code (see Section 2.12 on Programming Languages)
- managing memory
- managing disk operation
- coordinating information flow between system
  components (keyboard, screen, printer, disk drive)

Standard operating systems have emerged. They may function on one or a number of computers. *MSDOS*, standing for Microsoft Disk Operating System, functions on the IBM PC and IBM PC look-alikes. However, the IBM PC also supports other OSs.

CP/M for 8-bit machines is the oldest of the small computer OSs, with a large base of software applications available at low cost.

UNIX is a product of Bell Telephone Laboratories and a powerful OS used primarily by system developers. But use in the business world is increasing as applications software becomes available.

The Apple Macintosh has a unique operating system that is more of a total environment in which icons are used to make the operation easier and more intuitive.

Some points need to be made here:

- OSs are supported by certain CPUs. MSDOS, for example,
  functions on the IBM PC 8088 processor. It does not function
  on the Z80 processors. The CP/M OS functions on the Z80
  series computers.

- Applications software developed under one OS may not function under another. If the same programming language exists for both OSs, and disk incompatibilities can be overcome—through program transfer utilities available—then the same application program will function under both OSs.

- Using more than one OS and applications that function under different OSs should be avoided. It can make system operation unnecessarily complicated, and may also degrade operation.

2.11-1 Utilities

These are the *housekeepers* of the system. They work closely with the OS, the general manager. They are used to test the system, format disks, provide directories, indicate the amount of space left on a disk, and so forth. The best utilities are those that are compact so as not to waste valuable disk and memory space, and easy to use so as not to waste valuable time.

2.11-2 Window managers

Window managers are a recent technology. They turn the screen into an electronic desk top. They provide multiple windows onto a single program, or multiple programs. This does not necessarily mean that the user can do more than one thing at a time (multitasking), but it does mean rapid and easy movement between different applications, or different parts of the same application.

Sometimes window managers are a part of the system, or an add-on to the system, or a part of an application. They are likely to become standard issue because they improve operation and they make systems easier to use. Programmers, however, often do not like window managers because they can interfere with the types of manipulations programmers need to make, or they are unfamiliar to programmers who are used to the more esoteric and cryptic commands of traditional computing. "Friendliness," therefore, is a relative term.

2.11-3 Add-ons and shells

Add-ons and shells are programs that add features to an existing OS or applications, or provide a different interface to the operating system for the user. Often the features added are very useful and we can wonder why they were not in the original OS in the first place. One highly useful set of utilities for the IBM PC are the *Norton Utilities*. The add-on or shell might improve the speed and/or the ease of operation. It might provide more information from the system, or allow for more to be added. It might improve the operation of a particular application. For example, program enhancements exist that add rulers, coordinates, variable image rotation, and perspective to the paint program (MacPaint) on the Macintosh, features it does not normally possess. Topview, Windows, and GEM for the IBM PC provide a graphics interface to the OS, similar to the one pioneered by Apple on the Macintosh.

There is an add-on utility for the Macintosh that provides a calendar, a useful enhancement to the day and time clock provided. Both are shown in Exhibit 2.24 and were activated while this page was being typed into the word processor. The calendar program is one of many *memory-resident* programs available; that is, a program always in memory as a desktop accessory and, therefore, always available. The ungodly hours kept by writers appear in the upper right corner of the screen.

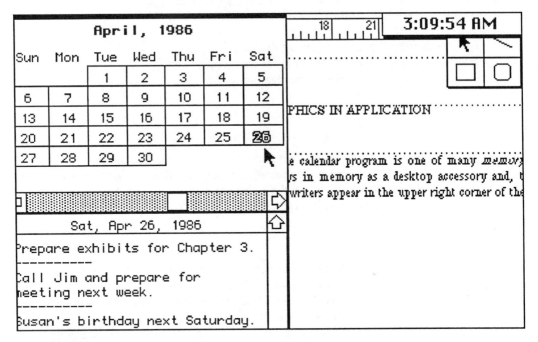

Exhibit 2.24: *CalendarBook* **accessory** (Part of Sidekick® for the Apple Macintosh; courtesy of Borland International)

2.12 PROGRAMMING LANGUAGES

Programing languages are software used to develop applications. Here are the names of familiar languages, the year they first appeared, and a brief description.

- **FORTRAN** (FORmula TRANslation); 1957; used primarily for engineering and scientific work.
- **COBOL**(COmmon Business Oriented Language); 1960; used for business applications, more "English-like" than other languages, but, by today's standards, as wordy and tedious as a Victorian novel. In its day it was a great innovation and remains a widely used language.
- **BASIC**; 1965; an easier language to learn, dominant on microcomputers, and exists in many "dialects" and expansions of the original.
- **Pascal**; 1971; highly structured (some say bureaucratic); prime tool for teaching programming.

- **LISP** (LISt Processing); 1960s; the language of Artificial Intelligence.
- **LOGO**; 1970s; a learning language; highly graphic; derived from LISP.
- **PROLOG**; 1970s; a research and artificial intelligence language.

There are many variations of the languages listed, and hundreds of other languages. The first four named are widely used, but it is estimated that less than 10 percent of the North American population will learn to use one effectively. They are called High Level Languages (HLLs) because they are closer to English than the machine code the computer "understands." But they still require some considerable effort to learn, and skill to use.

Computer languages fall into five generations; the fifth generation is in present development and part of the future.

2.12-1 First generation

At first those working with computers learned to "speak" machine code, that is sequences of instructions written in zeros and ones, the very bits the computer understood. Very tedious, time consuming, and error prone, as illustrated in Exhibit 2.25.

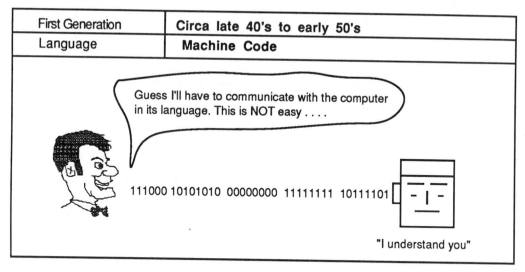

First Generation	**Circa late 40's to early 50's**
Language	**Machine Code**

Exhibit 2.25: First generation programming

Computers understand only one language: *binary code,* or ones and zeros, called *machine code.* When programmers first started programming they thought they had to speak the language of computers in order to communicate with computers. Understandable mistake. However, humans do not communicate well using two signals only; it is a poor way to say "I love you," "you owe me $100," or "draw a circle." The object is to get computers to communicate in our language, rather than us having to learn to communicate in theirs. This has taken, and is taking, a number of generations to develop.

2.12-2 Second generation

Programmers then thought of instructing the computer to recognize, and translate into machine code, short easy-to-remember mnemonic codes such as **ADD, SUB, MOV** (for add, subtract, and move). Programs are written using these mnemonics in a language called *Assembly*, and the program that translates assembly into machine code is called an *Assembler*, as illustrated in Exhibit 2.26. Assembly still serves important functions; programmers use it to develop highly efficient code.

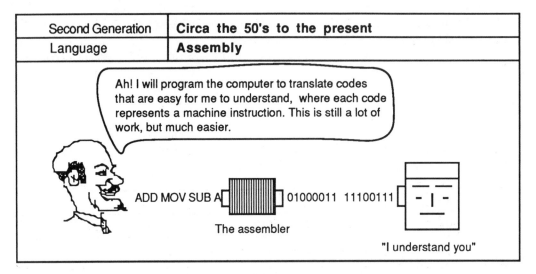

Exhibit 2.26: Second generation programming

2.12-3 Third generation

Following swiftly on Assembly, languages developed that allowed the programmer to write one line of instruction representing a complete procedure which in assembler might take several instructions. These are the High Level Languages (HLLs) like FORTRAN, COBOL, BASIC, and Pascal. HLLs are also known as *Procedural Languages*. They use instructions like:

NETPAY= GROSS - DEDUCT

Programs written in HLLs also need to be translated into machine code for the computer to understand them. The translation programs are called *compilers* and *interpreters* as illustrated in Exhibit 2.27.

Compilers translate all at once, something like a transcribed speech from a foreign language into English. Once you have the translation you do *not* need the original any more.

Interpreters translate one instruction at a time, something like having a foreign speaker and an interpreter present; for each comment by the speaker the interpreter translates the speaker's statement on the spot. You need *both present* all the time.

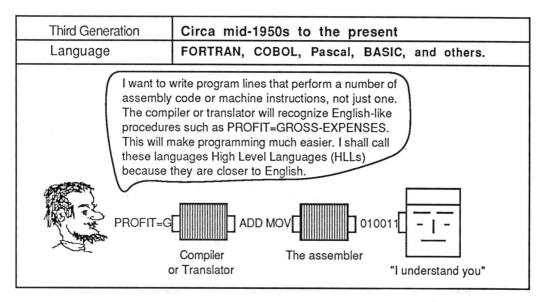

Third Generation	Circa mid-1950s to the present
Language	FORTRAN, COBOL, Pascal, BASIC, and others.

I want to write program lines that perform a number of assembly code or machine instructions, not just one. The compiler or translator will recognize English-like procedures such as PROFIT=GROSS-EXPENSES. This will make programming much easier. I shall call these languages High Level Languages (HLLs) because they are closer to English.

PROFIT=G | ADD MOV | 010011 | - | -

Compiler or Translator

The assembler

"I understand you"

Exhibit 2.27: Third generation programming

Compilers lead to faster and more efficient operation. Translators can be slow because of the necessary communication between program and interpreter. But interpreters allow for easier program development because they translate immediately, allowing for the immediate running of the program and, if it is not correct, immediate correction. Languages are tending to use a combination compiler and interpeter, that is, the best of both possible worlds.

We need to define two other terms: *Source Code* and *Object Code*. The program code written is the Source Code. The code produced by the translation program (assembler, compiler, or interpreter) from the source code is called the Object Code.

When a commercial software package is acquired, it is invariably the object code that we receive. There is no problem, unless we are dealing with an unsupportive or disreputable software producer or supplier. But, we should be aware that the object code cannot be changed. We must have the source code to make changes or corrections to the program. Therefore, if the object code purchased has "bugs," or errors in it, and the supplier does not provides us with support and changes, we are out of luck.

In any case, applications software is reaching such levels of complexity and sophistication that allowing any programmers, unless they are very skilled, other than the original programmers to work with the software is very dangerous indeed.

Since so few will learn to program, are we doomed to using other people's "canned" programs? Fortunately not. The separation between languages and applications is getting fuzzy because languages are being developed that allow for a broader base of users. For example, in Chapter 14 we discuss programming through the use of graphics itself.

2.12-4 Fourth generation

More recent developments include programs that are very English-like, or use procedures that are more intuitive (like icons), or are established to use menu choices, or table choices, and that can be used by nonprogrammers. They are called *Very High Level Languages (VHLLs)*.

All the applications software required by all the present and potential users of computers cannot be produced by programmers, and could not even if 25 percent of the total North American work population were all feverishly programming.

Therefore, new programming tools *had* to emerge. These new tools are not called programming languages, though in many respects they are. They are called *Generators* and often work in conjunction with *Database Management Systems*, as illustrated in Exhibit 2.28.

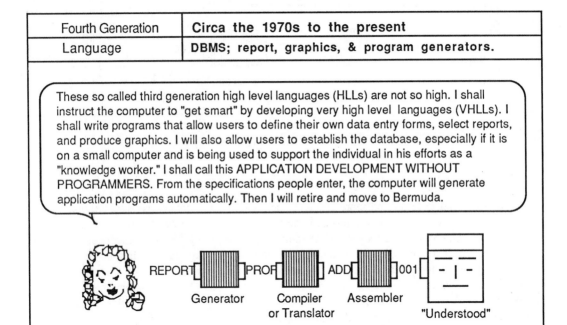

Fourth Generation	**Circa the 1970s to the present**
Language	**DBMS; report, graphics, & program generators.**

These so called third generation high level languages (HLLs) are not so high. I shall instruct the computer to "get smart" by developing very high level languages (VHLLs). I shall write programs that allow users to define their own data entry forms, select reports, and produce graphics. I will also allow users to establish the database, especially if it is on a small computer and is being used to support the individual in his efforts as a "knowledge worker." I shall call this APPLICATION DEVELOPMENT WITHOUT PROGRAMMERS. From the specifications people enter, the computer will generate application programs automatically. Then I will retire and move to Bermuda.

REPORT — Generator   PROF — Compiler or Translator   ADD — Assembler   001   "Understood"

Exhibit 2.28: Fourth generation programming

VHLLs are powerful, providing as much as a 100 to 1 improvement in the production of applications in comparison to traditional programming languages. Further, many more people are able to use them directly. They are important enough to be listed as a separate system component in Exhibit 2.9.

VHLLs appear in graphics systems. For example, a design, presentation, or analytic graphics system may contain a database of graphic images and related information and a command language that provides more capabilities—and requires more learning—than a simple menu driven application. For example, the *Graphic Decision Support System (GDSS)* from Data Business Vision, Inc. for the IBM PC is of this nature.

Engineers, designers, and architects use computer aided design systems involving icon command screens dedicated to a given design area (electrical, mechanical). Drawings are created by choosing from the menu of graphic symbols and the commands to manipulate them. Further, a database of information is associated with the graphic primitives that the engineer or designer can reference and use on direct command.

2.12-5 Fifth generation

Computers are being developed that do not use one CPU but many, that do not process one instruction at a time, but many in parallel. Parallel processing more closely emulates human brain functioning. Explorations in *Artificial Intelligence (AI)* involve explorations of parallel processing and related languages. Related languages are *non*procedural and are concerned with the state of objects in a problem, the relationship between objects, and the truth of a relationship as it relates to a solution or answer.

One such language is PROLOG, adapted by the Japanese, expanded, modified, and to be called HIMIKO as the basis for programs in their fifth generation computers. PROLOG is a knowledge representation language. A simple program line in PROLOG might read as follows:

likes(Joe, fish)

In the PROLOG language this means: *Joe likes fish.* Many statements like this might be entered, building a database of objects and relations. We may then query the database as follows:

?- likes(Joe, fish)

In the PROLOG language this means: *Does Joe like fish?* PROLOG will search the database to see if any data or facts relate. PROLOG would respond "yes" to the above.

Obviously, PROLOG is capable of far more complex logic and query than the above. It is not that procedural languages cannot perform such functions; it is that they do not do it as directly or cleanly—we might say as logically—as a language like PROLOG.

PROLOG is referenced briefly in Chapter 14 when we discuss research and development related to a graphics version of PROLOG. The aim is to design powerful and more intuitive means for instructing the computer. If there are many processes occurring in parallel some graphic means will be necessary simply to have a map of what is happening. Traditional linear lists of programming code will not suffice.

2.13 SOFTWARE ORGANIZATION

The software is organized hierarchically, as shown in Exhibit 2.29. When using the computer, we first encounter the initial intelligence of the system located in ROM, and are quickly transported to the operating system or environment. This general manager then provides us with access to all other software: applications programs, programming languages, housekeeping utilities, and so forth.

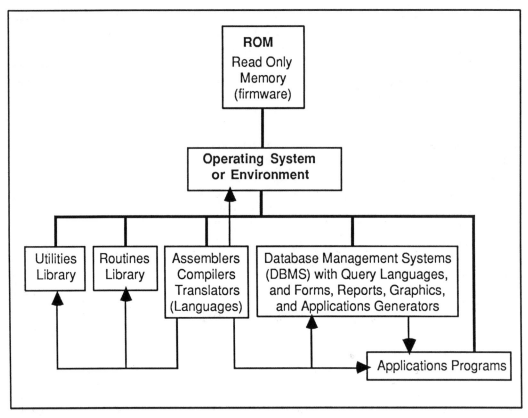

Exhibit 2.29: Software is organized hierarchically
(Note: The lighter lines with arrows indicate that languages are used to produce most software, except for applications programs which are created using either languages or applications generators.)

The light lines in Exhibit 2.29 show that languages are used to create most software, except applications programs which are created using both programming languages and applications generators.

The programs in ROM are not created using traditional programming approaches; they are placed there using a physical means for modifying the electronic circuitry, often involving the use of ultraviolet light to create binary coded circuits permanently "burned" into the system.* For most users, this level of involvement with the internal functioning of the computer is unlikely.

---

* With some systems it is possible to obtain ROM in a form that allows the technically inclined user to program it, and sometimes to program, erase, and reprogram it; called PROM and EPROM for Programmable Read Only Memory, and Erasable Programmable Read Only Memory, respectively.

3

Types of Graphics Systems

3.1 INTRODUCTION

We may obtain graphics from a computer system in different ways, based on the different types of processing: batch and interactive. These are called the *modes of operation*. Further, there are different *classes of graphics systems* which relate to these modes: large *mainframes*, *minicomputer workstations*, and *microcomputer-based systems*. These classes of systems are not mutually exclusive; a system's *configuration* might contain some mix of the three. The classes or categories help us make sense of the many system configurations possible. In this chapter we discuss modes of operation, classes of systems, and systems configurations. Further, we describe and compare a few systems from different classes.

3.2 MODES OF OPERATION

The modes of operation are based on categories provided by Stover (1984).We will relate batch and interactive processing, as discussed in Chapter 2, to the different means for obtaining graphics from systems.

3.2-1 Passive or batch

Passive, or batch, graphics is the oldest form of graphics. It existed on early large mainframe systems and, in most cases, it is not acceptable today. Input is in the form of data on punched cards, and output is in the form of a printout from a line printer or a plot from a pen plotter.

Passive graphics can be tedious, time consuming, and expensive in terms of human effort. Sometimes many repeat cycles may have to be made—repunching cards, reentering cards, processing, and reviewing output—absorbing many hours before a correct image is obtained.

In passive graphics, the computer generates an image from data entered by the user in the form of numbers, coordinates, instructions to join coordinates, and so forth. The computer, based on this data and under the control of a program, prepares and presents the images.

3.2-2 Passive or batch: conversational

Conversational graphics is an improvement over ordinary batch mode, but not much better. Input is through a *non*graphics (alphanumeric) terminal, and output remains the same: a printer or pen plotter. There is no graphics on the monitor, and the system remains clumsy. However, this mode is suitable for certain applications such as plotting numeric data (Stover, 1984).

3.2-3 Interactive: real time

Interactive graphics is a dialogue that takes place between the user and the system. Graphics appear on the monitor and can be changed in real time; that is, changes are registered immediately.

Real-time interactive computer graphics places a heavy demand on processing, memory, and storage. This is why large computers were for a long time the only ones capable of real-time, animated, three-dimensional, interactive graphics. These same capabilities now appear on mini- and microcomputers, as described in a later section of this chapter.

To understand this increased demand, let us assume we would like the computer to present a complex three-dimensional image immediately. Further, we need to interact, move, manipulate, explode, rotate, and scan the image at will. Consider what it takes by way of the number of com-putations to rotate a three-dimensional image composed of 1000 lines at a rate that will avoid any flickering of the screen. The data associated with the location of the endpoints of all of the 1000 lines must be recomputed and the screen must be refreshed 30 times a second to display the new end points of all of the 1000 lines once every 30th of a second. Up until very recently this kind of real-time interactive graphics was possible only on large systems because of the numeric calculation load placed on the system.

We may consider the following question: What is the load on memory when we increase the required resolution in a display from 320 by 200 to 640 by 400 and further to the resolution of 1,024 by 1,024 or more? The number of pixels and the number of bits in memory in the frame buffer increase as shown in Exhibit 3.1.

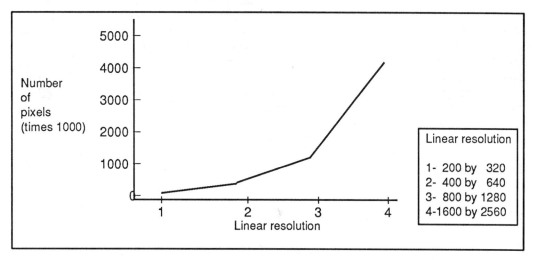

Exhibit 3.1: The number of pixels on the screen increases exponentially with a linear increase in resolution

The curve shows that the demands on memory, processing, and storage increase exponentially with a linear increase in resolution.

A resolution of 400 by 640 is available on a number of microcomputers, either as a part of the basic system, or through the use of add-on graphics cards that enhance the existing lower resolution of the basic system. The IBM PC, for example, provides a resolution of only 200 by 640. However, a graphics card added to the system can increase resolution to 400 by 640 (Tecmar, Cleveland, OH). This is an acceptable resolution for business graphics and some design work.

In order to obtain higher resolutions than this, it is necessary to enhance the microcomputer with a more powerful graphics card (for example, a card from Number 9 Computer, Cambridge, MA), or switch to another class of system in a higher capability and cost bracket altogether.

3.2-4 Interactive real time with database

In an interactive system with a related database the user has the following available:

- Libraries of stored graphic symbols, sometimes referred to as graphics primitives
  (dots, lines, circles, polygons)
- Libraries of icons or images of objects for a particular domain of design (desks,
  chairs, dividers, bookcases, plants, drapes for designing interiors)
- Related numeric and text data (sizes, colors, materials available, specifications,
  suppliers)

All of the above can be selected by the user—artist, designer, architect, engineer—to produce finished designs and related specifications.

In order to make this kind of application available, a programmer has spent time constructing what is known as an *Application Model*, that is, "a collection of data representing objects and relationships in that data. . . .These objects can be concrete or abstract and can be visualized in a two- or three-dimensional world—for example, a mathematical function, an integrated circuit, a floor plan, a gear train, or a molecule." (Foley and Van Dam, 1983). Application models are discussed further in Chapter 8.

Establishing a common database available for all users of a system in an enterprise is important. It leads to consistency of data, reduced redundancy of data and programs, more accurate applications, and faster applications development. If an operation moves to automated manufacturing, this becomes even more critical. The database serves as a collection point for all the research on products and product manufacturing which can then be used by the graphics designer in the design of products.

3.3 CLASSES OF SYSTEMS

All graphics systems consist of the following major components:

- Systems software.
- Graphics and related software.
- Graphics and related data.
- A CPU that is part of a micro-, mini-, or mainframe computer.
- A graphics processing unit (GPU) for handling all the interactive graphics
  functions. (Some systems do not possess a GPU and rely on the CPU to handle
  this function; this is unwise with small CPUs because the load is too great.)
- Internal or main memory to work with the CPU and GPU.
- Auxiliary storage—usually hard disk.
- Backup archive storage; in mainframe systems large magnetic tapes are used, in
  smaller systems a streamer tape or Winchester cartridge, and in smaller systems
  still, floppy disks.
- In large systems there is a separate control unit for the CPU, usually a keyboard
  printer or alphanumeric display console. In smaller systems it is the graphics
  station itself, or one of the graphics stations if there is more than one.

- Graphics workstations.
- Some hard copy output devices: printers and/or plotters.
- Output capture of other kinds—film, slide, and video (optional).
- Some form of communications with other systems (optional).

The *difference* between systems consists of size, number of stations, data capture, image display, speed of processing, and capabilities provided through applications software. For example, modeling realistic 3-D, solid, colored images in animation at rapid speed, and captured on high quality commercial size film requires the resources of Lucas Film or Walt Disney, not a personal computer system.

Graphic systems can be grouped into seven classes or categories:

- Centralized mainframe, multistation, time-share systems
- Distributed minicomputer, multistation, time-share systems
- Minicomputer or microcomputer graphics workstations
- Enhanced microcomputer systems
- Basic microcomputer systems
- Network systems
- Turnkey systems

The turnkey graphic system may be based on any of the above, with the possible exception of the mainframe. Turnkey is not a technical term; it simply means a system completely configured by a vendor and ready to use, that is, one need only *turn* the *key*.

3.3-1 Centralized mainframe

A mainframe computer is a large central computer system that supports many workstations. In the mainframe system, none of the stations is independent; they all share common resources such as memory, storage, printers, and plotters.

One possible problem with mainframe systems is the degradation that takes place as more workstations are attached. Reaction time slows down and the user may wait a considerable time queueing for different resources. A way around this is to move toward distributed processing; that is, a number of computers located at different remote geographic locations and connected together in some configuration.

Cost of graphics software for mainframes can run high; a single application can cost $5,000 to $20,000 for operation on a Data General, Digital Equipment Corporation (DEC), Prime, or IBM mainframe or large minicomputer. However, cost-performance benefits should be computed across all users, which may constitute a large number.

3.3-2 Distributed minicomputers

Distributed processing often uses minicomputers, but may involve mainframes, minis, and micros. The mainframe may act as a repository for shared data in a database and for archive data, the minicomputers distributed to support a number of stations, and microcomputers used in place of graphics terminals. The basic idea is to use more than one computer or CPU and have fewer graphics stations use the resources of each computer. This then reduces loads and queueing.

Each mini- or microcomputer-based system may support one or more graphics stations. Each station may operate in a stand-alone mode, with its own CPU, memory, storage, input, and output devices or as independent units that use certain resources such as a high quality plotter and a central database on a large storage medium in common. Distributed processing is a part of networking.

3.3-3 Graphics workstations

The graphics workstation can be based on a mini- or microcomputer. It can vary considerably in capability and cost, from $15,000 to $150,000. The graphics station is often used as the basis for a turnkey system. A turnkey system is a complete graphics system which includes the hardware, software, users guides and system documentation, installation, support, service, and training. It is a system designed with some specific dedicated end-purpose in mind (architectural drafting, publishing). Most Computer Aided Design (CAD) systems are turnkey systems. Very often a developer of an application will select a given graphics workstation on which to develop the turnkey system. For example, the *Interleaf Electronic Publishing System* by Interleaf (Cambridge, MA) is built around a *Sun Workstation* by Sun Microsystems, Inc. (Mountain View, CA), and discussed in Chapter 12.

Recent Sun Workstations are based on the 15MHz Motorola 68020 32-bit CPU, with 4 megabytes of main memory expandable to 8 megabytes, a built-in link to Ethernet (networks are discussed later in this chapter), a 19-inch monochrome display with a resolution of 1152 by 900 bit-mapped graphics and very rapid flicker-free screen refresh, a 71-megabyte disk drive, and a 60-megabyte 1/4 inch cartridge streaming tape drive. Streaming tape drives are capable of backing up large amounts of data very quickly. The Sun operating system is UNIX based and, therefore, very powerful, supporting multitasking (many tasks performed at the same time), and multiwindows on applications. The reader may wish to refer back to Chapter 2 and reread the sections on OSs, CPUs, memory, storage, bit-mapped graphics, and screen resolution. An image of the Sun-3/160C Workstation is given in Exhibit 3.3 and can be compared to the image of the Macintosh in Exhibit 3.4.

The difference in screen size between the two systems is shown in Exhibit 3.2.

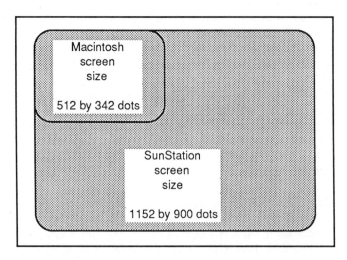

Exhibit 3.2: Big difference in size but little difference in resolution

Exhibit 3.3: The Sun Workstation (Courtesy of Sun Microsystems, Inc.)

Exhibit 3.4: The Apple Macintosh (Courtesy of Apple Computer, Inc.)

The *resolutions* of the screens of the two systems, however, are not very different at all: approximately 5,265 and 5,695 dots per square inch for the Macintosh and Sun Workstation, respectively. There are major differences in speed, multitasking, size of memory, and storage. The Sun system is superior to the Macintosh, but then so is its price, approximately six times higher. The Apple Macintosh and the Sun Workstation belong to entirely different classes of systems. Both, for their intended purposes and pocketbook, are excellent systems. Here are descriptions of three other graphics stations.

Applicon (Burlington, MA), a well-known supplier of graphics software for mainframes, produces the *Aria Standalone Color Workstation*. The Aria workstation is a system suitable for computer aided design (CAD), engineering (CAE), and manufacturing (CAM). It is based on a DEC VAX processor with 3MB of memory expandable to 4MB, a 160MB Winchester disk, and two cartridge tape drives. The display allows for eight colors at one time with a resolution of 504 by 672. The system costs approximately $90,000.

PERQ is another turnkey workstation produced by Three Rivers Computer Corp. (Wakefield, MA). It offers a screen in either portrait (higher than wider) or landscape (wider than higher) with orientations of either 768 by 1024 or 1280 by 1024 pixel resolution, respectively. The memory is expandable to 2MB, the operating system is a version of UNIX, and the system is specifically designed to support electronic publishing. It costs around $30,000.

ORCA, a series by ORCATECH (Ontario, Canada), provides systems based on the Intel 8086/8087 CPUs, or the M68000/68010, with both CPUs enhanced by a graphics processing unit (GPU). It has a resolution of 1024 by 1024, memories up to 8MB, Winchester drives up to 80MB, and prices range from $25,000 to $80,000.

The systems briefly described above are only a few of the many available. A short list of vendors of graphics workstations is provided in Appendix C. The reader may wish to write to selected vendors to obtain updated product descriptions and specification sheets in order to evaluate and compare different systems and systems configurations. The evaluation methods provided in Chapter 15 are designed to aid in this type of comparison.

3.3-4 Assembly of a system

The difference between a turnkey system and the assembly of a graphics system from various components of hardware and software is that a vendor has taken the responsibility of configuring a turnkey system for the user. Configuration can be a challenging task, and it may be wise to select a turnkey system with all of the inherent support that should be part of a complete package.

If the graphics requirements are standard, are met by standard or minimally enhanced micro-computer systems, *and* are supported by a local vendor, then assembly of a system is a safe alternative. The basic precautions provided by systematic analysis and selection should be followed as described in Chapter 15.

When the graphics requirements exceed those provided by a locally supported, minimally enhanced microcomputer, and when the building blocks or computer components are complex and expensive, then system integration may present too many hurdles and pitfalls for in-house or personal assembly. Integrating higher level graphics systems requires access to well-trained technical staff, knowing how to do it, or a willingness to learn.

3.3-5 Enhanced microcomputers

The enhanced microcomputer is an attractive alternative that provides good value. Options exist that were available in earlier days only on much more expensive systems. We should not be misled, however. Microcomputer systems will not replace mainframes or minicomputers. The improved graphics on microcomputers simply expands the base of choices and users, reduces costs for a number of graphic applications (business presentation graphics, graphics design) and allows a graphics station, connected or otherwise, to be microcomputer-based. An enhanced microcomputer system can easily run $15,000 to $50,000 or more, depending upon hardware and software options chosen.

For example, a microcomputer-based turnkey system, *Multidraw*, provided by Cymbol Cybernetics Corp. (Ottawa, ONT), includes either a 2-D or 3-D version, unbundled or as a part of a turnkey system using the IBM PC AT as the base unit. The turnkey system includes a 1024 by 780 resolution, 19-inch display, 512K memory, 20 MB Winchester, the IBM PC AT with an added math coprocessor (the 80287), a digitizing tablet with a puck (another name for a mouse), and systems and graphics 2-D software for $30,000 (3-D graphics would increase this price to $34,000).

The *XTAR Graphics Microprocessor* by XTAR Electronics (Elk Grove, IL), provides high resolution of up to 2048 by 2048. It has a fast enough refresh of the screen, namely, 130 to 300 times per second, that complex images may be drawn and animated on a microcomputer. The screen, of course, would have to be able to handle these levels of display, which would mean a higher investment in the monitor. The XTAR also allows for 4096 colors to be displayed at any one time from a palette of over 16 million colors. It is the number of colors that can be displayed, as much as the resolution, that provides for quality and realism. Further, the XTAR comes with a graphics command language for the programmer. These are impressive capabilities and compare favorably with systems costing a lot more. Flight simulation for small airports and flight schools, architectural drafting, animation, video production, and animated story boards for ad agencies are possible applications (Coleman and Powers, 1984).

Polycad/10 by Cubicomp (Berkeley, CA), appears to offer similar capabilities to the XTAR by expanding the IBM PC or IBM PC XT. They also offer 4096 displayable colors from a palette of over 16 million and *two* frame buffers of 512 by 512; one can be updating as the other is displaying. They offer software to support a graphics database, user-friendly interactive menus, a command language for the programmer, animation, macros (macros are a means for establishing sequences of commands which can then be initiated by a single press of a key, command, or program line), the storing and manipulation of models, and support for various output devices. The *Polycad/10* costs less than $19,000 for the base system.

The *Vetrix Midas Color Card* from Vetrix Corp. (Greensboro, NC) may be added to the IBM PC. It provides 672 by 480 resolution, 512 colors at any one time from over 16 million, supports an extensive library of graphics macros, comes with a "paint" program with an extensive end-user command language including color mixing, graphic primitives (e.g., lines, polygons, arcs, circles, patterns), and 3-D transformations around different axes. The hardware and software enhancements cost in the range of $6,000 to $7,500.

Two systems that fall between the high end graphics workstations and the low end PC systems are the *IBM 3270 PC/G* and *PC/GX*. They are suitable for some computer aided design (CAD) work and high end business graphics. The 3270 PC/G comes with a 14-inch screen with 720 by 512 resolution, and adds $4,500 to the cost of an IBM PC system. The 3270 PC/GX possesses a 19-inch screen and 960 by 1000 resolution. This upgrade adds $12,000 to the cost.

Inovion (Layton, UT) supplies a graphics system based on the same CPU as used in the APPLE IIe, the 6502. The system has a resolution of 512 by 483 and at a price of $4,495 appears to offer good price/performance. The system offers a color palette of over 2 million possible colors, and 780KB of graphics memory and may be used as a stand-alone system, a computer terminal to another system, or as an image processor, since it is capable of accepting and storing color input from a TV, video camera, or VCR. The images produced are impressive: three dimensional, good color renderings. Various graphics routines are built into the system's ROM. An optical mouse is also provided.

Graphics suitable for business are available in portable and lap top models. Consider the *Data General/One* system from Data General Corp. (Westboro, MA). The *Data General/One*, shown in Exhibit 3.5, weighs less than 11 pounds and fits into a briefcase.

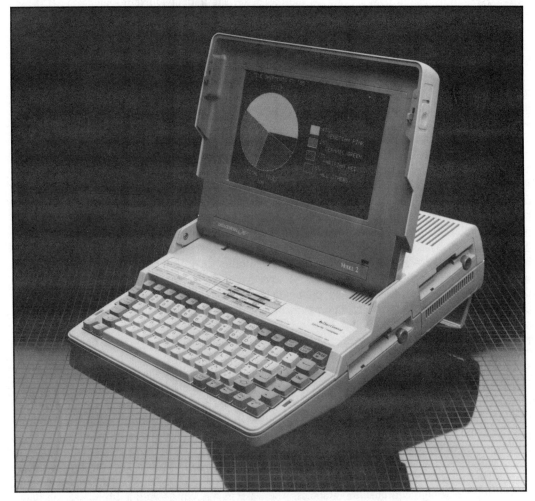

Exhibit 3.5: The portable *Data General/One* with business graphics
(Data General/One is a trademark of Data General Corporation. Photo used with permission)

It uses a full size flat screen, two 720KB disk drives, and memory which is expandable to 512K. A built-in modem, a portable printer, and an 8-hour battery pack are optional. Using a portable graphics system can extend the office to any location and provides the business person with the ability to create reports that include both text and images.

A transportable unit directed to the engineering and scientific community is the *Integral PC* provided by Hewlett Packard. The portable HP has a 9-inch screen, supports 3-D graphics and animation, comes with a built-in ink-jet printer, possesses 512K memory expandable to 1MB, a RAM disk that serves as the second storage device, and a UNIX operating system built into a 256K ROM. The unit has been well received but is definitely oriented to the technical user.

3.3-6 Microcomputers as mainframe terminals

Systems like the *Apple Macintosh* did not emerge from mainframe environments and therefore do not follow any standards that developed in the large system environment. However, a Macintosh is a low cost black-and-white graphics system of supreme quality. One group of terminals that has been used for graphics with large mainframe computers is the series from Tektronix. The Tektronix terminals are high quality, relatively expensive, and form a standard for working with mainframe computer graphics software. Through software such as *Tekalike* by Mesa Graphics (Los Alamos, CA), it is possible to have the Macintosh emulate the Tektronix terminals. *Tekalike* provides for communication with remote mainframes, for the accessing of mainframe graphics programs, and for the recording from the mainframe to the Macintosh.

3.3-7 Networks

Exhibit 3.6, based on a diagram by Stover (1984), shows the evolution to networked systems where each system is capable of functioning independently.

A network is important when sharing data and resources among different workstations is necessary. There are many network offerings. *Ethernet* from Xerox has been available for some time and is considered a standard. 3Com (Mountainview, CA) offers a network called *Ethermac,* which allows IBM PCs and Apple Macintoshes to be linked together. The network also allows Apple and IBM stations to share a 36MB Winchester and an Apple Laserwriter (laser printers and other output devices are discussed in Chapter 5).

Another alternative is to link computers via telecommunications. In fact, since this ubiquitous connection, the telephone, is already in place, some industry observers believe that it will become the primary basis for networking.

Most users require three things from a network: the sharing of information, the common use of high cost peripherals like laser printers or Winchester drives, and the transfer of files from one station to another. Further, many users do not need to tie together very many stations and peripherals. A wide variety of low cost networks now exist that provide for the networking of a small number of computers, some costing as low as $100 per station or node. Low cost systems offered include Lanpac by Racore (Scotts Valley, CA), Easylan by Server Technology (Sunnyvale, CA), and the Systemizer by Applied Creative Technology (Sunnyvale, CA).

The needs of users, the software, and the hardware must match. If, for example, several users are required to use a given database of information, then the software that manages the database must be multiuser. Very often such software is written so that it will support a given network or networks, but not all networks. For example, Omnis 3 on the Macintosh supports two networks:

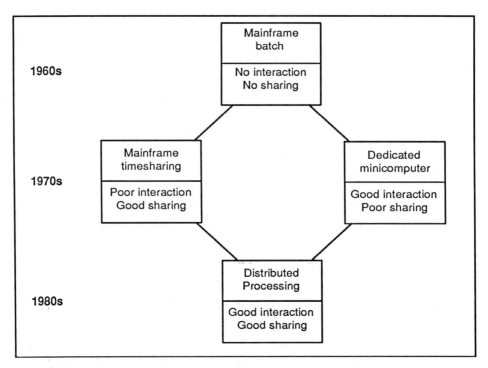

Exhibit 3.6: The evolution of systems (From *An Analysis of CAD/Cam Applications* by Richard Stover © 1984. Used by permission of the publisher, Prentice-Hall, Inc., Englewood Cliffs, NJ.)

Hypernet and Omninet, but not Appletalk. A similar situation exist for IBM PCs and networks. Compatibility among different software, hardware, and networks is a problem. Standards do not exist.

Different cabling can be used to connect computers: telephone wire, twisted pair (twisted because it cuts down on noise and interference), coaxial cable, and optic fibre (relatively new and highly efficient). Any method of connecting computers will allow for the transmission of digital signals, and those signals can represent letters, numbers, sounds, or bit-mapped images. The speed of transmission is partially dependent on the type of cabling used. Speed of transmission on networks can vary tremendously; from rates as low as 20 thousand bits per second to 10 million bits per second.

Sometimes high speeds are important; other times far less important. For example, if rapid transmission of high resolution color images between many points is required, then obviously the demand on the network is very great. However, if the network is required to transmit relatively low resolution, black-and-white business graphics, and delays of a few minutes are not critical, then an entirely different network is configured. In the first case coaxial cable is required; in the second ordinary telephone wire might be used along with a low cost means for connecting computer systems and requiring very little additional hardware.

The network configuration can be in the form of a bus, a ring, or a star to which different stations and devices are attached. The configuration is sometimes called a network *topology*. A bus configuration is shown in Exhibit 3.7.

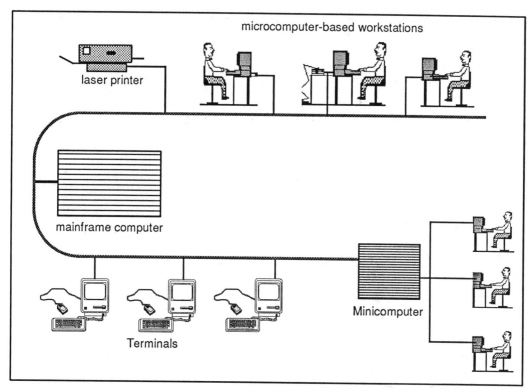

Exhibit 3.7: Bus network

The configuration shown is symbolic; it need not look like this at all. The diagram in Exhibit 3.7 symbolizes that a bus network can connect different kinds of computers, and different devices that serve users on the network.

A ring configuration is shown in Exhibit 3.8. The way users get on to the network is different with a ring from a bus network. With the bus network, users keep trying at random times to use the network, which, if busy being used by a given user, cannot be used at that precise moment by anyone else. This kind of use is like a group of people waiting at a bus stop that refuse to line up, but keep crowding the door trying to get on. By comparison with a ring network, one receives a "token," an electronic go-ahead, that keeps circling the network, and users queue to use the token and get on the network; like a more civilized queue-line of people waiting at a bus stop.

The star network is the simplest topology and is diagrammed in Exhibit 3.9. In a star network, one device is controlling and monitoring everything. A typical configuration is a number of microcomputer-based stations connected to a microstation that monitors the network, and controls access to the information in a Winchester disk, the use of a printer, and the file transfer between different stations. Expansion with a star network is limited after a certain number of nodes have been added. One can intuitively see why this is so; the load on the central system becomes too great.

Let us pose a problem: we need to transmit a black-and-white image created on a Macintosh to another Macintosh located 400 miles away. We are working with a graphics designer and we wish

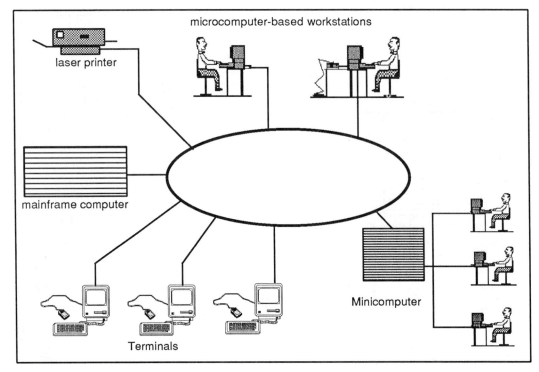

Exhibit 3.8: Ring network

to cooperate on the design of certain images. We create the image using MacDraw (a drafting program discussed in Chapter 9), save it in a file and then, using a communications program, we send the file to the other computer. The other computer is set up in receive mode, while our computer is set up in send mode. The communication software performs this task, and the modem connected to the telephone allows for the file to be transmitted. Using the same MacDraw software at the other end, the designer looks at our picture, adds things, makes corrections and sends the changed drawing back. This process might be repeated several times over some period. What is critical for the ease and success of this transmission and cooperative effort (besides a good telephone connect) is that *the two systems are identical, and they are functioning in the same mode.*

Now consider two IBM PCs. If configured *exactly the same,* then there is no problem; they would perform the above task with equal ease. But if configured differently in certain critical ways, then the kind of cooperative effort between remote stations could not take place.

3.4 IBM PC AND APPLE MACINTOSH COMPARED

For some considerable time the author has had access to the IBM PC XT, the Apple Macintosh, and a wealth of software for both. They are very different in how they operate and in their respective strengths and weaknesses.

The IBM PC has a memory of 128K expandable to 640K (a number of boards are now

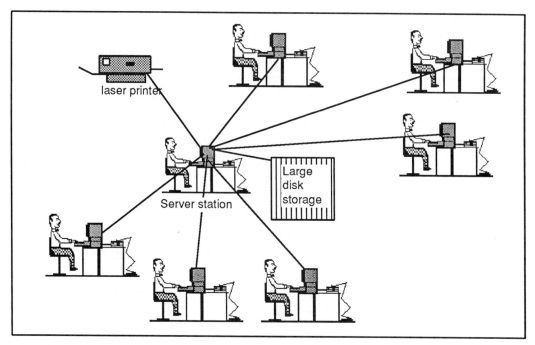

Exhibit 3.9: Star network

available for expanding memory beyond the IBM PC limit of 640K), uses the 8088 quasi 16 bit for its CPU, is largely menu driven, uses keyboard input and control, possesses dual 5-1/2-inch floppy disk drives for storage, has a mouse interface option, has optional graphics and color, and is a large desktop unit.

By comparison the Apple Macintosh has 128K, 512K, or 1MB memory; uses the M68000 32 bit for its CPU, an icon driven mouse interface, and 3-1/2-inch microdiskettes; is monochrome only (but an integrated graphics system of high excellence); and is transportable. The screen is smaller.

The Macintosh is technically a far superior machine in its design, operating environment, and its basic integration. It is a graphics system. The IBM provides for no graphics particularly, and equipment and software must be added to the IBM PC in order to make it into a graphics system. If imitation is the highest form of flattery, then the Macintosh designers should be highly flattered. For example, many window/mouse/drop menu interface systems now available for other machines, including the IBM, such as *GEM* from Digital Research, *Windows* from Microsoft, and *Topview* from IBM itself, are shameless imitations of the *Finder* and the *Desktop* applications for the Macintosh system.

However, none of the imitators on the IBM provide the integration afforded by the Macintosh because none of them were designed from the beginning along with the hardware. Macintosh's operation is *modeless,* which means that *the same commands and moves mean the same thing in all applications.* The Mac interface clones for the IBM PC are all grafts onto the existing IBM system. They may take up a lot of resources, may not support a lot of software, or support only a certain required set of software. Something that has been designed together from the beginning is bound to have a certain edge in operation.

The major disadvantage of the IBM is a lack of consistency in operation that grows uncontrolled as new applications are added. Each application has its own unique way of using the machine's resources, and presenting itself to the user. An analogy would be climbing into a car to find the stick shift moved from the column to the floor, the foot clutch changed to a hand clutch, the brake and the accelerator pedals switched, and the steering wheel changed to a joystick.

Further, since there is this lack of consistent operation due to the open architecture, software developers will write programs to function in a *non*graphics mode, so the program will run on the most IBM PCs. Thus software for the IBM often lacks the graphics which aids use and provides power, but is directed to the lowest common denominator: the 8088 CPU.

The major advantages of the IBM PC family of computers are their open architecture (they can be expanded, for a price) which is of value when a system needs to be configured for some *dedicated* purpose, the wealth of software available, the amount of industry support it receives from other manufacturers in the way of add-on products, and IBM's reputation for good service and support. It can also support color. Color has been shown to influence message impact, and the lack of color on the Macintosh might, for some applications, simply rule it out as a choice.

An argument made against the Macintosh has been the lack of applications software, but this is no longer the case. The Macintosh now has a wealth of software available, and software that takes full advantage of its graphics capabilities. In fact, the recent arrival of the Macintosh plus with its 1MB of memory, 880K minidiskettes, improved speed, and ability to connect to more peripheral devices is answering many of the criticisms.

The Macintosh's recent penetration into the corporate area is evidenced, for example, by its acceptance at *GEISCO* (The General Electric Information Systems Corporation), a large supplier of database and networked systems and services to Fortune 5000 enterprises in North America. The Macintosh will serve as a base unit upon which a telecommunications system supporting text and graphics sharing will be designed for GEISCO clients.

Also recently, *Peat Marwick*, a prominent chartered accounting and auditing firm in the United States and Canada, acquired many hundreds of Macintoshes for their auditors to take to their respective clients. Ease of use and graphics capabilities were the factors that influenced the choice. The Macintosh simply needs less written documentation to operate and is more intuitive in its functioning.

But Apple's penetration into corporate America will not be easy. As Richard Shaffer (*Personal Computing*, August, 1985), former technology and science editor for the *Wall Street Journal,* comments: "Will corporate America spend $4,000 or so for a computer system called Fat Mac from a company called Apple in order to run a program called Jazz from a company called Lotus?" Shaffer recommends that Apple pay attention to building its sales and support organization. This appears to be happening.

Regardless of the attitude of corporate America, the Macintosh's increased applications software offerings, expanded memory, expanded storage, ease of use, high quality laser printer option, and networking make it a highly viable office system choice. Only two things might rule it out: lack of color and multiprocessing. As for the latter, most other microcomputers, with the exception of the ATT PC, do not possess this feature.

3.5 ADDITIONAL SYSTEMS CONSIDERED

There are many other systems including the *Amiga* by Commodore, the *520ST* by Atari, and the

PC/IT by Sperry. The systems selected for discussion are only a very few of the many available. The low cost Atari and Commodore systems, for example, may serve well as alternate low cost graphics workstations to a larger system in place of ordinary terminals possessing no on-site processing and storage capabilities. They are both low cost graphics systems, with more software becoming available. The PC/IT, an IBM PC/AT clone, but with superior processing speed and more auxiliary storage, is a good value and suitable as a server or central computer for a small network.

The above systems, and the IBM PC and the Macintosh family of computers, are all relatively low cost. In Exhibits 3.10 and 3.11, we list some low- and high-end graphics systems, respectively, which are, however, all on the high end.

Name:	APOLLO	DEC	IBM	SGCS	SUN
Cost:	$15,000	$42,000	$25,000	$28,000	$12,000
CPU:	MC68020	MicroVAX II	RISC	MC68010	MC68020
Memory:	2-4MB	2-9MB	1-4MB	2-12MB	4MB
Display size:	19 inch	19 inch	14 inch	15 inch	19 inch
Color:	B & W	B & W	color	color	B & W
Resolution:	1280X1024	1024X864	720X512	1024X768	1152X900
Storage:	-	31MB disk	40MB disk	22MB disk	-

Exhibit 3.10: Low-end graphics workstations
(Based on a more extensive table from Peter Bulas, "Barrage of new 32-bit workstations," *Computing Canada*, 12,7, April 3, 1986)

Name:	APOLLO	DEC	IBM	SGCS	SUN
Cost:	$108,000	$64,000	$72,000	$88,000	$87,000
CPU:	MC68020	MicroVAX II	RISC	MC68010	MC68020
Memory:	2-4MB	3-9MB	2-4MB	2-16MB	4-16MB
Display size:	19 inch	19 inch	19 inch	19 inch	19 inch
Color:	color	color	color	color	color
Resolution:	1280X1024	1024X864	1024X1024	1024X768	1152X900
Storage:	86MB	71MB disk	70MB disk	170MB disk	71MB

Exhibit 3.11: High-end graphics workstations
(Based on a more extensive table from Peter Bulas, "Barrage of new 32-bit workstations," *Computing Canada*, 12,7, April 3, 1986)

4

Capturing Data

4.1 INTRODUCTION

This chapter discusses the various input devices available today in relation to graphics. Other devices used for *non*graphics input, such as bar code readers and specialized keyboards, are not discussed.

   Data capture sounds like a game. In a way it is, with a highly important objective: how can we get data into the computer easily, accurately, and rapidly? Data capture occurs at the interface between man and machine. It involves building a path between people and computers that fits people. Data capture includes both hardware and software; that is, various physical devices which are then programmed to function in a given way.

   In this chapter, we briefly discuss data capture in relation to the sciences of *Ergonomics,* the fitting of machines to people, and *Semiotics,* the study of signs and their interpretation.

4.2 ERGONOMICS

When computers first emerged, few people used them and those who did were scientists and researchers. They were not concerned with the effects of the video on eye fatigue, the angle tilt of the monitor, designing easy ways to instruct the system, icon type keyboards, or touch-sensitive screens; they were simply trying to get the computer to do some processing. As the early processing problems were solved, and more people began to use computers, attention turned to the ergonomics of the situation: how could the machine be made to fit people? Research, for example, on improving the person-machine connection through the use of the now ubiquitous mouse, began at Stanford Research Institute in the mid-sixties (see the history chart in Exhibit 1.7).

   Ergonomics is reflected in the many devices for data capture discussed in this chapter. Each device is another attempt to build a better bridge between man and machine. Should the user press a button, push a lever, turn a wheel, roll a mouse, or talk? What works best in which situations, and how is it best designed? These are some of the concerns of ergonomics.

   These devices should function within some consistent environment, that is, modeless operation; the same press of a button, roll of a mouse, should always mean essentially the same thing. It is the aim of systems designers—or should be—to make computers so that they virtually can be any machine, but the operation of each virtual machine, that is, each application, is close to being identical.

4.3 SEMIOTICS

Semiotics is the theory of signs and symbols and their function in both natural and artificial languages. Semiotics includes *semantics,* the study of signs and their meaning; *syntactics,* the formal relations between signs; and *pragmatics,* the relations between signs and the people who use them. The relations named here are diagrammed in Exhibit 4.1. Essentially, signs relate meanings to people.

   Interactive graphics is becoming the standard medium of communication with computers. Why? Because signs in the form of images, or icons, often speak more clearly than signs in the form of words. Icons communicate faster and better, and they can be designed to communicate rapidly either to a specialized audience, or to a very broad audience. They are highly pragmatic.

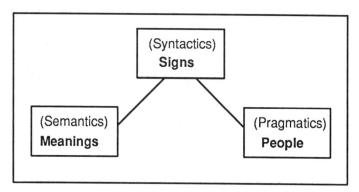

Exhibit 4.1: Signs relate people and meanings*

Letters, mathematical notations, specific signs used in industry, signals, and symbols are all graphics. Obviously only the initiated can understand specialized languages. However, the specialized language communicates very well to the initiated group. For all others, it is obscure and difficult. This may well explain why computer programmers sometimes find the icon-driven interface suitable for the end-user to be irritating; they prefer the cryptic and, for them, easier to use interface of a previous generation of computers.

This gives a different perspective to the meaning of "user-friendly." No interface is user-friendly in any absolute sense.** For example, some users feel that the language used in the friendly icon interfaces are user *insolent*; they object to terms like "fatbits" (the exploded display of the pixels in a screen image) and refer to the use of such terms as "California cuteness." However, in large measure, the icon-driven system with its easy-to-remember images, use of terms like "fatbits," mice, and pull-down menus is a great improvement over earlier user interfaces with cryptic operating system messages like PIP B: = A:*.COM, meaning "copy all the compiled files identified by the extension COM in their file names, from the disk in the A drive to the disk in the B drive." The icon interface may be user insolent, but that is better than an interface which is user hostile. The command PIP means "peripheral interchange program." On most systems COPY has been substituted for PIP, but the interface remains cryptic.

For the purpose of this discussion we will group languages as

√ Specialized
√ Vernacular
√ Symbolic
√ Iconic

For many years, the Church maintained its influence because to read and write meant understanding Latin. A discipline remains a discipline partly because of a specialized language, which within the discipline can serve an important "shorthand" function but, unfortunately, often fails to communicate well with others outside the discipline. Before the use of icons, computers, in large measure, used specialized languages. Specialized languages prevent broad computer use,

---

* The author wishes to thank Scot Gardiner of Gamma (Montreal, PQ) for suggesting this image.
** The term *user-friendly* should be dropped in favor of *user-servile*. Computers are not our friends; they are our servants.

and they facilitate use by specialized groups. The specialized groups became "the high priests of a low cult" (Alan Kay quoting Robert S. Barton, 1984).

The vernacular languages—English, French, Spanish, and so on—allow for communication to a broader audience. We have symbolic languages (road signs, colors, shapes) which allow for communication to a still broader audience. Symbols may be culturally learned but sometimes seem to transcend culture and mean the same to many people (hand waving). Then we have icons, images of the actual objects, for example, an image of a garbage can on the screen into which the

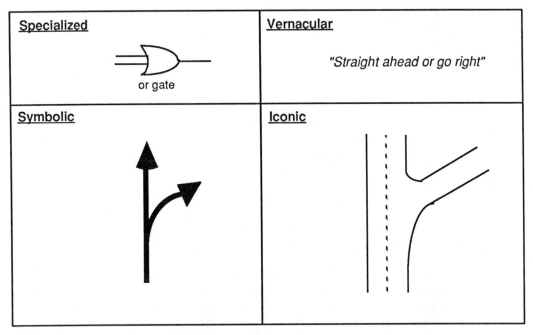

Exhibit 4.2: Different classes of languages

user "throws" an image of a disk, folder, or file to delete it. A comparative example is provided in Exhibit 4.2.

Icons, when they are well designed, communicate most clearly and quickly to the most people. It is possible to design specialized icons for different professional groups, as well as more general icons familiar to members of a given culture or subculture. It is upon these facts that the latest developments in the design of the computer interface depends. We have come full circle in an evolutionary sense; our earliest languages were iconic, and increased in abstraction over the millenia. Now we return to iconic languages in communicating with a machine that uses the most abstract language of all: binary code.

4.4 KEYBOARDS

The QWERTY keyboard is familiar to anyone who types. "QWERTY" refers to the first six letters in the upper left-hand section of the keyboard. It was designed to *slow typists down* in the age of mechanical typewriters. There exists an alternate keyboard called the Dvorak keyboard that is *not* designed to slow typists down, but habits are strong and we continue to use the QWERTY keyboard with ultrafast electronic computers.

Keypunch operators use the same keyboard to punch cards. Later on various command keys were added (escape), then dedicated control keys (cursor control keys), followed by programmable soft, or function, keys (Danish, 1984).

Keyboards are a flexible means for entering data, and special keyboard programs can facilitate data entry. This is a boon for the many people who cannot type or cannot type well, and with some large applications that requires the use of many commands that are difficult to recall. A single keystroke or command is used to represent the data, or set of commands. For example, there is a program called *QuickWord* for the Apple Macintosh that works in conjunction with a word processor. The user builds quickword tables; series of user-defined mnemonics that are keyed to chunks or modules of text that the user might need to enter often. For example, this author uses various mnemonics, like "PH" for Prentice Hall, and "SG" for Scot Gardiner, and so forth, to reference the many companies and people with whom I often correspond. When I activate the table, the entry "PH" into my open text document will command the computer to enter the full name and address of Prentice-Hall. The flexibility and time-saving capabilities of these types of programs are obvious.

4.5 TOUCH SYSTEMS

4.5-1 Touch screens

Exhibit 4.3 shows a touch screen by Carroll Touch, Inc. (Round Rock, TX).

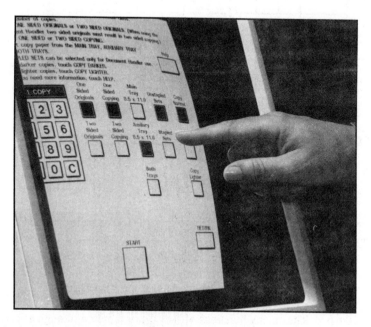

Exhibit 4.3: A touch screen (Courtesy of Carroll Touch, Inc.)

The touch screen is being displayed on a Xerox monitor and shows some of the commands required to operate a Xerox 5700 electronic printer. It would have taken 129 buttons to activate the functions of the printer. The system uses a matrix of LEDs (light emitting diodes) and phototransistors mounted around a video screen. A grid of infrared beams of light, which are invisible to the user, cover the screen. A finger or stylus touching the screen breaks a beam of light and the system is signaled as to the location on the screen. Commands exist at given locations.

Control Data Corporation (CDC) has been using touch-sensitive screens on its Plato computer aided instructional system for 15 years. Hewlett Packard uses an infrared system on its latest microcomputer. Concerns are that extended use causes tired arms, smudges on the screen, and is based on an ongoing conspiracy with the manufacturers of Windex.

4.5-2 Touch pads

Carroll Touch Technology has produced a system that consists of a "single plastic mylar membrane silkscreened with a silver conductive grid and two resistive strips," and works in a similar fashion to the touch screen, but on a flat pad (Danish, 1984). When a key is pressed, two electrical resistances are reflected between a common line and the x and y output lines, as diagrammed in Exhibit 4.4.

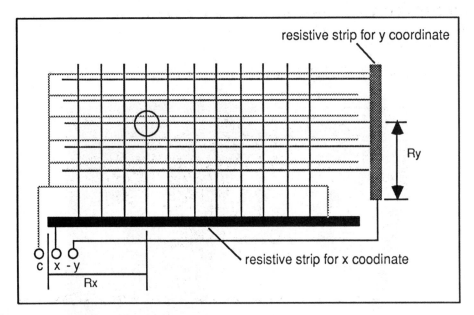

Exhibit 4.4: The workings of a touch pad (Reprinted by permission of the Publisher from the Winter 1984 edition of *Computer Technology Review*®.)

Software monitoring the touch pad and measuring the resistances identifies which key has been pressed. Different overlays representing the commands for controlling different software are placed on top of the pad. Thus many hundreds of "keys" are supplied through a single input device. In addition, custom keyboards are possible.

4.6 LIGHT PENS

The light pen is about the same physical size and shape as a fountain pen. It is connected to the monitor by a cord extending from one end of the pen to the computer system through a controller board. The user points at the screen with the pen, the light is sensed on the screen, and a message is sent back to the computer. The computer then determines the location and performs accordingly, depending upon the software being used. For example, in Exhibit 4.5, the pen is being used to design a floor plan through the selections provided by a menu.

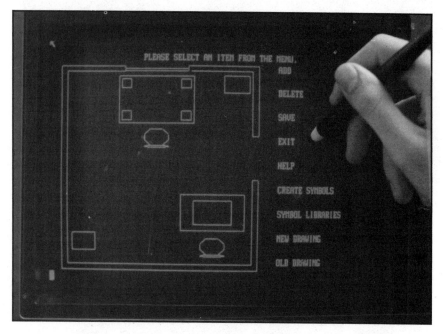

Exhibit 4.5: Use of light pen in computer aided design (Courtesy of Sun-Flex)

The light pen can also be used to draw as shown in Exhibit 4.6. The idea behind the light pen is the familiarity of ordinary writing. It is a direct and natural form of input. No desk space need be set aside for movement, as with the mouse. Possible disadvantages are that, for accuracy, the pen must be held perpendicular to the screen and may block the user's view. Holding the arm up may be tiring, and its wire connection to the computer may be restrictive. The light pen must be used with a refreshed Cathode Ray Tube (CRT) as described in Chapter 5.

4.7 DIGITIZING TABLETS AND TABLES

A digitizing tablet (small) or table (large) consists of a stationary flat surface and a positioning tool. The positioner is either in the shape of a fountain pen with a sharp point for surface contact, called a pen or stylus, or in a hand-held box shape with a cross-hair sight known as a cursor, puck, or mouse. A tablet is shown in Exhibit 4.7, and a table in Exhibit 4.8 on page 87.

Exhibit 4.6: Use of light pen in art and design (Courtesy of PTI Industries)

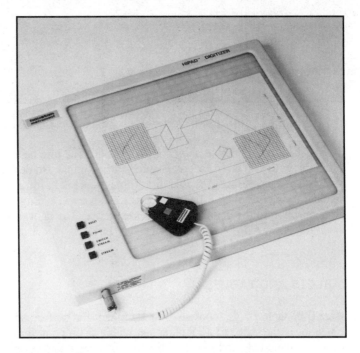

Exhibit 4.7: Digitizing tablet (Courtesy of Houston Instrument)

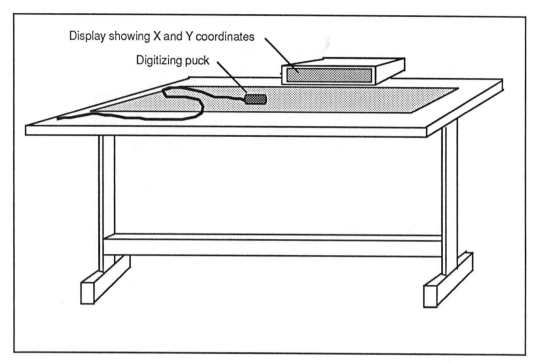

Display showing X and Y coordinates

Digitizing puck

Exhibit 4.8: Digitizing table

Digitizing tablets (and tables) convert location or movements of the pen or mouse into digital information which can then be processed by the computer. The user moves the pen or puck across a photo, map, or drawing, and the image is entered into the computer. The location of the pen or puck is determined in terms of the reference provided by the edges of the tablet and a pair of X Y coordinates. Therefore, digitizing tablets (and tables) are a means for taking physical location data, turning it into numerical coordinates, and allowing this spatial information to be input to the computer. Most handle points in two dimensions; some digitizers can handle three dimensions.

The major quality criteria for tablets (and tables) are *resolution, accuracy, linearity,* and *repeatability* (Kuklinski, 1985). Resolution varies between 100 to 1,000 points per inch. The resolution determines accuracy. Variability over a given area is a measure of linearity. When one draws a line on the tablet, will the cordinates digitized into the computer also describe a straight line? That is the issue here. Linearity usually suffers most near the tablet (or table) edges. Repeatability is reliability; that is the same measure obtained when the locator is in the same position. Low repeatability means high "noise."

Some digitizers use an electric grid of wires embedded in the tablet or table to generate a magnetic field. A control unit picks up the signal through the pen or puck and the location is determined. Other devices use a grid of light produced by LEDs where the stylus blocks the light and identifies the location; or, the stylus creates a tiny spark and the related sound is picked up by microphones around the edge of the tablet. An older method uses relative movement along the X and Y axes, a method that depends upon a combination of mechanics and electronics.

Tablet (and table) digitizing resembles writing and drawing. The input of graphs and images is as easy as tracing with a pencil. It is the most popular device for Computer Aided Design (CAD) and avoids the fatigue associated with screen digitizing. In all cases, needs determine the device chosen. Sporadic menu selection from a large number of choices might call for a touch or screen pad; long-term use in preparing drawings, a digitizing table or tablet.

Exhibit 4.9 shows a diagram of a transluscent tablet for backlit projection and digitizing.

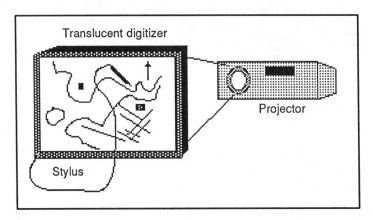

Exhibit 4.9: Backlit digitizer

Exhibits 4.10 and 4.11 illustrate two systems, called respectively, the *Space Tablet* and the *Perceptor,* electromechanical digitizers from Micro Control Systems (Vernon, CT), and used for digitizing three-dimensional objects. The Perceptor records 3-D points at the rate of seven **X, Y,** and **Z** coordinates per second, and possesses its own microprocessor. They both allow systems that are limited to 2-D digitizing to expand to 3-D.

On the other end of the scale, low-cost digitizing of images is provided using a strictly mechanical approach that works in conjunction with the mouse on the Apple Macintosh. *Mouse-Artist* from Village Computer Resources, Inc. (Lakewood, CA) provides a clear acrylic board that is highly resistant to breakage and scratching. The mouse fits into the pointing device as shown in Exhibit 4.12 on page 90, and entry is increased in accuracy through tracing.

4.8 MICE, TRACKBALLS, DIALS, AND JOYSTICKS

These devices are similar in that they are hand-held, and perform cursor control movements on the screen. By comparison, tablets, tables, and pressure-sensitive pads and screens locate the cursor in terms of absolute coordinates established by the physical sides of the screen or tablet.

Each device described here has some kind of handle which can be used to create and translate an analog signal to a digital signal that the computer can use. The names "mouse," "trackball, " "dial," and "joystick" refer to the type of handle used. Puck is a synonym for mouse.

The *mouse* is becoming a standard optional input device on most microcomputers. There are many varieties including those that work on the basis of mechanical movement (older and not used any more), optics, and a combination of both, like the Apple Macintosh mouse. A ball on the bottom is in friction contact with some surface and with two rotating rollers connected to vanes, which interrupt beams from light emitting diodes (LEDs) picked up by light sensitive phototransistors. The two vanes track the forward and side movements of the mouse (*not* vertical

Exhibit 4.10: A 3-D digitizer (Courtesy of Micro Control Systems)

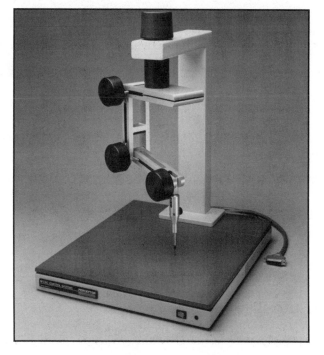

Exhibit 4.11: A more capable 3-D digitizer (Courtesy of Micro Control Systems)

Exhibit 4.12: A low-cost digitizer (Courtesy of Village Computer Resources)

and horizontal; that is, forward is any direction the mouse happens to be pointing). Illustration of operation is shown in the top half of Exhibit 4.13 and, by contrast, a similar device, called a *puck* or a *cursor*, is shown in the bottom half of the same exhibit. The difference between the mouse and the puck is that the puck does not need a ball because it works in conjunction with a digitizing tablet or table. The puck possesses cursor hairs set in a plastic see-through window for more accurate digitizing, and a variety of buttons for entry of data and commands.

Scientists at Bell Telephone Laboratories have developed a language called *Squeak,* so that the mouse can be programmed; that is, some simple sequence of moves will generate a multiple number of parallel operations. An analogy would be driving a car where we shift gears, depress brakes, activate signals, and turn on the radio, all at the same time (Canadian Datasystems, February, 1986).

A *trackball* is a sphere mounted in a base so that it rotates in all directions. A little less than half of the ball is exposed and can be easily rotated with the hand. The trackball controls the position of the cursor on the screen with the direction of rotation controlling the direction of cursor movement and the distance the cursor travels controlled by the number of revolutions of the ball.

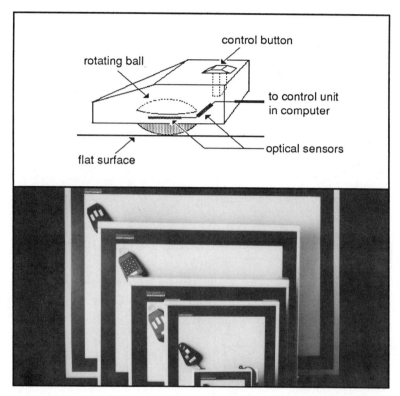

Exhibit 4.13: The mouse and its relative the puck (Pucks courtesy of Houston Instrument)

Four sensors are located in the base of the trackball, corresponding to each direction of the compass. Each sensor counts the number of rotations in its direction. Four analog signals are generated, converted to digital, and used to calculate direction and distance. A diagram and picture of a roll ball are shown in Exhibit 4.14. A *dial* is a small rotating wheel mounted in a base or in the monitor casing itself, as illustrated in Exhibit 4.15. Each wheel provides single axis cursor control. Clockwise or counterclockwise rotation of a horizontal or vertical dial causes the appropriate movement of the cursor in that direction, with the distance being determined by the number of revolutions. For full screen movement the nimble rotation of both wheels is required.

A *joystick* may be used with graphic systems but is familiar to most of us as a control device in computerized games. It functions on the basis of a vertical shaft that may be moved in any direction, with the direction and degree of displacement translated into the speed and direction of the cursor movement. A diagram is shown in Exhibit 4.16.

4.9 SCANNERS

Scanners may possess one or both of two capabilities: to digitize images at a given resolution, and to act as an optical character reader (OCR). Scanners are now available in the $1,000 to $2,500 range with resolutions that match the laser writer: 300 dots per inch. It is the software that deter-

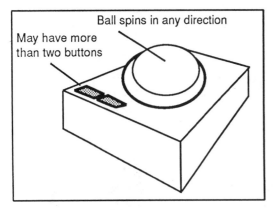

May have more
than two buttons

Ball spins in any direction

Exhibit 4.14: Roll ball

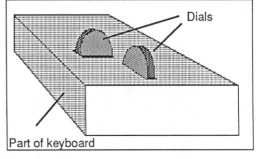

Dials

Part of keyboard

Exhibit 4.15: Dials

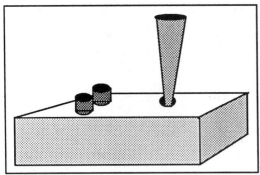

Exhibit 4.16: Joystick

mines the capabilities. These devices consume a lot of processing and require powerful micro-processors, like the Intel 80286 or Motorola 68000. A scanner that works with the IBM PC and the Macintosh by Microtek Lab (Gardena, CA) is shown in Exhibit 4.17. The Microtek scanner digitizes images at 300 dots per inch, but does not act as an OCR device.

The object is to capture text and images so that they do not have to be entered manually. A prime application is desktop publishing, where the scanner might take on as much importance as the word processor, the page layout software, and the laser printer.

Scanners are also used in conjunction with large optical disks that can hold an encyclopedic amount of text and graphics information. Pictures are memory- and storage-intensive; they take up a lot of bits and bytes. Write-Once, Read-Many (WORM) optical storage disks are capable of storing a lot at low cost. Scanners would help build the large database. There are many applications including education, training, reference, and information update.

Thunderscan for the Apple Macintosh from Thunderware, Inc. (Orinda, CA) is a unique low-cost optical scanner. It fits into the printer of the Macintosh system temporarily replacing the usual print ribbon cartridge. Images on paper are fed into the printer, through the scanner, and then into the computer. It displays good quality resolutions. Images can be reduced by 25% at the time

Exhibit 4.17: Scanner for digitizing images (Courtesy of Microtek Lab., Inc., Gardena, California)

of scanning, and the result is an improved resolution of 300 dots per inch. The images in the history chart in Chapter 1 were captured using Thunderscan.

OCRs are usually limited to the number of font types they can read. In order to expand capabilities beyond a few fonts requires a more sophisticated and more expensive device; something in the range of $50,000, rather than $2,000. Scanners of this quality possess intelligence, for example, the *Kurzweil 4000* from Kurzweil Computer Products, a subsidiary of Xerox, reads characters by analyzing their shape, and actually "learns" the characteristics of different fonts. Other scanners use preprogrammed templates representing the different fonts and styles, to which a match is then made by the system. The Kurtzweil first goes into a "training session," scans a few lines, begins to give feedback, and asks the operator for assistance on smudged characters—which are shown enlarged—or unusual characters. Then, following training which with clean copy can take a few minutes, high speed scanning begins. The machine can handle thousands of fonts between 6 and 24 points. Points is a measure of font size (Canadian Datasystems, December, 1984).

4.10 DIGITIZING VIDEO SYSTEMS

A digitizing video system is a video camera attached to an input controller which converts the video signals to digital data. The camera is pointed at the image to be recorded, the video signal is digitized and then sent to the computer monitor. Here the user can adjust size and shade, cut and paste, add other pictures or text, and then store the resulting image, or print it. An example using a black-and-white video camera, the *MacVision* system from PTI Industries (Santa Clara, CA), and the Apple Macintosh computer is shown in Exhibit 4.18.

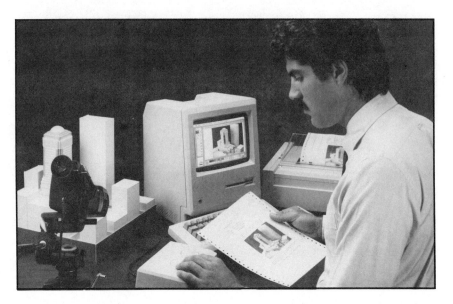

Exhibit 4.18: Digitizing video system (Courtesy PTI Industries)

Digitizing video cameras are a quick and easy way to enter data. Applications on small systems for low- to medium-resolution video images occur in real estate, police work, employee records, bank records, and so forth. High resolution video input is also possible. It may be used in high quality solid 3-D graphics image processing, or in vision systems for pattern recognition. An example of a control guidance application is diagrammed in Exhibit 4.19. The system is "trained" to match the actual pattern to a given pattern in its memory, and then transmit a signal to a robot to perform selection and placement. Other applications of high resolution video digitizing include inspection, measurement, guidance, placement, and removal in an assembly-line operation.

4.11 DIGITIZING CAMERA SYSTEMS

These systems differ from video-based systems in that they use lens cameras. The *Micro D-Cam*, a system which costs less than $300, resembles a 35mm camera with no body, shutter, prism, film, or rollers. It resembles a rifle scope on a tripod (Christopher, 1984). Images are recorded in RAM memory in two arrays of 128 by 256 pixels, and each array is sent to the screen for display. A menu allows for change of size and exposure time.

Electronic digitizing camera systems, however, can be very expensive and cost many thousands of dollars. One professional level system for a microcomputer is the *Datacopy Model 90*, a system that provides images with resolutions of 1,728 by 2,846 pixels, costs $10,000, and works

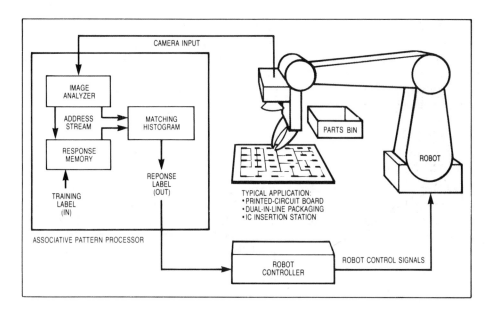

Exhibit 4.19: Pattern recognition and computer aided manufacturing
(Reprinted by permission of the Publisher from the Summer 1984 edition of *Computer Technology Review*®.)

with the IBM PC or PC XT. The manufacturers of the Model 90 see it as being a part of a complete in-house publishing system in large enterprises.

4.12 VOICE ENTRY

A voice entry system (VDE) consists of a microphone attached to a speech recognition device, which in turn transmits voice command information to a computer. The workings of a VDE system are essentially explained by the name; data are entered through voice commands. A user speaks a command which is interpreted based on a preprogrammed definition of its meaning.

A predefined vocabulary is programmed into a library by having the future user repeat a word a number of times while the command is being entered via the keyboard. The average speech pattern becomes associated with the command, allowing some room for deviations in the vocals from time to time. These signals are stored digitally in a library. A number of libraries can be made for different functions. When the user speaks a command, it is compared with the library of preprogrammed patterns and, if a match is found, the action associated with the word is performed.

The idea behind VDE and the benefits of its use are obvious; a person can communicate orally with a computer in very much the same way as with another person. Also, VDE systems allow the user to keep both hands free for other purposes and devote more attention to the monitor or digitizing table. For example, data from drawings might be entered vocally as drawings are being prepared. VDE also provides obvious benefits for the blind, paralyzed, or limbless. In addition, users with hearing or speech impediments can have telephone conversations converted to text or to synthesized speech.

VDE is limited by the current state of the technology. Speaker dependent systems are current; speaker independent systems, that is, systems that can recognize the patterns of a wide number of speakers, are a much more difficult technical challenge. Mike McMahan, head of the Speech Systems Development Program at Texas Instruments, a pioneer in the area, states, "In 10 years . . . speech will be a very common mode of interfacing with a machine." (McMahan, *Personal Computing*, January, 1984)

4.13 CONCLUSION

Every tool that man invents progresses through many stages of refinement, even a device as simple as the screwdriver (The reader is challenged to think of all the various types of screwdrivers of various end shapes, manual through automated.). If a simple tool like a screwdriver can take on so many forms, input and data capture devices as we know them today might constitute only the second or third generation of "screwdriver" available for opening up the computer to our input.

5

Displaying Images

5.1 INTRODUCTION

The *output* from a system is the most important part of the system. All other parts—input, processing, storage, operating system, applications software—are in its service. Systems design and
designer ingenuity are motivated by the output desired, obtained economically and simply.

Output is information, whether in the form of text, graphics, sound signals, or messages to
other machines. It involves the use of hardware and software; that is, the media for producing the
output, and the instructions for what is produced (namely, the content or the messages). The
hardware determines the form; the software determines the content.

In this chapter we discuss the various media for displaying graphic information, how they are
used, their basic design, advantages, and limitations. We also present findings related to human
perception, and show how those findings influence the design of output devices and graphics
system and software development.

5.2 A TAXONOMY

In Exhibit 5.1, a taxonomy of output devices is given. All but one, full character printers, are used
to produce images as well as text.

Hard copy involves the production of something tangible: a document, an overhead transparency, a 35mm slide, and so forth. Display involves something transient, namely, a screen display.

There are three classes of hard copy devices; paper, video, and film. We include images
produced on acetate overhead sheets under paper. The paper devices include plotters and printers.
Plotters are either vector or matrix; that is, pens either draw lines (vectors), or dots are deposited on
the paper to represent lines and objects. If dots are close enough, they look like lines to the naked
eye. Printers fall into two major categories: dot matrix and full character. There are four types of
printers that form images using a matrix of dots: pin or wire, ink jet, laser, and thermal. The other
category of printer uses a fully formed character on a ball or daisy wheel, like a typewriter, and is
not used in graphics.

Video cameras can be used to record images for input to the computer, as described in Chapter
4, and then modified for the output required; from simple black-and-white digitized images on
microcomputers to highly specialized effects on television.

A specially configured Polaroid camera may be pointed at the CRT screen and a picture taken
for the purpose of producing a 35mm slide. Or, using a computer, special effects may be recorded
on film; consider *Tron* by Walt Disney and the *Star Wars* series by Lucas Film.

5.3 DISPLAY SCREENS

Display screens or Cathode Ray Tubes (CRTs) act as both an input and an output device. An input
use of the CRT is when we draw with a mouse or a light pen and our drawing appears on the
screen. Output is when the CRT acts as a temporary display device. We discuss displays in the
order of chronological development. They are listed in the taxonomy in the order of frequency of
use today.

We see things on a screen because of the activation of phosphor in the screen. Phosphor
glows when hit by high voltage electrons. The electrons shoot outward from an electron gun in the

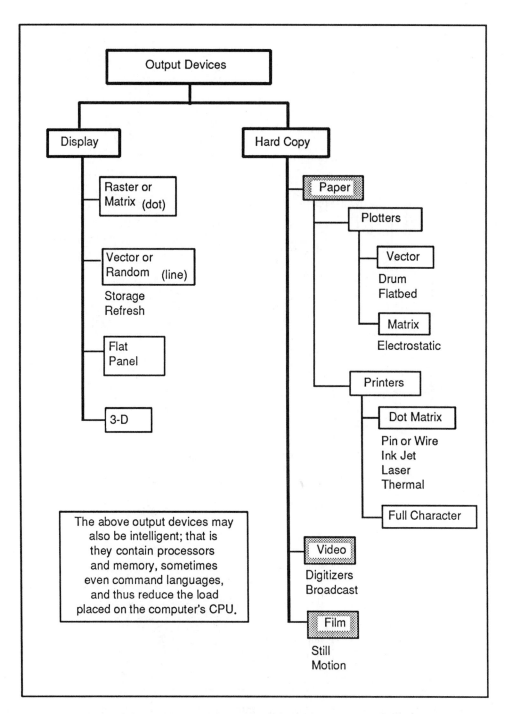

Exhibit 5.1: A taxonomy of computer graphics output

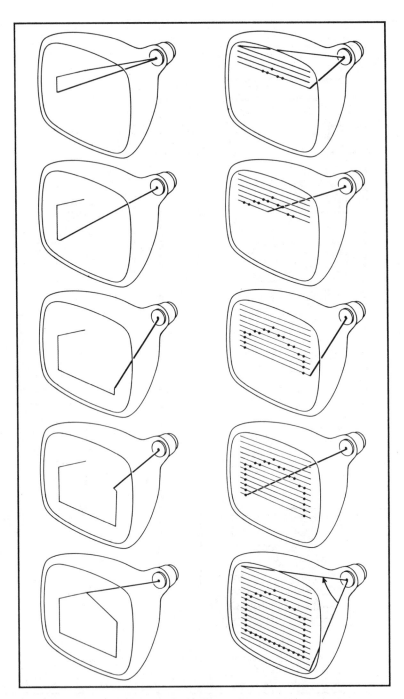

Exhibit 5.2: Vector and raster displays (From "Computer Software for Graphics"
by A. VanDam. Copyright © September, 1984 by Scientific American, Inc. All rights reserved.)

neck of the CRT (Gibson, 1984a). Phosphor lights up for different periods of time, depending on whether it is a slow or a fast fade phosphor. We will see how fast and slow fade phosphors work in different monitors.

5.3-1 Vector: refresh

The vector, stroke, random, or calligraphic CRT display is used to plot graphics by drawing lines on the screen. It is actually joining endpoint coordinates stored in a refresh buffer or memory. An illustration is provided in Exhibit 5.2, comparing it to the dots used in raster scan displays. When the dots are close they look like a line to the naked eye.

In a vector display, the electron beam portrayed in Exhibit 5.2 is like an electronic "brush" creating drawings by activating the phosphor. The "brush" is controlled by the X and Y coordinate amplifiers or magnets that deflect the beam.

The screen is redrawn or "refreshed" every 30 seconds, because refresh CRTs use a short decay time or fast fade screen phosphor. Anything less than this speed of refresh causes the human eye to detect a flicker rather than see a continuous picture.

The vector refresh CRT has a resolution of up to 4,096 by 4,096 lines on a screen, and is used in applications requiring high resolution. It is relatively expensive because it requires a refresh controller and consumes a lot of processing power, especially if the image is complex. It is susceptible to instability and flicker. But it allows for selective erasure and the display of motion, functions with a light pen, and is highly interactive.

5.3-2 Vector: storage

The Direct View Storage Tube does not use a refresh buffer, but stores images semi-permanently in what is called a storage mesh, a device embedded with a slow decay or slow fade phosphor. An illustration is given in Exhibit 5.3.

The main electron gun traces the image on the slow fade phosphor in the mesh, and the flood gun activates the screen. Wherever the main electron gun has traced a pattern, there is more phosphor activity and, therefore, more light.

Very detailed images can be drawn. The vector storage tube display is suitable for many engineering applications requiring detailed drawings. It is less costly than the vector display (but not as inexpensive a technology as raster scan terminals). High image precision and stability in complex displays are possible using very little computing power. But, there is no selective erasure and no motion. The light pen cannot be used because there is no rapid change in the light on the screen. However, digitizing tablets, mice, and dials can all be used.

5.3-3 Raster displays

In 1975 raster scan graphics terminals became available. They are the dominant and growing form of display used. They are less expensive, based on standard television technology, and growing in capabilities. The raster scan draws by using dots. It is the ultimate pointillist.

In a raster scan display, the screen is refreshed by scanning top to bottom and left to right 30 to 60 times per second, as illustrated in Exhibit 5.4.

The refresh allows the image to appear constant. Gibson (1984a) uses the analogy of writing a note in invisible ink that disappears every 60th of a second. We would have to rewrite the note

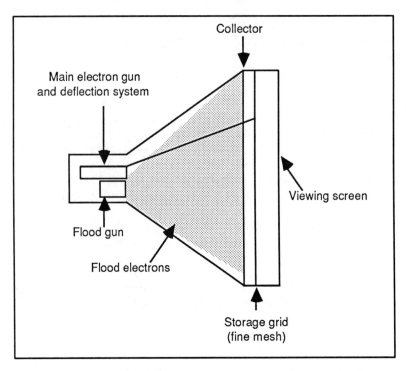

Exhibit 5.3: Direct view storage tube (based on a drawing in Harris, 1984)

every 60th of a second to allow the note to be read. That is what the computer is doing to the phosphor on the screen: reactivating it constantly. Actually the odd lines on the screen are activated followed by the even lines. This is called *interlacing*. Under certain circumstances an annoying flicker will occur, which can only be solved by higher refresh rates or resolutions.

The raster refers to the matrix of pixels, or dots, that covers the entire screen. As described in Chapter 2, the entire raster screen is bit-mapped in a refresh screen buffer in terms of pixels rather than endpoint coordinates. Whether a dot on the screen is activated or not depends on the state of the corresponding bit or bits in the buffer at some given time.

More memory is required for raster scan than for vector displays; it takes more data to store all the points or pixels on the screen than all the end coordinates of all the lines being drawn. But, low cost solid state memory makes it feasible. The present limit on raster scan display resolutions is 1,448 by 1,448 pixels and, therefore, cannot match the resolution of 4,096 by 4,096 in vector displays. But 1,448 by 1,448 pixels is a high level of resolution; many high quality systems use resolutions of 1,024 by 1,024 and lower.

A typical resolution used for business graphics and low end computer aided design, and considered "good" within the present limits of technology and economy, is 640 by 400 on a 12-inch screen. Anything less than this is not acceptable, leading to what is known as an extreme case of "the jaggies"; jagged lines that appear when drawing away from the vertical or horizontal; for example, an angled line or a circle. Various approaches or algorithms are used to solve this problem, including what pixels should be on and off leading to the best looking straight line or curve, and shifting the edges to create a fuzzy edge which then appears less jagged. An example is given in Exhibit 5.5. Exhibit 5.6 compares the three display technologies discussed.

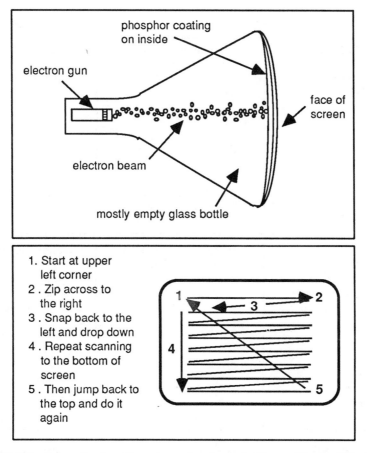

Exhibit 5.4: Raster scan display (Based on a drawing in S. Gibson, "Bottles Full of Nothing," *Infoworld*, 6, 24, July 11, 1984)

Exhibit 5.5: "Jaggies" counteracted by blurring pixels on the edges (From "Computer Software for Graphics" by A. VanDam. Copyright © September, 1984 by Scientific American, Inc. All rights reserved.)

Technology	Advantages	Disadvantages
RASTER REFRESHED Cathode gun refreshes screen in horizontal lines filling entire CRT screen. Data displayed based on bit-mapped memory.	1. Competitive cost with decreasing cost trend for future. 2. Digital accuracy. 3. Digital reliability. 4. Good brightness. 5. Good contrast between data and background. 6. Excellent gray scale. 7. Multitude of colors. 8. Selective update/erase. 9. Low maintenance cost.	1. Resolution currently limited to 1448 by 1448 addressable points (may have increased).
DIRECT VIEW STORAGE TUBES Cathode gun writes vectors on energized CRT screen, which then maintains image without refreshing.	1. High resolution (4096 x 4096) addressable points.	1. Higher maintenance cost. 2. Analog circuits require adjustment. 3. No gray scale. 4. No color. 5. Low contrast between data and background. 6. Limited to low ambient light working environments. 7. No selective updating or erasing.
VECTOR REFRESHED Cathode gun writes vectors on standard CRT screen, with phosphor persistence maintaining data until vectors can be refreshed by redrawing.	1. High resolution (4096 x 4096) addressable points.	1. Analog circuits require adjustment. 2. Flickers when too many vectors displayed.

Exhibit 5.6: Comparison of three display technologies
(From *An Analysis of CAD/CAM Applications* by Richard Stover © 1984. Used by permission of the publisher Prentice-Hall, Inc., Englewood Cliffs, NJ.)

5.3-4 Flat panel

The CRT technology will dominate through the 1980s. The flat panel display is able to present a flicker-free image, takes up less room, and uses less power than the bulky CRT. It is, however, more costly to produce. It is suitable for portable units and can display graphics. In fact, the screen display is stable, with high resolution, and can be polarized to achieve high contrast.

5.3-5 Three dimensional (3-D)

Earlier systems were based on producing two stereoscopic views of an object which were then placed on the same screen. When viewed through special glasses, the two views fuse into one 3D image. The method is tiring to the eyes, and we cannot view the object from alternate viewpoints.

Two alternative systems have emerged, one based on holographics and the other on the use of oscillating mirrors. Both are expensive, and the second, pioneered by Genisco Computers, can only produce monochrome images which are difficult to rotate and manipulate in real time (Harris, 1984).

The more usual 3-D graphics displays are those with the ability to accurately simulate, in 2-D space, the cues for depth perception, with hardware dedicated to the real-time processing of hidden-surface removal, color fill and shading, 3-D cursor movement, and transparency effects. These are high resolution raster scan displays with many color options. These types of graphics displays are expensive. An example is the Comtec DS-300 by Daikin/Comtec (San Jose, CA) costing approximately $30,000.

5.3-6 Quality of display

If we assign one bit to each pixel, as described in Chapter 2, then a dot or pixel on the screen can be either black or white. If we assign 2 bits to each pixel we can handle four messages, or four different states, and the pixel can be black and white and, if the system is set up to do it, the pixel can be one of two different shades of gray. Increasing the number of bits assigned to control each pixel increases the number of shades or colors, if color is involved, of each dot on the screen.

Six bits provides a full range of gray tones from black to white, that is, 2^6 or 64 monochromatic tones. Exhibit 5.7 shows four video-captured images with different resolutions and gray tones produced by *PC eye* and graphics software called *Imigit*.

The first image in Exhibit 5.7 was originally in four colors. Note that the resolution is quite poor; in fact, significantly poorer than the other black-and-white images in Exhibit 5.7 with the same resolution. The reason is explained when we discuss color. We can see the improvement in the quality of the other images with an increase in the resolution and the number of gray tones.

5.3-7 Color, RGB monitors, and standard TVs

High-resolution color display is more difficult than black-and-white display. As Gibson (1984b) points out, color monitors are kludges, that is "a mess of compromise and mechanical trade-offs." Now let us see why the first image in Exhibit 5.7 is so poor.

First we must distinguish between an ordinary color TV set and the RGB monitor. These are the two displays used in microcomputer based systems, but professional level systems require the RGB monitor, which is considerably more costly. The reason for the additional cost is superior resolution and the higher cost of production.

How does the RGB monitor work? A diagram is shown in Exhibit 5.8.

There are three different sets of cones in the eye, cells sensitive to color. They respond maximally to three different colors: red, green, and blue. Thus we have the name of the RGB monitor. Our detour later on into the psychophysiology of human perception will explain more of the human side. Let us continue with the technical side. Suffice it to say that all perceived colors, including white, are made up of different combinations of these three primary colors.

Through the display of various combinations of red, green, and blue on to a screen we see all

320 x 200 x 4 colors (in original) 320 x 200 x 16 levels of gray

640 x 400 x 16 levels of gray 512 x 512 x 64 levels of gray

Exhibit 5.7: Different resolutions (Courtesy of Chorus Data Systems)

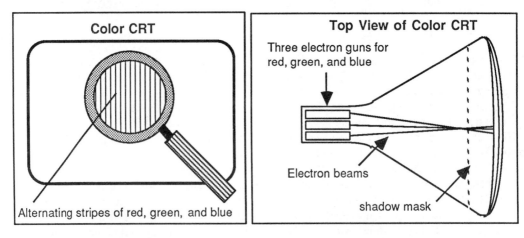

Exhibit 5.8: RGB color monitor (based on a drawing in S. Gibson, "Colors of the Rainbow," *Infoworld*, 6, 25, July 18, 1984)

the colors. As Gibson points out, in order to display all the colors everywhere on the screen, we would need three types of phosphor sensitive to the three primary colors everywhere. Since that is impossible, there is a compromise. The early RCA monitors placed triangular arrangements of tiny clusters of red, green, and blue dots all over the screen. That has been replaced by the in-line or Trinitron approach: the dividing of the screen into very narrow vertical strips of alternating red, green, and blue phosphor, as shown in Exhibit 5.8. Therefore, although all colors are not everywhere, they are nearby.

At the back of the color CRT are three electron guns, one for each of the colors. In between the guns and the stripes is a shadow mask of vertical slots. The slots line up with the stripes. The slots are placed so that the electron gun for a given color hits only that color phosphor and none of the other stripes; these are "shadowed" by the mask. Now it should be clear why accomplishing higher resolutions on color monitors is much harder than on black and white. Not all dots are everywhere. With black-and-white monitors they are.

The narrowness of the stripes is called the pitch; the narrower the stripes, the smaller the pitch, and the finer the resolution. For example, the Princeton monitor, compared to the IBM monitor, has a smaller pitch and, therefore, a superior resolution.

The RGB monitor is superior to an ordinary TV because of differences in the frequency of scanning, the number of raster lines displayed, the size of the slots in the shadow mask, the number of changes the transmitted signal must go through before it arrives at the TV, and the lack of independent channel handling of the three color signals.

High-resolution color monitors are expensive to manufacture because of the tolerances and alignments involved. Thus, color monitors on small computers are fuzzy while black-and-white monitors, such as on the Macintosh, are sharp. The value of the sharpness of a black-and-white monitor becomes apparent when enlarged displays are required as shown in Exhibit 5.9.

Exhibit 5.9: Projecting the screen (Courtesy of Professional Data Systems)

RGB monitors are raster scan, and to display color, more information must be stored for each pixel than with a black-and-white monitor. Information is stored in a bit-mapped memory buffer, as it is with a black-and-white monitor, but there are a number of memory buffers functioning in parallel. A diagram is given in Exhibit 5.10.

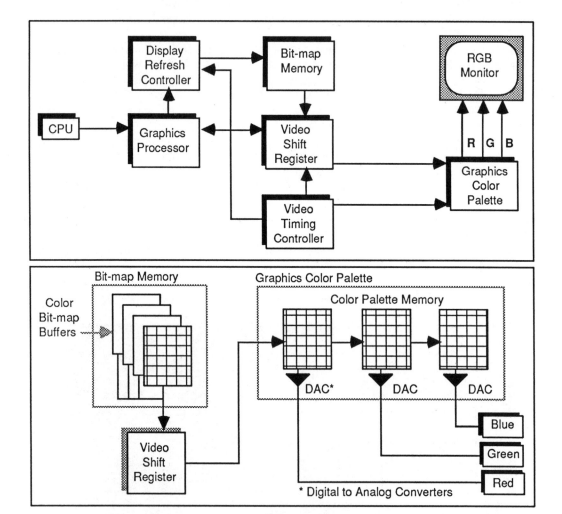

Exhibit 5.10: Display of color takes more computer resources

With more memory buffers we can produce more unique signals (the video shift register in the diagram) to send to a palette of encoded colors kept in memory (sometimes called a look-up table). Then messages from the palette, representing different colors, are converted from digital to analog signals to produce various combinations of red, green, and blue. Different levels of intensity in different combinations of the three produce all the colors we see.

5.3-8 Human perception

Computer graphics is related to the functioning of the human perceptual system. How we perceive color, depth, form, illusion, and so forth, helps determine the design of computer graphics systems, and the algorithms and graphics programs used to produce certain effects.

There are laws to the perception of color, depth, form, pattern, relationship, and continuity. *Perceptions persist in spite of our knowledge that our perceptions are wrong*; consider the illusions in Exhibits 5.14 through 5.17 (Rock, 1984).

Our perceptions are also remarkably constant despite massive sensory changes to the eye; consider the perception of a table top as "square" even though the image on the retina is a constantly changing trapezoid.

• Color

Exhibit 5.11 diagrams the fact that white is not the absence of color but the wavelength mix of all the colors.

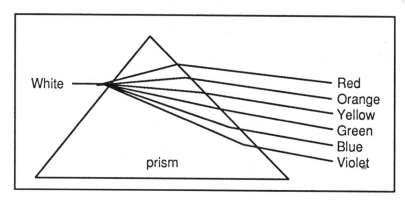

Exhibit 5.11: White is a mix of all the colors (Aftab A. Mufti, *Elementary Computer Graphics*, © 1983, p.9. Adapted by permission of Prentice-Hall, Inc., Englewood Cliffs, NJ)

Imagine all the colors on the right in Exhibit 5.11 being fed through the prism to create the white light on the left. Exhibit 5.12 diagrams the result of additive mixing of the three primary colors, red, green, and blue. Exhibit 5.13 diagrams the result of filtering using the secondary colors produced by mixing the primary colors. The result is the primaries. The filtering of colors comes into play with printers and color production, discussed in a later section.

• Depth Perception

A number of visual cues give rise to the experience of depth (Armstrong and Burton, 1985; Rock, 1984). They include:

Motion parallax, the changes in the retinal image caused by a movement of either the object or the perceiver

Size, the absolute and relative size of the retinal image

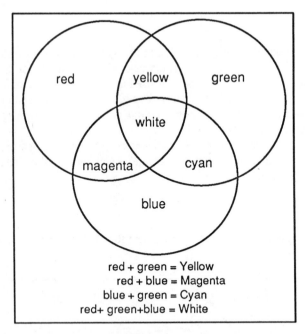

Exhibit 5.12: Additive color mixing (Aftab A. Mufti, *Elementary Computer Graphics*, © 1983, p.10. Adapted by permission of Prentice-Hall, Inc., Englewood Cliffs, NJ)

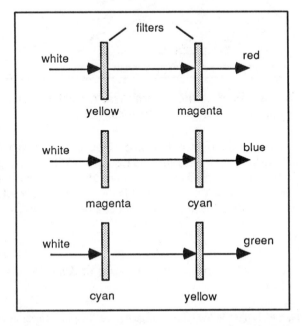

Exhibit 5.13: Subtractive color mixing (Aftab A. Mufti, *Elementary Computer Graphics*, © 1983, p.11. Adapted by permission of Prentice-Hall, Inc., Englewood Cliffs, NJ)

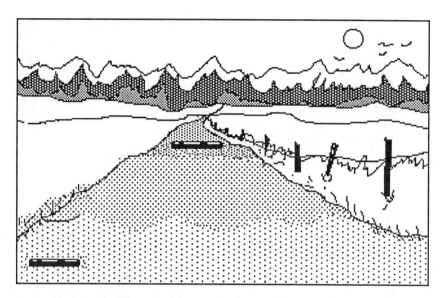

Exhibit 5.14: The two logs in the road are the same size
(Drawn using MacPaint on the Macintosh; software applications capable of more realistic
3-D effects are discussed in Chapter 9; the reader should compare the effect here with the
more dramatic effect in Exhibit 5.15 based on the use of more depth cues in the image.)

Linear perspective, the convergence of parallel lines in the distance
Angle of regard, the angle of view of an object; distant objects tend to be closer to
  the center of the field of vision
Interposition, further objects are blocked by closer objects
Aerial perspective, the blurring of more distant objects, or a blueing or atmos-
  pheric effect
Light and shade, reflections, highlights, and shadows add to the perception of depth
Texture, closer is larger; further is finer
Binocular Disparity, the two eyes receive a somewhat different view of the same
  object; also called stereopsis
Convergence, the angle of each eye when viewing an object
Accommodation, differences in focusing required by near and far objects

Some of these clues can be used more than others by the graphics system designer and
programmer to convey the impression of depth, shape, size, and so forth.

Armstrong and Burton describe various procedures for portraying multidimensional space as
an aid to the mathematician, the physicist, the engineer, and others for imagining or visualizing n-
dimensional functions and relations in their respective disciplines.

If we know the clues for depth, we can play with them and create various perceptual effects or
illusions. The illusions perceived inform us further as to how the human perceptual system works,
and how we can create illusions using computer graphics. The experience of motion on a screen is
a major illusion.

**Exhibit 5.15: Figures at end of hall and base of column are the same
drawn height and extend the same retinal angle** (Reproduced by permission of the
Bettman Archives, New York, NY)

• Perceived size

The perception of size, within a certain limit of distance, is experienced according to the *perceived* distance and the size of the retinal image. At long distances this is not so; consider the tiny houses and people perceived from an aeroplane. Therefore, if we can make the perceived distance *appear* to be greater, the perceived size of an object will look larger regardless of its actual size. The illusions in Exhibits 5.14 and 5.15 are demonstrations of this fact.

• Perceived form, pattern, relationship, and continuity

There are many variables, too many to discuss, that influence the perception of form. They include figure and ground, proximity, similarity, continuity, and recognition. Examples in Exhibits 5.16 through 5.22 demonstrate a variety of effects from Rock (1984).

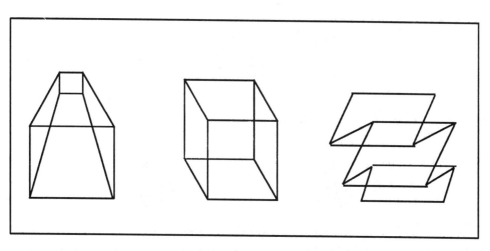

Exhibit 5.16: The above figures are ambiguous and demonstrate the importance of hidden line and surface removal in computer graphics
(From *Perceptions* by Irving Rock. Courtesy of W. H. Freeman and Company Publishers.)

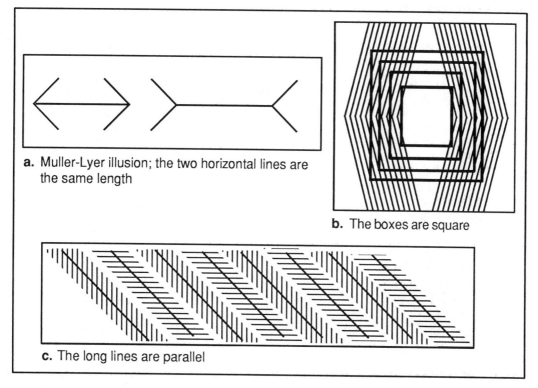

a. Muller-Lyer illusion; the two horizontal lines are the same length

b. The boxes are square

c. The long lines are parallel

Exhibit 5.17: Perceptions persist in spite of knowledge to the contrary
(From *Perceptions* by Irving Rock. Courtesy of W. H. Freeman and Company Publishers.)

Exhibit 5.18: Nonexistent border and whiter inner figure are perceived
(From *Perceptions* by Irving Rock. Courtesy of W. H. Freeman and Company Publishers.)

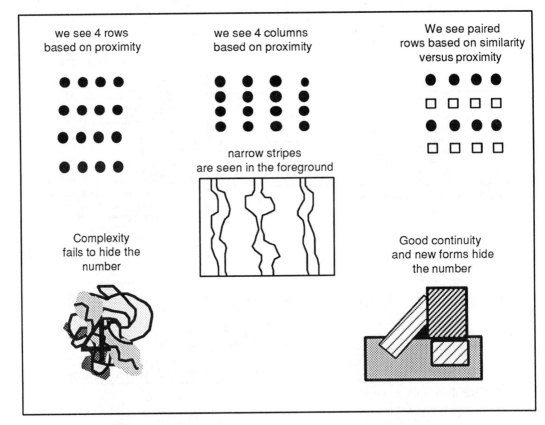

Exhibit 5.19: Some principles of form perception
(From *Perceptions* by Irving Rock. Courtesy of W. H. Freeman and Company Publishers.)

Exhibit 5.20: The two heavy vertical wall lines are equal in size
(From *Perceptions* by Irving Rock. Courtesy of W. H. Freeman and Company Publishers.)

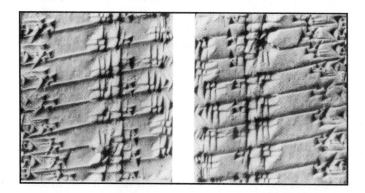

Exhibit 5.21: Two identical images show effect of shadow placement
(Turn the text upside down to see that one picture is the inverted image of the other. Courtesy of the Yale Babylonian Collection, Yale University)

Exhibit 5.22: Recognition leads to perceptual organization (Left image from P. B. Porter, "Another Picture Puzzle," *American Journal of Psychology*, 67, 550-5, 1984. Right image courtesy of Mr. Ron James.)

5.4 PLOTTERS

The quality produced by hard copy devices is important because we are still a paper dominated world, and appearance makes an impression, good or bad. In fact, it can be quite frustrating when the screen displays such beautiful forms and colors, and the hard copy device produces a mediocre output in black and white. However, low cost color plotters (and printers) capable of producing good to excellent quality color drawings are now available.

There are two types of plotters: vector and matrix. The vector plotters draw lines; matrix plotters draw dots. Plotters usually produce superior quality output in comparison to printers. Plotters can produce, if properly programmed, any type or size font desired. However, a more recent technology, the laser printer, provides very high quality and comparable output. Plotters can handle much larger and more complex drawings than printers. Plotters range in cost from one to many thousands of dollars, depending on the size of drawing created, speed, volume, resolution, pen control, scaling available, adjustments for humidity and different media, and so forth.

The plotter may contain enough intelligence to plot intermediate points between the end-points of lines. The software for drawing graphic primitives (lines, arcs) and different fonts may be relegated to microprocessors in the plotter. Some plotters may use high level languages and be able to reproduce a part of a diagram, stored as a procedure or a routine, anywhere in the larger diagram.

5.4-1 Drum plotters

Drum plotters are vector plotters and are usually used for drafting applications with mainframes or minicomputers. They are capable of producing complex, multicolored, and very large diagrams. Exhibit 5.23 shows a complex drawing being produced on a Houston Instrument's high speed, 14 pen plotter. The paper wraps around a drum or roller and is fed beneath pens. The control panel for the plotter is on the front, as shown.

5.4-2 Flat-bed plotters

Flat-bed plotters are of two types: small desktop units and larger table plotters. A picture of a Houston Instrument's desktop plotter is shown in Exhibit 5.24. The pen moves in the Y axis and the X axis movement is controlled by a moving bar or gantry. With some desktop plotters, paper movement in and out of the plotter forms one dimension for plotting, and movement of the pen across a track forms the other. The Hewlett Packard 7470 and 7475 plotters are of this type and handle 8-1/2 by 11-inch and 11 by 17-inch paper, use two and six pens, respectively, and produce high quality output at modest cost: around $1,000 for the 7470, and $2,000 for the 7475. Exhibit 5.25 shows that the HP units are about the size of a wide carriage printer.

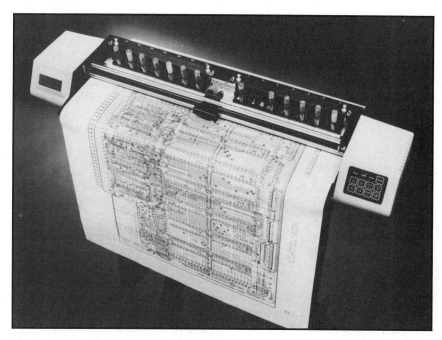

Exhibit 5.23: Drum plotter (Courtesy of Houston Instrument)

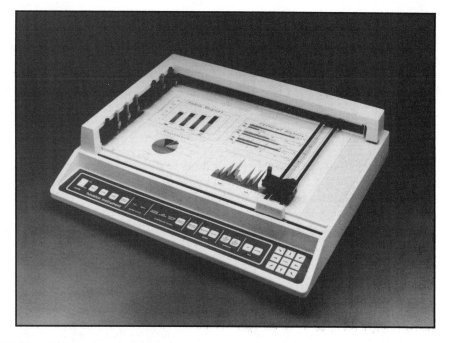

Exhibit 5.24: Flat-bed plotter (Courtesy of Houston Instrument)

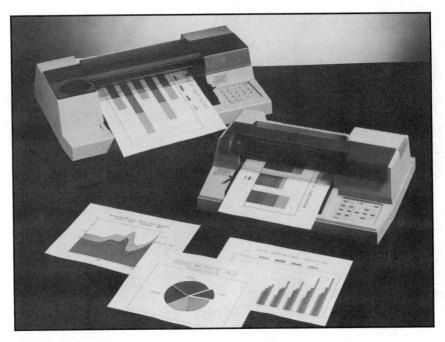

Exhibit 5.25: Small plotters (Courtesy of Hewlett Packard)

All HP plotters are controlled by the Hewlett Packard Graphics Language (HP-GL). An HP-GL command may look as follows:

    PA 133,315
    PD
    PA 215,435
    PU

This sequence instructs the plotter to start at an absolute point (PA) with X and Y coordinates of 135 and 315, then put the pen down (PD), draw the line or vector to absolute point with X and Y coordinates of 215 and 435, then raise the pen up (PU).

The HP-GL commands can be generated using BASIC or other languages. Since the HP 7470 and the HP 7475 are popular plotters, most graphics applications for small computers contain a driver for these plotters (and many others), making the writing of printer commands superfluous.

5.4-3 Electrostatic plotters

Electrostatic plotters form diagrams by adhering dots to paper. As the paper passes through the plotter, electrodes deposit charges on chemically treated paper. The paper then passes through a toner bath and black toner adheres to the charged areas, followed by drying. Resolutions are not of high quality, but these plotters can produce complex diagrams very quickly.

5.5 PRINTERS

There are four classes of matrix printers: wire or pin, ink jet, laser, and thermal.

5.5-1 Wire or pin matrix printers

Dot matrix printers, as they are called, are the most common. The diagram in Exhibit 5.26 illustrates how they work, in comparison to a nongraphics fully formed, character daisywheel printer.

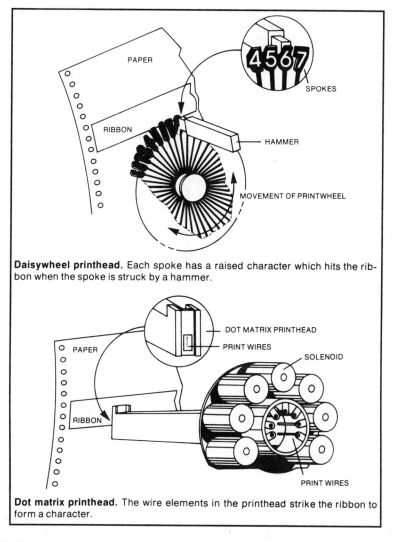

Daisywheel printhead. Each spoke has a raised character which hits the ribbon when the spoke is struck by a hammer.

Dot matrix printhead. The wire elements in the printhead strike the ribbon to form a character.

Exhibit 5.26: Dot matrix versus daisy wheel printer operation (Courtesy of Digital Equipment Corporation)

Pins or wires, under the control of a set of solenoids (magnets), shoot out in different patterns to form the letters. The density of the matrix used to form the letters, the ability to slightly shift the dot matrix, varying the speed of printing, and overprinting can lead to high print quality.

A comparison of character quality with print shift, and the effect of differences in the number of pins used on letter and graphics output is shown in Exhibit 5.27.

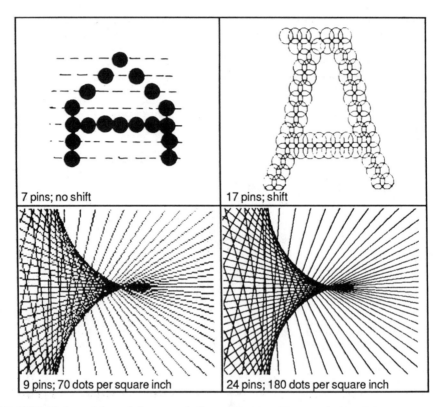

Exhibit 5.27: Dot matrix printer resolutions (Reprinted by permission of the Publisher from the Winter 1983 edition of *Computer Technology Review*®.)

Dot matrix printers under software control can be used to produce any graphic image desired, as well as any font type. The high quality dot matrix printer, for example, is being used to solve the problem of Japanese language processing. The Japanese written language uses over 6,000 ideographs called *kanji*. Dot matrix printers can produce kanji ideographs very readily, while an impact printer or typewriter would require 6,000 print heads!

5.5-2 Ink-jet printers

Ink-jet printers shoot tiny drops of ink on to the paper. Exhibit 5.28 diagrams their basic operation. With color ink-jet printers, barrels of ink are used containing the three colors cyan, yellow, and magenta. The diagrams in figures 5.12 and 5.13 show that these are the filter colors that produce the primaries red, green, and blue that are the basis for the perception of all colors.

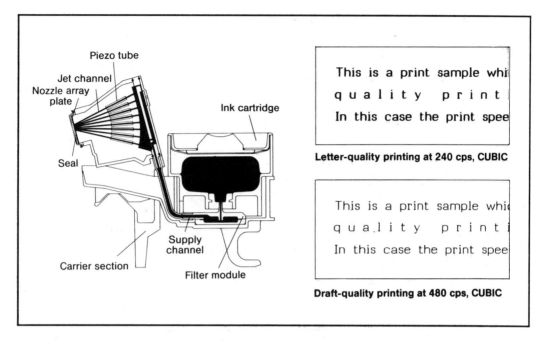

Exhibit 5.28: Ink-jet printer and sample output (Courtesy of Siemens Information Systems, Inc.)

Mixing pigments is a subtractive, or filtering, process. Software instructs the printer on the mix of colors. The printers are very quiet (how noisy can a jet of ink be?), produce good quality images, and require good absorbent paper to work well.

The cost/performance of ink-jet printers has improved tenfold in a few years. Color ink-jet technology may replace plotters, which operate at slower speeds. Ink-jet printers can print at speeds of up to 480 characters per second (cps), and produce resolutions of 240 dots per inch (dpi), as illustrated in the text output shown in Exhibit 5.28.

5.5-3 Laser printers

Laser printers use a laser beam to produce an image. The laser beam hits a photosensitive drum and produces an electrically charged dot; in fact, many dots, corresponding to the image being produced. Then black toner, as used in copier machines, is attracted to the charged dots and heat-fixed to a sheet of paper. Exhibit 5.29 illustrates the laser printer's operation.

When the first laser printer from IBM appeared in 1975, it cost $300,000. Desktop laser printers now cost under $4,000. Resolutions of 300 dpi produce quality that is excellent for in-house printing and some text production. However, laser print cannot match the 900 dpi of typesetting (this text is laser produced at 300 dpi).

Laser printers are fast with the big units costing $100,000 or more and producing 100 pages per minute; a senior bureaucrat's delight, they could bury the world in paper reports. The small desktop units produce 8 pages per minute, which is a highly respectable speed; suitable for a junior bureaucrat.

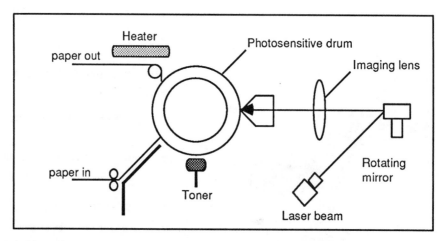

Exhibit 5.29: Laser printer operation (A simplified version of a diagram in Lu, 1984.
Reprinted by Permission of MicroSoft Press. Copyright 1984 by Cary Lu. All Rights Reserved.))

Small laser printers cannot handle high volumes; they are suitable for producing a few hundred or less pages per day. Further, the printed pages look like high quality copies rather than originals, and may not be suitable for all business correspondence and reports.

The new technology is introducing a new language and a new discipline into the office; namely, that of the typesetter (O'Connor, 1985). Are office workers willing to learn about font types, font sizes, points, true justification, and so forth? As O'Connor points out, users of the Macintosh will experience less difficulty making the transition, because the Macintosh uses different fonts, and the "what you see is what you get" concept is familiar. This is, in general, not the case for the IBM PC. O'Connor is of the opinion that, for microcomputer users, laser printers and personal publishing—at present and because of the above—introduce more complexity than they do increased production. It appears, however, to be the opposite case; people *are* willing to learn in order to improve performance. Further, software is appearing—and at a rapid rate—to facilitate instruction of the laser printer, and very accurate text and page layout. We will discuss this area further in Chapter 12.

5.5-4 Thermal transfer printers

Thermal transfer printers use a heating process that melts a waxy ink onto regular paper. The resulting image is susceptible to abrasion and high temperatures, but otherwise produces a clear image with strong colors. The printing element heats to a high temperature (185° to 300°) for a split second. The heated pins hit the special ribbon, black or colored, and transfer the wax-based ink to the paper. Some use a 24-element print head and therefore produce high resolution images.

A ribbon is used containing the three colors (cyan, yellow, and magenta) which, through subtractive color mixing, are able to produce the three primaries which, in turn, produce all the colors we see. The colored ribbons are divided into three *sequential* colored sequences of 8-1/2 inches long, the width of an ordinary sheet of paper. The printer must make three passes across the page to print the three colors and to produce a full-color image.

5.6 VIDEO AND FILM

This involves the placing of computer graphics images on film and video. The applications can be simple, for example, *photographing the screen* to make 35mm slides as shown in Exhibit 5.30.

Exhibit 5.30: Creating visuals from the screen (Courtesy of Polaroid Canada, Inc.)

Another simple use is the *digitizing of images* using a video camera and an analog to digital signal converter, as discussed in Chapter 4. Applications include showing images of real estate properties in a listing, or employee pictures in a company's staff files.

Other applications are more complex. One area that uses sophisticated and expensive computer graphics systems is *television broadcasting*. Images must be produced quickly—the industry lives on deadlines—and they must be of high resolution and good color quality. Major applications for computer graphics in broadcasting include weather, news, sports, and advertising. Visuals can be produced more quickly using sophisticated paint systems than shooting live pictures (Hutzel, 1985a). We discuss these applications in Chapters 8 and 9 under the topics of computer generated imagery, modeling and simulation, and computer aided design.

The key to successful broadcast systems is integration; the ability to move between different functions and perform each easily. Functions include image generation, text production, still work, and animation. The artist, for example, should be able to quickly take foreground objects and paste them electronically into a background, select images from a database and then, based on the cues for depth, create the appearance of depth.

Advanced broadcast systems include many brushes and colors, menu-driven interfaces, high resolutions, advanced cut-and-paste capabilities, sophisticated animation, full color video digitizing, 3-D capabilities, character generation, graphics database, flexibility, and upgradability. Systems range in cost from $30,000 to over $200,000.

An application still waiting to come to full life is *Videotex*, or *Interactive Television*. Videotex involves two-way communication. The user, through a monitor or a small computer and a modem, dials up a databank containing both text and image information, and selects the information required for display. The graphics standard for videotext in North America is *NAPLPS* (North American Presentation Level Protocol Standard). It was developed in Canada as *Telidon*.

An application used in agriculture is a videotex weather service called *Grassroots* aimed at farmers and others in the agribusiness. Grassroots provides detailed contour weather maps several times a day. A weather map is shown in Exhibit 5.31.

Exhibit 5.31: Videotex weather map (From G. Blackwell, "Videotex and the Office," *InfoAge*, April, 1985, p.19)

This is only one of many information services they provide. Others include commodity prices, stock prices, agricultural and related news, and so forth.

Another videotex service provided to electronic design engineers by Videolog Communications (Norwalk, Connecticut) is a databank of test specifications and detailed design diagrams on a half-million different semiconductor chips from 14,000 different manufacturers across North America. Electronic design engineers number over 300,000 in North America, and 70 percent of them have access to a computer. The subscribing engineer may search selectively, for example, and request a listing of all manufacturers who produce 256K RAM chips in the state of Colorado (Blackwell,1985).

5.7 SUMMARY

In this chapter we reviewed the media used to produce output; the final chapter of our introduction to graphics computer systems before discussing applications. We now have sufficient background to comprehend the use of graphics systems. Output is the most significant part of a system for the obvious reason that it is the system's response to the applications required. The sophistication of output devices, and the quality and variability of output, will continue to improve. We have not, for example, reached a point in the development of the technology where we are able to readily produce integrated multimedia presentations. It can be done, but cost and effort are high, and this capability is not generally available. But with the integration of different technologies (computers, laser disks, video, telecommunications) in a desktop unit, our personal and interpersonal communication capabilities will expand. We will be able to send each other complete productions, rather than a letter or a memorandum.

6

Presentation Graphics

6.1 INTRODUCTION

History states that chart representation of numeric data originated with René Descartes, the 17th century philosopher and mathematician; thus we have the *Cartes*ian coordinate system for plotting charts. It is difficult to believe that the Chinese, Phoenicians, Greeks, and Romans did not discover it earlier. Be as it may, it took another 100 years following Descartes' discovery for charts to be used as we know them today to represent scientific, business, and management information.

Presentation graphics in business and management is related to what one author calls the "Art of Persuasion." (DiCocco, 1984) The brief time spent by a manager, executive, or professional presenting past performance, current accomplishments, and future expectations to colleagues and superiors is extremely important; possibly critical.

We need to use good communication tools and use them skillfully. Otherwise the savings—and some estimate a cost of $10 per visual as compared to $35 to $100 using conventional methods or a professional graphics house—are completely wasted (Corr, 1985).

Now that we are capable of rapidly producing high quality images without first becoming skilled draftsmen, the door is open for the world to be inundated with terrible graphics presentations. The computer could amplify our lack of skill. The need for good design remains. Interactive computer graphics will help arouse our visual mind (Benzon, 1985).

The judicious use of computer graphics is an art. Computer graphics allows those of us who cannot sketch a cow or draw an oil well to create and manipulate images. What we create and present, however, and whether it is tastefully rendered and with high impact, depends upon how well we use the automated graphics tools. We will need to learn the syntax, semantics, and pragmatics of graphics just as we did with words, in order to express ourselves properly.

It is wise to follow the guidelines for graphics presentation that have emerged from past experience and are now codified in certain standards.* Then as skill, creativity, and confidence increase, more daring presentations can be attempted. Poor graphics blocks, rather than enhances, communication.

In this chapter we will briefly compare presentation and analytic graphics, describe the anatomy of a chart, discuss the rules for preparing good graphics, list the pitfalls to avoid, discuss and present examples of the major forms of presentation graphics and their principal applications, and discuss some major microcomputer-based systems.

6.2 PRESENTATION AND ANALYTIC GRAPHICS

The basic purposes of presentation graphics are to get a message across—to persuade, convince—not to analyze. *Consensus in the direction of the intended message* is the main goal, not discussion.

By comparison, the purpose of analytic graphics (Chapter 7) is to *clarify relationships* in data and information. Analytic graphics works in the service of the individual analyst, management group, task force, or work team. The important abilities of analytic graphics applications are to interface with database management systems and electronic spreadsheets, to produce charts from statistical analysis packages, and to display the results quickly and clearly at modest cost and quality. The objectives of presentation graphics are different. They are listed in Exhibit 6.1.

---

* In 1915 a *Joint Committee on Standards for Graphic Presentation* was formed in the United States to develop standards (Lambert, 1984).

• High quality
The quality must approach that of a graphics art house. Higher resolution, a variety of type fonts, variable line widths, good control over fill shading and borders, superior color separation if color is involved; these are some of the concerns. Quality is of more concern than speed.

• Flexibility
Wide choice of formats with rapid display for selection by the user, text insertion, adequate space for text, insertion of art work to enhance the message; these are some of the capabilities that add to flexibility.

• Balance
Layout, sequence, and balance between text and images are some of the issues here. Can text and images be readily integrated? Are there good facilities for page or image layout? Can a sequence be tested in animation on the computer? Some systems provide these capabilities.

• Varying media
Oversize screens or screen projection, hard copy on paper, overhead transparencies, slides, multi-slide presentation, film, video, coordination with sound, teleconferencing and remote graphics presentation are some of the media options that need to be considered.

Exhibit 6.1: Objectives of presentation graphics

The difference between presentation and analytic graphics is a matter of degree; presentation and analytic graphics capabilities do not exclude each other. The same system may provide both. But we need to be aware of the difference in order to use them properly. Consider the charts in Exhibit 6.2. The Lotus 1-2-3 *analytic* chart on the left is vastly improved in appearance in the *presentation* chart on the right, created using *Freelance* from Graphic Communications, Inc. (Waltham, MA), a very good graphics system functioning on the IBM PC.

Commentators on the use of graphics use different terms. The primary division is between presentation and analytic graphics. Some use the term business graphics to mean presentation graphics and others to mean analytic graphics. We offer the taxonomy in Exhibit 6.3 to put the issue of different terminology to rest at least for our discussion here.

Symbolic, or abstract, graphics is *representative* of real events (a bar or line chart of profits). Concrete graphics is an *image of something real* (a drawing of a pig of different sizes to reflect hog production). Symbolic or concrete images can be used in all three basic classes of graphics: analytic, presentation, and design.

Presentation hard copy graphics may be produced on a printer for modest quality or on a plotter for high quality. Display graphics may consist of a simple overhead, a single slide projector, thirty slide projectors with animation effects (and sound), video, or film.

Design graphics includes structured (interior and exterior building design, product design, modeling using 2-D and 3-D CAD systems) and free form graphics (interactive art using paint software, pattern generation programs).

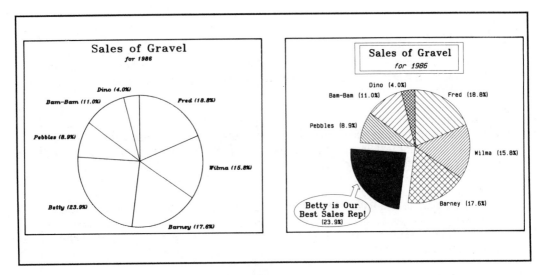

Exhibit 6.2: Analytic and presentation graphics

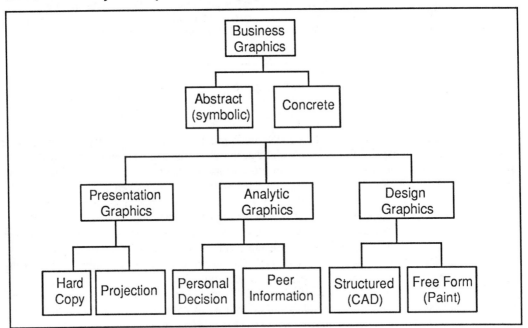

Exhibit 6.3: Taxonomy of business graphics

We will not cover here all that is represented in Exhibit 6.3. The taxonomy represents a size-able chunk of the media, communications, and computer graphics technology. Some topics are discussed in other chapters (design graphics in Chapters 8 and 9).

The *alternatives* in presentation graphics, and the process of creation from idea to output, is diagrammed in Exhibit 6.4, and discussed in this chapter.

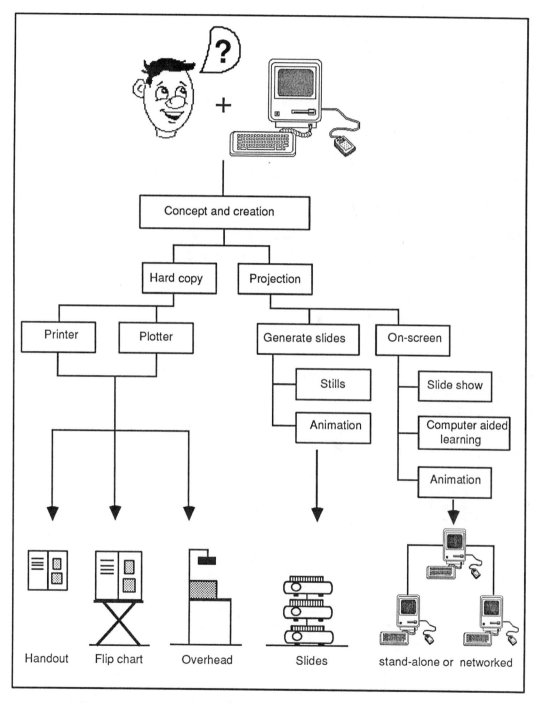

Exhibit 6.4: Alternatives in presentation graphics (Based on a diagram from Crider, 1984)

6.3 THE ANATOMY OF A CHART

Most of us are familiar with the garden variety charts used to present information, namely, the pie, column, bar, and line charts. In the last three kind of chart two variables are related; the *independent variable* (the categories) usually plotted on the horizontal **X** axis, and the *dependent variable* (the values) usually plotted on the vertical **Y** axis. The values are plotted as points in the body of the chart.

Various text items are added to transmit the meaning of the chart, including a heading or chart title, axes labels, and a legend defining the various columns, bars, and lines in the chart. The columns, bars, or lines are differentiated by different black-and-white textures and/or colors. The plots are usually a representation of some recorded observations maintained in a table of data.

Different typefaces and *styles,* or **BOLD TYPE** may be used in a judicious manner, as well as symbols (♀♂), icons (☠), lines, boxes, shadows, and textures, may be used to enhance communication. Exhibit 6.5 summarizes our brief discussion of a chart's anatomy.

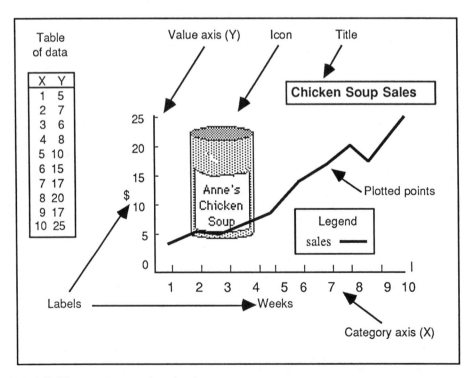

Exhibit 6.5: The anatomy of a chart

6.4 GOOD PRESENTATION PRINCIPLES

The good presentation principles listed in Exhibit 6.6 have been extracted from the sources listed in the references to this chapter. The list is not exhaustive, simply suggestive. The principles relate to audience identification, simplicity, directness, and the use of space, text, color, and balance.

• **Who is the audience**: an important consideration. What, for example, is the audience's level of knowledge concerning the content of the presentation, and what is its general experience with graphs? We might use symbols that are well known to persons in a particular industry, for example, company logos or industry symbols. We would avoid using a scatter diagram with an audience unfamiliar with such things, unless we felt it to be necessary, and that it could be explained simply and quickly. How many are viewing the presentation and what are their ages? If there are five or six in the audience, direct viewing of the computer screen may work, especially if it is oversized. More people than this will require projection. Further, an older audience might require letter sizes at a given projection distance that is twice the size required for younger audiences (see Exhibit 6.7).

• **Keep it simple:** do not present any more or less than is required to persuade successfully.

• **Identify the point**: are we clear as to the message we need and want to communicate? More time spent here is worthwhile time.

• **Start with the familiar**: then work towards the unfamiliar. We would not necessarily follow a chronological or logical development.

• **Each chart is independent**: that is, each chart stands by itself as a complete message and does not rely on any other charts for an understanding of its meaning.

• **Use space**: be aware of the placement of elements in the chart and use white space to set things off and guide the eye.

• **Use balance**: not too much information should be included in any given chart or graphic, and text and image should be in good balance.

• **Use text judiciously:** not too much and not too little, but enough to explain directly. Further, use one or two typefaces and not too many sizes.

• **Use color judiciously**: use only a few colors, and avoid colors that clash or resonate with each other in a psychodelic manner, or that are too extreme or sharp.

Exhibit 6.6: Good presentation principles

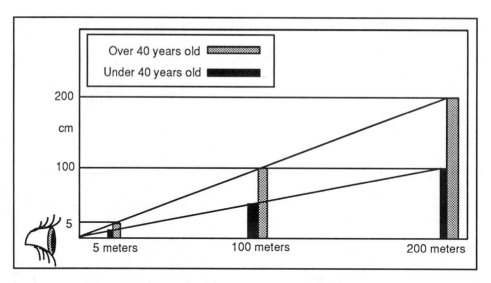

Exhibit 6.7: The size of lettering required for different age groups
(one meter = 39.37 inches, or a few inches over a yard)

6.5 PITFALLS TO AVOID

Figures lie and liars figure; and, since we do not want to consciously or unconsciously mis-represent, we should be aware of how figures can lie. The pitfalls are based primarily on the obser-vations of Francis (1962), and are listed in Exhibit 6.9. Exhibits 6.8, 6.10, and 6.11 are referenced in Exhibit 6.9.

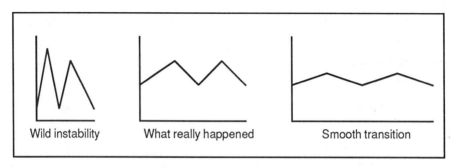

Exhibit 6.8: Bending the results

• **Avoid using disproportionate sizes unwittingly.** For example, we might use the height of a person to represent population in an area. If population doubles, do we double the size of the image? The answer, of course, is *no,* because that would imply a *fourfold* population increase rather than twofold. We would double the height only.

• **Avoid misleading chart proportions.** The recommended proportion is that the height of the chart should be three quarters of the length or width. By changing these proportions we can seriously distort the information in the chart. An example of distortion is shown in Exhibit 6.8.

• **Avoid misleading scales.** In a similar fashion we need only change the scales to obtain a similar distortion obtained by changing the chart proportions.

• **Avoid dual scales, or use carefully.** For example, plotting net sales and income per share on the same chart may improve communication. The two plots would use different scales as shown in Exhibit 6.10. Another exception is described in Chapter 7; when comparing the fiscal *patterns* of two companies from different countries and, therefore, using different currencies, two scales may be used.

• **Avoid nonzero baselines.** That is, start with a value of zero if it is possible. There are exceptions. For example, if an enterprise has always captured at least 10 percent of the market share, and it is not expected that the market share will exceed 20 percent, then the scale can legitimately go from 10 percent to 20 percent.

• **Improper or missing labels.** This occurs more than we might imagine. Testing a chart on a willing subject or two can be revealing.

• **Show the whole picture.** Based on an example provided by Lambert (1984), the first chart in Exhibit 6.11 shows recovery; the second implies growth only.

• **Avoid redundancy.** This relates to the knowledge level of the audience. If all the data being presented are about a single division of a enterprise, then there is no reason to keep repeating the division name on every chart.

• **Avoid plotting on the scale line.** Sometimes a graphics system does not allow one to avoid making the first plotted point appear on the y axis. This is poor form.

• **Use easy-to-read scales.** For example, do not use scales such as 7, 14, 21, 28, etc. Use 5, 10, 15, 20, 25, 30, etc.

• **Use simple messages.** For example, use terms like good/bad, up/down, more/less, fast/slow.

Exhibit 6.9: Pitfalls to avoid

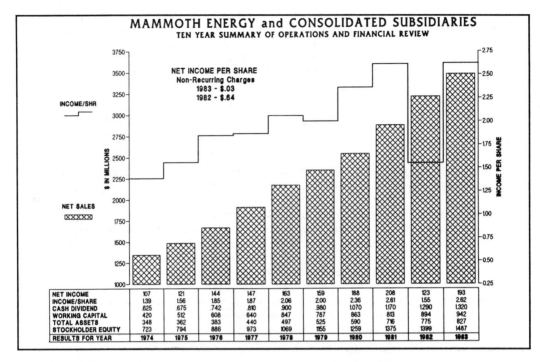

	1974	1975	1976	1977	1978	1979	1980	1981	1982	1983
NET INCOME	107	121	144	147	163	159	188	208	123	193
INCOME/SHARE	1.39	1.56	1.85	1.87	2.06	2.00	2.36	2.61	1.55	2.62
CASH DIVIDEND	.625	.675	.742	.810	.900	.980	1.070	1.170	1.290	1.320
WORKING CAPITAL	420	512	608	640	847	787	863	813	894	942
TOTAL ASSETS	348	362	383	440	497	525	590	716	775	827
STOCKHOLDER EQUITY	723	794	886	973	1069	1155	1259	1375	1399	1487
RESULTS FOR YEAR	1974	1975	1976	1977	1978	1979	1980	1981	1982	1983

Exhibit 6.10: Net sales and income per share; an example of the *proper* use of dual scales (Produced using *Picture Perfect* from Computer Support Corp.)

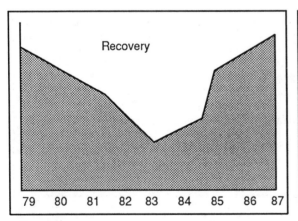
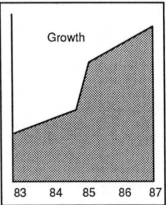

Exhibit 6.11: Not showing the full picture (based on a diagram from Lambert, 1984)

6.6 TYPES OF CHARTS

There are several basic chart types. Lambert (1984) discusses six types and *MSChart* from Micro-Soft (Bellevue, WA) on the Apple Macintosh provides a menu of 45 different variations of these six basic types that format automatically once selected. The name, characteristics, typical purposes, and examples of each are given in this section.

6.6-1 Column charts

Column charts show variations in values (**Y**) across categories (**X**). They are often used to show variations across time. They may be presented side by side or stacked. Exhibit 6.12 is a stacked example.

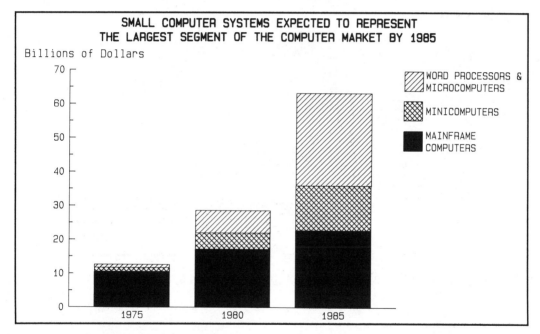

Exhibit 6.12: A stacked column chart
(Produced using *Graphwriter* from Lotus Development Corporation.)

6.6-2 Bar charts

Bar charts show variations in values (**X**) across categories (**Y**). They are often used to show data independently of time. They are suitable for portraying progress, or lack of it. Exhibit 6.13 shows a simple bar chart, and Exhibit 6.14 a more complex use.

Bar and column charts are most suitable for representing values for *discrete* data (sales data by regions, manufacturing costs by product type). By comparison line charts are suitable for *continuous* data (profit by time, temperature by season). Line charts should *not* be used to represent *discrete* data; that implies a continuity that does not exist (market testing of a product and the different reactions of different consumer groups; one set of data bears no relationship to another set.).

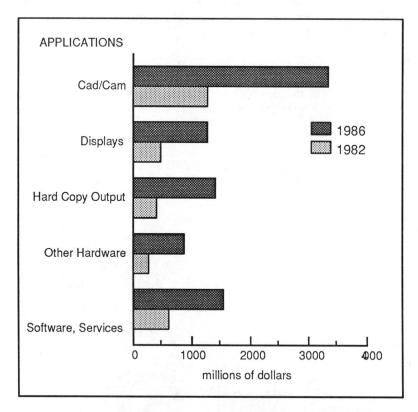

Exhibit 6.13: Worldwide shipments of computer graphics systems by U.S. manufacturers

6.6-3 Line charts

Line charts plot quantitative data to show and compare trends. Line charts allow for rapid information evaluation and comparison, and are suitable for portraying *continuous* data. A line chart of growth in sales, expenses, and fixed assets is shown in Exhibit 6.15.

6.6-4 Pie charts

Pie charts are suitable for showing *relative proportions* of parts to the whole. They are the simplest and easiest charts to understand. An example is provided in Exhibit 6.16.

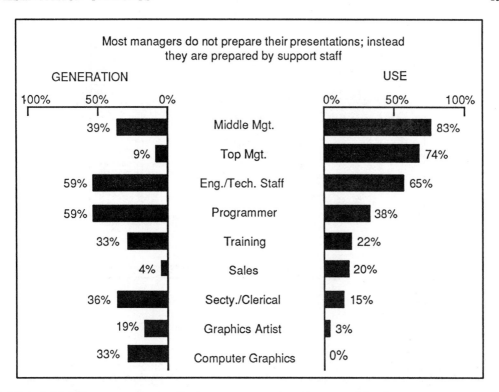

Exhibit 6.14: Who prepares and who uses presentation graphics? (Based on a diagram from D. L. Wilcox, "The Boom in Business Graphics," *PC World*, 2, 9, August, 1984)

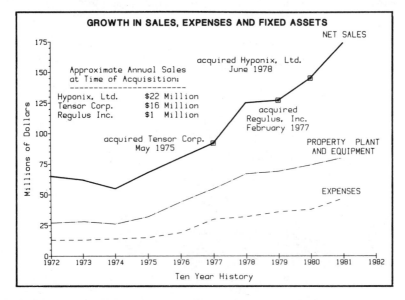

Exhibit 6.15: Line chart of growth in sales, expenses, and fixed assets
(Produced using *Diagraph* from Computer Support Corporation.)

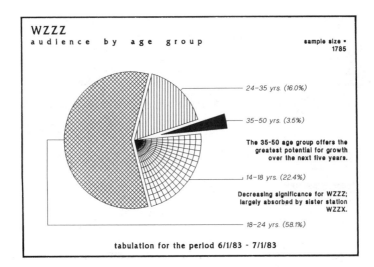

Exhibit 6.16: Pie chart (Produced using *Picture Perfect* from Computer Support Corp.)

6.6-5 Area charts

Area charts reflect both trends and proportions. The area chart resembles a line chart with shading below. The *order of plotting is critical;* it will change the appearance of the chart and the way information is communicated. An example is provided in Exhibit 6.17; the "B" plot is superior to the "A." Area chart "B" in Exhibit 6.17, where the largest *decrease* in sales (hulls) is plotted at the base, and the largest *increase* in sales (motors) is plotted at the top, appears to portray the data the clearest.

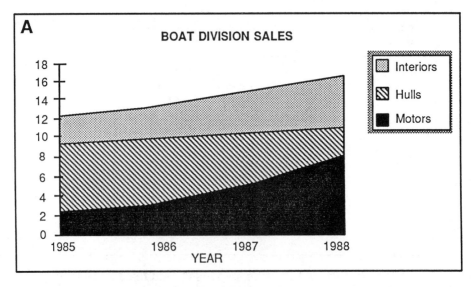

Exhibit 6.17A: Area chart *not* showing the data as clearly as it could

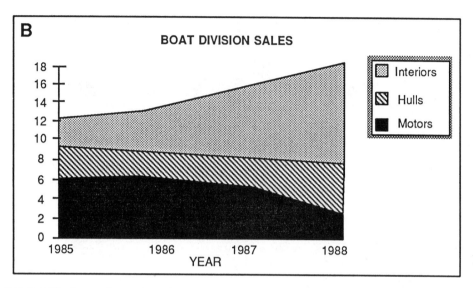

Exhibit 6.17B: Area chart showing the data in a clearer manner

6.6-6 Scatter charts

Scatter charts, or diagrams, show the relationship between two variables. The relationship may vary between being perfectly positive (measures in inches and centimeters), through no discernible, or zero, relationship, to a perfectly negative relationship. Scatter charts are the visual equivalent of the correlation coefficient, **r**, which can possess values between +1.0 and -1.0. An example showing the relationship between the consumption of coffee, hot chocolate, and lemonade with an increase in temperature is shown in Exhibit 6.18.

6.6-7 Bubble charts

Bubble charts add a third dimension to the usual X and Y axes, namely, the *size* of the bubble. In Exhibit 6.19 the bubble sizes are proportional to the total assets of an enterprise.

The diagram shows that the company with the highest assets and close to the highest growth shows the *least* return on sales. Bubble charts are not particularly easy to read and should, therefore, be selectively used with an audience that will readily understand them.

6.6-8 Combination charts

Combination charts may be judiciously used to further improve communication and impact. For example, the combination of a column and line chart can be very effective. The combination of a pie with a column chart can improve communication. Consider the two applications in Exhibits 6.20 and 6.21.

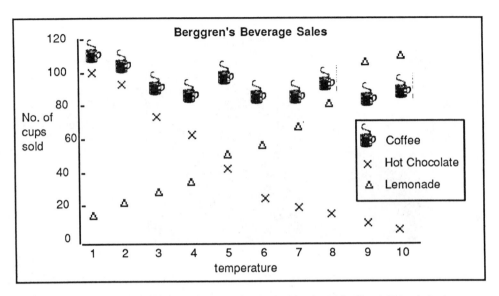

Exhibit 6.18: Scatter diagram (cup icon based on drawing from *Art Portfolio* by Axlon)

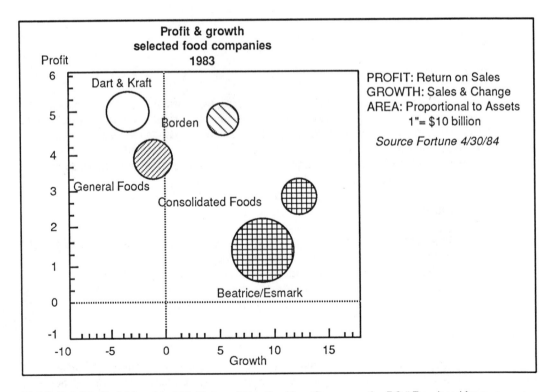

Exhibit 6.19: Bubble chart (J. Bishop, "Charting Your Course on the PC," Reprinted from *PC Magazine,* 4, 1, January 8, 1985; Copyright © Ziff Communications Company)

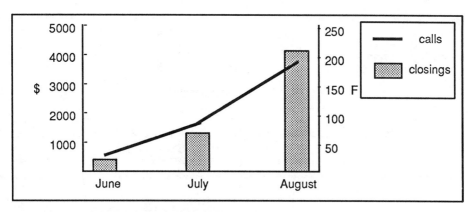

Exhibit 6.20: Combination column and line chart

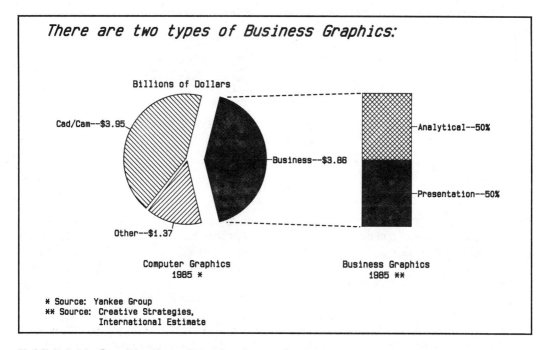

Exhibit 6.21: Combination pie and column chart (Produced using *Graphwriter* from Lotus Development Corporation.)

6.6-9 Organization charts

Organization charts show the hierarchy and formal lines of communication in an enterprise. Exhibit 6.22 provides an example.

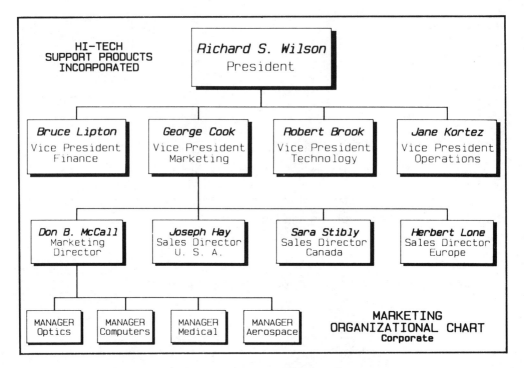

Exhibit 6.22: Organization chart (Produced using *DIAGRAPH* from Computer Support Corp.)

6.6-10 Text charts

Text charts improve communication although they do not use images as such. They should be used to present key ideas, and they should not be too extensive. They are the most abused aspect of presentation graphics; that is, attention must be paid to the capabilities and limitations of human perception—there is only so much we can take in at any one time. In fact, it is limited to about seven "chunks" of information, plus or minus two.

Exhibit 6.23 provides an example of a *plotted* text chart, and Exhibit 6.24 shows the variety of fonts possible with dot-addressable systems and the proper software.

Exhibit 6.24 contains far too much information, if the intent was to present the *content*; and/or if it were being projected on a screen. But in this case the intent is to convey an *impression* of the capabilities of a particular piece of software, rather than information to read and remember.

6.6-11 Map charts

Maps are an excellent means for exhibiting certain types of data: locations, routes, networks, and densities; geographic, geologic, and atmospheric data; and all types of demographic statistics. *MacAtlas* by Micro:Maps (Morristown, NJ), functions on the Apple Macintosh, and *STATMAP* from Ganesa Group International, Inc. (McLean, VA), on the IBM PC. Exhibit 6.25 provides an

Job Performance and Job Satisfaction

What is their bottom—line value to an organization?

DESIGN CONCERN	HAS AN EFFECT ON		
	Job satisfaction	Job performance	Ease of communication
Degree of enclosure			✔
Layout			✔
Temperature/air quality	✔		
Lighting	✔	✔	
Windows	✔	✔	
Access control		✔	
Noise	✔		
Speech privacy			✔
Comfort	✔		
Participation	✔	✔	
Flexibilty	✔		

Exhibit 6.23: A text chart (Produced using *Sign-Master* from Decision Resources, Inc.)

Exhibit 6.24: Fonts (Produced using *Fontrix* from Data Transforms, Inc.)

example of the accurate bare maps provided by *MacAtlas*, to which a variety of information may be added using various graphics means including dots, lines, shades, symbols, and icons. Exhibit 6.26 shows the distribution of educational software sales in the United States.

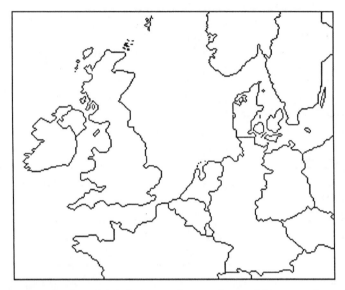

Exhibit 6.25: A bare map to which information and graphics may be added
(Produced using *MacAtlas* from Micro:Maps)

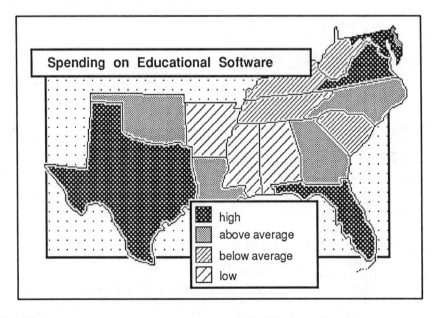

Exhibit 6.26: An enhanced map (Produced using *MacAtlas* from Micro:Maps)

6.6-12 Other charts

Other charts used in presentations are described elsewhere in this text. They include *project management charts* such as *Gannt* and *PERT* (chapter 11), *2-D and 3-D layout or design charts* (chapters 8 and 9), and *flow charts* as used in system analysis (chapter 15).

6.7 CHARTS WITH ART

It enhances communication when artwork is added to a chart. The chart itself is a visual and an improvement over text alone, but it remains abstract or symbolic. Adding related images and artwork increases the concreteness and the impact. Images are used to enhance the message in Exhibit 6.27.

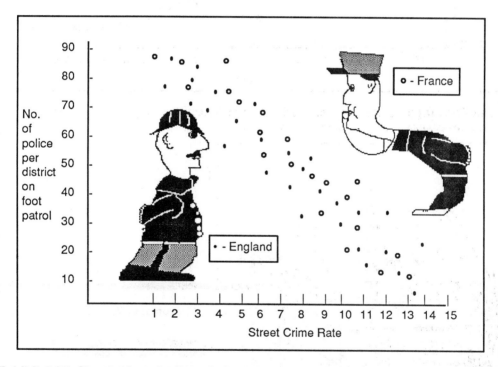

Exhibit 6.27: Street crime declines in both England and France with an increase in foot patrol officers (Illustrations by Adam Marshall)

In Exhibit 6.28 the artwork produced through *Fontrix* from Data Transforms, Inc. (Denver, CO), an extensive paint and design program for the IBM PC, shows dragon sales are slipping in Transylvania. As the reader can see, highly detailed drawings are possible on microcomputers. In Exhibit 6.29 a piece of fine artwork produced using *MacPaint* on the Macintosh is used to enhance the message of increased tourism in Devon and Wales. The purpose of art in charts is to emphasize a point and increase the message impact. Some of the available paint programs are listed in Appendix C.

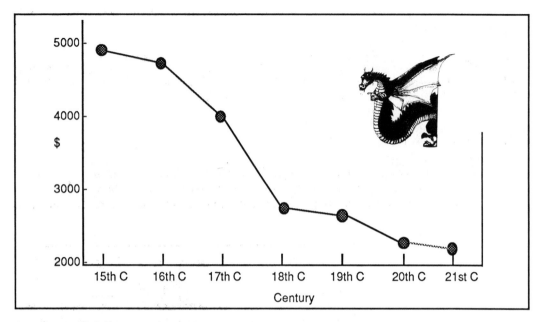

Exhibit 6.28: Dragon sales have slipped in Transylvania (Dragon produced using *Fontrix* and reproduced courtesy of Data Transforms, Inc.)

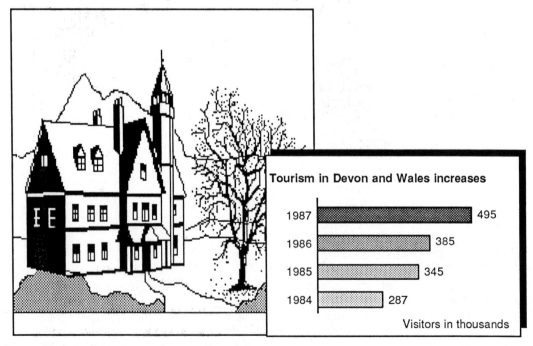

Exhibit 6.29: Tourism in Devon and Wales on the rise (Image from library in *PictureBase* and reproduced courtesy of Symmetry Corp.)

6.8 COMPUTER AIDED LEARNING (CAL)*

A computer aided learning system is defined when an author of some learning materials is able to control the sequencing of screens (often called *frames* and sometimes called *tableaus*), display a mix of text and images, and *branch* to different sequences on the basis of different *responses* by the learner. These type of systems go beyond the traditional definition of presentation graphics, but they are an alternative to the use of paper graphs, overheard charts, and computer-generated slides for convincing and instructing. Further, CAL systems on small graphics computers are only a recent innovation. One such system is *LightSource* from Computer Learning Systems, Inc. (Concord, NH), that functions on the Apple Macintosh. It turns the Macintosh into a CAL authoring and learning station. The author designs tableaus of text and images. Various locations on the screen can be designed to be "active"; that is, when the user places the cursor on an active location and presses the button on the mouse, some action will take place: the next sequence of frames, branching to an alternate sequence, a quiz, termination; some action of some kind. The action location on the screen can be a sentence, an object, part of an object, or a box. The sequences of frames, the various branchings, different flags that indicate when certain things should take place, plus the content, all make up the *script*. In addition, LightSource provides for testing and scoring.

It is obvious that the development of a script in this context is far more demanding than writing a textbook, or preparing a lecture. There are more capabilities and flexibility and, therefore, more demands on creativity. The next capability, animation, makes further demands.

6.9 ANIMATION

Many systems provide some form of sequence animation. On personal computers they are often primitive but allow for testing sequences prior to actual production in another medium (broadcast video), or the setting up of computer-based learning. The latter offers some interesting possibilities. If a picture is worth a thousand words, then what is an animated sequence of images worth? Most likely a lot when it comes to showing people how to do something. Training films and videos have existed for quite a few decades. The advantage of the computer, of course, is flexibility and control.

One system for the Apple Macintosh is called *VideoWorks* from Hayden Software (Lowell, MA). VideoWorks turns the Apple Macintosh into a desktop animation station. Using either images provided by VideoWorks, or created using MacPaint or *CheapPaint* (VideoWorks scaled down version of MacPaint), we assemble the necessary frames. In Exhibit 6.30 we see the sequence required to show a man doing the broad jump. VideoWorks is as much a learning environment for acquiring the knowledge and skills necessary for creating successful animated sequences, as it is a tool for doing the job. For example, in Exhibit 6.31 we are told to pay attention to the matching required between frames in order to create the illusion of locomotion. VideoWorks can be used for lighthearted animation (Exhibit 6.32), or for more serious learning (Exhibit 6.33). Further, VideoWorks provides various backdrops (Exhibit 6.34) upon which one is

---

* Other terms used include *Computer Based Training (CBT),* and *Computer Aided Instruction (CAI).* This author prefers *Computer Aided Learning* because it defines the automated learning system from the perspective of the learner, not the teacher.

Exhibit 6.30: Animation sequence of the broad jump (Produced using *VideoWorks* and reproduced here courtesy of Hayden Software)

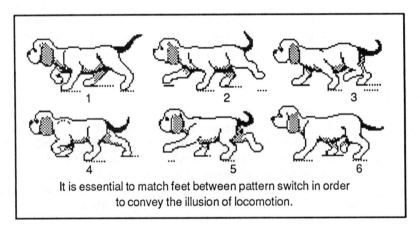

It is essential to match feet between pattern switch in order
to convey the illusion of locomotion.

Exhibit 6.31: Animation systems as an environment for learning about animation (Produced using *VideoWorks* and reproduced here courtesy of Hayden Software)

able to superimpose various action figures. Further, it is possible to animate business graphs (show rising profits in animation).

VideoWorks is inspiring, but there is much to learn; as a recent reviewer pointed out, "you grasp the potential before you have the credentials" (McCandless, 1985). Creating an animation of any substance requires many frames, and takes a considerable investment of time and effort.

A powerful authoring system would consist of some combination of the capabilities of computer-aided learning and animation, coupled with the ability to draw upon a variety of presentation media (video sequences, music, film, and computer-stored materials). Such systems are not, as yet, generally available.

Exhibit 6.32: King Kong (Produced using *VideoWorks* and reproduced here courtesy of Hayden Software)

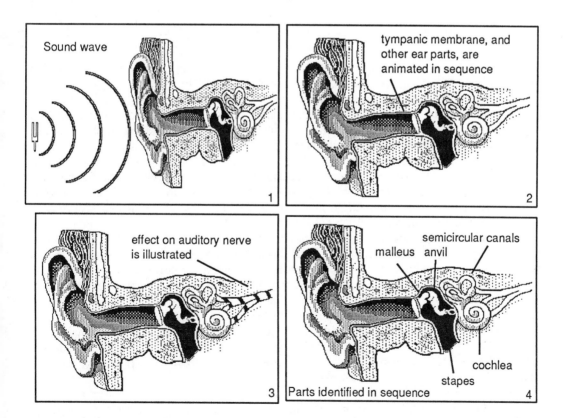

Exhibit 6.33: The workings of the ear (Produced using *VideoWorks* and reproduced here courtesy of Hayden Software)

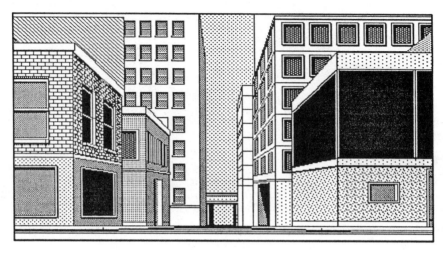

Exhibit 6.34: City backdrop (Produced using *VideoWorks* and reproduced here courtesy of Hayden Software)

6.10 COMPARING SOME SYSTEMS

We formally review the criteria for evaluating graphics systems in Chapter 15. Here we look informally at a few available presentation systems to get some idea of the range of capabilities.

Since presentation graphics is meant for public display and must look artistically prepared and not look like it came from a computer, some microcomputer-based graphics systems may not make the mark. This is as much a function of the output device used as of the graphics software selected. But if the software cannot emulate the freedom of the graphic artist and provides too few graphic content and layout choices, high quality output from a plotter will not help too much.

It may be necessary to select two or three packages. Howitt (1984) describes the vice-president of a bank who uses computer graphics extensively and regularly uses *eight* different graphics systems. The point is that one package may offer a wide selection of type fonts; another more attractive chart layout; and a third better color control.

Graphwriter is an impressive graphics package for the IBM PC. Exhibit 6.12 was produced using Graphwriter. It has the ability to create graphics not possible with other systems (bubble charts). It includes a command language. *Chart-Master* offers "a fair degree of flexibility within a menu operation" (Bishop, 1984). It allows for different scales on the Y axis, multiple charts on the same page, and may be obtained with a companion system called *Sign-Master* for producing text charts only (see Exhibit 6.23). Examples of *Picture Perfect* and *Diagraph* have also been included (Exhibits 6.10, 6.15, 6.16, and 6.22). Diagraph provides extensive libraries of different images.

Graftalk is both menu- and command-driven, as is *GDSS*, which provides an extensive language of over 120 commands. This, of course, means more power, more flexibility, and more to learn. The question is always: do we need it?

Some systems possess a wide range of capabilities such as *Energraphics* from Enertronics Research, Inc. (St. Louis, MO), which is able to create analytic, presentation, freeform, and design graphics. By comparison, systems like *PFS-Graph* and the *Executive Picture Show* on the IBM PC, and *MSChart* on the IBM PC and the Apple Macintosh, are relatively easy to use, with more limited capabilities, but at lower cost. These systems can be used immediately by the end-user with little or no training. These systems offer a lot of variety (many choices of charts and chart formats), but little flexibility; that is, anything outside of what they offer specifically cannot usually be produced. The use of preformatted charts and graphs is in response to limited user knowledge of graphics design.

Execuvision is directed at producing slides and allowing the user to develop the graphics and the animation. The slides are created from extensive stored libraries of images. However, the images are not high quality; they look as if they came from a computer, as shown in Exhibit 6.35.

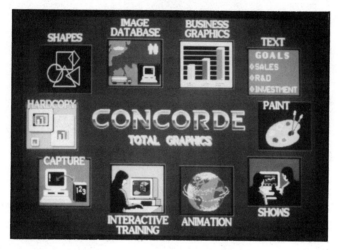

Exhibit 6.35: Medium resolution image (Courtesy of Visual Communications, Inc.)

By comparison, the images produced by much more expensive systems namely *Videoshow 150* (not a slide production system but a dedicated graphics processor that connects to a personal computer and creates high quality color images on a wide range of monitors) from General Parametrics Corp. (Berkeley, CA), and the *Samurai Image Processor from Image Resource Corp.* (Westlake Village, CA) are of far superior presentation quality. These systems are cost-effective and the images produced compare favorably to graphics generated by systems more expensive still. Both systems are easy to use. Videoshow 150 hardware and software adds approximately $4,000 to the cost of a system; Samurai about $10,000.

Exhibit 6.36 shows an image produced using *SIGHT*, a graphic command language based on the GKS standard which is a part of Samurai.

Slide graphics production is becoming a PC-based technology (Hutzel, 1985b). There are two approaches to obtaining high quality computer-based slides: use a service, or use software and hardware on a microcomputer. Using a PC *without* graphics, it is possible to send instructions via a modem to a central service, by responding to various queries related to the slide or slides desired. Twelve to twenty-four hours later the slide is delivered. Or, using a PC *with* graphics, one can create the slide, do some of the design, get an idea of how the slide will look like in its final form, and then transmit the information on the slide to the central service to obtain superior resolution and color. Further, one can establish a *fully independent system* costing $15,000 to $40,000, in comparison to the $75,000 or so of several years ago. There are a number of vendors of these

Exhibit 6.36: High resolution image (Original in color courtesy of Calcomp)

services, and software and hardware, including 3M/Artronics, Autographix, AVL, Aztek, Bell and Howell, Dicomed, Genigraphics, Imapro Management Graphics, and MGI (see Appendix C).

6.11 CONCLUSION

John Naisbitt in *Megatrends* (Warner Books, New York, NY, 1982) reports that a major trend is the movement from an industrial society to an information society, where work and value produced are not related to hard commodities but to soft information. The value of information can be enhanced by the proper use of the syntax, semantics, and pragmatics of presentation graphics, supported by the personal interactive computer system. Maybe we will "get the picture" sooner through the use of more images in our communication with each other. The purpose of personal computers is to provide paths between people. And it is the larger context of understanding and wisdom that should connect us. People must provide this larger context, but graphics computers might help provide a clearer content. It will take time for us to learn to use this new medium effectively. The reader may wish to turn to the beginning of Chapter 15 and review Exhibit 15.1, which illustrates the content-context dichotomy.

7

Analytic Graphics

7.1 INTRODUCTION

In this chapter we sample some of the analytic uses of computer graphics. Graphic images similar to those used in presentation graphics are used in analytic graphics; their purpose is different. *Analytic graphics is used to make decisions rather than influence others on decisions already made*, one of the purposes of presentation graphics.

We will first discuss the electronic spreadsheet, the prime tool used on computers for manipulating numbers, and then demonstrate the translation of the numbers to graphics. We will then present two applications, one on price sensitivity, and the other on break-even analysis. A relatively new application of graphics is then presented: the visual income statement and balance sheet. Following this, we will explore integrated systems that include multiple functions, followed by a discussion of descriptive and inferential statistical analysis and the use of graphics. Our discussion is only a small sample of an expanding field.

7.2 THE ELECTRONIC SPREADSHEET (ESS)

An ESS is used to create, edit, and print out spreadsheet calculations, a tedious procedure when performed manually. An ESS would be used by an accountant, a businessperson, or a manager to predict profits, estimate costs, study cash flow, make forecasts, create operating statements, plan financing, produce price lists, and plan inventory. With an electronic spreadsheet, when conditions change or when the effect of possible changes in different variables need to be studied, the impact on profits, cash flow, and so forth can be obtained nearly instantaneously.

The first electronic spreadsheet was *VisiCalc* and it is credited with being responsible for more sales of the Apple II family of computers than any other program.* Today there are a great many ESSs ranging in cost from fifty to several hundred dollars. Most are integrated in some fashion with other functions, including some or all of the following: database, word processing, tele-communications, and business graphics.

When using an ESS on a computer, we can imagine the monitor or screen as a window on a large flat sheet of grid paper with many rows and many columns. This is illustrated in Exhibit 7.1.

We can further imagine that we have immediate control over the labeling of any row or column. We can specify the relationships between any row, column, or cell in the matrix, enter data, specify formulae, transfer data or the results of calculations from other spreadsheets, transform the results into a graph, transfer the results to a word processor for adding explanatory text, and finally print it, or possibly transmit the completed report to another computer location.

---

* VisiCalc was the brainchild of Dan Bricklin, at the time an MBA student at Harvard University, who—so the story goes—was inspired to develop the ESS after suffering through various classes on the making of economic projections; the professor was constantly changing figures on the board, ending with a hard to read "mess," and a chalk-smeared coat! It seems that Bricklin approached a Harvard professor in finance with his idea, and the professor thought the concept lacked merit. Bricklin and his associates went on to form a company, Software Arts, which then successfully marketed VisiCalc; the program was a huge success. Bricklin recently developed a program called *Demo Program*, a computer-based training (CBT) development system with some clever twists, and discussed briefly in Chapter 8.

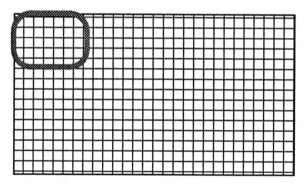

Exhibit 7.1: Window onto a large matrix

These capabilities allow for highly flexible and rapid data analysis and "what if" projections. "What if" projections are the study of different assumptions and the impact of potential changes on the enterprise. Integrating graphics with spreadsheets allows for the results of "what-if" projections to be communicated better.

7.3 A START-UP VENTURE APPLICATION

Let us assume we are starting a business. We have designed an automated system for evaluating consumer products, and we will sell this system in the form of a program on a disk with related data about different consumer products on other disks. We wish to present to the bank and venture capital investors some idea of first year start-up costs. Exhibit 7.2 shows the ESS in a stage of development using *Multiplan* from MicroSoft Corp. (Bellevue, WA) on the Apple Macintosh.

FIG. 7.2

		1	2	3
1	ITEM	TOTALS		HOW COMPUTED
2	Sales	$800		Given or estimated
3	Cost of Goods	$600		75% of Sales
4	Gross Sales			Sales − Cost of goods
5	Distribution			Given
6	Marketing			Given
7	Salaries			Given
8	Overhead			Given
9	Total Costs			Sum of all costs
10	Net Profit			Sales − Total Costs
11	Percent			Net/Profit/Sales * 100

Exhibit 7.2:   Developing projected start-up costs and expected income

Column 3 in Exhibit 7.2 is not necessary to the ESS. It is documentation to describe how each cell is calculated. Exhibit 7.3 shows the completed spreadsheet based on the assumption that cost of goods is 75 percent of sales. All other data are either given or calculated as shown. It appears that we expect to come close to breaking even the first year.

	1	2	3
Fig 7.3			
	1	**2**	**3**
1	ITEM	TOTALS	HOW COMPUTED
2	Sales	$800	Given or estimated
3	Cost of Goods	$600	Percent of Sales
4	Gross Sales	$200	Sales – Cost of goods
5	Distribution	$15	Given
6	Marketing	$80	Given
7	Salaries	$95	Given
8	Overhead	$12	Given
9	Total Costs	$802	Sum of all costs
10	Net Profit	($2)	Sales – Total Costs
11	Percent	–0.25%	Net/Profit/Sales * 100
12			

Exhibit 7.3: The completed spreadsheet for year one

However, some recent news changes the picture. Distribution costs are rising because of the increased cost of transportation. We estimate an increase of 10 percent the first year. Exhibit 7.4 shows this change, and the ESS reflects this change immediately in all other affected cells.

	1	2	3
Fig 7.4			
	1	**2**	**3**
1	ITEM	TOTALS	HOW COMPUTED
2	Sales	$800	Given or estimated
3	Cost of Goods	$600	Percent of Sales
4	Gross Sales	$200	Sales – Cost of goods
5	Distribution	$17	15*1.1
6	Marketing	$80	Given
7	Salaries	$95	Given
8	Overhead	$12	Given
9	Total Costs	$804	Sum of all costs
10	Net Profit	($4)	Sales – Total Costs
11	Percent	–0.44%	Net/Profit/Sales * 100

Exhibit 7.4: The spreadsheet reflects an expected 10 percent increase in distribution costs

It is obviously important that the "what if" analyses, like what if the costs of transportation rose 10 percent, are based on some empirical knowledge, not simply playing with numbers. One-year estimates are of limited value. We therefore use the ESS to project income and expenses across six years as shown in Exhibit 7.5.

Decrease salary increases!   *Cost of goods should drop in 1987.*

1	2	3	4	5	6	7
ITEM	1985	1986	1987	1988	1989	1990
Sales	$800	$960	$1152	$1382	$1659	$1991
Cost of Goods	$600	$720	$864	$1037	$1244	$1493
Gross Sales	$200	$240	$288	$346	$415	$498
Distribution	$17	$18	$20	$22	$24	$27
Marketing	$80	$96	$115	$138	$166	$199
Salaries	$95	$114	$137	$164	$197	$236
Overhead	$12	$13	$15	$16	$18	$19
Total Costs	$804	$961	$1150	$1377	$1649	$1974
Net Profit	($4)	($1)	$2	$5	$10	$16
Percent	-0.44%	-0.14%	0.13%	0.38%	0.61%	0.82%

Exhibit 7.5: The expected picture for six years with some "what if" remarks added

The picture is not very positive. On sales of close to two million in 1990, after six years of operation, we show a profit of only $16,000, which is less than 1 percent of gross sales. Inspection of the ESS shows that we increased people's salaries 20 percent each year, an unreasonable amount. Further, we have good reason to assume, even conservatively, that costs of goods will decrease by 1987 from 75 percent to 70 percent of sales. Exhibit 7.6 reflects these expected changes.

1	2	3	4	5	6	7
ITEM	1985	1986	1987	1988	1989	1990
Sales	$800	$960	$1152	$1382	$1659	$1991
Cost of Goods	$600	$720	$806	$968	$1161	$1393
Gross Sales	$200	$240	$346	$415	$498	$597
Distribution	$17	$18	$20	$22	$24	$27
Marketing	$80	$96	$115	$138	$166	$199
Salaries	$95	$106	$119	$133	$149	$167
Overhead	$12	$13	$15	$16	$18	$19
Total Costs	$804	$954	$1075	$1277	$1518	$1806
Net Profit	($4)	$6	$77	$105	$141	$185
Percent	-0.44%	0.65%	6.66%	7.60%	8.47%	9.28%

Exhibit 7.6: A new spreadsheet reflecting the changes in projections

7.4 FROM SPREADSHEET TO IMAGE

The effects of assumptions captured in spreadsheets are easier to see in a graph. In our example, the numbers are transferred to a graphics program and the resulting graph is shown in Exhibit 7.7.

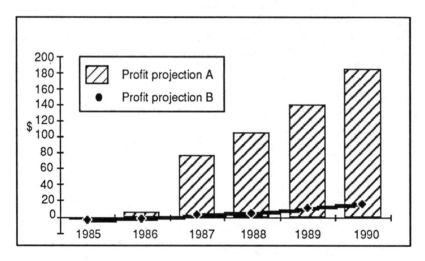

Exhibit 7.7: Profit projections

Profit projection A is based on a 12 percent salary increase, and a 5 percent reduction of the cost of goods in 1987. Profit projection B is based on a 20 percent salary increase, and no reduction of the cost of goods in 1987.

With some software the transfer from table to image is easier to do than with others. For example, with *Multiplan* and *Chart* as used on the Apple Macintosh, it is necessary to go through the scrapbook function, and it is somewhat clumsy and time consuming. With fully integrated systems, creating graphs from spreadsheet data is close to immediate, and very easy.

It is better to show the profit projections as a *percent* of gross sales as diagrammed in Exhibit 7.8. In comparison to the profit projection in Exhibit 7.7, the picture presented by the percent figures shows a *less* dramatic increase in profits. Finally, in Exhibit 7.9 the total costs for the two different projections are shown. The projections of cost do not appear very different. However, the higher costs, as we have already seen, lead to a loss or very little profit over six years, versus a growth to some acceptable level of profit.

The above is a simple example of the use of the ESS and analytic graphics. More complex examples and additional techniques for analysis are provided by Koff (1984). "What-if" analyses are a part of making projections. Projections are a part of modeling an enterprise and simulating different conditions to see how the enterprise might respond. The model and the simulated conditions are represented by mathematical formulae. The question is, how do we know that our mathematical equations accurately reflect reality? Usually this is determined by evaluating predictions against actual data, or is based on knowledgable opinion. We touch again on this point when we discuss price sensitivity and break-even analysis.

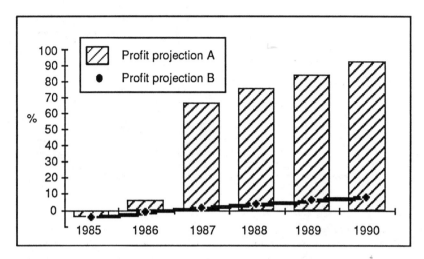

Exhibit 7.8: Profit projections as a percent of gross sales

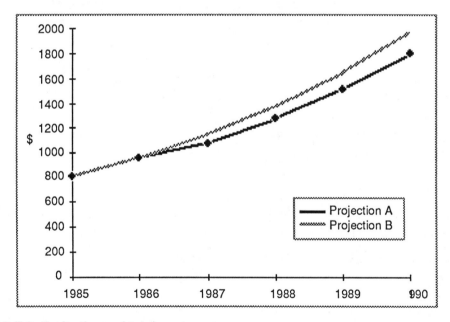

Exhibit 7.9: Projections of total costs

The effectiveness of the ESS is extended through the use of templates. *Integrated Profit Planning Systems* from Softouch Software, Inc. (Lake Oswego, OR), is a set of templates that works with *Multiplan,* and a set of guides for relating business objectives to operating, expense, and income plans. This then leads to consolidated profit plans. A diagram showing the relationship between objectives and plans is given in Exhibit 7.10, and a part of an income plan is shown in Exhibit 7.11. The income plan results would lend themselves to the same kind of graph as shown in Exhibits 7.18 through 7.21 to visually present accounting data.

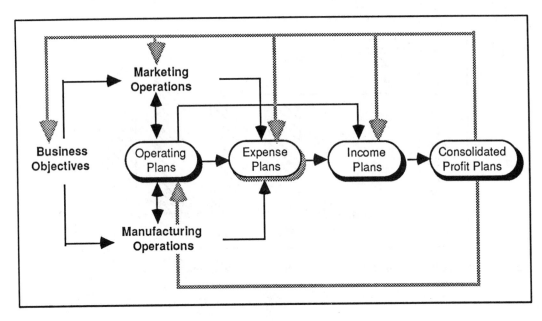

Exhibit 7.10: Profit planning diagram

Income Plan				
BUSINESS UNITS	BU1		BU2	
1 BU INCOME PLANS	%%%	$$$$	%%%	$$$$
2 GROSS SALES	100.00%	50000	100.00%	80000
3 (LESS).............				
4 DISCOUNTS	1.40%	700	1.00%	800
5 ADJUSTMENTS	1.00%	500	0.75%	600
6 (=) NET SALES	97.60%	48800	98.25%	78600
7 (LESS).............				
8 MANUFACTURING	20.00%	9999	25.00%	20003
9 VARIABLE C.O.S	4.00%	1999	15.00%	12000
10 FIXED C.O.S	7.00%	3500	4.38%	3501
11 PERIOD C.O.S	9.00%	4500	5.63%	4502
12				

Exhibit 7.11: Part of an income plan

7.5 PRICE SENSITIVITY

We demonstrate the use of some simple equations to derive a relationship between the selling price of an item, and profit. The example is based on one provided by Koff (1984). The item in question is a kite. Different profit levels are computed as follows:

Profits = -18000 + 1300 * price - 20 * price^2

where "*" means multiply and "^" means raise to the second power. The formula for profits is based on other formulae discussed next.

The kite manufacturer experienced 100 sales at a price of $45 and 500 sales at a price of $25. This provides two data points and a straight line function representing the relation of sales volume to unit price. The formula is as follows:

Sales volume = 1000 - 20 * price (e.g., SV = 1000 - 20 * 45, which equals, 100)

Further total revenues are computed as follows:

Revenues = volume of sales * price

The cost of manufacturing each kite is $12, the cost of shipping each kite is $3, and overhead costs are $3,000. This is reflected in the following formula:

Costs = 15 * volume of sales + 3000

Profits are obtained by subtracting costs from revenues or:

Profits = revenues - costs

Combining the above formulae using simple algebra leads to the formula already stated, namely:

Profits = -18000 + 1300 * price - 20 * price ^ 2

Using this formula in a spreadsheet we are able to generate different levels of profit for each unit price as shown in Exhibit 7.12. Transferring this data to a graph provides us with a price sensitivity curve as shown in Exhibit 7.13.

The unit price that leads to the highest level of profit is $32.50. The question remains whether the formulae represent reality. For example, is the relationship between price and volume of sales correctly reflected in the function shown? Would sales be zero at a price of $45 as indicated? It is doubtful. A normal curve function might be more realistic (Koff, 1984). Further discussion takes us beyond the scope of this text. Koff provides a good review of relating this type of modeling to business strategy.

Prices	Profits	Prices	Profits
20.00	0	33.00	3120
21.00	480	34.00	3080
22.00	920	35.00	3000
23.00	1320	36.00	2880
24.00	1680	37.00	2720
25.00	2000	38.00	2520
26.00	2280	39.00	2280
27.00	2520	40.00	2000
28.00	2720	41.00	1680
29.00	2880	42.00	1320
30.00	3000	43.00	920
31.00	3080	44.00	480
32.00	3120	45.00	0
32.50	3125		

Exhibit 7.12: Price sensitivity table (based on a spreadsheet analysis)

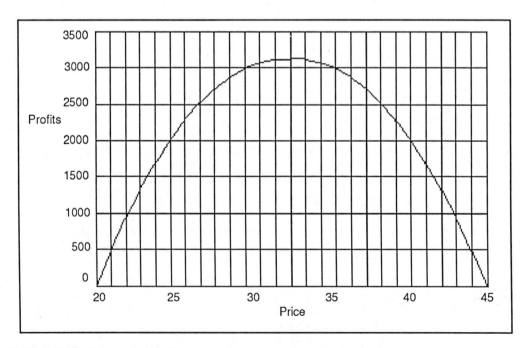

Exhibit 7.13: Price sensitivity curve

7.6 BREAK-EVEN ANALYSIS

The application software program called *Profit Projections/Breakeven Analysis* from Harris Technical Systems, Inc. (Lincoln, NE), hereafter referred to as *PPBEA* and which functions on the Apple Macintosh, is the basis for this part of our discussion.

PPBEA provides a number of useful templates and break-even graphs for analyzing profit as a function of income and expenses. Its value is in its simplicity and speed. Unlike a spreadsheet, which requires that the user create the template and pass the data to another program to format the graphics, the above contains both. Further, many graphics packages would not be able to handle this type of analysis graph at all.

PPBEA provides the user with templates already set up to enter income and expenses for different classes of business. Exhibit 7.14 shows the template for a retail operation with data entry completed and produced as a report for a shoe store operation.

PROFIT PROJECTIONS REPORT

Enterprise Qty
52 weeks

Taylor's Shoe Store
Hometown, America

Income Sources	Rate ... per week	Price per ...	------Income------	
			per week	total
Ladies Shoes	500 shoes	$30.00/shoe	$15,000.00	$780,000
Mens Shoes	350 shoes	50.00/shoe	17,500.00	910,000
		Total Income	$32,500.00	$1,690,000

Variable Expenses	Rate ... per week	Cost per ...	------Expense-----	
			per week	total
Cost of Goods	75 %		$24,375.00	$1,267,500
Dept. salaries	3 clerks	200.00/clerk	600.00	31,200
Commissions	5 %		1,625.00	84,500
Advertising			150.00	7,800
Other expenses			50.00	2,600
		Total Variable Expense	$26,800.00	$1,393,600

Fixed Expenses	------Expense------	
	per week	total
Admin. salaries	$1,500.00	$78,000
Rent	300.00	15,600
Utilities	169.00	8,788
Depreciation	100.00	5,200
Equip. repairs	150.00	7,800
Other expenses	100.00	5,200
Total Fixed Expense	$2,319.00	$120,588

Profit	$3,381.00	$175,812

Exhibit 7.14: Profit projection report for a retail shoe store

Exhibits 7.15 through 7.17 show three break-even analyses generated *immediately* by *PPBEA* from a simple menu.

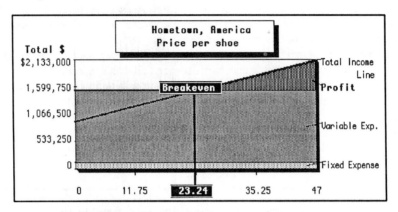

Exhibit 7.15: Break-even graph: price per shoe

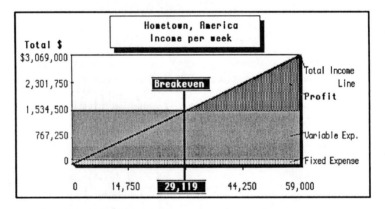

Exhibit 7.16: Break-even graph: income per week

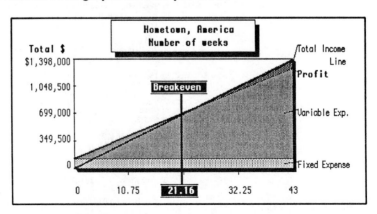

Exhibit 7.17: Break-even graph: number of weeks

PPBEA provides the small business with a method for constant and rapid monitoring of the effects of price, volume of sales, and costs on operation. Further, the business person is liable to perform more careful analyses if the tool is easy to use and provides results rapidly.

The question remains whether the traditional straight line break-even analysis reflects reality. Koff (1984) thinks not and suggests that "It is a neat and elegant graph, but so poor a representation of the real world that it may do more harm, in a strategic sense, than good." Koff suggests that the cost line is curved, intersects the revenue line at a higher unit volume, but produces more profit once the break-even point is passed.

Two blank worksheets taken from *PPBEA* are provided in Appendix A as a part of questions and exercises for this chapter, to allow the reader to explore break-even analysis starting with data collected in paper form.

7.7 VISUAL ACCOUNTING REPORTS

If an accountant presented us with financial statements in a narrative document, we would consider him or her mad. It is simply the wrong metaphor. Similarly, a memorandum presented in tabular form would be equally inappropriate. It could be done, but the metaphor is wrong.

But what if an accountant presented us with financial statements in a *graphic* form? Would we think him or her mad? Today, most likely not. With the analytic, graphic, and interactive capabilities of computers, graphic accounting reports are becoming a valuable complement to the traditional financial statement. *Computer graphics can allow for the study of patterns in a way that is very difficult or impossible with numeric data presented in tabular form.*

Spielman (1983) and Jarett and Johnson (1983) report on a graphics method for performing financial comparisons of international corporations, a difficult task because of differences in currency and rates of inflation. Jarett and Johnson point out, "Financial accounting is no more than a fiscal representation of a physical reality. In accounting, however, we only present the numbers without the translation to a pattern."

When income statements and balance sheets of different international corporations are translated into a graphic format, *where the size of the graphic is held constant and the currency scale is allowed to vary,* fiscal *patterns* can be readily compared. Exhibits 7.18 and 7.19 show two statements of income in a bar graph format of two companies, one in Japan and the other in Holland.

The bars represent either an addition to income or a subtraction from it. The graphs are read from top to bottom. The similarity in operating patterns, in spite of differences in scale, are obvious.

In Exhibits 7.20 and 7.21 the balance sheets are shown in graphic form. The value of the visual accounting statement is the improved ability to communicate. The method was discovered in the search for a solution to a problem: the difficulty comparing the *relative* performance of companies in the same industry located in different countries independently of differences in currency used and inflation rates. The success of the method depends upon agreement on a set of financial graphics standards. In this case, the standard involves keeping the window or graph size standard, allowing the scale to vary, and plotting the data in the manner shown.

The graphic accounting report, however, has other values. It is very easy to understand, communicates immediately and, therefore, might be very valuable to the nonaccounting executive and student.

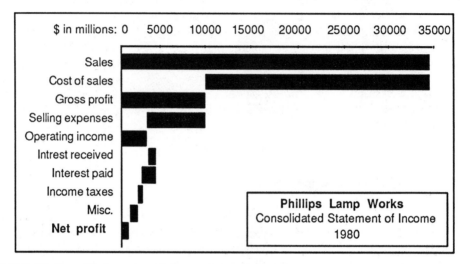

Exhibit 7.18: Graphic income statement (Jarett and Johnson, 1983. Courtesy of
Springer-Verlag, New York.)

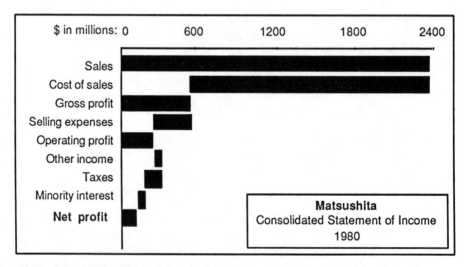

Exhibit 7.19: Graphic income statement (Jarett and Johnson, 1983. Courtesy of
Springer-Verlag, New York.)

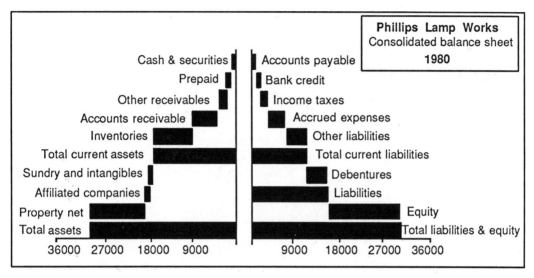

Exhibit 7.20: Graphic balance sheet (Jarett and Johnson, 1983. Courtesy of Springer-Verlag, New York.)

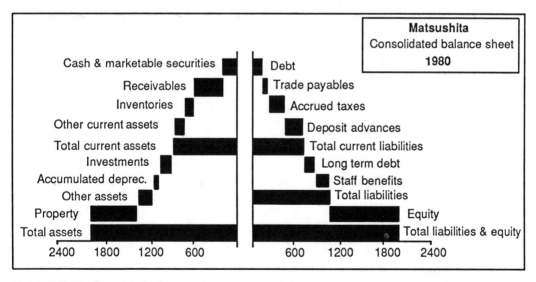

Exhibit 7.21: Graphic balance sheet (Jarett and Johnson, 1983. Courtesy of Springer-Verlag, New York.)

7.8 INTEGRATED SYSTEMS

We will use the *Excel* program from MicroSoft Corp. (Bellevue, WA), and the *Jazz* program from Lotus Development Corp. (Cambridge, MA), both for the Apple Macintosh to demonstrate the capabilities of an integrated systems. There are many integrated programs that could have been selected. A reference list of integrated software systems that include graphics is provided in Appendix C.

Integrated systems are suitable for the user who requires a broad set of capabilities that work together; flexibility versus a lot of computational power. For example, *Jazz* does not contain, as of this date, macro capabilities (the ability to instruct the computer to perform a set of tasks or commands on demand, rather than having to re-enter each command again when some application is required). *Excel* from MicroSoft (Bellevue, WA) for the Apple Macintosh does contain macro capabilities, but does not possess a word processor. *Jazz* has an integrated word processor. The *Excel* spreadsheet is fast and complete; it is considered one of the best spreadsheets available on any computer. What factors are important? User needs are again the key guide.

The first example uses three of the five integrated functions represented by the six icons that first appear when *Jazz* is used as shown in Exhibit 7.22, namely, the worksheet, graphics, and word processing. The other two are communications and database. Form works with the database.

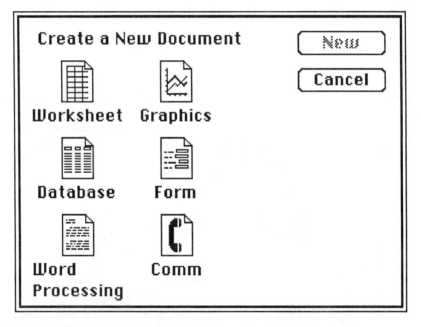

Exhibit 7.22: The first screen when using *Jazz* showing six icons representing different applications

The example is based on a lesson included with *Jazz* that shows the electronic spreadsheet being used to track ticket sales for a series of films at a movie theater. The spreadsheet screen is shown in Exhibit 7.23.

	A	B	C	D	E
1	January, 1987			Goal:	$70,000
2					
3	Title	Ticket Price	No. Sold	Sales	% of Goal
4	Tom Jones	$3.75	3570	$13,387.50	19.12%
5	Diva	$3.50	3776	$13,216.00	18.88%
6	Citizen Kane	$4.00	3154	$12,616.00	18.02%
7	Annie Hall	$3.75	4068	$15,255.00	21.79%
8	Star Wars	$4.50	4572	$20,574.00	29.39%
9					
10	Mean	$3.90	3828	$15,009.70	
11	Total		19140	$75,048.50	107.21%
12					
13					

Exhibit 7.23: Spreadsheet of movie ticket sales

The spreadsheet is easy to use and the data can be immediately translated to a graphics format. We do not have to transfer ESS data to some intermediate work file (the scrapbook on the Apple Macintosh), then close the ESS application, open a graphics application, transfer the data to the graphics application, and then produce a chart. It is the memo in Exhibit 7.24 that reveals one powerful purpose of an integrated application like *Jazz*.

The electronic spreadsheet data and a selected chart have been transferred to a memo, and the word processor used to explain the data. It is possible to do this with some unintegrated applications in some systems environments, but can be clumsy and time consuming. With *Jazz* and other integrated systems, it is very direct and simple.* The integration of graphs, tables, and text in *Jazz* is dynamic; Lotus calls it *Hotview*. Using Hotview we can add graphs, tables, and other data to word processing documents and, when changes occur to data in other functional parts of *Jazz* (ESS, database), the information in word processing documents is immediately updated.

The second example uses three integrated functions in *Excel*: electronic spreadsheet, database, and graphics. Exhibit 7.25 shows a few records of over a thousand from a database in *Excel*, namely records of expenses by date, amount, and vendor.

The top part of the spreadsheet in Exhibit 7.25 is a work area where various calculations, based on the data in the database, can be performed and recorded. For example, in Exhibit 7.25 we show the computation of overhead for a given period of time. Obviously, this requires finding all the overhead expenses for a given period, and summing them. This process is repeated for each of the three categories of expense listed in rows 5, 6, and 7: salary, inventory, and overhead. The calculation procedure in *Excel* is simple and powerful: select a function from a list of available functions, in this case, "DSUM" (see top of Exhibit 7.25) and upon selection the function is

---

* Some operating environments, like *Windows* from MicroSoft for the IBM PC or *Switcher* from Apple Computer for the Macintosh, allow the user to integrate *any* set of programs, up to some limit. This is a viable and attractive alternative to the fully integrated systems described which do *not* allow the user to select a particular word processor, or ESS, and so forth.

MEMO: February 2, 1987

TO: Rick Barker

FROM: Sammy Stone

Sales were superb in January. They exceeded expectations by over 7 percent as you can see by the spreadsheet reproduced here.

Month: January, 1987   **Goal: $70,000**

Title	Ticket Price	No. Sold	Sales	% of Goal
Tom Jones	$3.75	3570	$13,387.50	19.12%
Diva	$3.50	3776	$13,216.00	18.88%
Citizen Kane	$4.00	3154	$12,616.00	18.02%
Annie Hall	$3.75	4068	$15,255.00	21.79%
Star Wars	$4.50	4572	$20,574.00	29.39%
Averages:	$3.90	3828	$15,009.70	
Totals:		**19140**	**$75,048.50**	**107.21%**

Below is a chart of the income generated by each film we showed in January. Star Wars was the big income generator. Let's see if we can't get the Star Wars series again in July. Should help pick things up during the usual summer slump.

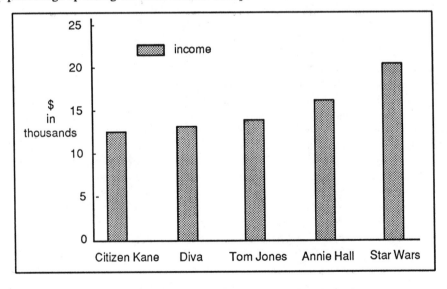

Exhibit 7.24: The final memorandum integrating spreadsheet, graphic, and text

B4		=DSUM(Database,"amount",Criteria)	

Expenses

	A	B	C	D
1	Date	Expense	Amount	Vendor
2		overhead		
3				
4		$91,840		
5	salary	$282,625		
6	inventory	$93,897		
7	overhead	$91,840		
8				
9				
10	Date	Expense	Amount	Vendor
11	1/1/84	overhead	$1,000	A.B. Properties
12	1/5/84	overhead	$566	Ace Power & Light
13	1/5/84	overhead	$600	Wheelin's Gas Co.
14	1/5/84	overhead	$200	Ralph J Cook Garbage

Exhibit 7.25: Database (partial view) and work area

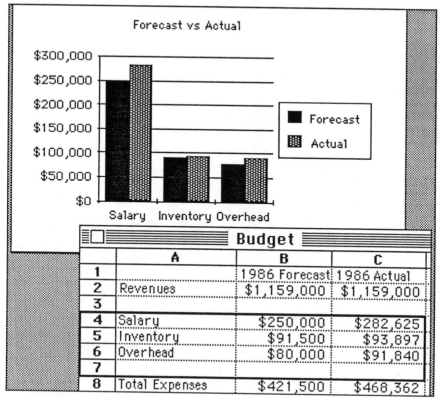

Budget

	A	B	C
1		1986 Forecast	1986 Actual
2	Revenues	$1,159,000	$1,159,000
3			
4	Salary	$250,000	$282,625
5	Inventory	$91,500	$93,897
6	Overhead	$80,000	$91,840
7			
8	Total Expenses	$421,500	$468,362

Exhibit 7.26: Forecast and actual data

pasted automatically into the formula as shown; select the "Database" (this tells *Excel* where to look for the data); inform *Excel* what data to sum, in this case "amount"; and finally what "Criteria" to use (this is specified in another screen for each of the three categories of expense).

Exhibit 7.26 shows the results of actual expenses pasted into another spreadsheet that also lists forecasted expenses. From this data *Excel* will quickly generate the graph shown. Further, if changes are made to any of the data in the spreadsheet, they are immediately reflected in the graph. Only a few of the many capabilities of both integrated systems have been covered here.*

7.9 DYNAMIC ANALYSIS

Approaches to analysis on computers are becoming dynamic. By dynamic we mean animated. A "still-frame" primitive form of animation has already been discussed, namely, the ability of integrated systems to update graphics in documents as the data changes. Another example is *DecisionMap* from SoftStyle, Inc. (Honolulu, HI), one of a burgeoning number of DSS packages on microcomputers for managers. Using a tree structure that contains factors and subfactors, one names criteria and subcriteria for evaluating any set of data. Then the criteria are weighted according to their relative worth or importance by varying the height of a column. One can then change data on the basis of different facts or assumptions, and the graphics change accordingly, a visual "what if" analysis. In this fashion one creates a model, and selected solutions or decisions are compared, shown to others for consensus, used to justify decisions, and used to support group decision making. A screen from DecisionMap is shown in Exhibit 7.27 in which various candidates for promotion to project manager are being assessed according to certain criteria.

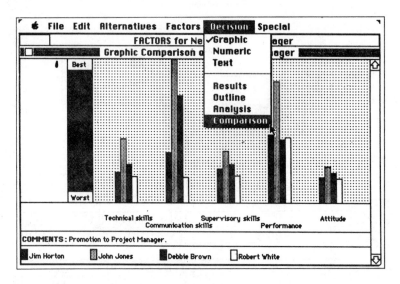

Exhibit 7.27: A dynamic chart from *DecisionMap* (Courtesy of SoftStyle)

---

* *Excel* is a joy to learn and use; it stands as a lesson in computer generated training (CGT) for educators. Its power is smooth; it provides a sense of involvement, a *desire* to learn.

MacSpin from D^2 Software (Austin, TX) is a "unique and powerful graphic analysis program (that) handles multivariate data in an intuitive, highly visual manner." (E. Hiram, *"Look at it this Way,"* *MacUser*, 1, 9, June, 1986, p.153). As Hiram points out in her review of *MacSpin*, for a mere eighty dollars the program provides dynamic data analysis only found previously on half million dollar lab machines! Animation reveals changes graphically across time, or differences between the state of different events at any given time. Hiram uses the example of the horsepower and fuel efficiency of automobiles from 1971 through 1983. *MacSpin* would show plotted points (similar to the plot shown in Exhibit 7.32), with a different plot symbol used for each dependent variable (horsepower and fuel efficiency); the change in horsepower and fuel efficiency across the years is immediately obvious in animation.

7.10 STATISTICAL ANALYSIS

Statistics are summaries of sets of data, and analytic graphics are capsule images. Statistics are traditionally classified into two main groups: *descriptive* and *inferential*. Under descriptive we have two main groupings: measures of *central tendency* (mean, median, mode), and measures of *variability* (range, standard deviation). Under inferential there are a large number of statistical methods (t-test, anova, chi square) related to *making predictions or inferences from samples to the populations to which the samples belong*. Obviously, we cannot measure the heights and weights of all children, now and in the future, but we can take a sample and relate such data to sex, age, nutrition, and so forth and, on the basis of sample statistics, predict for the whole population. There is another group of measures related to prediction, namely, *covariation* (correlation, multiple regression, cross-tabulation), that cut across the two main groups, descriptive and inferential, which, in any case, overlap. Covariation measures how well variables relate or predict. (Do people who do well in math use a computer better, or learn faster? The answer is "no.") The *generation* of statistics is a task for the computer; the *interpretation* of statistics is a task for the human (however, we must know how and why a statistic is generated in a given manner).

Statistical analysis packages have been available for some time on all sizes of systems, from mainframes to microcomputers. More recent offerings add ease of use and superior displays made possible by bit-mapped graphics. We will use *StatView* to demonstrate some analytic graphics capabilities.

In our example we are comparing the effect on sales over a 12-week period of two different marketing approaches: Market Plans 1 and 2. We track sales and the results of our tracking are shown in Exhibit 7.28. A t-test reveals that there is a significant difference between the average sales created across the 12 weeks by the two marketing approaches. *StatView* produced the results shown in Exhibit 7.29. However, it is not the average difference alone in which we are interested. A comparison line plot may reveal information that is not shown in the averages and the t-test, namely, differences in the pattern of sales across time. We instruct *StatView* to produce a line chart from the two distributions. They are both diagrammed in Exhibit 7.30.

It seems that with Market Plan 1, sales take off faster but drop off quickly after about seven weeks. Plan 2 functions in an opposite manner; early sales are slow, build steadily to a peak, and then drop sharply. We would want to analyze these results carefully and search for causes. If we had compared plans 1 and 2 after only 5 weeks, a far different picture would have emerged.; after 5 weeks only the means for plans 1 and 2 are 19.22 and 12.54, respectively. But now we know more. Even though plan 2 leads to higher average sales over a 12-week period, plan 1 might still

Market Plan 1	Market Plan 2
25.7	17.8
24.6	23.6
23.7	29.8
12.8	35.6
6.7	47.8
5.0	45.6
3.4	34.6

Exhibit 7.28: Average sales across 12 weeks for two marketing plans

Unpaired t-Test	**X: Market Plan 1**		**Y: Market Plan 2**		
DF:	X Count:	Y Count:	Mean X:	Mean Y:	Unpaired t Value:
22	12	12	12.62	25.43	-2.65 (.005 <p< .01)

Exhibit 7.29: T-test results produced by StatView

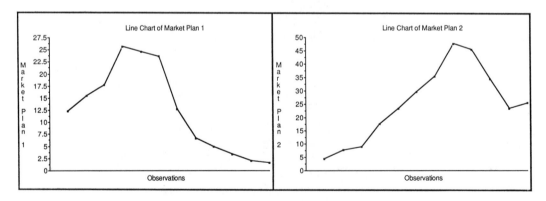

Exhibit 7.30: Sales by week for market plans 1 and 2

be our choice. Maybe there is something we can do to reinitiate plan 1 every five or six weeks. Maybe it should be rotated geographically, and so forth.

Another demonstration of statistical graphics analysis is shown in Exhibits 7.31, 7.32, and 7.33. Exhibit 7.31 shows some national data including GNP, unemployment, number of personnel in the armed forces, population levels, and employment for a number of years starting in 1947.

GNP Deflator	GNP	Unem-ployed	Armed Forces	Popu-lation	Year	Employed
83.0	230.000	235.6	159.0	107.608	1947	60.323
88.5	259.426	232.5	145.6	108.632	1948	61.122
88.2	258.054	368.2	161.6	109.773	1949	60.171
89.5	284.599	335.1	165.0	110.929	1950	61.187
96.2	328.975	209.9	309.9	112.075	1951	63.221
98.1	346.999	193.2	359.4	113.270	1952	63.639
99.0	365.385	187.0	354.7	115.094	1953	64.989
100.0	363.112	357.8	335.0	116.219	1954	63.761
101.2	397.469	290.4	304.8	117.388	1955	66.019
104.6	419.180	282.2	285.7	118.734	1956	67.857
108.4	442.769	293.6	279.8	120.445	1957	68.169
110.8	444.546	468.1	263.7	121.950	1958	66.513
112.6	482.704	381.3	255.2	123.366	1959	68.655
114.2	502.601	393.1	251.4	125.368	1960	69.564
115.7	518.173	480.6	257.2	127.852	1961	69.331
116.9	554.894	400.7	282.7	130.081	1962	70.551

Exhibit 7.31: Some national data: 1947 through 1960

Exhibit 7.32 shows the correlation between population levels and GNP, and population levels and unemployment. There is an obvious stronger relationship between population growth and GNP.

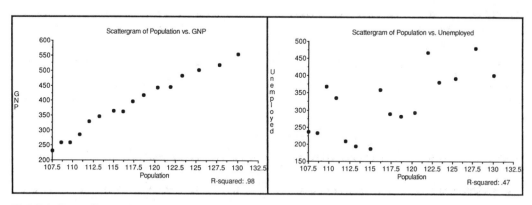

Exhibit 7.32: Scatter diagrams

StatView takes full advantage of the Apple Macintosh environment to create an easy-to-use system. Further, it is quite complete. It is capable of accepting downloaded text and data files from other systems, or from other applications on the Apple Macintosh (e.g., database and spreadsheet programs). It is capable of having four documents open at any one time. The amount of data that can be handled at any one time is basically limited only by the memory of the system. Readers interested in this area may wish to consult one of a large number of introductory texts on statistics. Using a program like StatView would certainly add learning.

Some statistical packages can create complex graphics not possible with other statistical systems, or with an ESS. For example, *EXEC*U*STAT* from Statistical Graphics Corp. (Princeton, NJ), was used to create the graphic shown in Exhibit 7.33.

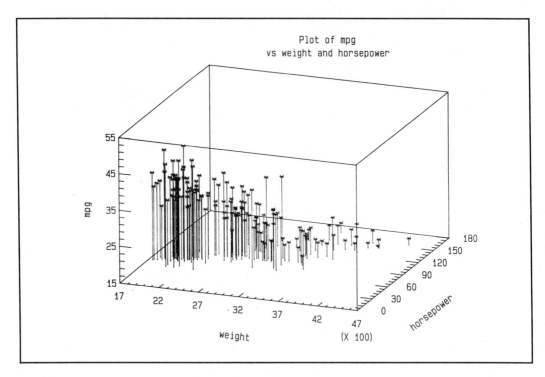

Exhibit 7.33: Miles per gallon (MPG) as a function of car weight and engine horsepower

The graph shows the effect of weight and horsepower on miles per gallon, a graphic portrayal of multiple regression with two independent variables. *EXEC*U*STAT* is menu driven, supports color, functions with a number of graphics boards on a variety of systems (IBM PC, ATT 6300), and provides a broad range of statistical, financial, and graphics analysis. Exhibit 7.34 shows a set of column data fitted with a normal curve distribution. (However, the normal curve does not fit very well, and we might have a bimodal distribution as indicated by the two columns that peak to a frequency of over 13; also the "Y" scale is not identified; it contains no labels.)

In similar fashion to presentation graphics, we might have to use a number of analytic systems to meet our needs. For example, *StatView* does not contain a number of functions we might require, including curve fitting (the drawing of a line that best fits a set of plotted points), and multiple regression, such as predicting the values of some variable (the *dependent* variable) from a number of other variables (the *independent* variables). However, the Engineering Tool Kit (ETK) from *Soft-Ware Tools* (Boise, ID), performs these and other functions.

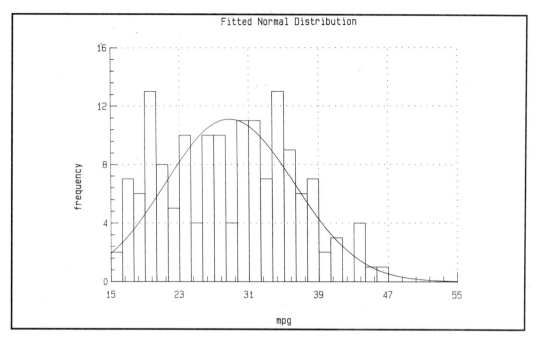

Exhibit 7.34: Normal curve fit of column data

7.11 CONCLUSION

In conclusion, we have touched upon some traditional and new methods for analyzing data using graphics. However, there are important areas *not* covered here, including access to databanks to obtain statistical, economic, and fiscal information available through common carriers such as Dialog, Dow Jones, Compuserv, The Source, Telenet, and others; and investment analysis. Analytic graphics is a large subject and we have covered a small sample of its many applications.

8

Models and Simulations

8.1 INTRODUCTION

We are familiar with models and simulations. As children, most of us possessed a model aeroplane, a car, or a model baby that even "wet" itself. We knew intuitively that the model was a representation of the real thing. We constructed towns out of building blocks, ran our model train or
racing car track though the town, and staged various disastrous crashes. Thus, we became simulators and play with models became simulations of real situations.

All our further discussions of models and simulations are grown-up versions of these child-
hood events. Users have matured, the toys have become tools, the tools are more sophisticated, and
the objects studied are sometimes more abstract. Nonetheless, the basic relationship that exists
between toy trains and crashes remains.

In this chapter we define simulation and modeling, the different types, their functions, and
how computers and computer graphics are used. As we shall see, some simulations using graphics
allow us to *make the abstract more concrete* and act as visual aids to the understanding, analysis,
and prediction of some process in real life (weather). In other simulations and models, the object
is to *generate a realistic graphic image of an object or scene* (appearance of the sky, the landing
field, and other aircraft during flight simulation in pilot training). Exhibit 8.2 diagrams a variety of
applications for models and simulations.

8.2 DEFINING SIMULATION AND MODELING

We design and implement models which reflect properties of real entities. The design is a boot-
strap operation, a constant iterative process of going back and forth between reality and model as
diagrammed in Exhibit 8.1.

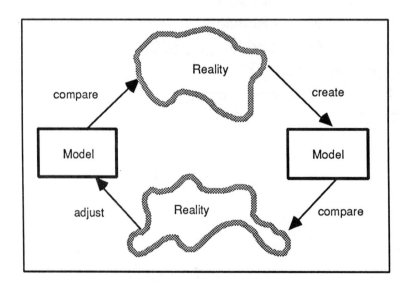

Exhibit 8.1: Model creation: a boot-strap operation

	Simulation/Model		
Who	**Data or Conditions**	**Model of System**	**Model's Response**
Weather Bureau	Weather measurements	**Local weather**	Weather?
Universities	Tuition	**Financial model**	Financial aid?
International Studies	Exports and imports	**Macro-economic**	Increased capital flow?
Sports and Dance	Digitized actions	**Body movement**	Correct?
Multi-discipline	Policies; decisions	**Urban development**	What happens?
Nuclear Engineering	Plant malfunction	**Nuclear plant**	What happens?
Auto Industry	Model of passenger	**Model of car**	Effects of crash?
Aviation	Pilot	**Flight simulator**	Reaction? Learning?
Space Program	Astronaut	**Space simulation**	Reaction? Learning?

Exhibit 8.2: Some example models, simulations, and users

Simulation is the process of designing a model of a real system, and experimenting with the model to understand and influence the real system. Computer-based simulation is the process of representing or modeling the behavior of a system on a computer. The software model mimics the original as nearly as possible. Then conditions represented in terms of data are fed into the model and the system's responses are recorded and analyzed.

Simulations contain models, and models, based on the information obtained from a simulation and its interpretation, are changed in the light of the information which is, hopefully, accurate and leads to a closer model of reality.

A model is a mathematical/quantitative, conceptual/verbal, diagramatic/organizational, geometric/design, or physical representation of an entity, a process, a system, or a subsystem. Descriptions and example applications of the different types of models are presented in this chapter.

8.3 TYPES OF MODELS

In relation to time and space, models fall into different classes as follows:

• Continuous time
The model represents the changes which occur to the model with relation to changes across time. For example, the trajectory of a rocket changes its position every second along with other variables (velocity, elevation).

• Continuous space
This refers to the model's ability to reflect continuous changes in location, usually expressed in some mathematical form. For example, a space rocket functions in continuous space.

• Discrete time
The model represents the occurrence of events at some discrete point in time. For example, the population growth of a country might be assumed to follow a queuing model with births representing arrivals and deaths departures occurring continuously over time. Since births and deaths occur every second, we would need to update our files every second: an awesome task. It might be better to consider a more discrete time period, maybe a year, and look at population growth as a function of other variables (land erosion, reclamation, and crop yield).

• Discrete space
Here it is assumed that whatever is being modeled is residing in some discrete fixed location. Models of mechanical, economic, or social systems, for example, are considered to be of this type.

Models may also be categorized as follows:

• Icon
The model looks like but does not act like the object being modeled; for example, a model of a car for 1990 made of plastic, or modeled on the computer using computer-generated imagery, discussed later in this chapter.

• Analog
The model acts like but need not look like the object being modeled; for example, the simulation of fuel flow through a pipeline in a process control system.

• Abstract
The model neither looks like nor acts like the object being modeled; for example, a mathematical model where the model consists of manipulated numeric parameters, coefficients, and exponents.

8.3-1 Mathematical models

Math is a formalization of the decision-making process. The movement is towards the application of mathematics to create a wide range of models, and simulations using the computer to do the computational work, thus improving accuracy and utility. Before computers, calculations were manual and tedious and thus often not performed. Karplus (1983) provides an overall taxonomy of models, diagrammed in Exhibit 8.3.

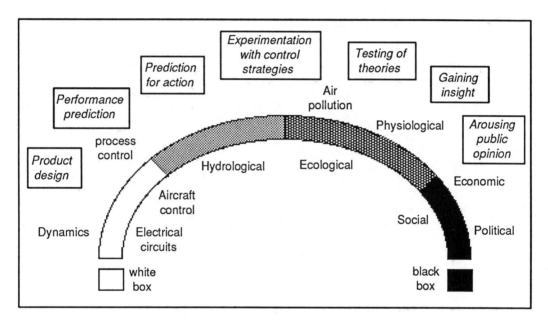

Exhibit 8.3: The motivations for modeling and shift from quantitative (white box) to qualitative (black box) models (From Karplus, 1983; copyright IBM, 1983)

Karplus is concerned with illustrating the use of mathematics in modeling. Therefore, the illustration does not include computer-generated imagery, which is related to generating realistic images, and is, therefore, a modeling of a different kind. The reader may wish to refer to the diagram in Exhibit 8.3 as we discuss the various types of models.

Disagreements exist as to the validity of applying math to the soft areas diagrammed towards the black end of the chart in Exhibit 8.3. The black represents the "black box" nature of a system being modeled; that is, there is little or no actual information on how the system functions. However, we may know how the system responds when a given input is made to it. By comparison, we know something about the internal functioning of electrical circuits located at the white end, and we can describe the functioning accurately through mathematical formulae.

There are two types of information: experimental data, and knowledge and insight about a system being modeled. The more *deductive* the modeling process, the more valid the mathematical model approach; the more *inductive*, the less valid the mathematical model approach. Further, the more accurate the observations or measurement of input and output, the more valid the mathematical approach. A classification of mathematical models is provided in Exhibit 8.4.

Model parameters	Abstractions		
	Continuous-space continuous-time (CSCT)	Discrete-space-continuous-time (DSCT)	Discrete-space-discrete-time (DSDT)
Typical applications	Heat transfer Air pollution Meteorology Hydrology	Electric circuits Mechanical systems Control systems	Traffic flow systems Management systems Economic systems Social systems
Pictorial	Drawing of field boundaries	Circuit diagram	Block diagram Flowchart
Model type	Partial differential equations	Ordinary differential equations	Algebraic equations Heuristic descriptions
Languages[a]	PDEL LEANS	CSMP CSSL MIMIC	GPSS SIMSCRIPT

Exhibit 8.4: Mathematical models classified according to three types of abstraction (From Karplus, 1983; copyright IBM, 1983)[b]

[a] It goes beyond the limits of this text to discuss the various simulation languages.
[b] A selection from a more extensive table by W. L. Karplus, "The Spectrum of Mathematical Models,"*Perspectives in Computing*, 3, 2, May, 1983. The reader will note that a fourth possible category is missing, namely, continuous space/discrete time. An example might be the study of the heavenly bodies (continuous space), at discrete points in time, noting whether expected location and appearance of stars meet with the actual. No other example comes to mind.

8.3-2 Conceptual/diagrammatic model

These models are represented by organization charts and flow diagrams of great variety. An example is provided in Exhibit 8.5 of a simple process known to all of us.

Model types may overlap. Exhibit 8.5, based on a drawing in Kantowitz and Sorkin (1983), is a conceptual model that is also diagrammatic. We may use such models to show the information paths in an organization, the logical flow of data through a computer system, the structure of a computer program, the sequence of instructional steps to operate a piece of machinery, and so forth.

8.3-3 Mathematical/design model

Here is an example of another mixed model combining mathematics and graphics design. The simple sine wave, a mathematical function that describes a number of natural phenomena including

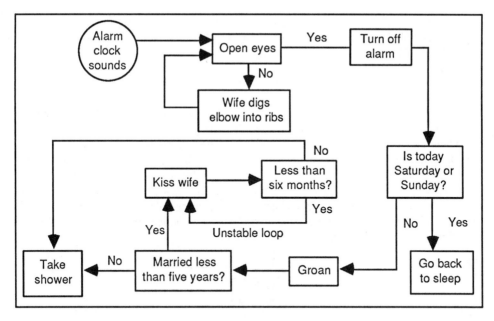

Exhibit 8.5: A conceptual diagram modeling a familiar process (From B. H. Kantowitz and R. D. Sorkin, *Human Factors*, John Wiley & Sons, New York, NY, 1983)

the behavior of light and sound, has been chosen by Cooper (1984) as the basis for designs in serigraphy, the fine art of silkscreen printing. As Cooper points out, we can use a paint program, or a digital camera, or a program to create images; each has its own particular qualities. Cooper chooses to program because "...(it lets) me use mathematics to create images in unexpected ways, bringing together the hard logic of math and the mysterious intuition of art." Using a personal computer and the program listing reproduced in Chapter 14, Cooper generated images similar to the one shown in Exhibit 8.6 to end up with designs for silkscreens.

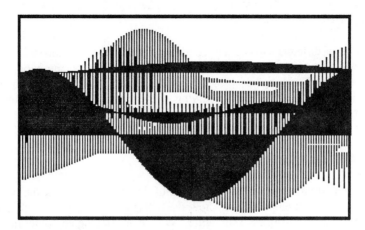

Exhibit 8.6: A design based on the mathematics of the sine curve

Cooper wrote the program so that the computer generates random numbers for entry into the sine equation and thus creates, as he says "happy accidents . . not chosen because of habits in our usual ideas of balance and texture."

8.3-4 Geometric model

Entities are composite, not monolithic; that is, they are made of parts (Foley and Van Dam, 1982). In engineering design using manual drafting systems, it is customary to use plastic templates with cut-outs of standard images of components to help create larger images.

In a computerized system, the standard shapes or symbols representing the given building blocks are stored in a database. The graphics program specifies relations between building blocks where the building blocks are organized hierarchically. This is a widely used model with many applications which include creating flow charts, logic diagrams, electrical circuits, buildings, interiors, faces, and designs. An example using an office layout application is diagrammed in Exhibit 8.7 with a floorplan and icon menu shown in Exhibit 8.8.

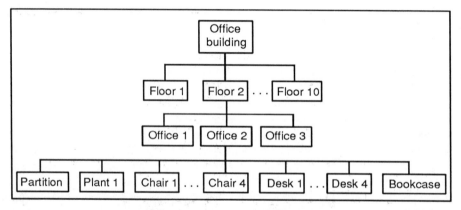

Exhibit 8.7: An application model (Foley and Van Dam, *Fundamentals of Interactive Computer Graphics*, © 1982, Addison-Wesley Publishing Co., Inc., Reading, MA. Fig. 1.13, p. 24 and other excerpts. Reprinted with permission.)

Offices can be of different layouts and contain different basic components or objects (chairs, tables, bookcases). The application model contains descriptions of these objects along with placement information. The graphics program uses the data to serve a number of functions, including the building, monitoring, and modifying of the model; traversing the model to analyze and display information; and providing for display and dialogue, that is, the user interface (Foley and Van Dam, 1982).

8.3-5 Models of natural phenomena

Fastook and Hughes (1982) report on the modeling of the disintegration of the present-day West Antarctic Ice Sheet in an attempt to study how the collapse of the polar ice sheets might affect worldwide sea levels and coast lines. They write, "We are developing computer models that allow us to conduct, in simulation, the experiments that Nature may ultimately perform in actuality."

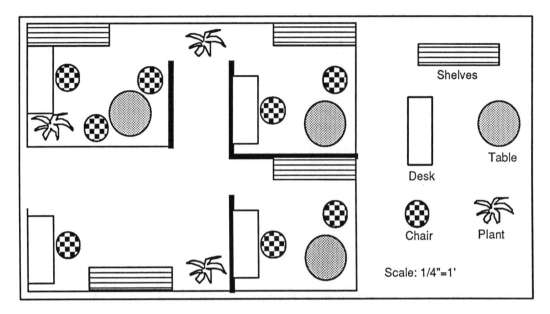

Exhibit 8.8: Floor plan and icon menu

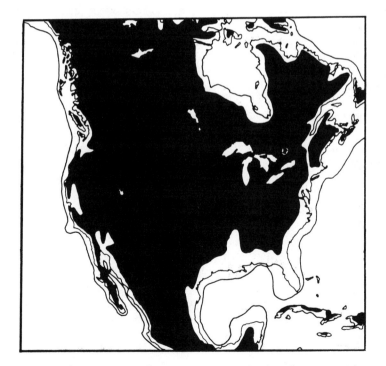

Exhibit 8.9: North American coast line: past, present, and future (From Fastook and Hughes, 1982; copyright IBM, 1982)

Formulae representing ice velocity, ice thickness, the slope of an iceberg, the rate of sea level rise, and a myriad of other factors constitute the model and are represented in the computer. Various data are fed through the model, reconstructing events as they existed 20 centuries ago when glaciation was at its maximum, and looking at events as they might be in the future.

Their model predicts that we are at present midway in time between the position of shorelines during maximum glaciation 18,000 years ago and the assumed shoreline for complete deglaciation some time hence. An image of the simulated coastline of North America, if the present ice sheets in Greenland and Antartica (not shown) melt, is illustrated in Exhibit 8.9. It appears that 20,000 years from now, the residents of Florida will have to relocate or be washed out to sea, and an island much larger than Manhattan appears where New York City used to be.

8.3-6 Network models

There are *operations research* methods which help us solve and understand certain problems, including the movement of people, goods, or resources (*transportation or transmission*), the flow of information (*communication*), the coordination of enterprises (*organization*), and the impact of these through time (*timetables*).

All these situations can be represented or modeled, and conditions simulated, using a basic tool: a *network*. The network may exist on computer along with related numeric and descriptive data. Various models of a system, simulation of conditions, evaluation of changes, and the playing of "what if" games can take place.

In the past such systems were batch-oriented and functioned on large mainframes. But now it is possible to do such work in interactive mode on small but powerful desktop graphics computers. We discuss one such system created by Dr. Richard Giles* called *Path* and which functions on the Macintosh.

8.3-7 Network design

Giles used the language C on the Macintosh to develop methods for analyzing networks. His aim was to identify methods for optimal network design, for example, the shortest path method. He used graphics to show the effects of the mathematics in his algorithms, because it is easier to see effects and patterns in pictures than in lists of numbers. He also chose to prototype in MBASIC rather than in C because it is easier to use; we can obtain a result and see an effect more readily. After identifying what appeared to be a good program development approach, he developed the program in C for purposes of speed and efficiency. As an interpreted rather than a compiled language, MBASIC is slow in comparison to C. But MBASIC is useful for prototyping and language learning.

Further, MBASIC on the Macintosh possesses built-in capabilities for creating pull-down menus. (This is a menu of choices in an application contained in a window on the screen that, under normal use, remains closed. However, by pointing the cursor at the heading or name of the pull-down menu, and by pressing the button on the mouse following pointing, the pull-down menu appears.) Thus the user interface can be modeled or created quickly. Creating pull-down menus in C or in MacPascal, for example, takes more effort because simple means for doing so are not provided. Pull-down menus are a powerful feature for developing applications.

---

* Jodrey School of Computer Science, Acadia University, Wolfville, Nova Scotia B0P 1X0

8.3-8 Some methods used in operations research

Operations research includes methods to determine or take into consideration:

- **Shortest Path**
- **Minimum Spanning Tree**
- **Maximum Flow**
- **Matching**

In a network a beginning or ending point of a path is called a *vertex*. The paths or lines are called *edges*. An edge may represent either distance or time. *Shortest Path* is the sequence of network edges from some defined start to a finish that is the shortest in comparison to any other route chosen. *Minimum Spanning Tree* is a minimal length subnetwork connecting all the vertices in the network. *Maximum Flow* is the largest amount of units of whatever is being studied, that can flow through the network, where each edge has a given flow capacity. *Matching* is the establishment of a pairing of vertices where each vertex may only be matched with one other vertex. For example, the vertices could represent sales territories of varying size, and salesmen of varying abilities, and the two need to be matched by size and ability.

Following various algorithms, that is, steps to the solution of a problem, a network analysis program will resolve various problems, such as shortest path, minimum spanning tree, the limits of flow, and so forth, and provide answers in both a graphic and a numeric form.

8.3-9 A network problem

We will use a simple example to demonstrate a network analysis. Let us assume we need to determine alternate routes through a communications network provided by two different common carriers with different trunkline rates between Los Angeles and New York. Obviously, we would want to use the lowest cost route. We can use *shortest path* to determine *lowest cost*. Exhibit 8.10 shows the two routes under consideration.

The network shows the shortest path in a heavier line, from designated start to finish. The drawing of this network is performed on the screen, with or without a grid, by the use of the mouse, the selection of "insert" from one of the drop menus, and a process of clicking and dragging. Maps, like the map of the United States shown, may be inserted from MacPaint documents. The text and numbers are typed in by the user into boxes provided next to the edges. In this case the text names the two carriers, and the numbers indicate the trunkline rates. The "S" in the Los Angeles vertex indicates "start," and the "F" next to the New York vertex indicates "finish." The numbers next to the vertices *not* in boxes are computed by the program and indicate, in this case, the lowest trunkline rate between any two cities (319 between Los Angeles and Dallas via St. Paul).

The user can scale the network to the window size, or scale up by a variety of factors using a zoom feature provided. In Exhibit 8.11, the original network in Exhibit 8.10 has been scaled up by a factor of two. *Path* files may be saved in various forms for interfacing to programming languages and to spreadsheet programs. This allows for further manipulation of the data. *Path* also allows for large networks to be printed, as shown in Exhibit 8.12.

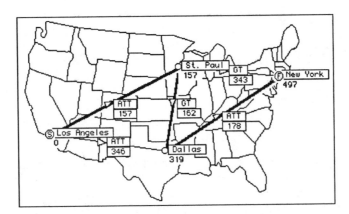

Exhibit 8.10: Network 1 (Courtesy of Dr. R. Giles, Acadia University, Wolfville, NS)

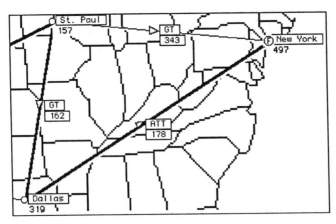

Exhibit 8.11: Network 2 (Courtesy of Dr. R. Giles, Acadia University, Wolfville, NS)

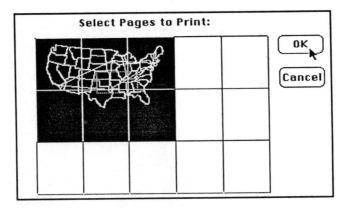

Exhibit 8.12: Networks covering 15 letter-size pages are possible
(Courtesy of Dr. R. Giles, Acadia University, Wolfville, NS)

8.3-10 A conceptual model

The purpose of the conceptual model is to provide a framework for dialogue and thought. Large problems often cannot be neatly measured. We cannot avoid studying major issues because we have not as yet designed an acceptable ruler. The example presented briefly here is a model suggested by Gardiner (1985) and used to guide exploration by 25 international institutions developing an integrated approach to human and social development. The model is whimsically entitled "The Three Interfaces of Adam." A quote from Gardiner will clarify why.

> Imagine Adam all alone on our planet before it became so complicated. He had to deal only with his natural environment. Let us call it the *ecosphere*. When Eve arrived and they prospered and multiplied, a second major system was introduced into Adam's environment—consisting of other people. Let us call it the *sociosphere*. As Adam and Eve and their progeny made discoveries about and inventions from their environment, they built up a third major system in Adam's environment—consisting of person-made things and ways of doing things. Let us call it the *technosphere*.

A diagram of the model is shown in Exhibit 8.13.

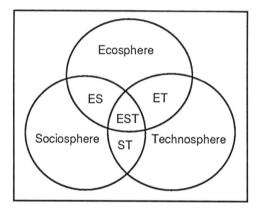

Exhibit 8.13: The three interfaces of Adam (from W. L. Gardiner, "On the need for planners to see things whole," *Canadian Associations*, November, 1985)

    Adam representing Everyman exists at the center of the model (the initials of the three spheres by some coincidence spell EST, meaning, "he is" in Latin). The purpose of the model is to provide a framework for studying the impact of all three spheres on all three spheres. There are, if one considers all the possible overlaps and combinations, a total of "49 possible patterns of impact studies."

    Gardiner then goes on to reference and classify according to the model described, studies, reports, and major texts relevant to the problem including such works as Toffler's *The Third Wave*, Jenkins and Sherman's *The Collapse of Work*, Russel's *The Electronic Briefcase*, Ellul's *The Technological Society*, and many other references. For example, as Gardiner points out, Ellul "presents the most articulate exposition of technological pessimism. . . . He presents the tragedy of a society dominated by technicians whose influence spreads beyond the technosphere into the socio-sphere and the ecosphere. . . . *Know-how* rather than *know-why* is the ultimate value."

A criticism of Gardiner's model, pointed out by Gardiner himself, is that it is so broad as to include everything and, therefore, says nothing. What does it simulate; what can it predict? Not very much; but then, these are not its functions. Its functions are to organize large masses of infor-mation into knowledge and understanding—to provoke dialogue.

8.4 FUNCTIONS OF MODELS

Models serve important functions which include:

• Making predictions
The model predicts in situations where relevant data are not available. For example, it is difficult to jump 18,000 years back or forward in time, to obtain data on coastline erosion and measure the effects of melting ice caps on sea levels and coast lines.

• Guiding research
The model suggests pertinent experiments or data collection. For example, what modifications to a building will incorporate solar energy but allow for the retention of desired aesthetics?

• Providing a framework
The model provides a framework to manage complexity and to help organize data into information and knowledge. Gardiner's model described above is of this nature.

• Modeling reality
Through the use of computer-generated imagery (CGI) and animation, the computer imitates reality. Several examples are offered later in this chapter.

8.5 PROBLEMS AND APPROACHES

Different problems call for different approaches. The approaches fall into three major categories which can be described as follows (Karplus, 1982):

- Given the input and system, what is the obtained output? This is a model of *analysis.*
- Given the input and output, what is the required system? This is a model of *synthesis or design.*
- Given the system and output, what is the required input? This is a model of *control or instrumentation.*

Different approaches, therefore, serve different functions: to study a systems response, to de-sign a system, and to control it. Exhibit 8.3 shows that the models at the black end of the scale, in the "softer" areas, are used to provide general insights that are often counter-intuitive; that is, they go against so called common-sense. This does not make them right; simply different and, there-fore, provocative and providing us with reason to pause and reflect. In fact, simulations in the black end are used in place of mathematical modeling because so little is known about the system that it defies being modeled mathematically. Models that do not use mathematics are often called *heuristic models*, meaning they have an intuitive construction. This is different from having a formula available that you know for certain accurately describes the functioning of a system.

8.6 COMPUTER VERSUS HUMAN

We are always using models, creating simulations, and making inferences in our mind; from how our girl- or boyfriend might react to a forgotten birthday and how we might handle the situation to pacify it, to drawing our dream house, car, or yacht. Our implicit and intuitive models, simulations, and projections can be wrong, due often to the hardening of the categories—a kind of mental arteriosclerosis; we simply do not take enough into consideration.

But this does not mean the computer is invariably superior, as some observers appear to conclude, because of the inadequacy of human intuition or mental modeling and simulation. After all, the computer model is derived from human thought. The superiority of computer-based models and simulations may reside in their ability to reflect data and information entered by a broad base of users, and this *may* improve the knowledge base. But a hundred Frenchman *can* be wrong; whole governments and nations have been wrong. Psychological studies show that it is possible for large groups to hold to a collective deception (the world will end in thirty years), in spite of incontestable evidence to the contrary. Accurate information in the computer depends upon the accurate perception of the *individual* who enters the data; no amount of collective knowledge refutes this basic fact. For example, if I am the only one who has been married to my wife for the past thirty years, I may be the *only* expert on reducing bruised feelings, and all the computer modeling and simulation, and shared knowledge of a thousand psychiatrists will predict no better.

8.7 COMPUTER-GENERATED IMAGERY (CGI)

By the 1990s it will be possible to conjure up almost any kind of scene from a digital description (Sørenson, 1984). It is difficult to execute flawless perspective with shadows and highlights by hand, but this can be efficiently accomplished using a computer. The computer requires information to generate a 3-D picture: the measurements, colors, and reflective properties of objects, the point of view of the *imaginary camera* (called by Foley and Van Dam the *synthetic camera*), the imaginary lens (closeup, wide angle), and the location of light sources. Locations are given in terms of X, Y, Z coordinates. The 3-D computer-generated image is portrayed in 2-D space like a photograph.

Why not take a picture? Sometimes it is not possible; a shot of the moon's surface with a lion on it, or a refrigerator spinning through space. With the computer there are no limits. The images in Exhibit 8.14 are not photographs; they are completely computer generated and exist only as mathematical formulae.

Sometimes surface textures are added to the mathematically generated images using digitized mapping techniques. In digitized mapping a video camera is used to capture different surface textures (metal, glass, wood), digitize, store, and then map them onto the CGI. Although expensive, CGI is often less expensive than conventional film or animation techniques.

Exhibit 8.14: Computer-generated images (Courtesy of WACS Productions,
Toronto, Ontario)

With CGI it is possible to simulate glass, plastic, metal, trees, plants, clouds, mountains,
and coastlines sometimes so realistically that the viewer cannot tell the difference from photographs taken of the real objects. The image in Exhibit 8.15 looks real, but exists only in the
computer's memory.

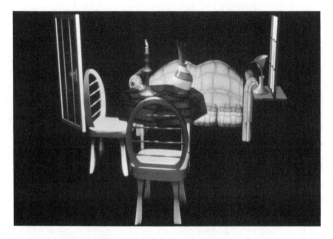

Exhibit 8.15: An image that exists only in the computer's memory (Courtesy
of WACS Productions, Toronto, Ontario)

8.7-1 Applications of CGI

The applications for CGI are enormous. Here we will mention only a few by way of example, and
then discuss further applications in Chapter 9 when we discuss computer aided design (CAD).

Design and test products in production

With CGI we can view, test, change, and approve a product without incurring the cost of
prototypes (MacLeod, 1985). The same database used to graphically construct products can be used

as data to numerically control the machines to produce products. This process is also the basis of CAD/CAM. Professor Kunii of the University of Tokyo has used CGI to define and make visible the entire manufacturing process with simulation and animation. It is then possible to assess the efficiency of the production process, the ease of use of tools, and the fit of components produced (MacLeod, 1985).

Show architecture and interiors

Architects can walk clients through and around buildings, look inside and out, overview to detail, simulate different weather conditions, display different surface textures, color schemes, interiors, decorations, and styles, all without the benefit of physically building a model. Most important is that the system is interactive and can be changed upon demand, unlike going to the movies, viewing a set of slides, or working with physical models. Negroponte's Spatial Data Management System at MIT (Foley and Van Dam, 1982) and Backer and Lippan's work at the same institution are total environments responsive to the viewer's tactile, gesture, and vocal input, providing, under user control, dynamic, photorealistic, animated, sound output, that is a "dialogue personal computer movie house with a databank" (MacLeod, 1985). Systems can contain a combination of many technologies, referred to by some researchers and developers as *hypermedia*.

Art and design

Artists create images of awesome simplicity or mind-boggling complexity using CGI. CGI is computed art, different from using the computer as a "paint brush" in a paint program, and different from inputting an image by digitizing it in some manner. However, all three methods may be used individually or in combination. Some examples of computer-generated art are shown in Chapter 9. Related CGI applications include applications of animation in film and television, represented, for example, by the work of George Lucas and the *Star Wars* film series, and by many television advertisements.

8.7-2 Tools and techniques of CGI

Realistic looking images—nature scenes to fantasy spaceships—can be generated through a computer using mathematical models, the laws of optics and physics, and a knowledge of the laws of human perception; not painted or sketched, but *generated*. Here we discuss some of the major tools and techniques.

Polygons

A surface, flat or curved, can be represented or approximated by a number of polygon surfaces. If the polygons get small enough we will not be able to tell the difference between a sphere, for example, and the model of the sphere represented by all of the tiny flat polygon surfaces. Of course, as we increase the number of polygon surfaces, we increase storage, computation, and the load on the system. But from a geometric database we can build all the surfaces—many thousands of them—to create a realistic image of an object. We then need control over texture, including shading, transluscence, blurring, fuzzy shadows, and dual reflections, to add further realism.

Further, we need control in relation to other objects in the scene—a man in front of the tree, and a house behind. A computer's vision is like x-ray vision; it sees through things. But images in front normally block images behind; therefore, we need to eliminate hidden lines and surfaces, and add texture to the surfaces in the line of vision. Exhibit 8.16 demonstrates this process. The difference in quality is obvious, and the algorithms and programming in the more realistic images in Exhibit 8.16 are correspondingly more complex. These two aspects of CGI, hidden line removal and the texturing of visible surfaces, are critical.

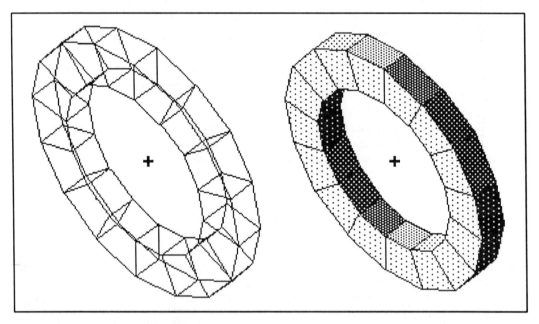

Exhibit 8.16: Hidden line removal and texturing of surfaces are critical in generating realistic images (Produced using *Minicad 3D-Designer* from Diehl Graphsoft Inc. on the Apple Macintosh)

Ray tracing

Ray tracing is based on the simple fact that light travels in straight lines which reach our eyes by reflection from objects in our view. Ray tracing programs determine the dots of color and shade required to display a certain image by working backwards from the eye to the object on the screen represented by thousands of small dots, or pixels. What must each dot's value have to be to arrive at the scene perceived? Ray tracing is like a pointilist painter's view of reality.

Mirrored spheres and highly realistic computer graphics of objects are the result of ray tracing. Ray tracing takes time, as we might imagine, since each dot must be specified and computed. We cannot simply texture a whole surface by filling it in, as we can in the above described polygon approach. But, in ray tracing, we do not have to be concerned with hidden line or surface removal, or one object blocking another. As the image in Exhibit 8.17 shows, ray tracing can lead to some impressive CGIs. The orginal was in color and much of the impact is lost presenting the image in black and white only.

Exhibit 8.17: Ray tracing (Courtesy of Numerical Design Ltd., Chapel Hill, NC)

Fractals

Fractal stands for *fractional dimension*. A snowflake is a simple fractal shape that can be modeled by taking an equilateral triangle and continually modifying its outer perimeter by adding further triangles. Its perimeter following this process approaches infinity. But, interestingly enough, *its surface area remains roughly constant*. This mathematical conundrum leads to the notion of not a single, or a two-dimensional shape, but something between; that is, a fractional dimension, abbreviated to fractal. Consider the illustration in Exhibit 8.18.

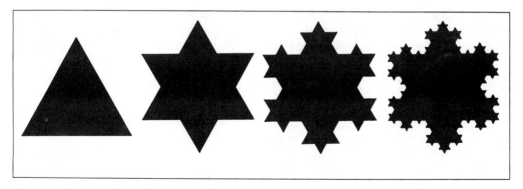

Exhibit 8.18: Creating a snowflake; the length of the sides approaches infinity; the area stays roughly constant (From Jankel and Morton, © 1984. Reprinted with permission of Cambridge University Press.)

Consider another example; if we were asked whether the illustration in Exhibit 8.19 was two- or three-dimensional, what would we say?

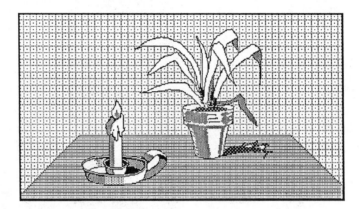

Exhibit 8.19: A three-dimensional image

We would say three-dimensional. But what about the illustration rendered in Exhibit 8.20?

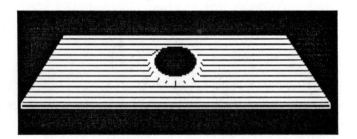

Exhibit 8.20: Two- or three-dimensional?

Here the decision is not so easy. In fractal terms, it might possess a dimension of 2.078, something between two and three dimensions. Nature is full of fractals. Using the mathematics of fractals and fractal geometry discovered and reported by Benoit Mandelbrot (1977), the computer is able to simulate many diverse phenomena of nature; clouds, trees, grass, flowers, and mountain peaks. The more complex and realistic the image the larger and more sophisticated the computer needs to be; but fractals of up to two dimensions are possible on a microcomputer. Consider the image produced by Ron Brunton* in Exhibit 8.21 using a Texas Instruments, desktop micro-computer and a dot matrix printer. Compare it to the mountains produced through a more sophisticated system and originally in color in Exhibit 8.22.

Traditional, or Euclidian, descriptions of nature using perfect forms appear less rich than the geometry of fractals. Mandelbrot states, "Clouds are not spheres, mountains are not cones, coastlines are not circles, and bark is not smooth; nor does lightening travel in a straight line" (Sørenson, 1984).

---

* Sociology Department, Acadia University, Wolfville, NS B0P 1X0

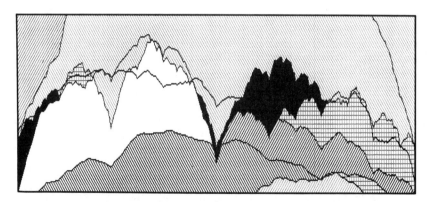

Exhibit 8.21: 2-D fractal mountains from a desktop computer and dot matrix printer (Courtesy of Mr. Ron Brunton, Acadia University, Wolfville, NS)

Exhibit 8.22: 3-D fractal mountains from a larger system (Excerpted with permission from "Fractals" by P. Sørenson, published in the September 1984 issue of *BYTE* magazine. © McGraw-Hill, Inc., New York, NY 10020. All rights reserved.)

Through the amplification of fractals, a space may be filled with "similar" constructions based on the computation of a simple formula repeated many times. This would not be possible without a computer, and it would be almost impossible to draw manually.

Fractals are both random and nonrandom; the former produce organic beauty, and the latter geometric beauty. The branching of trees, the meanderings of a stream, the expanse of the galaxies are all natural fractals. CGI allows us to mathematically model them visually (Sorenson, 1984).

8.7-3 CGI impact

Applications using CGI are expanding rapidly as costs keep dropping and systems increase in sophistication. Desktop systems may soon appear with 32 bit CPUs, array processors capable of doing 10 million instructions per second, and displays, in color, of 480 by 720 resolution or better, palettes of 16 million possible colors, 2 and 3 Megabytes of memory and very large auxiliary storage capacities, a variety of input and output devices, and networked to other similar units, all at a reasonable cost.*

If the above seems farfetched, consider our reaction to a description of a system like the Macintosh just prior to its announcement.

CGI is beyond reality; it is a world created with its own rules. We know that paintings and drawings reflect the artist's interpretation. We tend to believe photographs to be more veridical; therefore, photographs can lie even more. CGI gives new meaning to communication, propaganda, influence, and the perception of reality. CGI is an extension of what the wise have always known; our perceptions are an illusion.

Realistic, animated, 3-D CGI is the present zenith of computer graphics. 2-D line drawings, 3D wire drawings, and static solids modeling are more readily available capabilities and will be discussed further in Chapter 9.

8.8 FLIGHT SIMULATION

8.8-1 Simulated flight: large systems

Landing a fighter plane on an aircraft carrier at night is a risky and nerve-racking business (Tucker, 1984). Flight simulators provide realistic training in safe conditions.

The simulators of today are a great improvement over the first one invented in 1929 by Edwin A. Link. The original had a simple single motion system, and no sound or visual effects. Later flight simulators of the 1950s included TV cameras which scanned 100-foot-long model boards representing a few hunded square miles of terrain, and fed the visual images to the pilot in the trainer.

The above are now replaced by CGI systems and a totally computer-controlled environment. The basic layout of a flight simulator is shown in Exhibit 8.23.

Professional flight simulators used in the air force or flight schools for a single type of craft are very sophisticated. They include closed cockpits on hydraulic legs to physically simulate

---

* The above "dream machine" is based, in part, on a system described by Richard Moszkowski, formerly a programmer with John Whitney Sr, who is considered the "father" of computer animation (Quoted by Sørenson, 1984).

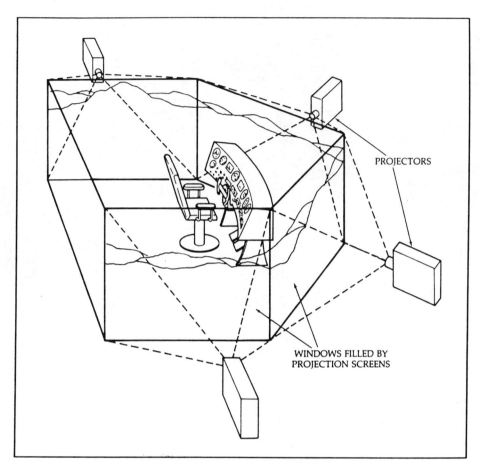

PROJECTORS

WINDOWS FILLED BY
PROJECTION SCREENS

Exhibit 8.23: Layout of a flight simulator (*Computer Graphics User's Guide*, A. Glassner, © copyright 1984, used by the courtesy of the publisher, Howard W. Sams & Company.)

movement, high-resolution graphics projected onto screens surrounding the pilot in training to simulate view, a complete instrument panel, and computer sound effects. The total system might be controlled by a large minicomputer such as the DEC VAX. The simulation and subsequent training are so realistic that the hours accumulated are counted as flight time by the FAA (Federal Aviation Commission). The U.S. Navy flight simulator for the AV8-B Harrier cost $100 million with $50 million alone for the visual system (Tucker, 1984).

CGIs of flight scenes have a realistic appearance, as shown in Exhibit 8.24. Recent developments using fractal geometry and digitized satellite images, however, are adding further realism to surface textures. For example, a system developed by Ivex (Atlanta, GA), uses fractal-based software for transforming digitized Landsat satellite photographs into landscape databases for storage on high capacity laser videodiscs. Ivex has also developed an interactive real-time operating system for the videodisc. From the stored database of landscapes, various animated scenes are possible. The result is high quality imagery at an acceptable cost and performance level.

Exhibit 8.24: A frame from an animated series of computer-generated images (Courtesy of Evans and Sutherland. A U.S. Navy T-45 trainer is shown approaching the U.S.S. Nimitz aircraft carrier.)

More recent developments include head-mounted systems feeding images to the trainee's eyes via fibre optics, as illustrated in Exhibit 8.25. These systems are still in the research stage.

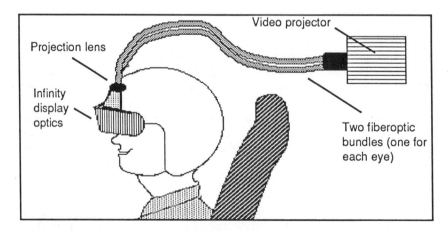

Exhibit 8.25: Head-mounted flight simulator system (J. K. Yan, "Advances in Computer-Generated Imagery for Flight Simulations," *IEEE Computer Graphics and Application*, 5, 8, August, 1985. Image reproduced courtesy of Digital Scene Simulation (sm) by Digital Productions, Los Angeles, CA, Copyright, 1985. All Rights Reserved.)

8.8-2 Simulated flight: microcomputer systems

Much can be learned from flight simulator systems that function in color, use animation, and cost $50 for the application software. Our discussion here is based on the *MicroSoft Flight Simulator* for the IBM PC as reported by Miastkowski (1984).

The *MicroSoft Flight Simulator* works only in color with a color TV. All other monitors, including an RGB display, will only show black and white. Color is important since the pilot uses color as visual cues for the instrument panel and the window view. Miastkowski suggests the system is not worthwhile without color. The system is accompanied by a manual with many of the maps and charts used in real flying. An example of the display is shown in Exhibit 8.26 with the outside view on top and the instrument panel below.

Exhibit 8.26: Microcomputer-based flight simulator (Excerpted with permission from "MicroSoft Flight Simulator" by S. Miastkowski, published in the March 1984 issue of *BYTE* magazine. © McGraw-Hill, Inc., New York, NY 10020. All rights reserved.)

The panel includes the instruments used in standard operation and instrument flying, engine monitoring gauges, a NAV/COM (navigation/communication radio), and a radar responder activated when radar signals hit the plane.

Controls normally activated by the use of hands or feet are controlled in the simulator through the keyboard; a drawback that interferes with the good qualities of the program. A good input option would be a joystick for the yoke control, the "steering wheel" of the plane.

The simulator allows the user to set up a very large number of different flight conditions including season, day, cloud, wind, turbulence, and location. In regard to the latter, the user can "fly," for example, into Seattle, Los Angeles, Chicago, or New York. There are ten preset flight condition modes and the user can add another twenty.

Miastkowski reports that the response in the window and on the instrument panel are realistic, and the simulator acts like a real plane.

8.9 COMPUTER-GENERATED TRAINING (CGT)

Computer-generated training was previously touched upon in Chapter 7 under the author's preferred title of computer aided learning (CAL), and discussed here under the more generic name. In many respects CGT is modeling and simulation, when it progresses beyond the flash card stage.

There is a serious movement in business and industry towards the use of computers to help train staff. It is the availability of low-cost graphics systems that is pushing the interest and software development (although some systems have been available for many years, the best known being the PLATO training series from Control Data Corporation, now available in a micro-computer version). CGT is also receiving a boost from the use of laser videodiscs which are capable of storing volumes of text and graphics information, which can be selectively retrieved and displayed during the training session. We will describe two classes of CGT: *business simulation software*, and *tutorial generators*.

8.9-1 Business simulation software

Why use business simulation software? The reasons are given in Exhibit 8.27.

Business simulation software:

• Is interactive, promotes involvement, and people practice immediately what they learn
• Provides more flexibility than books and viedeotapes
• Costs less than seminars and other traditional labor-intensive approaches; around five years ago, labor costs began to exceed computer costs
• Provides an overall picture of an operation that is difficult to teach otherwise
• Fine-tunes management skills, teaches how to make business trade-offs, and responds appropriately in crisis situations
• Allows the manager to deal with a changing environment and analyze problems; traditional case studies are too static
• Counteracts the problem of losing trained employees by providing for a broader base of trained employees
• Provides compressed learning, experiences it might take a manager six months to encounter
• Can be tailored to meet specific training contexts and needs (change the problem; change the enterprise).

Exhibit 8.27: Reasons for using business simulation software

Those using business simulation software include business schools, banks, trust companies, insurance houses, manufacturers, retailers, wholesalers, computer companies, and investment houses. A recent survey by "John Wiley & Sons (New York) shows that the Fortune 500 companies expect as much as 50% of their training efforts to use some sort of individualized interactive technology within five years" (D. B. Davis, "Learning with Technological Tutors" *High Technology Special Report*, Winter, 1985-86).

We will use *Entrepreneur* developed by Harvard Associates, Inc. (Harvard, MA) and available from MicroSoft Corp. (Bellevue, WA) for the Apple Macintosh to illustrate learning through simulation. In *Entrepreneur* two to nine companies, either human or computer-controlled, may play against each other. The simulation is of the software industry and the game calls for monthly decisions in five critical areas: product pricing, production levels, marketing expenditures, investments in plant operation, and research and development. There are two levels of play: basic and advanced, and the game may be played for as long as 36 months. The game ends when the allotted number of months have been played or all players, save one, are bankrupt. The winner, at any point, is the player with the highest total profit.

Entrepreneur makes good use of graphics. One of the initial screens is shown in Exhibit 8.28, where the three windows show last month's profit, the garage operation all players start with, and the desktop in each player's "office."

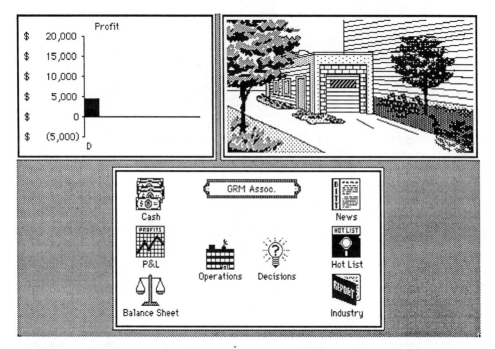

Exhibit 8.28: The initial play screen (from the *Entrepreneur* manual courtesy of MicroSoft Corp.)

The success of the company is shown by successive growth in the plant; from the garage shown in Exhibit 8.28, to the operations shown in Exhibit 8.29.

Each icon on the desktop shown in the lower window of Exhibit 8.28, when clicked, leads to another screen where various enterprise conditions may be viewed or decisions made. A click on the "Decisions" icon leads to the screen shown in Exhibit 8.30. Each player enters amounts for the five expenditure areas; the previous month's amounts are shown next to the new entries for the current month. Exhibit 8.30 shows that marketing and plant investment were increased, and the upper part of the screen shows that cash has been completely depleted (all money icons are black), and credit is nearly all depleted. In this short game of two months with only two players, GRM Associates lost to the computer as shown in Exhibit 8.31.

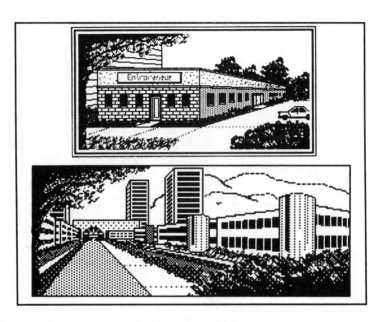

Exhibit 8.29: The plant expands in size as profits increase (from the *Entrepreneur* manual courtesy of MicroSoft Corp.)

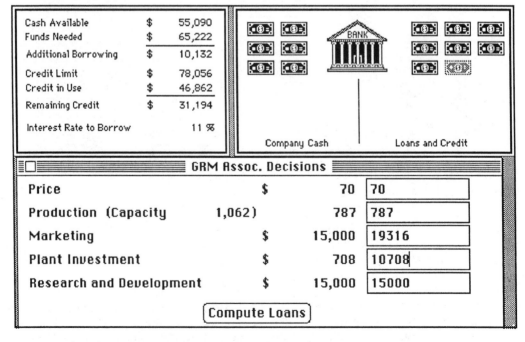

Exhibit 8.30: The screen for determining monthly expenditures by expense category (from the *Entrepreneur* manual courtesy of MicroSoft Corp.)

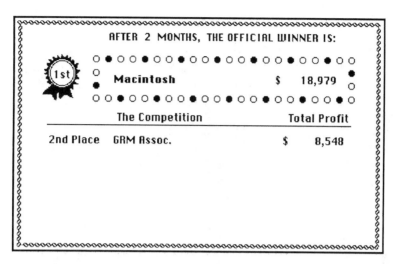

Exhibit 8.31: GRM Associates loses to Macintosh (from the *Entrepeneur* manual courtesy of MicroSoft Corp.)

8.9-2 Tutorial generators

Tutorial generators are a means for building interactive software tutorials; they simulate the operation of some given software (dBASE III, Lotus 1-2-3). A *general* tutorial generator for developing any form of CGT, namely *LightSource,* has already been discussed in Chapter 7. The programs described briefly here are specifically designed to develop tutorials which emulate application program operation. These programs markedly reduce the cost of training material development.

One program is the *Automentor* from Software Recording Corp. of America (Dallas, TX), a memory-resident program that works with most existing MS-DOS applications. *Automentor* allows nonprogrammers to develop tutorials, leading the developer through the process using various dialog boxes. For example, a dialog box may ask the developer to indicate when he or she wishes various keystrokes to be recorded. This is then used to show the user in training some sequence of choices and keystrokes required to perform some function (that is, as it actually occurs during operation).

A similar program is *Demo Program* from Software Garden, Inc. (West Newton, MA). *Demo Program* has been said to function like a slide show (J. Walkenbach, "Dan Bricklin Crafts a Demo Program," *InfoWorld*, 8, 13, May 31, 1986). The sequence of screens may be predetermined, or determined on the basis of some response by the user. The uses of Demo Program are to

- Develop prototypes of proposed software
- Design user interfaces
- Develop realistic demonstrations of existing software
- Use as a programmable slide show for presentation

One apparent limitation of both programs is that they do not support graphics, except those that are strictly character-oriented and, therefore, quite limited.

8.10 CONCLUSION

Through computer simulation and modeling we may better understand the world we live in. We can also create another world in the computer, a world that in some sense is less bounded; where we can make up the rules and see what happens, and explore desirable futures, rather than predicting enexorable trends. The question remains: do we know what future is desirable? Working towards any goal that does not include the answer to this question is, as Gardiner (1985) points out, "like playing chess in the drawing room of the Titanic."

How is computer graphics related to such grand schemes? It may assist, as it expands in power and simulation of reality, in providing so real a view of madness to avoid, and sanity to approach, that we may learn better and more quickly than we have in the past. Maybe.

9

CAD and Paint Systems

9.1 INTRODUCTION

A few years ago, CAD was available only on large and expensive computers costing $50,000 and more. Now sophisticated CAD capabilities are available on microcomputer-based systems for $3,000. However, as we shall see, there are major differences between low-and high-cost systems. They each have their value and application; otherwise both would not be extant.

In this chapter we define *computer aided design (CAD)* and related activities, compare CAD to *paint systems*, describe CAD applications, users, and the advantages of CAD, demonstrate the use of CAD through various case studies and example applications, and reference some of the prominent CAD and paint systems.

9.2 DEFINITIONS

Computer Aided Design (CAD) is the design and drawing of images using a computer system. Through a variety of input devices (keyboards, mice, tablets), drawings are rendered or sketched directly, or numeric data are entered on the drawing and the computer constructs and displays the drawing, or an image is digitized (with a video camera or scanner) into the computer and then manipulated, modified, and finally displayed. These are the three methods for rendering computer images: *sketch, specify,* and *digitize*.

CAD may be a part of *Computer Aided Engineering (CAE)*, which includes other related activities using a computer, such as cost analyses, production planning, specifying material requirements, quality control, and the direct control of machines for product manufacturing. We then arrive at *Computer Aided Manufacturing (CAM)* which uses the designs produced through CAD and the data specified through CAE to produce products or product parts. This larger context for CAD is illustrated in Exhibit 9.1.

All the information, images, numbers, and text may be kept in a *database* from which users may selectively choose information to create other drawings, specifications, and numeric control sequences to produce products. The database may be shared through a mainframe or minicomputer, or through a network of systems, which may include microcomputers in the configuration. The system might function as an independent, stand-alone station.

The value of database-supported CAD is obvious: production of drawings in some cases faster than real time, since, upon command, the computer can select subpictures from the database, construct the image, and update all the related support data. Further, the database provides for more consistency and less redundancy in the data, images, programs, work procedures, and final drawings and images produced.

The relationship between CAD and the stages in the design process is illustrated in Exhibit 9.2. Exhibit 9.2 is based on a diagram from a CAD/CAM text and in the original the "analysis" box was labeled "engineering analysis." It appears, however, that the diagram applies to many forms of computer aided design, including engineering.

9.3 APPLICATIONS AND USERS

CAE is not the only use of CAD, as the simulation and modeling discussed in Chapter 8 make obvious. The full complement of CAD applications includes product design, drafting, architecture,

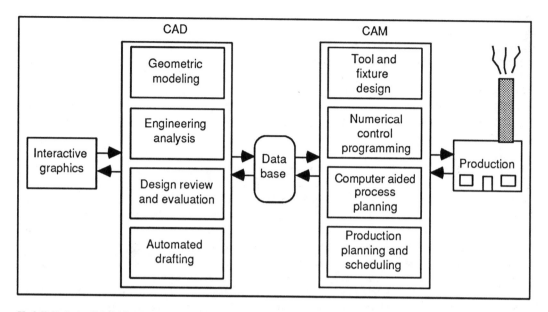

Exhibit 9.1: CAD/CAM: from interactive graphics to production
(Mikell P. Groover/Emory W. Zimmers, Jr., *CAD/CAM: Computer-Aided Design and Manufacturing*,
© 1984, p.59. Reprinted by permission of Prentice-Hall, Inc., Englewood Cliffs, New Jersey.)

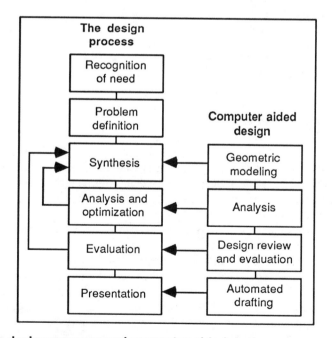

Exhibit 9.2: The design process and computer aided design
(Mikell P. Groover/Emory W. Zimmers, Jr., *CAD/CAM: Computer-Aided Design and Manufacturing*,
© 1984, p.66. Reprinted by permission of Prentice-Hall, Inc., Englewood Cliffs, New Jersey.)

illustration, map making, chart creation, forms design, block diagrams, flow charts, free form design, fine art, package design, advertising, photography, films, and TV graphics. CAD is used by engineers, architects, landscapers, product designers, artists, demographers, geographers, anthropologists, historians, language researchers, theatrical designers, and film animators.

The point is that a system so basic in its functioning may be used in any field. CAD systems are to images what word processors are to words and electronic spreadsheets are to numbers. We use CAD to create, edit, and cut and paste images for display on or in various media. Exhibit 9.3 shows an engineer working at a graphics workstation.

However, less than 10 percent of individual or small firm architects and engineers have adopted CAD. The experience of those who have adopted CAD is to soon want more capabilities. Large firms have been using CAD for a decade. For example "at Chrysler, more than 3000 users in 18 design centers share a huge engineering database on a network of 550 workstations connected to 27 large computers" (Krouse, 1986). However, with the low-cost systems available now, there is nothing to prevent the small company from establishing a similar operation on a smaller scale. The advantages will be similar to a large system: low redundancy of data, common and agreed upon procedures, high speed during revisions, and a network that supports enterprise cooperation.*

The trend is towards professionally oriented interfaces; meaning the computer becomes a clone of the engineer, the architect, and the designer and, in each different clone, a different language and graphics library is used suitable for the particular class of user. CAD is another language medium. Producers of CAD systems create CAD databases and user interfaces containing the images and languages of given industries. The database and interface may contain images of electronic components, and electronic engineers will build diagrams of electronic systems from the icons representing the different components. In a similar fashion, a system may contain icons of walls or wall subparts, doors, and windows, and all the other components needed by an architect; or chairs, tables, drapes, colors, and textures required by an interior decorator; or noses, mouths, eyes, hair textures, and skin coloring required by a police artist generating mug shots from victims' descriptions. The applications are endless.

9.4 CAD AND PAINT SYSTEMS COMPARED

CAD systems store data about images on the basis of coordinates and/or attributes. Information on a line is stored in terms of thickness, length, location, and orientation; a circle by its center and diameter, a rectangle by the placement of two of the coordinates, and so on.

Paint programs store images in bit-mapped form. On the screen a line is simply a line of dots, a circle, a circle of dots, as represented by the on and off messages in the bit-mapped buffer that controls the screen display and discussed in Chapters 2 and 5. The images in a paint system are not defined by data points or attributes.

Paint programs are easier to use; they are more flexible, but less powerful; for example, they cannot be integrated into a CAE system. Many of the capabilities of the two types of graphics systems often overlap. But, with the CAD system the numeric data is in the database and can be used for other purposes; to produce a bill of materials, to act as numeric control data (NC) to machines and, if it is part of a shared database provide data on objects to other users of the

---

*Put in a road or a communication link and people will use it; this constitutes change and coopera-tion using design science rather than moral admonition.

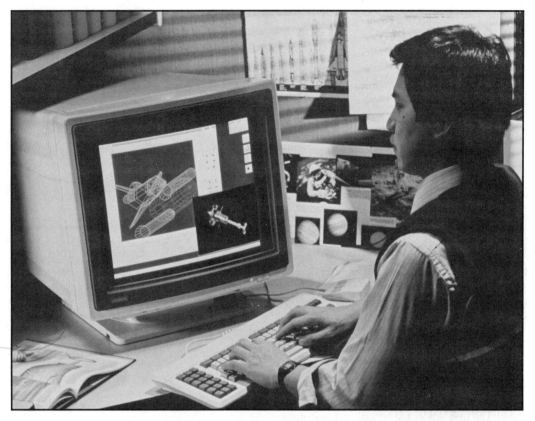

Exhibit 9.3: An engineer using a graphics workstation (Courtesy of Apollo Computer Inc. Apollo's DN580 high-performance workstation designed for real-time, 3-D color graphics applications.)

database. However, there is no inherent reason that paint programs cannot share a database of images, or users cannot create files of images for later use. Further, some software developers have created systems that share the features of both CAD and paint systems, for example, *Draft Math* by DM Systems (Bayshore, NY), a low-cost but complete system for the Apple Macintosh. *Draft Math* uses the eraser icon, which is usually a part of paint programs. The output from *Draft Math* is impressive, as illustrated in Exhibit 9.4.

The orientation and uses of paint programs differs from CAD systems. A summary is given in Exhibit 9.5 on page 217 based on a report by Hutzel (1985b).

There are over 50 different paint systems available. A number of paint programs are listed in Appendix C. Paint systems vary in capabilities and price. The monochromatic Macintosh with its MacPaint (pixel-based) and MacDraw (object-based) systems costs around $3,000 and for that price provide excellent resolution and good paint and draw capabilities. But a paint system can cost over $200,000; there must be a difference. The difference includes color, resolution, 3-D, anti-aliasing methods, animation, methods of input, methods of display, speed, multiusers, and multiprocessing.

The difference can be stated thus: CAD and paint systems on microcomputers automate 75

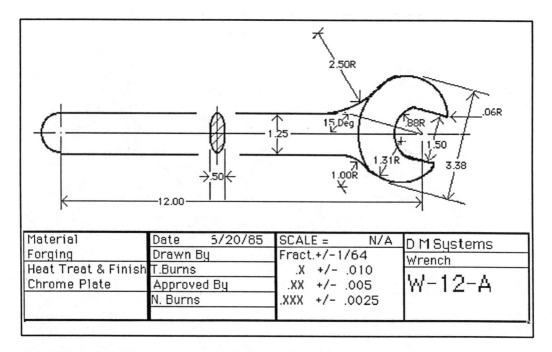

Material	Date	5/20/85	SCALE =	N/A	D M Systems
Forging	Drawn By		Fract.+/-1/64		Wrench
Heat Treat & Finish	T.Burns		.X +/- .010		
Chrome Plate	Approved By		.XX +/- .005		W-12-A
	N. Burns		.XXX +/- .0025		

Exhibit 9.4: Wrench drawing and specifications using *Draft Math* for the Macintosh (Courtesy of DM Systems)

percent of the job, and to automate the balance increases the cost of a system by a factor of ten or more. The question is user needs and resources.

9.5 HUMAN CREATIVITY AND COMPUTER POWER*

Humans can scan visually, very rapidly and accurately. Further, humans can rapidly coordinate fine motor movements to the visual sensations; otherwise, we could not drive cars or fly airplanes. Computers can perform some functions like this under special circumstances (autopilots in airplanes) where the situation is basically simple or straightforward (there is nothing to bump into up in the air). But we do not have autopilots for automobiles.

We possess extensive pattern recognition capabilities. For artificial intelligence researchers, this is a knotty problem. For example, we can interpret badly scrawled handwriting. The United States Post Office has spent millions trying to develop a computer system to recognize hand addressed envelopes with no success (Stover, 1984). We possess a powerful visual memory and can make matches, and "looks like" decisions.

A CAD system may use many symbols or subpictures to represent objects which, when integrated properly, form a larger image or drawing. The human operator is able quickly to recognize and select the subpicture for inclusion in the larger drawing.

---

*Inspired by the title of J. Weizenbaum's text on artificial intelligence entitled, *Computer Power and Human Reason: From Judgment to Calculation,* W. H. Freeman, San Francisco, CA, 1976.

CAD	Paint
• Object or vector based • More powerful • Capable of generating higher resolution hard copy on plotters and slides based on data instructions • Generating and scaling fonts is harder • Integrated into database and related applications (CAE, CAM) • Used to produce slides and high quality hard copy for drafting and design	• Pixel based • More flexible • Lower resolution but can fill areas; shade and airbrush much easier • Generating and scaling fonts is easier • Graphic images database possible, but serves no related functions • Used to produce medium resolution illustrations, fine art, enhance business presentations, and video frames

Exhibit 9.5: CAD versus paint systems

The computer is good at storing innumerable images, much better than we are. It can repeatedly draw the same symbol very quickly and with perfect accuracy, much better than we can. It can calculate length of lines and angles, and coordinate locations much faster. In fact, as Stover points out, the computer in CAD can perform the repetitive and time-consuming tasks, leaving the designer to do what he or she does best; be creative. The computer, in its history of application, is first used to do old things in new ways, before being used to do new things inconceivable before the existence of computers.

We humans are very slow, with poor memories, but capable of promethean leaps of creativity; that is, we can see patterns, make connections, envision possibilities, and imagine desirable futures. The computer has a near pefect memory, is extremely fast, but is poor at recognizing patterns or envisioning desirable futures. It is when humans and computers interact that creativity and power are realized. Humans and computers complement each other well.*

---

*A fishy serendipity story: direct interactive use of paint, draw, and CAD programs leads to creative synergies that are impossible when interaction is not so intimate, as in batch processing. For example, a biology professor purchased an Apple Macintosh and came across the illustration of a fish provided by Apple to demonstrate the capabilities of MacPaint. The biologist, exploring how to use the mouse and the commands, began to stretch and pull the fish drawing into alternate shapes. The different shapes took on the appearance of different species of fish. This suggested to the biologist an alternate theory to explain the variety in fish species.

9.6 CAD BENEFITS

There are work and productivity benefits to CAD. The benefits discussed are based on lists provided by Stover (1984) and Groover and Zimmers (1984).

9.6-1 Precision drawing and drawing placement

CAD programs use grid lines, and the image "snaps" to the grid established. Or, the image is defined numerically and the computer draws the image based on the coordinates stored or given.

9.6-2 A menu of images

Graphic primitives, or symbols, are displayed and selections made using the keyboard, a graphics tablet, a mouse, or a light pen with the screen. The images are stored as program procedures, as images in a file, or as data structures in a database; that is, the images are either "computed" each time they are needed, or are retrieved from a simple file or sophisticated database system.

The menu of images is like an automated "template," the kind used widely in manual drafting and design and full of different cut-out symbols used to guide the pencil or pen. In the computer based system, we select a primitive or image from the menu to build up our drawing. The selection screen from *MacDraw*, illustrated in Exhibit 9.6, shows various menus around the perimeter of the palette available for drawing. In Exhibit 9.6, a menu of subpictures (tables, desks) has been created in one file (lower window) that may be copied and pasted into a drawing in another open file (top window).

Menus of drawing primitives (lines, circles, rectangles), drawing components (chairs, tables, desks), and other drawing tools (texture fill) help increase consistency and productivity.

9.6-3 Lettering

Lettering is a very tedious and time-consuming manual operation that takes many hours and requires a lot of skill to do well. Using Rapidograph pens, lettering guides, and press-on letters helps, but even with these aids lettering remains tedious and clumsy. The computer can allow for the generation and scaling of many typefaces, and can produce lettering with flawless precision.

9.6-4 Editing and revision

Redrawing originals based on revisions is tedious work and difficult. Repeated erasure of lines made in pencil or ink on fine cloth vellum or high quality drafting paper leads to all kinds of damage to drawings. Sometimes an old drawing has to be completely redrawn. Some shops using CAD are working towards the elimination of drafting originals, and will store drawings strictly in the form of digital data. This makes complete sense; the drawing can be produced or reproduced using a plotter at any time. Consider the experience related in Exhibit 9.7.

AutoCAD referenced in Exhibit 9.7 is the best known CAD system on the microcomputer. *AutoCAD* uses the automated "plastic template" approach to build up images from other images. Further, it allows for many levels of detail design. One can build layers, then strip layers away to look at the next layer of construction. Vewing from different perspectives is possible, and 2-D and 3-D versions of *AutoCAD* are available. The system has a full-bidirectional zoom of 1:1,000,000;

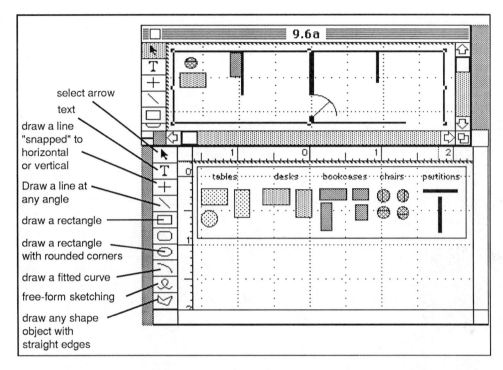

select arrow
text
draw a line "snapped" to horizontal or vertical
Draw a line at any angle
draw a rectangle
draw a rectangle with rounded corners
draw a fitted curve
free-form sketching
draw any shape object with straight edges

Exhibit 9.6: Menu of tools in MacDraw and windows on two different files

You lose accuracy whenever you trace by hand, especially after several generations of tracings and retracings. In a revision usually less than 20 percent of the information is being changed. For direct design sketching and drawing, your speed is about the same. Where the computer speeds things up considerably is when you have many repetitive details. With a program like *AutoCAD,* I can pull out the information for the contractor from one layer, the building department from another, client information from another layer, and so on.

(T. Reveaux, "C.A.D.: Elements of Structure," *COMPUTERLAND Magazine*, 1, 3, March/April, 1986).

Exhibit 9.7: CAD speeds up revisions involving repetitive details

one is able to zoom from a full view of the Challenger space craft to a close-up image of the astronaut's instrument panel.

   AutoCAD requires the speed provided by the IBM PC AT and clones, which some industry observers believe will become the CAD workstation of choice on the low end. However, the

Apple Macintosh is also a viable choice for low-end black-and-white work. It takes one week to learn to use *AutoCAD* with some proficiency. By comparison, *MacDraw* takes a few days, and *MacPaint* a few hours. Capabilities are similarly distributed. A drawing produced using *AutoCAD* is shown in Exhibit 9.8.

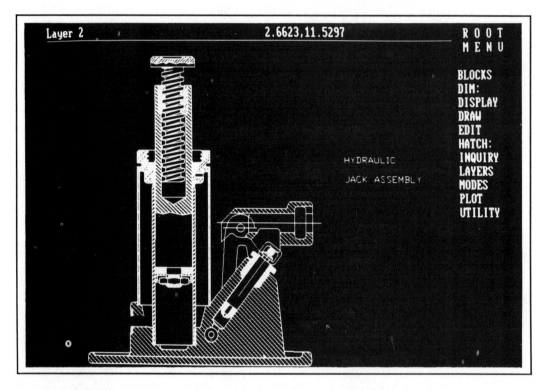

Exhibit 9.8: Drawing produced using *AutoCAD* on a WY-700 high resolution (800 by 1280) monochrome monitor (Courtesy of Wyse Technology)

9.6-5 Design analysis

It is possible with more advanced CAD systems to maintain accurate numeric data on objects as they are being drawn. Further, the numeric data generated along with the drawing can be subjected to various analyses, such as tracking the weight of components as they are developed in the CAD system and computing the total weight and mass as the object develops. Another application is determining the stress reactions of the object. Stress reactions can be displayed through the CAD system. Often a different color is used to show the effects of the stress on the object.

9.6-6 Flexible output

The computer can output the same drawing each time, on a variety of media, on different size drawings, and at various plotted scales. Further, if CAD is tied to CAM, the numeric data that produced the drawing may also be used to drive the drill press, the lathe, the shaper, the weaving machine, and other tools used in manufacturing.

9.6-7 Standardization of design, drafting, documentation, and output

CAD systems help facilitate standardization and are especially effective when drawings are complex, detailed, repetitive, and use a large number of different subpictures, and the CAD system is being used in a multistation environment.

9.6-8 Use of libraries

Designs and layouts can be created using libraries of images. For example, *daVinci Building Blocks* from Hayden Software Company, Inc. (Lowell, MA) is a series of disks containing buildings, building components, landscapes, and interiors for use by architects and interior designers. Exhibits 9.9 provide a sample from this collection of MacPaint documents.

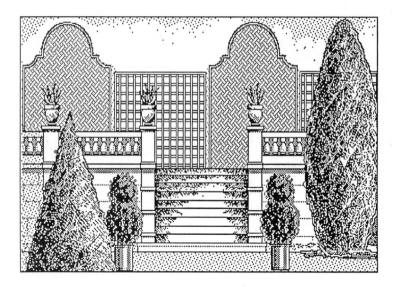

Exhibit 9.9: An example from a library of images

9.6-9 Savings in drafting time

Drawings that took 10, 16, and 50 hours to complete using manual methods, took 3, 4, and 20 hours, respectively, with a CAD system, thus leading to savings in time of 7, 12, and 30 hours. (Cortes, 1983). In general, users experience about a 30 percent improvement in time, somewhat less than the above figures indicate. Further, CAD-produced drawings compare favorably to manually made drawings. A comparison of two drawings of a cross-sectional view of a fireplace, one computer-generated and the other drawn manually, is shown in Exhibit 9.10.

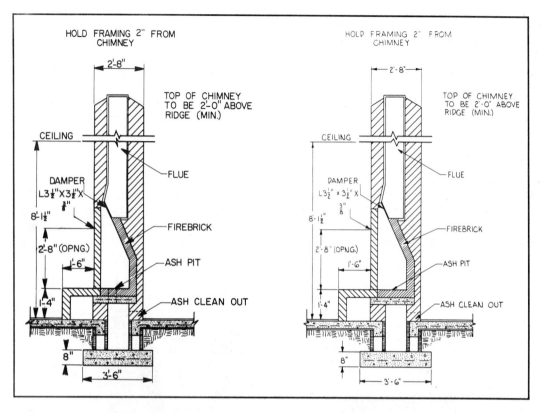

Exhibit 9.10: Computer (left)- and manual (right)-produced drawings (From
David L. Goetsch, *Introduction to Computer Aided Drafting*, © 1983, p.73. Reprinted by permission
of Prentice-Hall, Inc., Englewood Cliffs, New Jersey.)

9.7 CAD CAPABILITIES

The benefits of CAD depend on the capabilities of CAD. Systems vary greatly in capabilities, and
our discussion here describes some main features of a broad range of available systems. Further,
the capabilities of CAD systems are improving. A low cost system on a microcomputer that could
at one time handle only two-dimensional drafting, may be upgraded to generate and manipulate
three-dimensional drawings. The major gradations of capabilities that differentiate one CAD system
from another are, in order of CAD power, as follows:

- 2-D drafting
- 3-D drafting; wire frame only
- 3-D with hidden line and surface removal added
- 3-D with shading and texture capabilities; alternate perspectives
- 3-D with multiple views, color, animation; the works

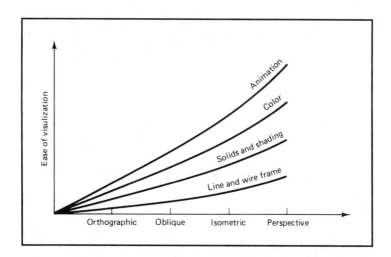

Exhibit 9.11: Improvement in visualization of images for various drawing types and computer graphics features (From David L. Goetsch, *Introduction to Computer-Aided Drafting*, © 1983, p. 73. Reprinted by permission of Prentice-Hall, Inc., Englewood Cliffs, New Jersey.)

The relationship between ease of visualization, type of perspective, and major features is shown in Exhibit 9.11, showing that animated, solid-shaded objects in true perspective are the easiest to comprehend. Examples of the different capabilities of CAD follow. An example of 2-D drafting is provided in Exhibit 9.12.

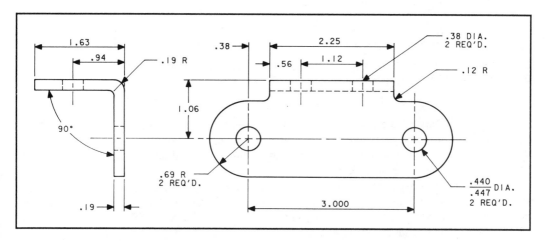

Exhibit 9.12: 2-D drafting (From J. C. Lange and D. P. Shanahan, *Interactive Computer Graphics Applied to Mechanical Drafting and Design*, John Wiley and Sons, New York, NY, 1984)

This type of drafting, using the traditional plan and side elevation views, serves a wide variety of technical uses. However, 2-D drafting systems obviously do not allow the user to render realistic views. An example of a 3-D wireframe view is provided in Exhibit 9.13.

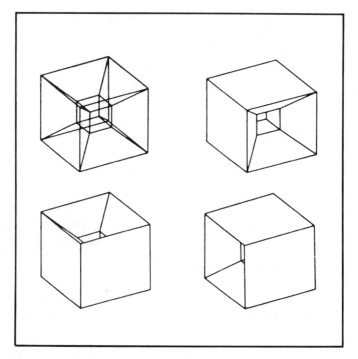

Exhibit 9.13: Wireframe: ambiguity leads to three possible interpretations
(From Solid Modeling—Key to Integrated CAD/CAM," *Tekniques*, 9, 2, Winter, 1986)

We see the shape of the object, but removal of lines and surfaces normally blocked by other parts of the object would make the rendition more realistic. An example of 3-D solid modeling with hidden line and surface removal is shown in Exhibit 9.14, and an example with shade and texture added is shown in Exhibit 9.15.

When a plotter is used in conjunction with a CAD system, the filling of polygons or surfaces with shade, texture, or color is performed by the repeated drawing of lines, and/or the changing of the pens used. For example, a fine-line pen can be substituted with a broad felt-tipped pen. Various color inks can be used and also overlaid.

Textbooks do not lend themselves too well to the demonstration of animated computer graphics. Viewing television for 30 minutes should provide more than one demonstration.

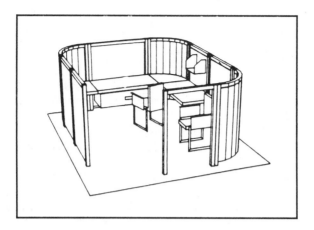

Exhibit 9.14: Hidden line and surface removal (produced using *EXECADD* courtesy of Tritek Vision Systems)

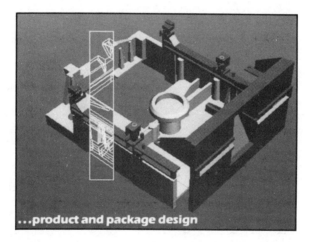

Exhibit 9.15: Solid modeling: surface textures and colors added (© 1985 Cubicomp Corporation. Artist: Wilson Burrows)

9.8 CAD FEATURES

The features listed here provide more detail to the major features discussed under CAD benefits and capabilities. In no manner can the list be considered complete; it is indicative. Some of the illustrated features were created using *MacDraw* on the Macintosh. *MacDraw* can be considered a 2D drafting system, not a CAD system. It is very good at what it does, and there are some things that it was never intended to do, but which are a part of more powerful CAD systems. For example, it does not contain a database, perspective, zoom and pan, user-defined macros or menus, mirroring, automatic fillets (small rounded corners), placement of an object or subpicture on the basis of parameters, or tagging. We describe all of these features here.

9.8-1 Drawing and editing

A mouse, and a stylus and tablet, are common drawing and editing devices. Images can be *selected* from a menu, the location, size, and other attributes (width of line, texture) specified, and either drawn, placed by pointing, or generated by command. The latter is the least interactive. A line may be *rubberbanded*, that is, drawn from some fixed endpoint and then stretched by moving the mouse or stylus to some other selected point and then fixed in place. We can move, resize, reshape, rotate, or delete drawing elements or the total image. Systems often possess an *undo* command that will undo the last command entered. A *mirroring* capability may exist, whereby the mirror image of an object is automatically generated on command. Or, a *repeat* command will duplicate a selected sub-picture. The last feature was used to create the trees in Exhibit 9.16.

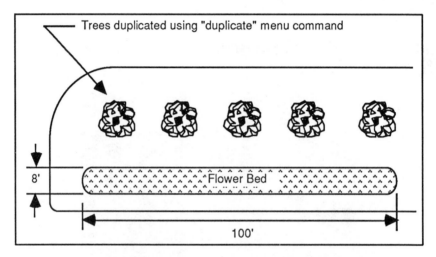

Exhibit 9.16: Duplicate command allows for rapid production of detail

9.8-2 Text handling

The type font, size, location, and angle of orientation are text handling features required to annotate a drawing properly. The availability of fonts, and the quality of the printed output, depends upon a number of factors including the output device used (plotter, laser printer, dot matrix printer), and the software available for producing the fonts (on a laser printer the fonts are often stored on a ROM chip in the printer itself). This textbook is a good example of font types and sizes available on a laser printer, in this case the Apple LaserWriter. Some more examples of type fonts, sizes, and faces are shown in Exhibit 9.17.

9.8-3 Display control

On-screen status display, such as the current coordinate location of the cursor, the status of the grid if being used, the scale being used, and so forth can be very helpful. Further, snap, zoom, and pan features can be valuable.

Courier plain 10 point

Courier bold 12 point

Helvetica plain 14 point

Helvetica bold 14 point

Times italic 18 point

Times   bold   24 point
with   outline

Exhibit 9.17: Some type fonts (Note: The range of high quality fonts is limited, in the case of laser printer output, to the availability of a given font for a given printer)

Snap, as we have discussed, provides for the automatic correction to a defined ruled grid of all graphic objects entered into the drawing. Snap can include line end points, midpoints, the horizontal or the perpendicular, some specified angle, and others.

Zoom acts like a camera zoom lens on the drawing. We can zoom in to enlarge a part of the picture, or zoom out to take more of the picture in. *Pan* is comparable to moving the automated camera lens across the drawing and looking at different parts. Pan is a convenient approach to viewing different parts of a drawing that is too large to be viewed on the screen at one time. Vertical and horizontal scrolling perform the same function, but with pan you can move diagonally. *MacDraw* does not possess zoom or pan features. A more complete system is *MacDraft* from Innovative Design, Inc. (Concord, CA) for the Apple Macintosh. The features possessed by *MacDraft,* not a part of *MacDraw,* include zoom, pan, one degree axis rotation, 16 different scales, automatic dimensioning, and several circle and arc functions. *MacDraft* is a more serious drafting program and is also more difficult to learn. Exhibit 9.18 illustrates the zoom function in *MacDraft.*

Aspect ratio is the ratio of display height to width. The system should correct for this so that displayed circles and squares look like circles and squares and not elipses and rectangles.

9.8-4 Fillets, complex curves, and fitted curves

A lot of manual drafting time can be taken by drawing small curves connecting two lines (fillets), by drawing complex curves, or by fitting curves to a set of points or parameters. But on a computer this can be automated. Exhibit 9.19 shows the stages in a CAD system for the creation of fillets at a street intersection.

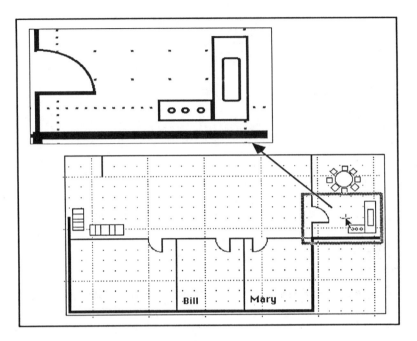

Exhibit 9.18: The zoom function in *MacDraft*

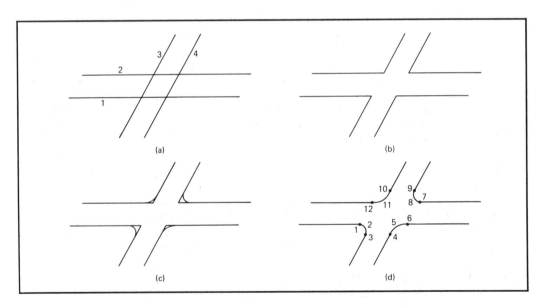

Exhibit 9.19: The automation of adding detail: a) computer identifies corners, and user keys in radii of corners; b) unnecessary lines are removed; c) computer adds fillets; d) computer removes extensions (Bruce A. Artwick, *Applied Concepts in Microcomputer Graphics*, © 1984, p.172. Reprinted by permission of Prentice-Hall, Inc., Englewood Cliffs, New Jersey.)

9.8-5 Hatching, shading, and filling

MacDraw demonstrates this feature well. An illustration is given in Exhibit 9.20 showing filled lines and areas, along with some other drawing capabilities available, including shapes, arrow lines, and smooth curves.

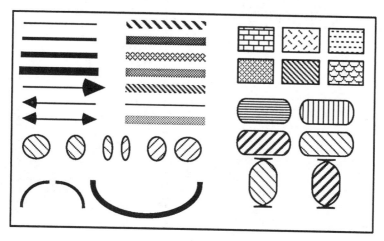

Exhibit 9.20: Patterns, curves, arrows, and lines available in MacDraw

In many systems, the user may define the pattern. In some systems, the pattern choices are displayed; in some, they are not and must be selected by commands entered through the keyboard.

9.8-6 User-defined macros and menus

Some objects in a drawing may require a sequence of commands to create. Macros are groups of program instructions that can be initiated by simple selection from a menu, or by a single stroke of a defined key. They assist in improving drawing time and consistency. Quite often, a macro program is not a part of a given application package, but is a separate program that can be used with any application software; *AutoMac* for the Apple Macintosh from Genesis Micro Software (Bellevue, WA) is a program of this nature.

9.8-7 Dimensioning

The location of dimension lines, selection of arrowheads and arrowhead sizes, dimension stacking, and, sometimes, automatic entry of dimensions, are available on CAD systems. The exact size of an object may be displayed as it is being drawn. An example is given in Exhibit 9.21 using MacDraw; most CAD systems possess this feature, and there are add-on memory-resident utilities that add this feature to paint programs that do not normally possess this feature.

CAD systems also provide custom rulers, including inches, centimers, locked or unlocked zero points, and choice of major and minor division spacing, for example, inches divided into 1/12ths as shown in Exhibit 9.21. Division into twelths is particularly useful because a *pica*, a unit of measurement equivalent to 1/6th of an inch, is used to format pages for publishing (discussed in Chapter 12).

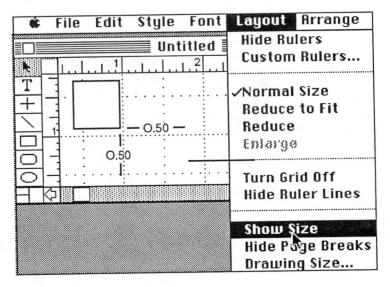

Exhibit 9.21: Some display options

9.8-8 Sketch mode

Sketch mode allows for freehand drawings to be entered. This is useful for entering contour lines, trees, bushes, and other objects best rendered in freehand form.

9.8-9 Object placement by parameters

Some objects are best entered according to a set of parameters. For example, the distance between two floors in a building might be specified (the parameters) and the computer will automatically compute the number of steps, the rise in each step, and then draw the staircase in the specified location. The drafting systems discussed (*MacDraw, MacDraft, Draft Math*) do not possess these features. But *MacSurf* from Graphics Magic (Perth, Western Australia) possesses this important feature. *MacSurf* is a specialized CAD "program that enables the user to manipulate curved surfaces (and) is particularly suited to marine hull shapes such as ships, yachts, and sailboards." (MacSurf User's Manual, 1985) *MacSurf* is a bundle of integrated programs specially tailored for the naval architect. The system works in conjunction with a wide variety of other Macintosh applications including all 2D and 3D drafting software for the Macintosh plus: *MacPlot,* a driver for a number of plotters; a digital circuit drawing and simulation package, allowing the user to design and detect design errors prior to actual circuit construction; *MacProject,* for project planning (discussed in Chapter 11); electronic spreadsheet, for manipulating hydrostatic data (hydrostatics deals with the pressure of liquids exerted on an immersed body); and word processing, for creating reports with integrated images. The program functions very rapidly and an example of the type of drawings produced is given in Exhibits 9.22 through 9.24.

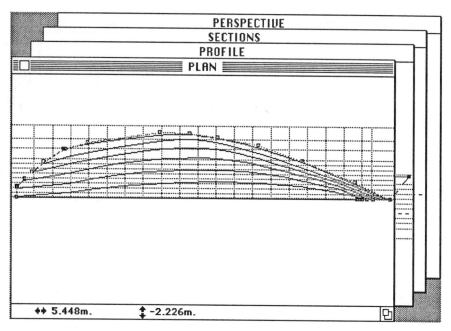

Exhibit 9.22: Plan view of hull

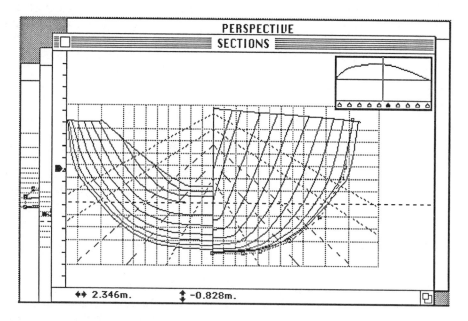

Exhibit 9.23: Section view of hull

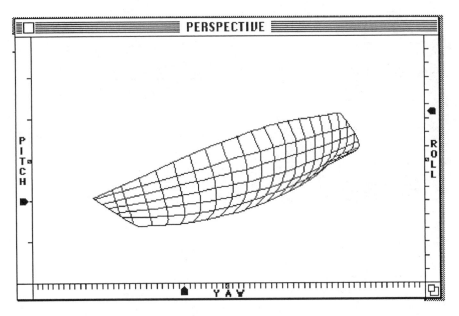

Exhibit 9.24: Perspective view of hull

The exhibits reveal three of the four views it is possible to obtain: *plan, sections,* and *perspective*. The fourth (not shown) is *profile*, or side view. The plan in Exhibit 9.22 shows only one half of the vessel; it is possible to show both halves. The small window in the upper right corner of the section's window in Exhibit 9.23 shows where the section is located. A click of the mouse moves the section view along the hull. The perspective view in Exhibit 9.24 may be changed immediately by moving the three pointers on the *pitch, yaw,* and *roll* scales. Pitch, yaw, and roll are explained using the diagram in Exhibit 9.25.

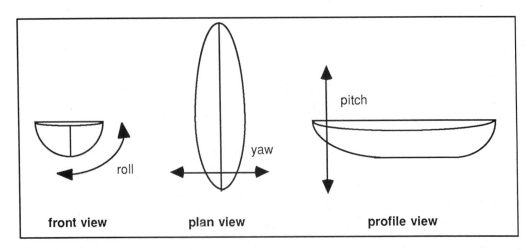

Exhibit 9.25: Roll, yaw, and pitch

9.8-10 Tagging

Tagging is the process of identifying drawing elements or objects. For example, some may be made of steel, and others of wood, glass, and so forth. The CAD system may allow for the maintenance of a related dictionary of object identifiers, including materials, tensile strengths, other descriptors, suppliers, and so forth.

9.9 CASE STUDIES

The applications of CAD to some specific tasks are presented here. We have included cases that fall outside of the engineering discipline because they may not be so obvious.

9.9-1 Population studies

One CAD application is to plot population densities on the basis of family last name, comparing figures extracted from MacAlpine's *Nova Scotia Directory of 1914* with current data gathered from phone directories. Exhibits 9.26, a and b, and 9.27, a and b, show plots for a Scottish and a French family name, respectively.

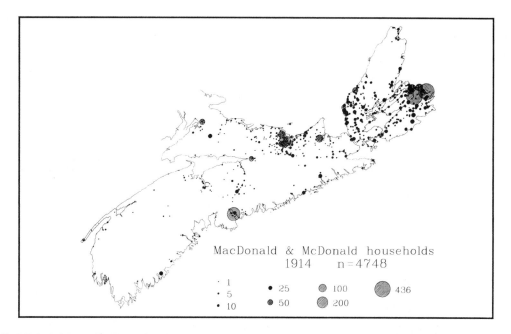

Exhibit 9.26a: MacDonald/McDonald households in Nova Scotia and Cape Breton in 1914(courtesy of Dr. Hugo Blackmer, Acadia University, Wolfville, Nova Scotia)

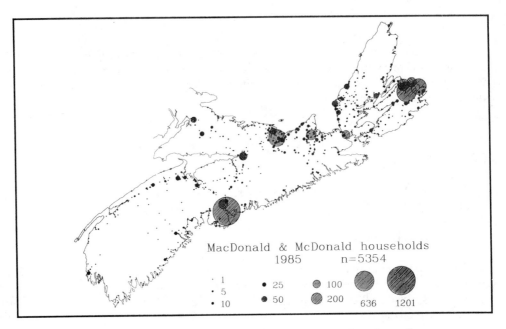

Exhibit 9.26b: MacDonald/McDonald households in Nova Scotia and Cape Breton in 1985 (courtesy of Dr. Hugo Blackmer, Acadia University, Wolfville, NS)

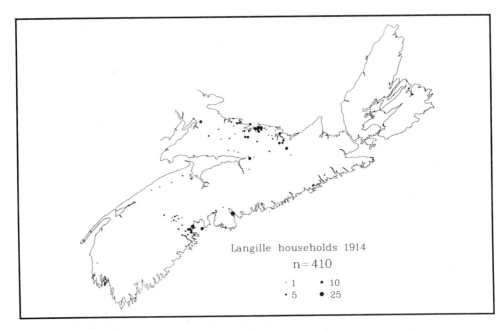

Exhibit 9.27a: Langille households in Nova Scotia and Cape Breton in 1914 (courtesy of Dr. Hugo Blackmer, Acadia University, Wolfville, NS)

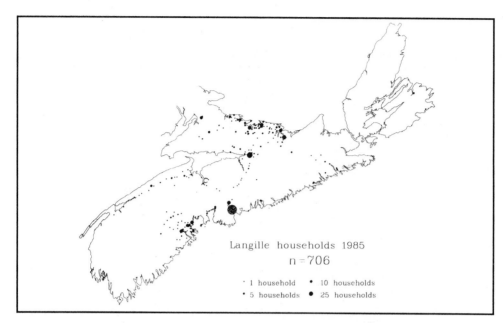

Langille households 1985
n = 706

· 1 household · 10 households
· 5 households · 25 households

Exhibit 9.27b: Langille households in Nova Scotia and Cape Breton in 1985 (courtesy of Dr. Hugo Blackmer, Acadia University, Wolfville, NS)

The exhibits show all of Nova Scotia and Cape Breton. In 1914, there was a heavy concentration of MacDonald/McDonald households in Cape Breton, the Halifax area on the South Shore, and another concentration on the Cumberlands Straits to the north. These same concentrations remain in 1985. There is some movement from the country to nearby cities. The Langille households are *not* located where the MacDonald/McDonald households are located, except in Halifax to the south.

Very little movement has taken place for these families. There has been some movement to towns and cities. Few have moved in or out of the area. Unlike national figures of family mobility, or mobility in other local areas of North America, the *lack of* mobility over the past 71 years in population distribution and densities for these families has been remarkable. Dr. Blackmer has identified the same stability (some might call it stagnancy) in Nova Scotia for other families of English, Scottish, and French origins.

People in Nova Scotia often locate places by family name, and do not pay too much attention to highway numbers, or directions given on the basis of mileage distances. For example, a local tradesman trying to locate the author's residence inquired, following a lengthy explanation in terms of highway numbers and turns to the right and to the left, "Do you live near the Berggrens of Belmont and Avondale?" This is a highly personal and communal way of relating to geography, one that most of us do not have an opportunity to experience because of constant movement. In the light of the stability identified by Dr. Blackmer, the locating of places by family name is quite understandable. Otherwise it is not.*

---

* Another related custom is to identify a house by the name of the orginal owner. The house where the Berggren's lived was known as the "old Blackburn house." No Blackburns have lived there since 1924!

9.9-2 Isodemographic maps

Another type of population map is shown in Exhibit 9.28.

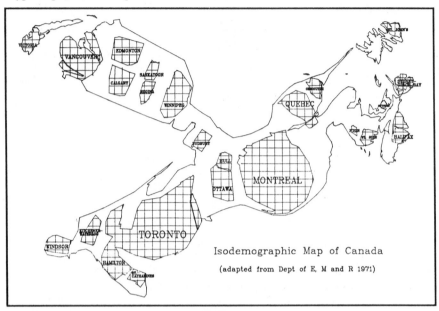

Isodemographic Map of Canada

(adapted from Dept of E, M and R 1971)

Exhibit 9.28: Density of population as reflected in size of geographic area displayed (courtesy of Dr. Hugo Blackmer, Acadia University, Wolfville, NS)

Exhibit 9.28 shows a map of Canada distorted to reflect population densities rather than mileage areas. It would appear that Toronto, Montreal, and Vancouver account for more than half the Canadian population! The map in Exhibit 9.28 communicates this fact better than any table, verbal description, or a map that uses density of fill or shade to represent density of population, rather than area distortion. The map in Exhibit 9.29 of population densities per square mile in the United States was created on an IBM PC using a program called *Atlas*. The maps by Dr. Blackmer were created using AutoCAD on a Texas Instruments Professional Desktop System, a digital tablet by Koala Technologies, and a plotter by Bausch and Lomb. The above does not reflect on the relative merits of the two CAD programs referenced. *Atlas* is used for producing maps, while *AutoCAD* has broader applications.

9.9-3 Theatrical stage sets

At the University of Nebraska, theatrical stage sets are being designed and modeled using *Microcad*, a 3-D CAD program, on a Compaq, and a Bausch and Lomb DMP-42 plotter (Martin, 1985). Wire frame models are made of stage props in various groupings and viewed in various perspectives by the stage designer and the director. When agreement is reached, the stage designer produces drawings of each prop for the construction crew. Libraries of icons representing stage props are maintained in a database and used to quickly construct various set designs on computer. CAD may also be used in a similar manner for costume design.

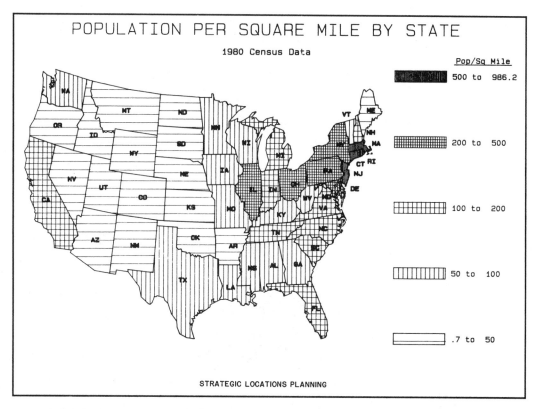

POPULATION PER SQUARE MILE BY STATE

1980 Census Data

Pop/Sq Mile

500 to 986.2

200 to 500

100 to 200

50 to 100

.7 to 50

STRATEGIC LOCATIONS PLANNING

Exhibit 9.29: Density of population as reflected in density of fill or shade

9.9-4 Film and video animation

The deadlines imposed by the television and film industry are making CAD a necessity; manual production takes too long. At Cinematte in San Francisco, a company that produces television station identification spots and television commercials, *Artwork* and an IBM PC are being used. Artwork is an animation 3-D CAD System. Martin (1985) reports on a specific ad use, where a wire frame model of a Black and Decker drill was first created, and then a move command used to animate the model. The effect of movement is enhanced by adjusting the scale of objects between frames. A picture is taken of each frame, with 24 frames used for each second of finished sequence of animation. Ad preview is possible on the screen display, enabling clients to request changes before filming.

9.9-5 Architecture and construction

This example is reported by Groover and Zimmers (1984). The top illustration in Exhibit 9.30 shows a three-dimensional view of a building section with a curved front facing. The standard projections of this building would present no problem in a manual *or* automated system. However, the construction of a three-dimensional physical model would be difficult. The CAD system, by contrast, can create a 3-D image as shown, or from any other desired viewpoint. The bottom illustration in Exhibit 9.30 shows a 3-D aerial view of a floor plan.

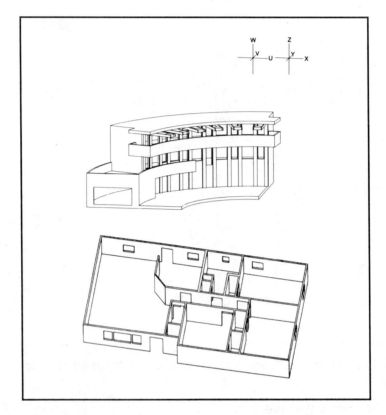

Exhibit 9.30: Architectural application of CAD (from W. Fitzgerald, F. Gracer, and R. Wolfe, "GBIN: Interactive Graphics for Modeling Solids," *IBM Journal of Research and Development*, 25, 4, July, 1981. Copyright 1981 by International Business Machines; reprinted with permission)

9.9-6 Art

The works of artists using the computer as a medium of expression are now represented in galleries. The first computer art gallery established in North America is *Beyond the Horizon*, Pittsburgh, Pennsylvania. The gallery was established by Elizabeth P. Van Dusen. The works of three artists represented by her gallery are shown in Exhibit 9.31 through 9.33: Rachel Gellman, a graphics art instructor at Pratt Institute and a freelance designer in New York City; Hervé Huitric and Monique Nahas of the University of Paris, and Ray van Buhler, an associate professor at the College of the Pacific, Stockton, California.

Exhibit 9.31: Art 1 (Courtesy of Rachel Gellman)

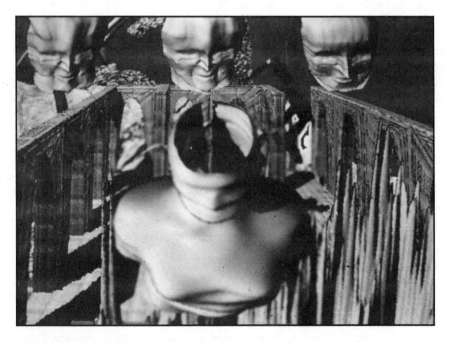

Exhibit 9.32: Art 2 (Courtesy of Hervé Huitric and Monique Nahas)

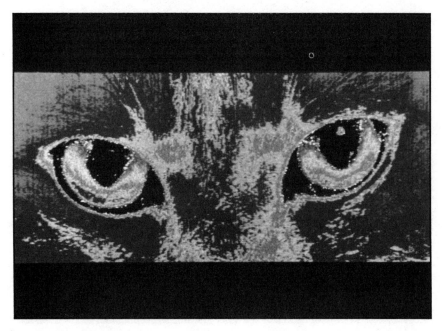

Exhibit 9.33: Art 3 (Courtesy of Ray van Buhler)

9.10 COMPUTER INTEGRATED MANUFACTURING*

Computer Integrated Manufacturing (CIM) uses CAD produced images, sometimes in animation, to simulate or demonstrate assembly, and to communicate the results. Then the engineer is better able to see the problems in the design and manufacturing process. Products with complicated designs require testing. Do they function properly? Have clearances been computed correctly? Traditionally, a physical model is constructed to help make these type of evaluations. Consider the bulldozer illustrated in Exhibit 9.34: a three-dimensional perspective, and a front view.

The purpose of the modeling and the various views is to analyze the range of motion—lift and tilt—the blade can accommodate without hitting some other part of the dozer; that is, clearance. The *front* view shows the blade in an extreme skew position.

A system in development reported by Noma and Kunii (1985) called *ANIMENGINE*, is based on the use of raster versus vector graphics because of the need to display solid areas of color and patterns to make components identifiable. The purpose was to animate product assembly. This requires high speed display. But the cost of real-time raster-graphics is expensive. Therefore, these researchers combined the interactive production of each frame with the storage of frames on a video recorder for later animation. Exhibit 9.35 shows frames from a sequence simulating the assembly of a roller unit in a copier machine.

---

* We are inundated with new terms. As we learn more, finer distinctions are required, and new terms are coined to identify those distinctions. For example, the Chinese have many names for the different varieties of rice they use. In the west, we have only a few: white, brown, long grain, Uncle Ben's. Who do you think discriminates better between different varieties of rice, the Chinese or the Westerner? It is similar with the different varieties of computer aided design work.

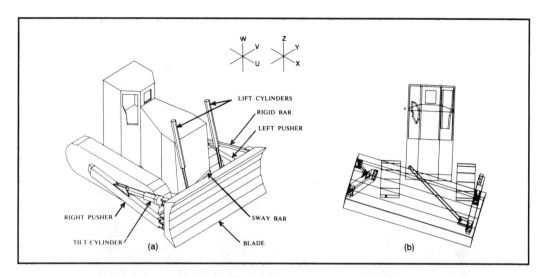

Exhibit 9.34: Product design application of CAD (from W. Fitzgerald, F. Gracer, and R. Wolfe, "GBIN: Interactive Graphics for Modeling Solids," *IBM Journal of Research and Development*, 25, 4, July, 1981. Copyright 1981 by International Business Machines; reprinted with permission)

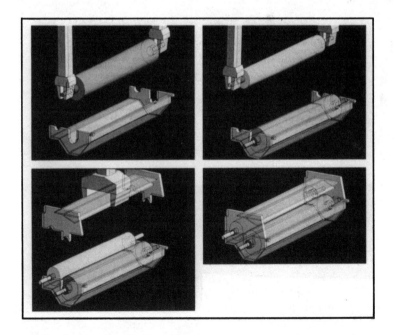

Exhibit 9.35: Selected images from an engineering animation series (From T. Noma and T. L. Kunii, "ANIMENGINE: An Engineering Animation System," *IEEE Computer Graphics and Applications*, 5, 10, October, 1985; © 1985 IEEE)

9.11 COMPUTER AIDED STYLING (CAS)

Another application is emerging, namely, *Computer Aided Styling*. In CAS the concern is with the look and the feel of a product; the contours, colors, textures, and balance in the industrial design of chairs, car phones, cars, motorbikes, and so forth (McGrath, 1986).* By contrast, CAD is concerned with the hard engineering aspects of design. CAS may be thought of as a marriage of CAD and computer-generated imagery (CGI); CAS involves both the engineering and the appearance of a product. Exhibit 9.36 shows two examples of CAS from *frogdesign* (Campbell, CA), using an Intergraph CAD/CAM system for the work shown.

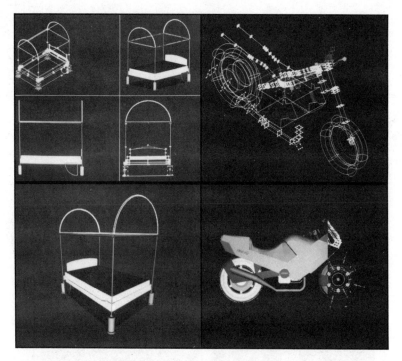

Exhibit 9.36: Study of a bed for the elderly and a study of a motorbike
(Courtesy of *frogdesign*)

9.12 CONCLUSION

There is no doubt that the CAD techniques discussed in this and the previous chapter constitute one of the most exciting areas in computer graphics. Many of us will not have access to the more advanced features for a few years; but soon, these capabilities will be widely available. They hold the promise of a new communication, a new language of great power.

---

* McGrath reports on the ALIAS/1 from Alias Research Inc. (Toronto, ONT), considered a technical breakthrough; it generates complex realistic 3-D images from a few defined elements or "patches," rather than addressing or creating all the individual elements of an image directly.

10

Visual Database

10.1 INTRODUCTION

A prime use of the computer is to store and organize information for selective retrieval later. We do not want all the information available all the time; only that portion relevant at a given time. Database and database management systems serve this need.

In this chapter we first discuss the relation of information systems to the real world; there are times when computers should *not* be used. This may be blasphemy in the age of technology, but there are applications in given situations that remain more effective if handled without the computer.

Next we introduce two concepts; one unique and the other mundane, but both useful. The unique application is a graphics-oriented filing system, and the mundane is a filing system for graphics. In the first, graphics are used as the very basis for finding things; in the second the graphic is the object being found. The second is no more than adding images as another data structure to other types of data that we store and wish to retrieve, such as alphanumeric data (names, dates, phone numbers) and real numbers used in computations (distance, time, amount).

Filevision, which functions on the Apple Macintosh and which has been used in a variety of applications to be described later in this chapter, is used to introduce graphics-oriented filing and database management. As far as the author knows, it is the only product of its kind which is generally available. *MicroSoft File*, which possesses images as an additional data structure, is used to introduce the storage, retrieval, and display of graphics images within the context of file management.*

10.2 MANUAL VISUAL FILING SYSTEMS

We sometimes forget that computer systems and the data they contain are models of the real world. That is, we become enamored of our technology and do not pay enough attention to relevancy, actual experienced efficiency, and what really works best. We tend to assume that automated is invariably better than manual. This attitude also makes us overlook how manual and automated systems can work together to form a superior system. As we shall see, *Filevision* lends itself to this kind of synergy very well.

The author has encountered a number of automated "index card" systems that search and locate files on the basis of keywords. However, the systems are set up to reference files only stored *inside* the computer, thus rendering the index system useless for all the other information we keep

---

* A third class of products, where graphics may be used to enhance the *appearance* of forms and reports, but does *not* include graphics as a data structure, is *not* discussed in this text. A prime example is *FileMaker* from Forethought, Inc. (Mountainview, CA), an excellent file, form, and report system for business. An interesting twist is provided by the integration of FileMaker and 3Com Corporations' network serving both IBM PC and Apple Macintosh computers. Data which resides on the IBM PC, for example, in dBASE II or dBASE III files, may be transferred to the Apple Macintosh to produce high-quality documents. The question one might ask is, why do we need two computers? The answer is, we should not. The IBM PC is the most widely used corporate microcomputer system, and, therefore, contains most of the data. However, the IBM PC does not possess the same graphics capabilities as the Apple Macintosh and, therefore, does not readily support high-quality document production based on the data it contains. As all systems become more graphic, including the IBM PC, this difference should disappear.

outside the computer. Did the designers of these systems think, consciously or unconsciously, that it was obviously better that all information should be transferred to storage in some digital form? Possibly, at some future date when we all have access to powerful low cost text digitizers and laser disc storage, this might be closer to the truth. But it is doubtful.

Humans can visually scan and identify a limited number of objects and patterns, rapidly and accurately; computers—except within highly restricted conditions—cannot. Computers can store and rapidly process lots of information; humans cannot. We need to use human capabilities supported by the computer's capacities.

An example will demonstrate the point being made. As a teacher, writer, and researcher, I require rapid access to information on a wide variety of subjects related to the functioning, application, and impact of computers. I have access to libraries, both manual and automated. But they are not my libraries. For my personal collection I obviously have books on shelves, and data and information on computer. But I am a dedicated, if not compulsive and possibly addicted, clipper of articles, pictures, quotes, and so forth. Where do these treasures go? They get deposited in my *Manual Visual Database,* which consists of the advanced technology known as the banker's box, a filing device which has been in existence since Victorian times, if not earlier. It is a cardboard box that one receives folded flat that takes approximately 30 seconds to assemble and label, and costs approximately $1.40 each. These boxes, uniquely identified, reside on library shelves.

One application of the manual visual database is to store reference materials for writing books, giving lectures, and doing research. Exhibit 10.1 shows the manual visual database for computer graphics that supported the writing of this text and other related work.

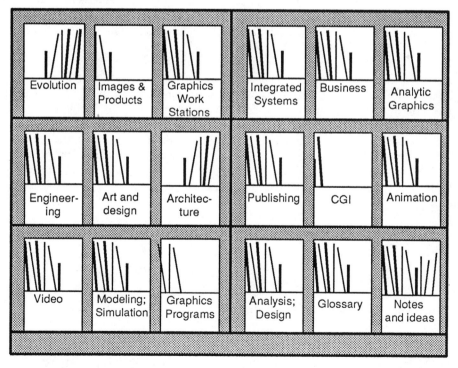

Exhibit 10.1: Banker's box manual visual filing system

Building upon the human capability to visually scan a limited set of data, my colleagues and research assistants and I—all of whom make periodic deposits and withdrawals from this and other manual visual databases organized by major subject—are able to select relevant information far more quickly than through any automatic DBMS. Data entry by a broad group of users helps keep the data current, and the user interface is very friendly and requires no training.*

We can retrieve an up-to-date set of information on Expert Systems and Artificial Intelligence as fast as the arm is able to raise and grab the banker's box marked "Expert Systems & AI." Cross-reference cards could be inserted in one box referring the user to related information in other boxes—a manual secondary index system—but it is usually not necessary. Therefore, for a personal (admittedly limited) database, supporting quick access to original sources, that requires no, or hardly any, data entry, or protocols for information retrieval, the banker's box visual database wins hands down. Building an automated database to do what the banker's box system accomplishes would be tedious indeed. Data entry would be enormous, and in large measure useless; information in general, and in the computer industry in particular, is rapidly out-of-date. With the banker's box system, removal of out-of-date information simply means scanning the boxes twice a year and removing anything older than one year.

10.3 THE AUTOMATED VISUAL DATABASE

But some combination of manual and automated is superior to either alone. The recent introduction of automated visual database systems on computer that can graphically represent the real world, and allow us to select information by pointing to given parts of that graphic representation, has created a new and powerful approach to representing and accessing data. Why? Because it combines the best that humans and computers can do.

With automated visual database systems we can directly relate the real world to models of the real world. We can combine the computer's superior capability to store, index, sort, select, search, and display with the human's superior capability to visually scan a limited set of organized data and, accordingly, accurately and rapidly select the information required. Think what it would take to configure a computer system to rapidly scan a set of articles, notes, and images—some printed, others hand scrawled, some high-quality images and others, rough sketched—select relevant materials, and discard the balance. With *Filevision*, the computer contains both information and images and displays the location of the records or objects of interest. With the image in mind, we can locate things very rapidly. Automated visual database systems are like navigation systems, broadly applied.

10.4 FILEVISION

Filevision has been described as a graphics-oriented information manager. The creators of *Filevision*, Telos Software Products (Santa Monica, CA), refer to it as "the fine art of filing by pictures," and to those who use it as "Filevisionaries."

---

* Manual filing systems in file cabinets are difficult to use because they do not allow for the scanning provided by the banker box system. This is not a trivial difference. File cabinets hide data; open libraries reveal it.

The concept is simple and the applications are many. Interestingly enough, application is not immediately obvious. We are strongly left-hemisphere and linearly conditioned. Many of us think in words, not pictures, and applying *Filevision* requires a visual imagination. On first viewing *Filevision,* two colleagues and I felt that it was an interesting product, but none of us could imagine how it could be used in a creative manner! So much for imagination. Thinking visually, graphically, or wholistically requires exposure, training, practice, and time. Visually oriented systems facilitate that learning.

Filevision is made possible only by the recent developments in microcomputer capabilities; namely, more powerful CPUs, larger memories, improved dot-addressable graphics monitors, and lower costs. *Filevision* functions only on the Apple Macintosh.

Telos programmers Howard Metcalfe and Howard Marantz, beginning in 1982, attempted to develop an earlier version called Geo-file for the Apple II. Metcalfe's original concept stemmed from his interest in history and a desire to display maps, the locations of different historical events, and link that visual data to information on the different historical sites. It could not be done so as to satisfy the requirements for an easy-to-use and powerful system. Microcomputer capabilities had to catch up with the imagination of systems designers. This occurred soon after with the appearance of the Apple Macintosh and its M68000 chip, superior graphics, and improved person-computer connection.

A list of applications where the graphics and file management capabilities of *Filevision* have been found to be useful is given in Exhibit 10.2.

- **Cable TV companies** map territories
- **Product sales managers** track their territories and salespeople
- **Delivery persons** map their routes and customers
- **City planners** track census and other demographic data
- **Franchise and chain stores** plan locations and sales territories
- **Electric companies** display power substations and transformers
- **Fire stations** record location information for display
- **Property management companies** track units
- **Systems analysts** display analyses and design diagrams
- **Photography studios** display steps in production process
- **Television studios** track ratings by county for program planning
- **County offices** locate voter registration information
- **City transportation** maps routes with related problem reports
- **Warehouses** manage inventories
- **Newspapers** map routes and sales data
- **Speech therapists** teach phonemes showing actual tongue position
- **Weather stations** display weather patterns and gradients
- **Medical researchers** graph cell structures and cell growth
- **Teachers** diagram the body with bone, muscle, and organ overlays
- **Doctors** diagram the body with links to information on diseases and treatments
- **Hotels** plan reception and seating arrangements
- **Tourist companies** generate restaurant locations and pricing
- **Reservation offices** display sports, theater, and concert events

---

Exhibit 10.2: Applications for visual database

10.4-1 How filevision works

We continue with our example of the visual database. Exhibit 10.3 shows two folder icons, one of them marked "LIBRARY." We click twice on that icon using the mouse; it opens, and the icons of files created using *Filevision* appear as shown in Exhibit 10.4.

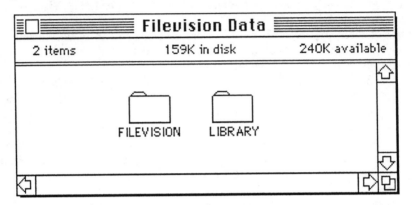

Exhibit 10.3: File folder icons on the *Filevision* data disk

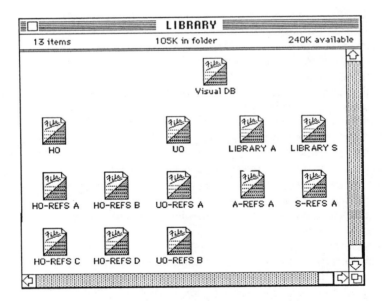

Exhibit 10.4: Files created using *Filevision* and arranged in hierarchical order

Each file contains an image, and data related to that image. The "Visual DB" at the top contains a map of the village where the author's offices at home ("HO" icon), at the university ("UO" icon), and the university arts library ("LIBRARY A" icon) and science library ("LIBRARY

S" icon) exist. These latter files contain layouts of these locations. Further, each of these locations contains various file cabinets and library shelves identified in the icons as "HO-REFS A", "HO-REFS B", and so on.

The village map is shown in Exhibit 10.5. Clicking on the office/library at home causes the home office to be displayed, as shown in Exhibit 10.6. In turn, clicking on the "Library A" icon causes the library shelves to be displayed, as shown in Exhibit 10.7. The large rectangles refer to shelves of texts, and the small rectangles to banker's boxes in the visual database.

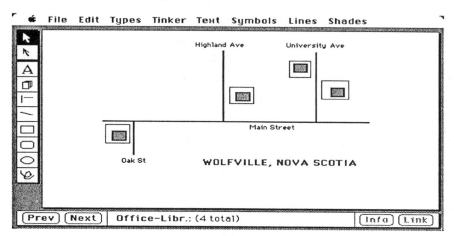

Exhibit 10.5: Map of the author's home village

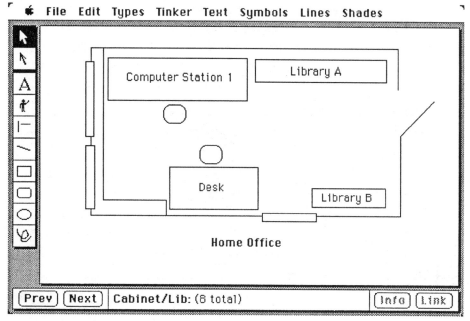

Exhibit 10.6: Office/library at home

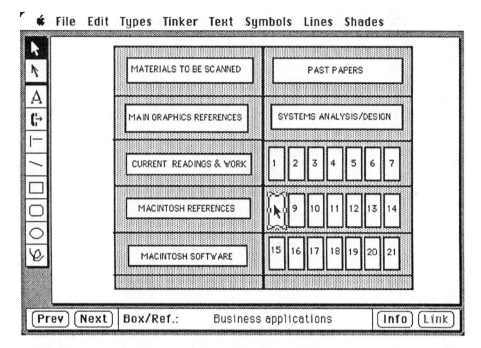

Exhibit 10.7: Library shelves in office at home

Going one level further, clicking on Box 8 in the library identified as "Business Applications," and then clicking in the "Info" button in the lower right corner of the screen causes the file record to be displayed, as shown in Exhibit 10.8. The references contained in Box 8 are listed in the record. The design of the fields contained in the records used in *Filevision* is under the direct control of the user.

Name	Business Applications: Macintosh & IBM	Link
Ref 1	MSChart review: Mac Buyer's Guide, Spring, 1985	
Ref 2	Excel reviews: several—plus references to use	
Ref 3	Lambert, S. Presentation Graphics on the Macintosh	
Ref 4	Filevision reviews and updates to system	
Ref 5	ChartMaster review	
Ref 6	Charts Unlimited product description	
Ref 7	Add-ons to Lotus 1-2-3	

Exhibit 10.8: References contained in banker box 8 in library at home

10.4-2 Selecting, reporting, and printing information

By using the various commands contained in the pull-down menus, the user can readily navigate through a visual database, adding, editing, selecting, and printing various data and information. For example, it is possible to highlight icons in images based on given criteria. This is illustrated using an example application, slightly modified, provided by *Filevision*. Exhibit 10.9 shows a map of the United States and the office locations for some imaginary service company.

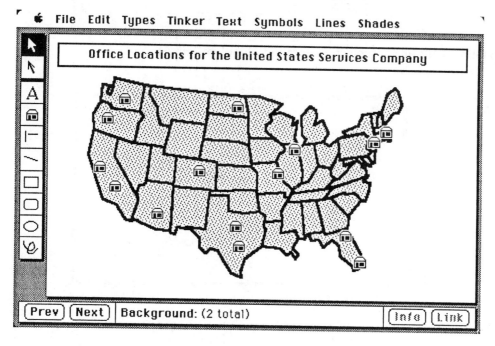

Exhibit 10.9: Office locations for service company in the United States

Exhibit 10.10 shows the selection screen provided in *Filevision* and a request made, namely, highlight "States" where the 1984 population was equal to or exceeded 8 million. The resulting display is shown in Exhibit 10.11.

We can select other information for display. Exhibit 10.12 shows a request to highlight "Offices" where revenues in 1984 were equal to or greater than 10 million dollars. The resulting display is shown in Exhibit 10.13.

All images can be printed, and various reports are possible. Exhibit 10.14 lists the office locations and revenues for 1984.

10.4-3 Limitations

There are limitations, as with all software. However, some limitations are overcome by Filevision's ability to work with other programs (described in the next section 10.4-4). In

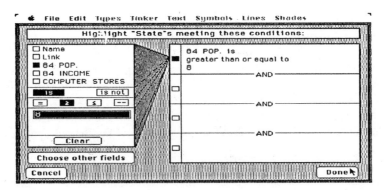

Exhibit 10.10: Report selection screen to highlight states

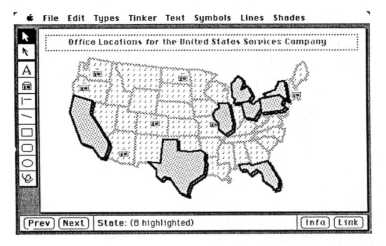

Exhibit 10.11: States highlighted with populations exceeding 8 million

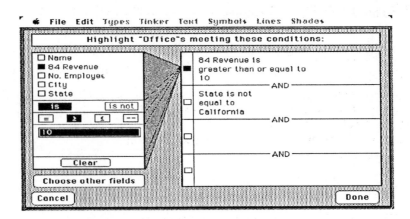

Exhibit 10.12: Report selection screen to highlight offices

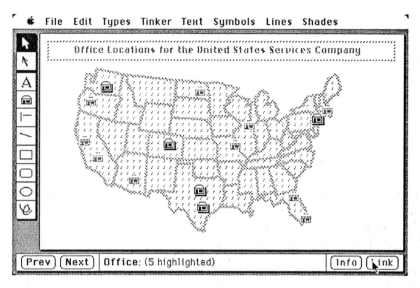

Exhibit 10.13: Offices highlighted with revenues exceeding 10 million

Name	State	84 Revenue
Princeton	NY	43.3
Middleton	CO	27.3
Dallas	TX	15.8
Garrington	TX	14.0
Simpton	WA	11.6
Railton	OR	9.0
Northington	FL	8.7
Harriston	MA	4.2
Tarriton	CA	4.2
Larrington	IL	4.1
Fankinton	CA	3.6
Winington	FL	2.6
Erickson	AZ	1.1
Killington	ND	0.9
Jacksington	MO	0.6

Exhibit 10.14: 1984 Revenues by office locations—in millions

Filevision it is *not* possible to store publisher's information in one file, and reference information in another, and relate the two sets of information through some common entry in all the records, for example, a publisher's code. That is, *Filevision* is not a relational database. (Telos does not claim that it is; see Chapter 14 for a discussion of relational database.) This limitation can be overcome by using *Filevision* in conjunction with a relational database. Cost may become a factor.

Another limitation is somewhat more serious. As with all data, it is important to download work in progress frequently. Otherwise a power loss or a system crash will lead to the loss of all the work since the last save. It appears, however, that a power loss with Filevision can be more damaging; a power loss may prevent the file from being reopened. No utility is provided for recovering damaged files.*

10.4-4 Capabilities

Business Filevision is a more serious version of the system. Capabilities include up to 32,000 records per file and a 4 megabyte file size, computed fields, automatic data entry and formatting, full 8 inch by 10 inch drawing area, custom forms, reports, and labels, combined text and graphics output, total and subtotal statistics (counts, sums, averages, running totals), mailmerge capabilities, and good search-and-sort capabilities.

An important capability has been added by an *Import/Export Data Exchange Utility* from Telos. This utility allows *Filevision* to work with a number of other applications including word processors (*MacWrite* and others), other file and database systems (*Odesta Helix, Omnis, OverVUE, MSFile, PFS:File*), electronic spreadsheets (*Multiplan*), and integrated systems (*Excel, Jazz*).

Templates of applications developed in *Filevision* are available from Telos. They include a system for developing instructional materials; science templates in astronomy, geography, history, physics, chemistry, biology, and physiology; time and billing; mapping; and a video production planner. A large library of public domain applications is also available from Telos.

A unique application is presented in Exhibits 10.15 through 10.21 created by Gary Himes of the Arizona Department of Transportation. The application consists of the mapping of airport locations in Arizona, and the storing of related data. The application opens with a view of the universe (Exhibit 10.15). The user first selects the earth's galaxy. Then a link to the next image in 10.16 occurs, where a click on the U.S.A. presents a map of the states (Exhibit 10.17).

A click on the state of Arizona and the link button reveals a map of airports in Arizona (Exhibit 10.18). From here one can descend to the layout of each airport (Exhibit 10.19), then to the specific hanger location (Exhibit 10.20), and then obtain related owner information (Exhibit 10.21). Creative systems like *Filevision* do not automatically lead to creative applications; they do, however, spark a lot of creativity in creative people, as this application well demonstrates.

10.5 MICROSOFT FILE

Our discussion of *MicroSoft File*, or *MSFile*, is not as extensive. Its graphics capabilities are less than Filevision's. *MSFile* is closer to the usual file manager available for small computers. Its one

---

* A representative of Telos Software explained that *Filevision* does not keep track of all data entries made because it would considerably slow operation. If incorrect data does happen to enter the file unchecked, then it is possible that *Filevision*, when it next goes to open that file, may not be able to open it. This is not as serious as it sounds if backups of files are made often. However, a utility program that allows the user to recover as much of the data in a damaged file or disk as possible, and transfer the recovered data to a new file, would be helpful.

Exhibit 10.15: View of the universe

Exhibit 10.16: View of earth

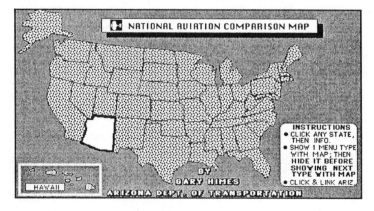

Exhibit 10.17: Major airports in the United States

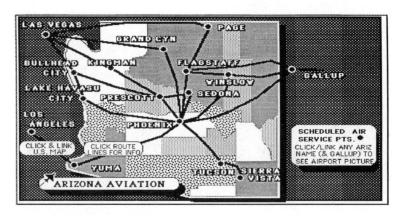

Exhibit 10.18: Air service in Arizona

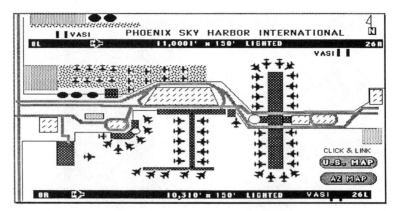

Exhibit 10.19: View of Phoenix Sky Harbor International Airport

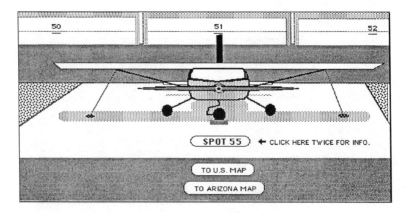

Exhibit 10.20: Specific hangar location at airport

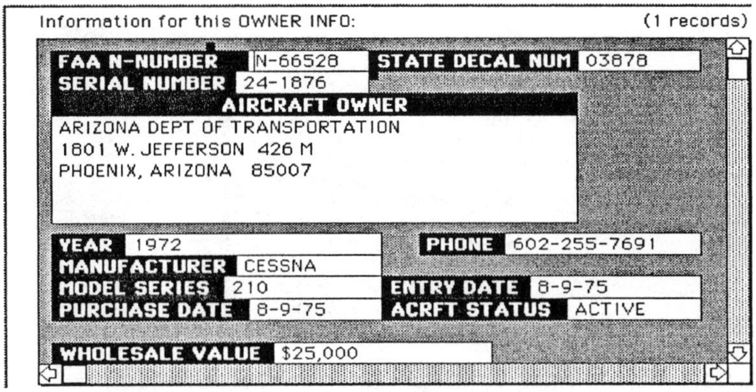

Exhibit 10.21: Aircraft owner information

distinction that calls for its inclusion here is that *MSFile* includes an additional and, for business-oriented file and database managers, an unusual data type: images. Images stored in *MSFile* are created outside *MSFile* using one of the available drawing programs such as MacPaint, MacDraw, or Chart. Then the image is pasted into a picture field in an *MSFile* record. *MSFile* does not possess any internal image creating capabilities such as those belonging to *Filevision*. Further, images cannot be related in a hierarchical nested fashion, as they can in *Filevision*. *MSFile*'s treatment of images is simply as an additional data item in a file. This can serve some important data capture and display needs.

Applications include the storage of images to increase communication impact. Graphics data items stored in different records may be included in printed reports, like any other item of data. An example provided by MicroSoft is the "*" assigned to restaurants to indicate level of recommendation, and "$" signs to indicate price levels. Exhibit 10.22 shows the records for two restaurants. In the first record, the use of images enhances communication impact in comparison to their absence in the second record.

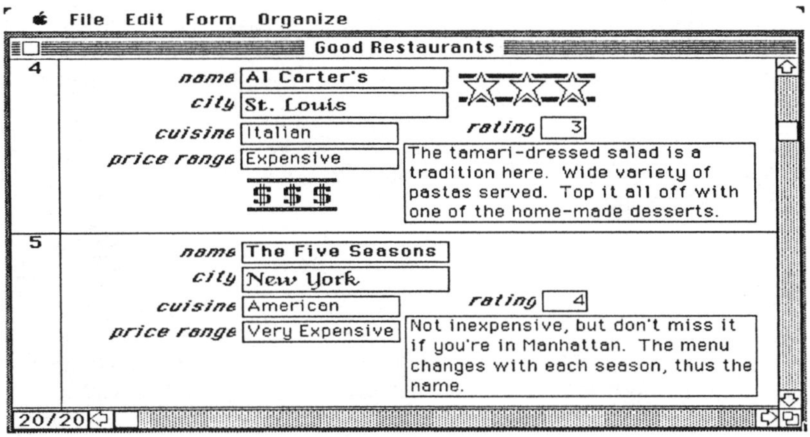

Exhibit 10.22: Records for two restaurants

CITY	NAME	stars	price range picture
Acapulco	Whitebeard's	⭐⭐	$ $
Chicago	A Bakery	⭐⭐	$ $
Miami Beach	Jill's Stone Crab	⭐⭐⭐⭐	$ $
Phoenix	The Golden Crow	⭐⭐⭐⭐	$ $
St. Louis	Henry VII Restaurant	⭐⭐	$ $
Vancouver, B.C	The Sea House	⭐⭐	$ $

Exhibit 10.23: Restaurants selected for good food at modest cost

Exhibit 10.23 shows a report using the graphics data from the same file of records. The author would have chosen simpler icons for the star ratings and price levels. Simplicity communicates better.

Other applications include

- The display of the floor plans of rental units
- Maps showing property locations in real estate listings
- Digitized images of properties
- Digitized images of employees in employee records
- Icons of items in inventory

An example record for a real estate listing is shown in Exhibit 10.24. Data in *MSFile* can be stored as lists or in a free form created by the user. The two formats lend themselves to different reporting; lists to a table form with total, subtotals, and other computed data displayed, and the free form to selected record display.

MSFile will compute sums, averages, counts, and standard deviations. *MSFile* readily interfaces to other applications, especially its sister products from MicroSoft such as Word, Multiplan, and Chart. One valuable feature when entering data is the ability to copy data from selected fields in the previous record to the record being entered. This can save considerable time. *MSFile's* reporting capabilities are quite extensive and will allow the user to define formats and summary fields, make selections using Boolean operators, use wild card symbols for making selections, and save report formats for later use.

10.6 CONCLUSION

Graphics database systems arouse the perceptual brain, provide a means for seeing patterns, allow for rapid and intuitive information selection (namely, by pointing), and are now a powerful computer graphics tool available to a broad range of users. We can expect to see a growth in these type of tools. They will enhance our ability to organize and perceive more wholistically.

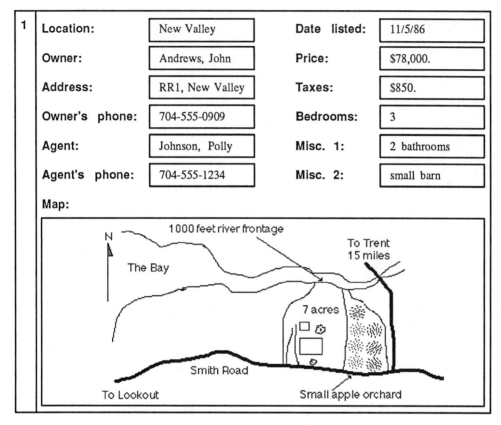

Exhibit 10.24: A record from a real estate listing application of *MSFile*

11

Project Management

11.1 INTRODUCTION

A project is a small or large job or task that can be subdivided into a sequence of subtasks. These tasks take time, consume resources, need people, and cost money. A project's success depends upon accurate anticipation of the tasks required, careful task sequencing, defining needed resources, tracking of past performance, monitoring of future steps, and effective action when actual expenditures of time, labor, resources, and money differ from those projected.

The purpose of project management systems is to plan, control, and communicate projects. The projects can vary in content or aim—establish a new venture, design a new product, plan a winning strategy—but the same purposes apply.

Sometimes the last purpose, communication, seems to be forgotten when it comes to the design and implementation of project management systems on computer. Graphics is the key. James Halcomb, an expert on project control, calls project management systems "a way of authoring destiny" (Shea, 1984). In most business situations, destiny is authored not by one manager but by many in concert, and the graphic diagrams produced by a project management system help build rapid consensus. If the system lacks good graphics, then communication and consensus are hampered.

The use of project management systems on computer requires some knowledge of project management itself. In this chapter we will discuss the goals and tools of project management in business, with an emphasis on the graphics techniques used. We will discuss the major functions performed by project management systems, illustrate project management using *MacProject* on the Apple Macintosh, and discuss some other systems that function on the IBM PC.

11.2 TWO CHART METHODS

Two major graphic methods used in project management are the *Gantt chart* and the *network diagram.*

The Gantt chart is a horizontal bar chart used to plot *activities* on its vertical axis and *progress* or lack of progress on the horizontal axis. In this type of application, a blank bar shows *scheduled progress*, and a shaded bar shows *actual progress.*

Another use of the chart is to plot the *critical activities* —activities which must be completed on time—and the *slack time*, that is, additional time available for given tasks that, if used, will not cause any delay in the completion of the project. A Gantt chart is shown in Exhibit 11.12.

The Gantt chart is a suitable method to use when there are a relatively few tasks to track. However, when there are many tasks, the method becomes unwieldy and we would use the method described next as the primary planning tool.

The *network diagram* is a planning chart used in the *Critical Path Method (CPM)*, and the *Program Evaluation and Review Technique (PERT).* The network diagram, sometimes called the *CPM/PERT Chart,* is a very good way of showing a comprehensive picture of a project involving many subtasks. The network diagram shows the following:

- *Tasks* and their sequence required to complete a project
- *Milestones*, the major events that indicate progress
- *The critical path*, the path formed by tasks for which there can be no delay in
  completion

The network may also show other subsidiary information, such as the dates when tasks are scheduled to begin, the latest dates tasks can begin without causing a delay in the scheduled completion, and the persons primarily responsible for given tasks.

11.3 A BUSINESS EXAMPLE

Let us assume we are faced with establishing a new venture, a library of software and systems on the microcomputer level. The library will function very similarly to a public library with the exception that all resources are used on-site or through some form of telecommunications hookup from remote locations.

Our potential clients are corporations, small businesses, and professionals, all seeking small systems and wishing to evaluate them before purchasing or leasing. Other clients of the library would be systems analysts and computer consultants.

We have developed an expert system that allows clients to evaluate computer systems and software in relation to their specific needs. The expert system functions like a navigation system, based on a large database of information on software and systems, and on the needs of clients. From the intersection of these two coordinates, clients needs and the systems and/or software available, relevant software and systems are rapidly identified. Following this identification, clients would then be able to test the software and systems in the library.

The details of the expert system are not of critical importance in our project management example. Let us assume that it works and that we want to build our business around the software and the operation of the library. There are major areas that we need to plan. They include:

- Prepare business plan
- Establish corporate structure
- Prepare a proposal and presentation to venture capital
- Establish roles of active principals
- Develop commercial software from prototype systems
- Hire key personnel
- Plan and initiate public relations work and marketing
- Establish a location

The above is not meant to be exhaustive. The list, from the viewpoint of the principals involved in this venture, lends itself to a *high level project management network diagram* as shown in Exhibit 11.1.

The tasks in this case are major areas of activity with many subtasks. The network diagram shows the sequence of tasks, the start date for each task, the number of days assigned to each task, and the major person responsible for a given task area. The dark boxes and lines show the critical path. Any delay in any of the tasks on this path and the whole project or venture is delayed. The rounded boxes show *milestones*, in this case only two, the beginning and the end.

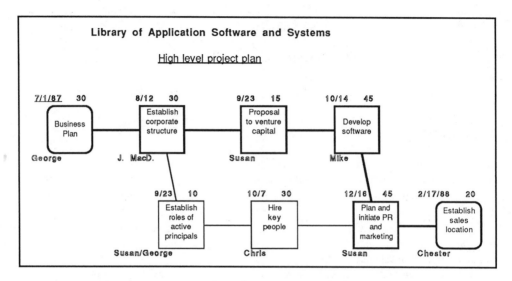

Exhibit 11.1: High level project management network

11.3-1 Defining operation

We have a choice as to what information to show in the network display. Exhibit 11.2 shows the menu of choices available.

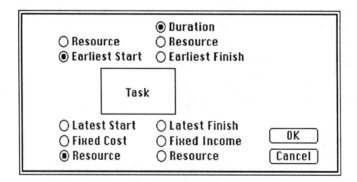

Exhibit 11.2: Network information display choices

Note that "earliest start" appears in the upper left of the task box, duration in the upper right, and resource in the lower left. In Exhibit 11.3 the project duration scale menu is shown. With this system we could track projects in minutes! We have chosen days.

Project Duration Scale. Set the time interval
for the duration and date display:
- ○ Minute
- ○ Hour
- ● Day
- ○ Week
- ○ Month

[OK]
[Cancel]

Exhibit 11.3: Project time duration choices

11.3-2 A top-down approach

It is valuable to take a top-down approach to project management. We use a hierarchical approach when analyzing systems (see Chapter 15), in writing (see *ThinkTank* discussed in Chapter 12), and in programming (see Chapter 14). It serves a similar purpose in project management, namely, modularity and a step-by-step refinement, or detailing, of tasks required.

Let us demonstrate additional features of project management and the use of graphics by looking at the subtasks required in order to develop the software. Exhibit 11.4 shows the network diagram generated. It is an expansion of the box labeled "Develop software" in Exhibit 11.1.

Arriving at a clear PERT chart or network diagram takes some thought. An automated project management system with a good user interface and superior graphics facilitates clear thinking. A bad user interface and poor graphics hinder clear thinking. For example, an earlier version of part of the final network is shown in Exhibit 11.6 on page 267, with recommended changes so that

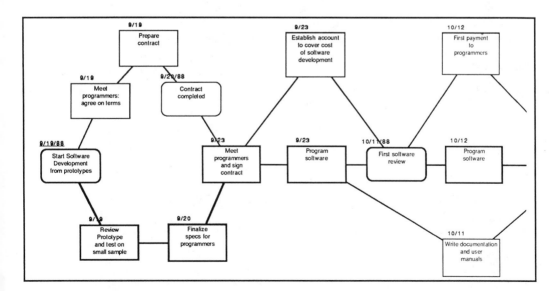

Exhibit 11.4: Schedule network chart for developing software

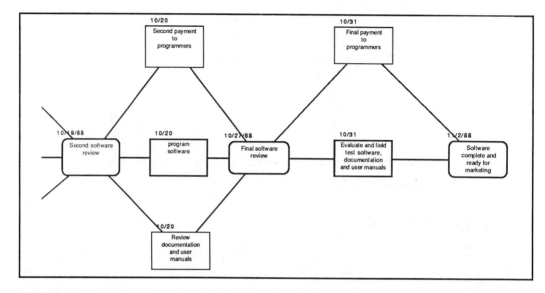

Exhibit 11.4: Schedule network chart for developing software (Continued)

documentation dovetails, as it should, with product development. Making this modification to the network diagram takes a few minutes, and *all other data files are automatically updated by the system.*

11.3-3 Support visuals

The screen is a window which may display only part of the total network. *MacProject* allows the user to view the structure of the total network as shown in Exhibit 11.5.

Further, we can print the network sideways on the paper, which allows us to draw networks of some considerable size. It might be wiser to avoid diagrams that are too big and use the top-down approach suggested. Exhibit 11.7 shows two examples of the chart size menu, and how our present project network would appear if it was a part of a six-page drawing in landscape versus portrait orientation. In the chart size menu, each block represents an amount of working space equal to an 8-1/2 inch by 11 inch sheet of paper.

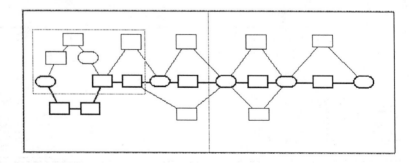

Exhibit 11.5: View of total network

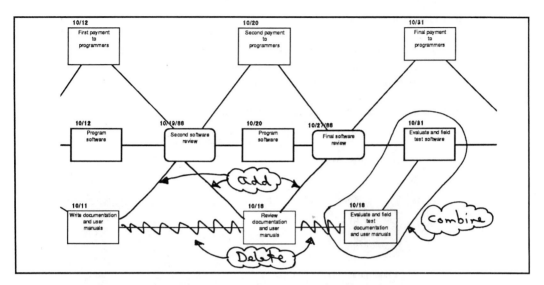

Exhibit 11.6: Earlier schedule network chart with changes indicated

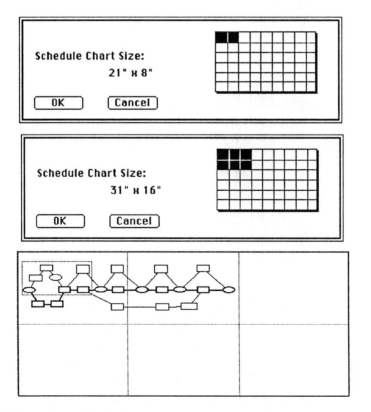

Exhibit 11.7: Choosing a chart size

11.3-4 Entering time frames

We need to specify the number of hours in a workday, and the calendar range, that is, the month and year in which the project is expected to start. Exhibit 11.8 shows the menu used here. We have chosen a 9 to 5 workday, and expect the work to occur in 1988.

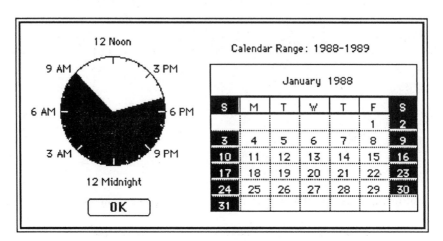

Exhibit 11.8: Establishing the workday and calendar range

11.3-5 Entering resource costs

MacProject provides two tables, one to enter fixed costs and the other to enter labor and other variable resource costs. The variable cost table is displayed in Exhibit 11.9; the fixed cost data entry table is *not* shown.

	Resource Name	Cost/Day	Accrual Method
1	George	600.00	Multiple
2	Mike	200.00	Multiple
3	John	200.00	Multiple
4	J. MacD.	600.00	Multiple
5	Susan	300.00	Multiple
6	Chris	250.00	Multiple
7	Chester	150.00	Multiple

Exhibit 11.9: Data entry screen for variable costs (In our example project, we have only used labor as a variable cost category.)

11.3-6 Assigning time and resources

Tasks, and sometimes milestones, use time and consume resources. Exhibit 11.10 shows the screen for making these entries along with the relevant part of the network. The relevant task is highlighted in the network window as the data related to that task is entered into the task information window.

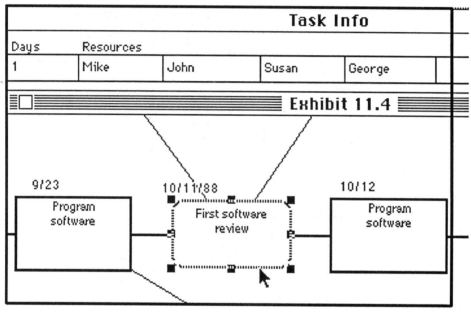

Exhibit 11.10: Entering task information

11.3-7 Other reports

After the network has been drawn, four other reports are automatically created:

- Task Gantt Chart
- Resource Gantt Chart
- Cash Flow Chart
- Project Table

Exhibit 11.11 shows the project schedule from the point of view of the task assignments. Mike is obviously facing a more critical time schedule than George. Critical time frames are shown as open bars, and slack time as gray bars. In Exhibit 11.11, we can see immediately that *reviewing the prototype, developing the final specs, programming the software,* and *reviewing the software* are the critical tasks.

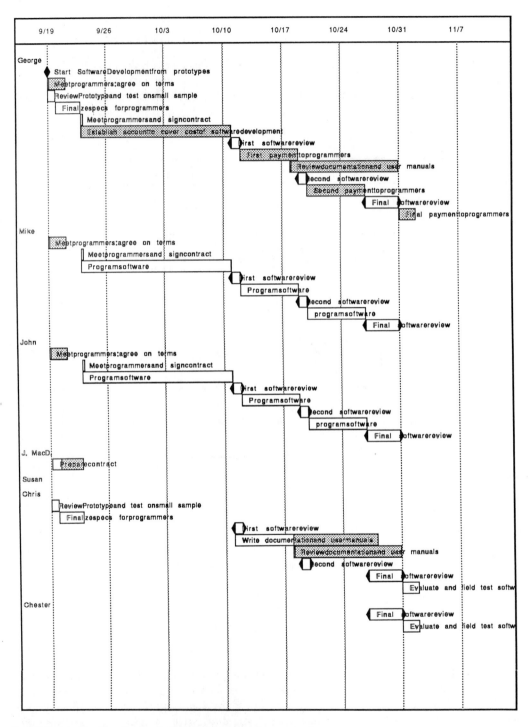

Exhibit 11.11: Gantt chart showing tasks by people

The Cash Flow in Exhibit 11.12 reports on the disbursement of funds across time, both incremental and cumulative.

Starting	Costs	Income	Ending	Cumulative
9/19/88	6300.00	0.00	9/26/88	-6300.00
9/26/88	2000.00	0.00	10/3/88	-8300.00
10/3/88	2000.00	0.00	10/10/88	-10300.00
10/10/88	4443.75	0.00	10/17/88	-14743.75
10/17/88	3631.25	0.00	10/24/88	-18375.00
10/24/88	3875.00	0.00	10/31/88	-22250.00
10/31/88	2050.00	0.00	11/7/88	-24300.00

Exhibit 11.12: Cash flow for software development

The Project Detail in Exhibit 11.13 shows all the information a *MacProject* document contains about a project. The dates refer to the scheduled start date (*Earliest Start*), earliest expected finish date for each task (*Earliest Finish*), the latest date a task can start without causing delay (*Latest Start*), and the latest finish date for each task without causing delay (*Latest Finish*).

	Task Name	Days	Earliest Start	Earliest Finish	Latest Start	Latest Finish	Fixed Cost	Resource Cost
1	Start Software Development	0	9/19/88	9/19/88	9/19/88	9/19/88	0	0
2	Meet programmers: agree on	0.50	9/19/88	9/19/88	9/21/88	9/21/88	0	500
3	Review Prototype and test	1	9/19/88	9/20/88	9/19/88	9/20/88	500	850
4	Prepare contract	1.25	9/19/88	9/20/88	9/21/88	9/23/88	0	750
5	Contract completed	0	9/20/88	9/20/88	9/23/88	9/23/88	0	0
6	Finalize specs for	3	9/20/88	9/23/88	9/20/88	9/23/88	100	2550
7	Meet programmers and sign	0.12	9/23/88	9/23/88	9/23/88	9/23/88	0	125
8	Establish account to cover cost of	0.12	9/23/88	9/23/88	10/11/88	10/11/88	0	75
9	Program software	12	9/23/88	10/11/88	9/23/88	10/11/88	500	4800
10	First software review	1	10/11/88	10/12/88	10/11/88	10/12/88	0	1300
11	First payment to programmers	0.12	10/12/88	10/12/88	10/19/88	10/19/88	0	75
12	Write documentation and user	5	10/11/88	10/18/88	10/21/88	10/28/88	500	1250
13	Program software	5	10/12/88	10/19/88	10/12/88	10/19/88	0	2000
14	Second software review	1	10/19/88	10/20/88	10/19/88	10/20/88	0	1250
15	Second payment to programmers	0.12	10/20/88	10/20/88	10/27/88	10/27/88	0	75
16	Program software	5	10/20/88	10/27/88	10/20/88	10/27/88	0	2000
17	Review documentation and user	0.50	10/18/88	10/18/88	10/28/88	10/31/88	0	425
18	Final software review	2	10/27/88	10/31/88	10/27/88	10/31/88	0	2800
19	Evaluate and field test	0	10/18/88	10/18/88	10/31/88	10/31/88	0	0
20	Evaluate and field test	2	10/31/88	11/2/88	10/31/88	11/2/88	1000	800
21	Final payment to programmers	0.12	10/31/88	10/31/88	11/2/88	11/2/88	0	75
22	Software complete and	0	11/2/88	11/2/88	11/2/88	11/2/88	0	0

Exhibit 11.13: Project table showing all the information in a MacProject file (additional columns *not* shown include fixed income figures, and names of resources)

11.4 THINKING VISUALLY

Both the use and report functions of *MacProject* are highly graphic. It is possible to become an expert on the use of *MacProject* in less than two days. Very few applications will allow such rapid learning. The good use of graphics, the excellent integration of software and system, and the excellent integration of the different modules of the program itself all contribute to this effect.

A project management system that is graphic functions in an opposite manner to an electronic spreadsheet. With the project manager, we draw the network chart and the system generates the data. With the ESS, we enter data and, if the spreadsheet interfaces with a presentation graphics system, the system draws the charts. This distinction is illustrated in Exhibit 11.14.*

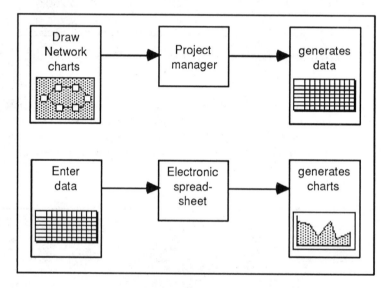

Exhibit 11.14: Project managers and electronic spreadsheets

With graphics-oriented systems we are given the opportunity to think visually. This takes practice, but it has decided advantages; relations between project components can be readily seen. In fact, we would not use terms like "components" and "seen" if we could not diagram and chart the abstract qualities of time, effort, resource expenditure, and goals reached. The concrete picture allows us to see when things are not in the proper place or sequence. The error portrayed in Exhibit 11.6 on page 267 was caught in this manner.

---

* Project management can also be conducted using other classes of software, including the electronic spreadsheet (ESS), and the idea outliner (see Chapter 12); in fact, we could use the word processor for very simple projects. Since the ESS allows us to define the rows, columns, and cells in any manner needed, we can define the columns in terms of some time frame (days, weeks), and use the rows to define tasks. An idea outliner is a useful alternative, especially for modest and small projects. The major headings can be milestones, the subtopics beneath each major heading become people, and sub-subtopics become tasks. The listed order could reflect time frame.

11.5 PROJECT MANAGEMENT ON THE IBM PC

The project management systems that function on the IBM are limited by the lack of graphics capabilities in the basic IBM PC system. Graphics may be added to the basic IBM PC unit, but none of the project managers reviewed extensively, namely *Advanced PRO-ject 6*, *Harvard Project Manager*, and *MicroSoft Project*, are configured to work with graphics. The reports from all three of these systems, since they work with *character-addressable* rather than *dot-addressable* systems, can only portray characters. In other words, in order to be used on the widest number of available IBM PC systems, the designers of these programs have chosen the lowest common denominator as the criterion for design. In reviewing briefly a number of other project managers for the IBM PC including TIMELINE from Breakthrough Software (Novato, CA), *SuperProject* from Computer Associates (San Jose, CA), and the *Project Scheduler Network* from Scitor Corporation (Foster City, CA) reveals that only the latter is written to take advantage of the IBM PC graphics adaptor and, therefore, displays superior charts. Exhibit 11.15 and 11.16 show small samples of output from the *Project Scheduler Network* with graphics, and *SuperProject* without graphics, respectively. Graphics are obviously superior to nongraphics. The graphics on the IBM PC lack the crispness of the graphics on the Apple Macintosh, but are able to take advantage of color.

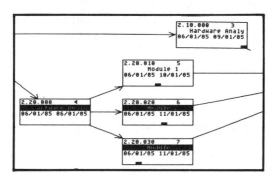

Exhibit 11.15: Project management on the IBM PC with graphics (Courtesy of Scitor Corporation)

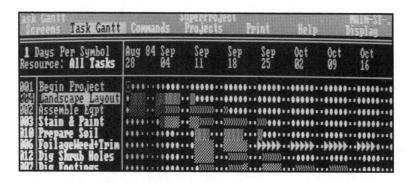

Exhibit 11.16: Project management on the IBM PC without graphics
(Courtesy of Computer Associates International, Inc.)

The differences in clarity and communication are obvious. The lack of graphics is a decided disadvantage for otherwise perfectly fine project management systems. Either the network diagram is bypassed completely, or it is of poor quality. For example, the critical path is often shown on the Gantt chart by the use of a different character, an "=" versus a "-", which has poor visual impact. None of these problems can exist on the Macintosh because its basic design includes graphics.

11.6 SYSTEMS OR SOFTWARE FIRST?

We are admonished by systems analysis sages that one must choose software before systems. This is no longer true. The first three named project management systems above were carefully compared. It took 100 hours to become familiar with the programs, make an evaluation and comparison, and write up a report. Following this fairly extensive exposure to these three systems on the IBM, the researcher* benchmarking the IBM-based systems was shown *MacProject* on the Macintosh. Immediately a new standard of excellence was established in the researcher's mind. Now the three project managers on the IBM, although quite excellent programs, appeared mediocre. The change in operating environment allows the functioning of applications to be experienced completely different. All three of the project managers, in a Macintosh-like environment, would be far superior products. The adage to choose software applications first and then the system has been rendered false by environments that dramatically improve application functioning. Obviously, if certain critical features do *not* exist in a given package, then, regardless of the system it functions on, it is not adequate. The point remains: project management on *non*graphics computers is inferior to project management on graphics computers.

11.7 SIMPLE AND SOPHISTICATED FEATURES

Although we have waxed poetic about the Apple Macintosh and *MacProject*, they are not without their limitations from a project management point of view. MacProject was not intended to be a complete system (which might cost 20 times as much). A system like *Primavera* that functions on the IBM PC XT is much more complete and costs much more.

There are three broad categories of features a project management system may possess:

- *Project Planning* is the process of setting up steps to do a job.
- *Project Monitoring* is the monitoring of how the job is going.
- *Project Tracking* is the close tracking of what is happening so that changes can be made and the project rapidly redirected.

11.7-1 Project planning features

Planning is a key feature of project management; therefore, the software must be capable of this. Some systems that support good planning, however, do not support good monitoring or tracking. On the planning level the following features should be available:

---

* The author would like to thank Mr. Edward Violette for his report on the IBM-based systems.

• Project Calendar

Tracking tasks over time is essential. Different programs allow for different time units; some will automatically adjust for weekends and holidays, others will allow for different time frames for different resources (accountants who work 9 to 5, and programmers who work all hours imaginable).

• Task Definition

Tasks differ. Some take time; others do not. Some consume resources and cost money; others do not. For example, "Waiting for Vendor's Response" takes time but costs nothing. "Proposal Completed," a milestone, takes neither time nor money. The assigning of resources differs from system to system. Some assume that resources are scarce, and the specified amount of resources assigned to a task determines the duration of a task. Other systems assume resources are plentiful, and the specified duration of a task determines the amount of resources assigned. Complex projects may involve subordinate plans, called "second level" tasks. The overall plan may specify second level plans only and the second level plans specify the tasks. Some project management systems lend themselves to this kind of level planning; others do not. We demonstrated second level planning when we discussed a top-down approach.

• Task Sequence

Tasks may start on a specified date or be triggered by other tasks or events. For example, "Build the Stairs" would be triggered by the task "Take Delivery of the Lumber." The latter is known as a *Prerequisite Task*. Some systems allow for only one prerequisite task; others allow for several, or even partially completed tasks to act as triggers, for example, the testing of a program upon partial completion.

• Resource Definition

Resources are assigned to projects and tasks within projects. Different systems allow for different numbers of resources to be assigned. If there is competition for limited resources between tasks, some more sophisticated systems allow for *Resource Leveling*, which adjusts the project schedule to allow enough time and resources for all tasks. The ideal for most projects is a slow build-up of resources with demand followed by a smooth cutback as the project draws to a close. Leveling algorithms reschedule a project's noncritical activities, that is, those with slack time, in order to come as close to this "S" curve of manpower across time as possible. Thus the algorithm is called *Resource Leveling*. This is to avoid people being assigned to projects faster than they can be assigned to tasks, or not being available when needed (Strehlo, *Personal Computing*, January, 1984).

• Cost Definition

The two categories of costs, fixed and variable, are assigned across different tasks on the basis of resource use. Each resource has its own charge rate. Some systems allow for rate changes during a project, and even inflation factors.

11.7-2 Project monitoring

Projects change, and the information in a system must be changed to reflect current status. Consider the following features:

- **Updating Project Information**

Insertion and deletion of tasks will invariably be necessary. Some systems will adjust the prerequisites. When resources and resource rates change, these must also be reflected in the project plan. Some systems will allow for resource redefinition and the creation of new resources. Calendars may need revision. Some systems allow for a change in the basic unit (hours to days).

- **Updating Task Information**

Information regarding task duration, start and end dates, and resources assigned may also require update. This is available with most project management systems.

11.7-3 Project tracking

Few systems on small computers have much in the way of project tracking. If they do, they are relatively expensive. The features in this area are as follow:

- **Resource Use**

Resources get used on tasks across time. Information by task, resource, and some small unit of time allows for an analysis of the cost of a resource for any given task.

- **Variance Reports**

A Variance Report is a way of seeing how well a project's progress matches against what was planned. For example, a rent increase is experienced in the middle of a project, or projected completion dates of tasks change based on actual delays.

11.8 SOME GUIDELINES TO USING PROJECT MANAGERS

Some guidelines to selecting and using project managers are given in Exhibit 11.17.

√ Do not choose a system that contains more features than you need.
√ Ensure that its operation is straightforward, obvious, easy to learn,
   easy to remember, and graphic.
√ Make rough sketches before you begin.
√ Take a top-down approach.
√ Keep layout as clean as possible.
√ Keep boxes a uniform size.
√ Draw all boxes and arrange them before connecting them.
√ Create concrete, brief, clear, and specific task and milestone descriptions.
√ Estimate time for tasks accurately: it affects everything else.
√ Display or project diagrams for superior communication and consensus.

Exhibit 11.17: Some guidelines

11.9 FUTURE OF PROJECT MANAGEMENT

The future of project management resides with the creative use of multiple technologies. For example, Dr. Boyd Paulson of Stanford University has developed a software system that maintains a file of data based on time lapse videotape of a particular construction job. A computer model of the operation is constructed from the data and studied and modified to see how the activities on the job could be improved to save resources, time, and money. Thus these types of methods go beyond merely keeping within some prescribed budget (Strehlo, 1984).

Another approach has been pioneered by the Japanese using real-time acquisition of on-site data. Paulson states: "They are designing the deep foundations of subway systems as they go. They monitor the alignment of a beam by optical means and use an a/d convertor to feed that into a desktop computer. If the beam alignment begins to go out of tolerance, that is, if it begins to yield too much, they simply shore up the beam as needed. It means there is no need to overdesign—they get close to the lowest possible cost without quality control problems." (Strehlo, 1984)

12

Computer Aided Publishing

12.1 INTRODUCTION

This chapter will discuss the shifting roles of the author and the publisher created by the new small computer technology; outline the traditional publishing cycle and compare it to a new alternate cycle; describe and compare a low cost and a high cost, microcomputer-based, writing and publishing system; and conclude with a brief discussion of applications and impacts.

Today the individual using a personal computer is able to be a publisher. From available software and hardware it is possible to assemble a user-friendly desktop system, at a cost as low as $10,000. With this system, we are able to store a library of text and graphics information, selectively and rapidly retrieve the text and images, integrate the text and images into page layouts, and produce near typeset quality camera-ready page proofs ready for reproduction.

Further, it is possible to operate a publishing business using the same system: perform accounting, plan and track marketing, promote mail-order, handle subscriptions, create mailings, and so forth. The availability of the microcomputer, low cost graphics, digitizing, and the desktop laser printer now make the production part possible; the business part has been available longer.

Will this development put traditional publishers and typographers out of business? Not at all. But it will increase the ability of the author to influence the design as well as the content of what gets published, increase the opportunity for the small business or enterprise to produce in-house publications at modest cost, and allow the individual and the small communities and networks of which he or she is a part to communicate and be heard through newsletters and newspapers.

The new technology supports (helped create?) a major trend: decentralization. The person as publisher is part of that decentralization. Naisbitt (1982) writes, "We now have 13,000 special interest magazines and no general purpose magazines." He further notes, "The new source of power is not money in the hands of a few but information in the hands of many."

In 1979 the *Point Reyes Light* won the Pulitzer Prize for public service, honoring its investigation of cultism at Synanon, the therapeutic community for drug addicts. The *Point Reyes Light* was a small operation made possible by computer technology. Computer aided photocomposition methods enabled the owners and their staff of one to prepare their own layouts and deliver them to a printing shop; they did not have to rely on expensive linotype equipment. In 1979 computer-technology provided the means for individuals and small groups to be heard. What was true in 1979 is even more true now.

12.2 SHIFTING ROLES

There are four basic stages in producing a book: *generate, design, print,* and *distribute.* Generation was always the province of the author and those who support the author in his efforts (secretaries, reviewers, editors). Now, design and format, and the preparation of camera-ready copy, is available to the author. Now, the author can generate, design, print and even distribute, by publishing electronically on-line, or making his text known via electronic bulletin boards.*

12.2-1 Traditional responsibilities

Traditionally, an author writing a book is responsible for producing a readable manuscript, a table of contents, an index, a glossary, pencil line sketches of drawings, and selecting photographs that might be included. However, the author is traditionally not responsible for—in fact, usually has no say in—artwork, page layout, font types, headers, use of white space, and design; all of the image qualities of a text which influence the impact of the message as much as the message itself. As we know, the structure of a page is as important for good communication as the content, and writers can now determine structure as well as content.

The last two basic stages, namely, printing and distribution, and related activities including binding, packaging, storage, publicity, and marketing, remain the province of the publisher. Text generation and design—the activities of authorship—are labor intensive and confined usually to the efforts of a few people. Printing, distribution, and marketing—the activities of publishing—are cost intensive, and require an extensive organization and a lot of people.

Authors and publishers are being provided with many automated tools that speed the process, from a gleam in the author's eye, to a fully born and distributed book. Writing a book, for example, might take two to five years using paper, pen, and/or a typewriter to prepare a completed manuscript, and nine to twenty-four months using a personal computer and a selected set of software, to complete the finished camera-ready copy. Finished camera-ready copy is much more than a completed manuscript; it is the book itself, ready for reproduction.

12.2-2 A metaphor for the new roles

Titles and roles adopted from the theater or film industry convey better the new functions of the writer and publisher. The *author becomes a director* with a set of automated resources available to him or her for producing a book; a "set," "stage crew," and "actors" of hardware, operating system, and integrated applications software. The author has available a production department on a desk; software for manipulating ideas, developing outlines, producing text and images, and then a final piece of software that allows for the integration of text and images into final camera-ready form. Much or all of this is accomplished without the benefit of drafting boards, light tables, parallel rules, electric erasers, manual paste-up, or typeset copy. Savings in the turn-around time for text production, labor, and costs are dramatic, ranging from 100 to 400 percent.

---

* One means by which authors can take over some of the marketing and distribution functions of publishers is when materials published are marketed via electronic bulletin boards; or are in electronic form, maintained in databanks, and accessed through terminals and computers. A recent newspaper article reported on an individual who was using electronic bulletin boards to sell his book. In a brief period of a few months, the individual had sold 7,000 copies to a potential market of 400,000 buyers, subscribers to the bulletin boards in the United States, Britain, and Canada. However, we will not use databanks and bulletin boards to read books, look at art masterpieces, or even search for the meaning of a word; databanks will be used for accessing current information, storing research documents, and to archive materials. Books will survive.

The *publisher becomes a producer*, the impressario who supports the director, owns the product, and knows how best to present and market the book. The publisher/producer, to an increasing extent, will become less and less involved with the technical production of the content and form of text pages (they will remain intimately involved in jacket design and production, book assembly, packaging, and so forth), except in one important but indirect way: the maintenance of standards of quality. As Strawhorn (1980) writes, "Most of them (publishers) are concerned with the establishment and preservation of quality in the system of formal communication. These contributions can probably not be replaced by authors and users acting on their own behalf."

12.3 THE TRADITIONAL CYCLE

It would not be atypical for an author to write the original text by hand, and then turn it over to a secretary for typing. The typed draft is then returned to the author for review and corrections. This process is repeated several times before an error-free document is produced. The completed document, along with any images required in the form of rough sketches and photographs, is sent to reviewers and copy editors. At this point, the overall design of the book is conceived by an expert in that field.

The edited manuscript showing corrections and suggestions is returned to the author for review and approval. Upon approval and return of the manuscript to the publisher, the document is typeset by a typographer using a monitor and a front-end computer system that controls the typesetter. From this process, galley sheets (an initial printout of the copy entered) are produced and sent to the author and editor for review and correction.

In the meantime, rough sketches of any drawings have been sent to a graphics art shop for the production of finished artwork by traditional drafting methods. In addition, any photographs required have been prepared in halftones suitable for reproduction. Then the text, line art, and photographs would be assembled into pages on boards using razor-blade and wax for photographing to prepare the master plates. Then the plates are used to produce the page proofs. These proofs are returned once again to the author for final review and correction. In the meantime, the art department of the publishing house has designed a cover, and possibly a jacket, for the text. The pages are reproduced, the cover is bound to the pages, copies are boxed and stored for distribution, and the book is ready to market and sell.

Automation can help at each stage of the cycle; CAD/CAM, for example, in the printing, collating, binding, boxing, storing, and other manufacturing processes. Here, however, we are concerned with that part of the cycle that affects the author.

In the traditional book production cycle, corrections or changes made at any point are tedious, and changes later in the process are very costly. However, if generation and design are automated, corrections and changes are electronic, and the automated system allows the user to see what the final pages will look like once printed, then errors are no longer a problem; they are simply a part of the development process. This is not a trivial difference; computers support a wide variety of creative approaches to writing (Marshall, 1984).

12.4 A NEW PUBLISHING CYCLE

The technology changes the manner in which printed materials are produced, and also creates new and important products (Strawhorn, 1980). The writer does not simply write a book when he is using a computer-publishing system. He or she creates a database of information that can be used to support a variety of writings and shared with other researchers and authors. Therefore, we can say that *when using computer-publishing systems, authors do not write books and articles as such, but they create both the structure and the content of organized databases of information—text and graphics—from which various publications are selectively created.*

Some computer-publishing systems now possess knowledge systems that help create graphics and documents; for example, automatic selection of colors that go together well, or automatic selection of image or document sizes appropriate for different media (overhead transparencies and slides). In the future, more systems will include electronic "colleagues" in the form of expert systems that help create the content and context of documents. We discuss future capabilities and impact in Chapter 16.

12.4-1 Function

In computers, the function or process is represented by the applications software being used. More than a word processor, the traditional tool of a writer using a computer is required. In fact, in the conception of the author as publisher as diagrammed in Exhibit 12.1, the word processor appears in a fourth stage following three other applications.

The boxes have been numbered for easy reference. The diagram is linear, but in reality applications are used in repetitive cycles. Boxes 1, 2, 3, and 4 represent *support functions,* and boxes 5, 6, 7, 8, 9, and 10 represent *production functions.* When the pressure of deadlines is felt, there is a tendency to bypass the support functions and jump right into production; it is a mistake, but sometimes an unavoidable reality.

12.4-2 Structure and content

Each application is provided with a *structure* by the author, and each application produces a particular kind of *content* related to that structure. For example, a database allows the author to establish the information stored on given entities (publishers, references, products, images), and how the information is retrieved and displayed. A brief discussion of the function of some specific applications programs in the context of an example will clarify our discussion. Exhibit 12.2 repeats the diagram of Exhibit 12.1, but with specific programs named and icons used to communicate their function.

12.5 EXAMPLE PROGRAMS

There are many programs that could have been selected for discussion; the author has chosen to discuss those used directly in his own work. Our example programs are the components for a low-end system; a high-end system is described later in this chapter.

12.5-1 On-line databanks

DIALOG (Lockheed Information Systems, Palo Alto, CA) is one of a number of databanks available. Others include *BRS* (BRS, Latham, NY), and *NLM* (National Library of Medicine, Bethesda, MD). Databanks of information are being created in all fields, archaeology to zoology;

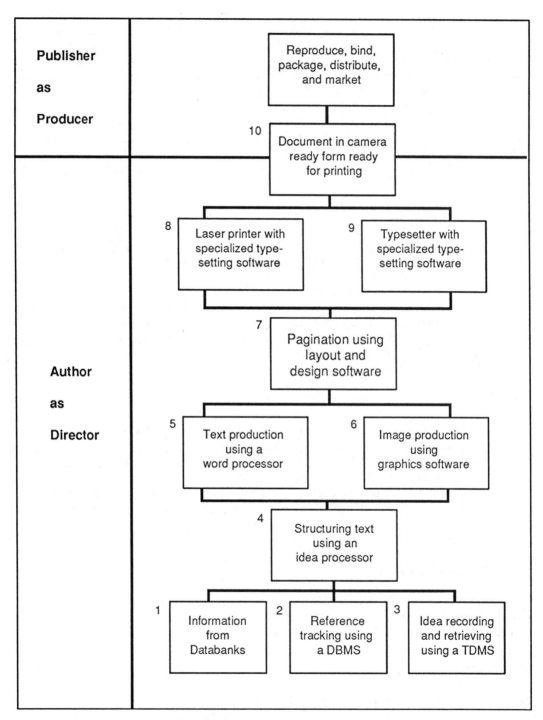

Exhibit 12.1: The personal publishing process

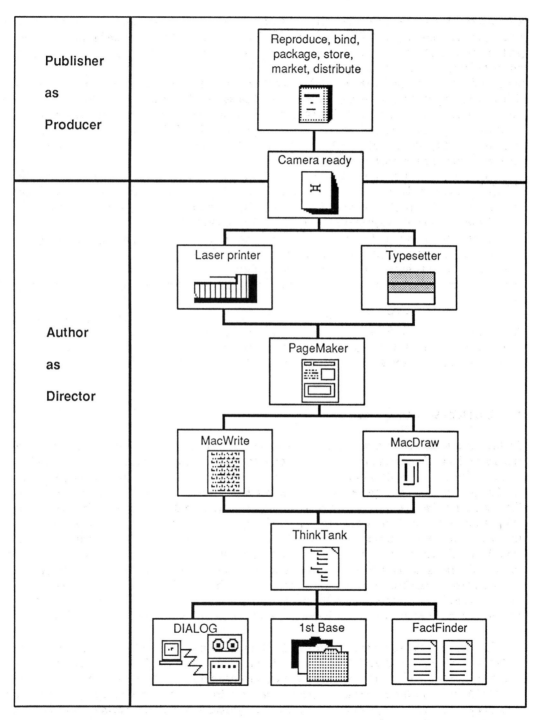

Exhibit 12.2: Tools for personal and in-house publishing

and in nonacademic areas such as weather, sports, travel reservations, restaurants, stocks, news articles, and so forth. By performing a search according to certain key terms and logical operators (and, or, not, greater than), we are able to scan and selectively retrieve a body of relevant and complete information. For example, "Give me all the articles written since January, 1986 on the subject of computers and publishing." The problem we face is not lack of information, but the difficulty finding it. This is the purpose or goal of databanks; but there are problems. The query must be made in the language of the databank. Programs exist to make the task easier such as PROSEARCH (Meno Corp, Santa Clara, CA) and SCI-MATE (Institute for Scientific Information [ISI], Philadelphia, PA) which allow the user to selectively access a variety of databanks using the same set of menus and menu choices.

The very fact that programs like PROSEARCH and SCI-MATE exist, pinpoints part of the problem. Access to databanks through telecommunications facilities, most often the telephone using a datapac line, is often bewilderingly complex. A librarian—librarians are the good samaritans of research— knowledgeable in databank searches is an invaluable ally.

There is much promise here but a lot of work remains to be done. The problems relate to ease of access, compatibility of equipment, the integrity of the databanks, whether the databanks being accessed contain the information desired (there are over 3,000 *public* information databanks, and many more private databanks), how selection is made, and how the information is retrieved and displayed.

Do we wish to be this well connected, with this much information at our finger tips? Unless the search and find functions are efficient, we will end up with too much information, and drown once again. Another factor is cost; high cost may prevent many of us from accessing certain databanks. If information is valuable we can expect it to be hoarded.

12.5-2 Database management

1st Base is a relational database management system (DBMS). It readily allows the user to name and define fields of information to store in records on any set or file of support information required when writing. For example, this author maintains records of information on publishers, books and articles, products, images, quotes, and people. *1st Base* allows for the rapid joining of different files of information (publishers with books, publishers with products, quotes with books), when information is required from *both* files to perform some support or production function (mail letters to publishers to obtain permission to quote from books and articles; produce a list of publishers and their products for inclusion in an appendix). These are the necessary functions in support of writing, and a DBMS, which interfaces easily to a word processor and includes mail merge and report capabilities, will allow for the rapid production of correspondence, request letters, release forms, bibliographies, and reference materials in appendixes. There are a number of database managers for small computers that could serve these functions; several are listed in Appendix C.

Exhibit 12.3 shows records from two files maintained by the author. The publisher's file includes fields called "contact," "title," and "salutation," since these fields of information are used to create letters and release forms. The mail merge program inserts the information from these and other fields in the database into the appropriate place in a letter (or any other created document) and each letter, when printed, appears to be a personally typed piece of correspondence. The databases also help in the indexing of the text.

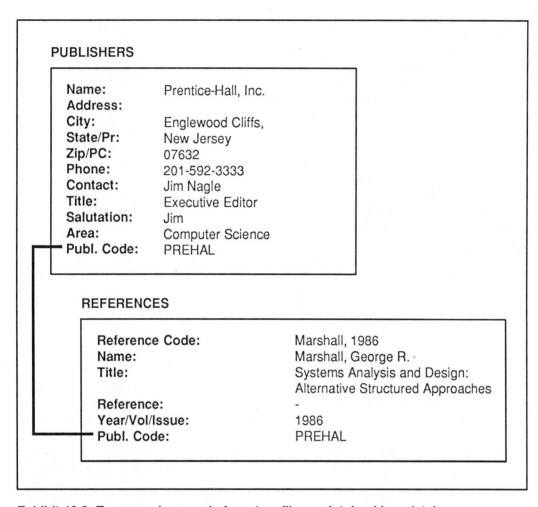

Exhibit 12.3: Two sample records from two files maintained in a database

The publisher's code in the two records shown in Exhibit 12.3 is used by *1st Base* to join the files and temporarily store the combined information in a third file. Once a report from the third file has been obtained, the joined file may be deleted. By always maintaining the information on each separate entity (publishers, books, products), we reduce the possibility of redundant information, a prime reason for using relational database management systems. For example, one publisher might be responsible for many books. We would want to store information on each publisher only *once* in the publisher's file, not each time we record information on books published by a given publisher, in the books and articles file.

Specialized file and database systems exist, for example, bibliographic software for both the IBM PC and the Macintosh (*Professional Bibliographic Systems*, Personal Bibliographic Software, Ann Arbor, MI). Bibliographic systems serve the needs of someone who does a lot of library and research work. The software provides many record formats specifically designed to record information on different types of references (books, newspapers, dissertations, conference proceedings); and produce bibliographies in one of a number of commonly used bibliographic formats (American National Standard, Modern Language Association, American Psychological Association, *Science* magazine). The software also allows for full text search of the bibliographic records. Link software available allows for the downloading of records from on-line databanks, such as DIALOG and DBS.

A general-purpose DBMS, with appropriately formatted input forms and report formats, should be able to replicate the specialized functions of the bibliographic software described. But there are negatives in using a general-purpose DBMS instead of a specialized bibliographic system. Using a DBMS would involve some sizeable effort establishing the variety of form and report formats required; some DBMSs limit the size of the fields and records; and most DBMSs lack the flexibility to create a single bibliography from a multiple number of files with different record formats. This last problem could be solved if output from the bibliography files in the database were transferred to text files, then pasted together, and the bibliography formatted manually using a word processor; a messy process, and alphabetical indexing would have to be created interactively, not automatically

But there are drawbacks to the specialized bibliographic systems. Possibly the biggest drawback of the bibliographic system, from the viewpoint of the individual writer, is that it supports one function, while a DBMS using the same established database will support many functions. If data from files in a DBMS could be readily transferred to files in the bibliographic system, then the required integration —and single data entry—is met.

12.5-3 Text data management

Factfinder is a text data management system (TDMS), or free-form filing system and information organizer. *Factfinder* functions particularly well when used with a RAM disk—as do many of the applications programs described—which speeds operation considerably. Similar to a file or database manager, the key difference is that the record is a free-format text file and is called a *factsheet*. Factsheets reside in *stacks* and are referenced and retrieved on the basis of key words assigned and then searched according to logical or Boolean operators, for example, display all factsheets that are referenced by the key words "Publishing" *and* "Graphics." Key words and logical operators are selected using the pointing capabilities of the mouse; easy and fast. The factsheet is analogous to a record, the stack to a file or database, and the key words to index keys.

Factfinder lends itself well to the recording of ideas and quotes which can then be selectively retrieved on the basis of subject, topic, and subtopic. Unlike the "start with an outline" approach most of us were taught in school, writing often starts with a stream of consciousness, a flow of ideas which associate and disassociate as they bubble forth. This bottom-up approach to writing is admirably supported by *Factfinder*, which allows the structure to emerge from the flow of thought rather than be dictated by a too-early designed outline. When pen, paper, and typewriters were our only tools, outlines prevented too much rewriting, or too much work with the scissors and gluepot. Computers, however, with their electronic cut-and-paste capabilities, are not hampered by any lack of early structure (Marshall, 1984).

Exhibit 12.4 shows a screen from *Factfinder* with four windows; one showing a factsheet on an "Ad Plan Summary" for the "Johnson Corp"; another the keys for the "Johnson Corp" factsheet; a third the names of all factsheets in the stack; and a fourth window used for specifying factsheet searches based on factsheet names or key words (Set to "all" in the window shown). The stack is called "Examples."

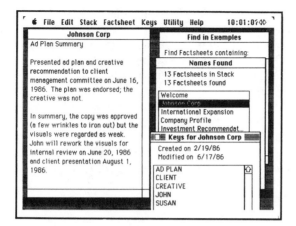

Exhibit 12.4: A screen from *Factfinder* showing four windows

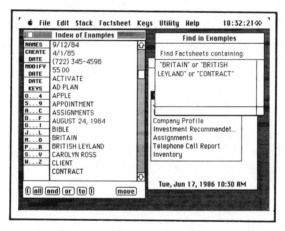

Exhibit 12.5: The index for the "Examples" stack

It is possible to expand the factsheet window to fill the screen by clicking on a convenient "zoom button" located at the bottom left corner of the factsheet window. The cursor in the form of an arrow controlled by movement of the mouse is shown near the zoom button.

Exhibit 12.5 shows part of the index for the "Examples" stack. All factsheets in a *Factfinder* stack are indexed on their names, date created, date modified, and the key words specified. The "A through C" key words shown were selected by clicking on the "A . . .C" choice on the left side of the index screen. Then by clicking on "BRITAIN," the "or" operator at the bottom of the screen, then "LEYLAND," then "or" again, and finally "CONTRACT," *Factfinder* will search and locate only those factsheets that contain any one of these three terms.

Factfinder is reminiscent of a manual retrieval system based on 5-inch by 7-inch index cards with many punched holes on the perimeter of the cards, a notcher for removing the cardboard between the holes and the edges of the cards, and a knitting needle used as the method for selecting cards. Each hole represents a category or topic. A notched hole means the information on the card falls into that category. The knitting needle and card system constitute a simple "operating system" with minimal chance of system errors—unless you clip the wrong hole; it is highly cost effective, quite friendly and user-servile, fast in retrieval, but somewhat messy as cards containing desired information waft to the floor. However, only the most recent small computer technology made it worthwhile shifting over to an automated system, because TDMSs did not exist on small systems until quite recently.

Document indexing software exists that has one powerful feature lacking in *Factfinder*; the ability to index *all* words in different documents, and then later search the index by specific words and retrieve the files containing the documents. *ZylNDEX* (ZyLAB Corp. Chicago, IL) for the IBM PC can index over 325K bytes of text located in 13 files in less than 8 minutes; and identify files on the basis of key words in less than a few seconds (Crider, 1985).

12.5-4 Idea processing

ThinkTank is publicized as an idea processor. *Thinktank* is used for a wide variety of applications including project management, scheduling, and calendar. However, in its application to writing it is better classified as an outline processor, albeit a powerful one that allows for both the manipulation of supertopics, topics, subtopics, text, and images.

If *Factfinder* is bottom-up, then *ThinkTank* is top-down. On a computer system the difference is unimportant; we can shift back and forth with relative ease. From the stream of ideas emerge topics. The topics form the basis for structure. The chapters and sections of the text emerge from the topics. The last stage is to name chapters and write the table of contents. An editor once passed by Scot Gardiner, a writer and colleague, while he was working at the computer and asked, "Scot, what are you writing?" Scot replied quite truthfully, "I don't know. It hasn't told me yet." *ThinkTank* allows the emerging structure of writing to become visible.

Exhibits 12.6 through 12.8 show sample work screens from ThinkTank used in the development of this text. Exhibit 12.6 shows the major parts of the text and an early rejected title. Exhibit 12.7 shows "Part 1: Introduction" expanded to reveal the next level of structure. Exhibit 12.8 shows a third level of expansion, namely, the insertion of some notes for Chapter 1.

ThinkTank will print out all or part of the contents of a work file in two forms; one showing the nested level of materials by number (1, 1.1, 1.1.1), and as a table of contents without numbers.

12.5-5 Image generation

MacPaint and *MacDraw* are, respectively, a free-form computer painting program, and a drafting and design program. The latter provides much better quality print of text and images on a laser printer, or a plotter, because *MacDraw* transmits coordinates as values, rather than pixel values. The printer's or plotter's internal language is able to translate coordinate instructions more accurately, for example, drawing a line between two points, and rendering the line with the highest accuracy possible. The printer's or plotter's resolution can be superior to the computer's or the screen's.

One can draw almost anything with *MacPaint*—in black and white—and then transfer the image to *MacDraw* to combine it with images that lend themselves more to drafting than drawing. *MacPaint* is an artist's tool, and it makes us all artists, though not necessarily good artists. It has created more personal interest in computers than any other product since VisiCalc on the Apple IIe

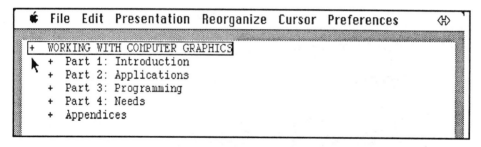

Exhibit 12.6: ThinkTank screen showing old title and major sections for this text

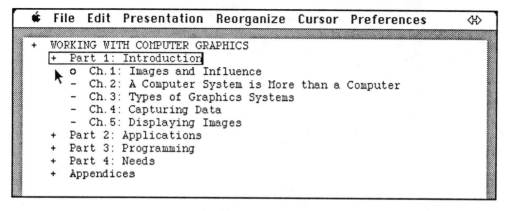

Exhibit 12.7: ThinkTank screen showing Part 1 expanded

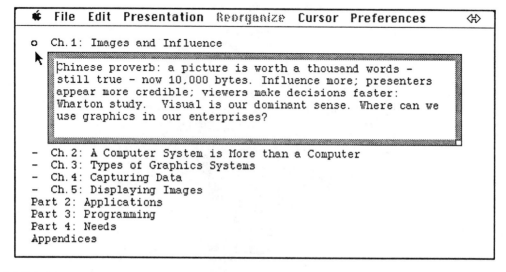

Exhibit 12.8: ThinkTank screen showing added text

back in 1981. Exhibits 12.9 through 12.12 show four illustrations of MacPaint art. The illustrations reveal the quality that is possible using paint programs, when used by a competent and talented artist, illustrator, or designer.

Exhibit 12.9: *Portrait of F.E.* **by Dave Meyers** (Copyright 1984 Apple Computer, Inc.)

Exhibit 12.10: *High Noon* **by Steve Momii** (Copyright 1984 Apple Computer, Inc.)

Exhibit 12.11: *Bamboo* **by Wan Chi Lau** (Copyright 1984 Apple Computer, Inc.)

Exhibit 12.12: *Beginning* **by Raymond E. Coia** (Copyright 1984 Apple Computer, Inc.)

Paint and drafting programs may be used to enhance written communication. Many exhibits in this text were produced using MacDraw and MacPaint. Exhibit 12.13 illustrates the use of borders and other graphics provided in libraries of MacPaint images. Graphics used to dress up presentations should be used judiciously.

Exhibit 12.13: Images for enhancing communication

Other graphics programs discussed elsewhere in this text, such as *MSCHART* and *MacProject,* may also be used at this stage to produce images for inclusion in the final camera-ready copy.

Images may be organized into a database; *Filevision* and *MSFile*, discussed in Chapter 10, are suitable for this purpose. Specialized programs are beginning to appear, for example, *PictureBASE* from Symmetry Corp. (Phoenix, AZ), which allow for images to be scanned and retrieved by image, title, key words, or source.

12.5-6 Word processing

MacWrite is a word processor. Sooner or later, most of the materials produced by the previous programs discussed will end up in a word processor file. *MacWrite* is not particularly sophisticated; *WORD* for the Macintosh contains many more features. *MacWrite* lacks features such as automatic table of contents (*ThinkTank* possesses this feature), automatic indexing (*Factfinder* can handle this), and automatic footnoting.

MacWrite is simple, and may actually be better than feature-rich word processors when materials for final form are going to be moved to a page layout system. Feature-rich word processors may take more time to learn to use, may cost more, and may contain features seldom used. It is the page layout system that needs to be highly sophisticated, to handle the complex process of page design and layout. However, some features which may be integrated into the word processor itself, or an available add-on, are highly useful; for example, spelling checkers.

The most dramatic difference between word processors on graphics and nongraphics computers is that on graphics systems what you see is what you get, often abbreviated to WYSIWYG. Exhibit 12.14 illustrates this point by showing the screen appearance using *MacWrite* and *WordStar*. The instructions to make the title bold, for example, are imbedded in the text in the WordStar program (^B), and make the text difficult to read. When the document is printed, the letters appear bold. But only on a graphics system do they also appear bold on the screen; or, WYSIWYG.

12.5-7 Fonts and faces

Fonts are an assortment of characters of one style and size type; faces are variations of a given font (boldface, italic, outline, shadowed). Word processors on graphics-based personal computer systems now offer a rich variety of font types and faces. Exhibit 12.15 shows a sample of the fonts available for the Macintosh.

For the IBM PC expanded to include graphics capabilities, fonts of great variety, including those supporting unusual applications such as electronic circuit symbols, are provided by a number of publishers of software (see Appendix C). An increasing number of fonts are available for laser printers configured to operate with the IBM PC.

It is the recent availability of commercial typefaces on microcomputers and desktop laser printers that expands the use of microcomputers in personal publishing. These fonts include Helvetica, Times Roman, Courier, and Garamond. Garamond has been around for several hundred years, and Times Roman, designed in the thirties for optimal readability, has become an industry standard. The text in this book is Times Roman. More fonts and faces will appear for laser printers in the near future. Unless a laser printer is configured to use a given font, the letters do not get printed in an acceptable quality.

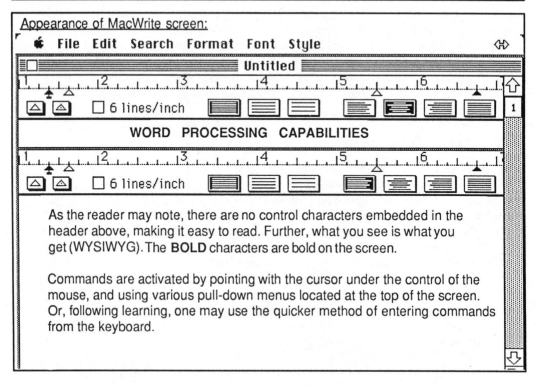

Appearance of WORDSTAR screen:

     C:TMP PAGE 1 LINE 11 COL 62   INSERT ON

L----!----!----!----!----!----!--- -!----!----!----!-------R

    ^B^^D^WORD PROCESSING CAPABILITIES^D^^B^

As the reader may note, there are control characters embedded in
the header above making the text difficult to read. Further, what
you see is not what you get. The "^B^" means BOLD, or strike three
times when printing; the "^D^" means double strike. The numbers
and commands at the bottom of the screen refer to function keys
on the keyboard that will perform the command in question
(e.g. "3SET LM" means "Press function key no. 3 to set the left
margin.").

1HELP 2INDENT 3SET LM 4SETRM 5UNDLIN 6BLDFCE 7BEGBLK 8ENDBLK 9BEGFIL 10ENDFIL

Appearance of MacWrite screen:

    File   Edit   Search   Format   Font   Style

    Untitled

   6 lines/inch

WORD   PROCESSING   CAPABILITIES

   6 lines/inch

As the reader may note, there are no control characters embedded in the
header above, making it easy to read. Further, what you see is what you
get (WYSIWYG). The **BOLD** characters are bold on the screen.

Commands are activated by pointing with the cursor under the control of the
mouse, and using various pull-down menus located at the top of the screen.
Or, following learning, one may use the quicker method of entering commands
from the keyboard.

Exhibit 12.14: *WordStar* and *MacWrite* appear differently on the screen

Font	Face	Size
Courier	Plain	9
Courier	**Bold**	**10**
Courier	*Italic*	*12*
Courier	Bold/outline	14
Helvetica	Plain	10
Helvetica	*Italic*	*12*
Helvetica	**Bold/shadow**	**14**
Helvetica	**Bold**	**18**
Times	Plain	10
Times	*Italic*	*12*
Times	Bold/outline	18
Times	**Bold**	**24**
London	Plain	18
Athens	**Bold**	**18**
Venice	Italic	14
Chicago	**Bold/shadow**	**12**

Exhibit 12.15: A sample of the fonts, faces, and sizes available on the Apple LaserWriter (Those below the line are *not* installed on the LaserWriter and, therefore, print in low resolution. Other fonts installed on the LaserWriter that print in high resolution include Palatino, New Century Schoolbook, Helvetica Narrow, ITC Bookman, ITC Avant Garde, ITC Zapf Chancery, and ITC Dingbats.)

In Exhibit 12.15, the fonts above the line are defined and stored mathematically and are called *spline fonts*. Spline fonts take full advantage of the high resolution of laser printers and typesetters. The fonts below the line are defined as bitmaps, as reflected in their low resolution.

Font editors are available, for both bitmapped and spline fonts, that allow the user to define his own fonts. Using a font editor introduces one to the world and language of letters and their formation; it is a rich world. Many have spent lifetimes creating different fonts and faces in wood and metal that we can now create with zeros and ones. The graphics computer provides a gate to this rich world. But we have to be willing to learn the terms and skills used to describe fonts, including ascent, baseline, descent, leading, kerning, and others; that is, learn the language and craft of the typesetter (the glossary contains definitions of these terms).

Let us discuss one term: kerning. Kerning describes the overlap between characters. High quality typography requires that some character pairs are closer than others, meaning that the placement of a given letter depends upon the letter that precedes it. For example, inspect the following sequence of letters: Word. The reader will note that there seems to be too much space between the "W" and the "o". There is, according to high quality typography. With high quality systems, not only is the print a higher resolution, but kerning tables are used along with a special text editor which references the table to calculate where the next letter should appear. These kind of capabilities are beginning to appear in desktop publishing systems.

12.5-8 Page layout

PageMaker from Aldus Corporation (Seattle, WA) is a page layout (pagination) system that automates the page design and pasteup process.* *PageMaker* allows the person unfamiliar with drafting, design, typesetting, and pasteup to perform these functions, and create professional looking copy. However, page makeup programs do not prevent us from creating unattractive layouts. The technology replaces technical, not design, skills. *PageMaker* allow the user to create or import from other applications:

- Headers, captions, and text of various sizes and fonts
- Line artwork, such as borders and boxes
- Illustrations and images, drawn or digitized

Further, the system allows for very accurate placement of the above, which together form a completed page, ready to be used as the master for creating the plates from which the final document is printed. *PageMaker* also allows the user to

- Mix type styles and sizes within a given block of text
- Move, reduce, or expand text and images for more accurate placement or design
- Adjust the flow of text across different pages
- View the layout of any two-page spread
- Interface to both laser printers and typesetters that use *PostScript* as the printer control language

PostScript is a page description programming language developed by Adobe Systems (Palo Alto, CA). PostScript provides for compatibility between many computers and printer devices that use it, and provides programmers with a powerful set of tools for combining text and images on pages, and creating friendly front-end systems like *PageMaker*. *PostScript* is described in more detail by Sprague (1985).

Exhibit 12.16 shows a page created in *PageMaker*, namely the face page of Chapter 10 of this text, overlayed with one of the drop menus from *PageMaker*. The drop menu shows that the "actual size" of the page has been selected for display; the smaller sizes are used for page layout

---

* Aldus Manutius was a printer, scholar, and patron of learning in 16th-century Venice. He was responsible for preserving many Greek classics that would have been lost or destroyed as a result of the Turkish invasion of Constantinople. He invented italic type and standardized the use of punctuation.

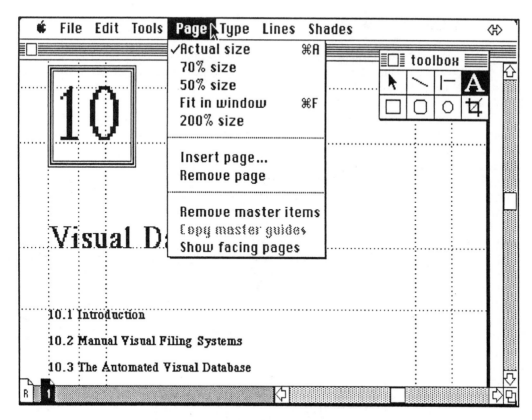

Exhibit 12.16: A screen from PageMaker

purposes, and the larger size for accurate text and image placement. The dotted lines on the page do *not* print, but are used to guide placement. The tool box in the corner is activated by pointing and pressing the mouse on the appropriate icon; an arrow to move and resize text and images, lines for drawing, letters for typing, boxes and circles to draw, and a cropping tool, in the lower right corner of the tool box, used to crop images. The page icon in the lower left corner of Exhibit 12.16 shows that we are working on page 1 of a single page document. Up to 16 pages are allowed in any one *PageMaker* file. The "R" labeled page refers to a master right page design, which can selectively act as a template for all right-handed pages in the manuscript. If this was a two-sided document, an "L" labeled page would appear and would act as a master left page design.

PageMaker is a sophisticated program; it offers a large subset of functions provided by a high-end, fully dedicated and integrated publishing system. We will discuss dedicated high-end writing and publishing systems costing upward of $45,000 later in this chapter.

Other available page layout software are listed in Appendix C and include *ReadySetGo, Mac-Publisher II,* and *JustText for the Macintosh,* and *Do-It, MagnaType,* and *ClickArt Personal Publisher* for the IBM PC enhanced with graphics. There are others on microcomputers that only produce galleys from various typesetters, and are not interactive design and page production systems. *JustText* is a powerful command-driven system that overcomes the tedious page-by-page text layout required by page-oriented systems *(PageMaker),* but it does not handle graphics.

12.6 A LOW-END SYSTEM

In the previous section we described different applications programs that could form a low-end, desktop, microcomputer-based authoring and publishing system. Exhibit 12.17 lists the hardware and software for a total low-end system configuration. The cost of the system described in Exhibit 12.17 can be reduced by sharing the use of the laser printer with several other systems.

This system, to some degree, is a "kludge," a term used by engineers to refer to a system created from a piece here and a part there which, however, works. In this case the system works remarkably well at modest cost. It lacks speed, and is, on a few occasions, clumsy in operation, for example, moving data between applications. However, recent changes in the operating environment of the Apple Macintosh are improving data movement, including a program called *Switcher* which allows for rapid movement from one application to another, and increased memory which allows for more programs and data to be used rapidly at any given time.

The configuration in Exhibit 12.17 is one of many. For example, another local author uses an IBM PC compatible *Compaq;* a *Mouse Systems* mouse; an *IBM Quietwriter*; one 360K floppy disk; a 30MB hard disk; *WordStar 3.3*, a widely used word processor; *Prokey*, a system for programming the keyboard and used for establishing compatibility with a large bibliographic databank; *Videoshow/PictureIt*, for graphic images; *Lotus 1-2-3*, to manage article lists; and *Sidekick*, a desk untility (calendar, notes, calculator) to "hold it all together." At the time, this author was looking for page makeup software as output to a laser printer to provide good previews of typeset galleys, and a high resolution graphics screen that would display a full page (66 lines) and support rapid on-screen editing.

12.7 A HIGH-END SYSTEM

Sometimes the term *Electronic Technical Publishing (ETP)*, or *Electronic Publishing* is used to refer to in-house publishing by a business or enterprise. The systems used may cost as little as $45,000, or as much as $250,000 (Jones, 1985). They hardly fit the image of the "person as publisher," but the low-end systems on this high-end scale are single-station desktop units that provide small enterprises with sophisticated publishing capabilities.

High-end systems may include any of the following capabilities:

- Provide input from digitizing pads or scanners
- Integrate input from CAD, paint, text, and other applications
- Function in both batch and interactive mode
- Maintain a database of text and images
- Accommodate frequent and rapid page changes
- Provide for highly rapid throughput and document production
- Interface to typesetting equipment and high production laser printers
- Provide for telecommunications and decentralized document production
- Contain sophisticated word processors
- Provide for color production
- Allow for sophisticated operations to be conducted by
  nonprofessional but skilled operators

Item		Retail Cost
APPLE Macintosh + with 1MB memory including black-and-white monitor, keyboard with pad, mouse, operating system, 800K disc drive, various ports (high speed for hard disk, etc.)		2,500.00
20 MB Winchester disk		1,500.00
ImageWriter	Dot matrix printer for preview & mailing labels	700.00
LaserWriter	For camera-ready copy	5,500.00
Modem	For connection to bibliographic sources, databanks, other researchers and authors, etc.	700.00
Digitizer	For image capture	230.00
Total for Hardware:		**$11,130.00**
MacWrite	Text processing	125.00
MacPaint	Free-form paint program	125.00
MacDraw	Computer aided drafting program	125.00
Hayden Speller	Electronic dictionary and thesaurus	80.00
1st Base	Database manager and report writer	195.00
1st Merge	File- or mail-merge system	95.00
Factfinder	Text data management system	150.00
Thinktank	Outline and idea processor	145.00
PageMaker	Page design and pasteup	495.00
JustText	Text layout command language	100.00
Cat Comm'n.	Access databanks, bulletin boards, etc.	500.00
Total for Software:		**$ 2,135.00**
Supplies, service contract, support, training		**$ 2,500.00**
TOTAL:		**$15,765.00**

Exhibit 12.17: A low-end system (In U.S. dollars—prices quoted are approximate and subject to change)

We will review one system that possesses most of the capabilities listed; it does not handle color printing: the *Interleaf* electronic publishing system from Interleaf, Inc.(Cambridge, MA). This relatively low cost, powerful, and fast turnkey publishing system has been well received.

Interleaf will handle four types of graphics: data-driven business charts, line illustrations and diagramming, external CAD system graphics, and digital scanning of preexisting artwork and photographs. As Exhibit 12.18 shows, the Interleaf screen is able to display a full page plus command menus and icons; it is the type of screen Apple Macintosh users dream about.

Interleaf is well designed ergonomically; it fits people. The system is 10 times faster than traditional word processing, creates a publishing house and print shop in the office, all sitting on a

Exhibit 12.18: The *Interleaf* screen (Courtesy of Interleaf, Inc., Cambridge, MA)

desk, and taking up no more room than a copier. Publishing systems will become as familiar in the office as typewriters and copying machines.

Interleaf is based on a 10MHz, MC68010, 32-bit Sun Workstation microcomputer from Sun Microsystems. It uses a 19-inch monochrome display with 900 by 1,152 pixel resolution, refreshed at 70Hz and supported by 128K of frame buffer memory. The memory management system and virtual memory capabilities allow for eight simultaneous active processes. The system uses the UNIX operating system, Imagen's software for pagination, and a Canon laser printer which produces 8 pages per minute at 300 dots per inch resolution.

Documents produced by other applications (WordStar, Lotus 1-2-3, Multiplan) on other microcomputers and word processors can be transferred to the *Interleaf,* merged with other text and graphics, and printed. Further, the system supports the storage of frequently used text and images in a database. A scanning device is available that takes any image up to 8 1/2 by 11 inches and places it in a document in less than 2 minutes. The image, once placed, may be sized, rotated, and edited on the screen. Text and free-hand graphics can be added, and retouching is possible using an extensive pallette of textures and electronic "brushes."

The *Interleaf* also interfaces with a variety of typesetters, and may be used in network mode. Savings in typesetting costs of 60 percent have been reported.

The *Interleaf* system's ease of use, power, and relatively low cost are a portent of the future for personal publishing; it will get easier, more powerful, and even cheaper. Individuals with minimal technical training—but with high skills in other areas—will be able to generate, design, print, and distribute high quality printed materials on a variety of media: paper, transparencies, film, and video. Further, we will be able to store text and graphic information on various high volume storage devices (laser or optical disc) for later retrieval and sharing.

12.8 LOW- VERSUS HIGH-END SYSTEMS

What are the differences between low- and high-end desktop publishing systems, and when should we consider one over the other? Basic capabilities do *not* differentiate them; that is, they can both do the same things. For example, the quality of output of text and images of the Apple Macintosh and the Interleaf systems described is identical. But, by analogy, so can a bicycle and a racing car; they both get us there. But, *how* they get us there is very different, and one is not necessarily better than the other; it depends upon needs and budget. It is the same with publishing systems. The differences between low- and high-end systems are

- Speed
- Number of applications operative at the same time (multi-tasking)
- Size and resolution of screen
- Level of integration of different applications
- Size of memory
- Efficiency with which memory is used (memory management)
- Efficiency with which storage is used (virtual memory capabilities)
- The quality and flexibility of image capture and manipulation
- The ease with which text and images can be integrated and page proofs created

This text was produced using the system described in Exhibit 12.17, a low-end Apple Macintosh-based system.*

12.9 SOME APPLICATIONS

Possible applications include the following: technical manuals, research reports, sales brochures, restaurant menus, stationery, cards, logos, and publicity materials, newsletters, and small newspapers, books not requiring the highest quality, and comic books.

The last represents a unique application deserving of special mention because it constitutes "the first change in production methods of the art form in 40 years" (C. McGeever, "The Mac Makes a Hit Comic," *Infoworld,* April 8, 1985, copyright © 1985 Popular Computing Inc.). First Comics (Evanston, IL) has published a comic book by Michael Saenz called *Shatter,* "a story of the life and times of a 21st-century cop in a tough computerized world." The comic book was produced entirely through MacPaint on the Macintosh. Color was manually added later to the black-and-white images produced. Saenz reports he has been able to double his normal output of one or two pages per day. Saenz further reports that one major advantage of the computer was the ability to store stock images which he could then call up and modify—shrink, expand, rotate—to produce additional comic-book frames.

12.10 CONCLUSION

In summary, the advantages of personal desktop publishing are more direct control by the user over the process—especially revisions and corrections, a costly and time-consuming activity; more involvement by the user in the total design of the output; a new and powerful environment and approach to organizing and producing media, whether individually or collectively generated; savings in time; and lower costs.

Technical advances create progress and confusion. Technology has no respect for traditional lines. As mentioned, authors take on the duties of publishers, and publishers become impressarios. Further, print shops offer computer services which can include art and layout work, non-professional (but skilled) workers operate sophisticated equipment, and the individual with his personal small computer may possess a full-fledged production department on a desk. That which distinguishes the secretary, the writer, the artist, the layout designer, the producer, the printer, the publisher, the typographer, the compositor, and the computer specialist is increasingly fuzzy.

The desktop publishing system allows for the learning and integration of the skills of all of these occupations; a broad base of knowledge is important in this area. There is always the matter of production know-how and artistic capability. There is a big difference between producing a two-page flyer, or a simple set of slides, and the production of a textbook, or a commercial show involving the use of 30 slide projectors. There is the need for good content and design on all levels. The availability of high quality systems expands professionalism; our criteria of excellence should go up.

---

* The capabilities and power of communication provided by the new low-cost technology to the individual is impressive. On some occasions, however, I cursed the lack of integration, slow speed, and the small screen of the Apple Macintosh 512. With the introduction of the Apple Macintosh +, the integration and speed problems have been alleviated; the small screen is still with us.

Programming Graphics: An Introduction

PART A

PART A

13.1 INTRODUCTION*

This chapter is presented in two parts. In **Part A**, we introduce the concept of programming, the basic building blocks used in the development of programs, and a series of simple programs in Pascal, BASIC, and LOGO. It is expected that readers will be able to follow and understand the program listings in Part A. **Part B** is more challenging, the programs are increasingly complex, and the reader is invited to enter the program listings into a computer and view what they do, *possibly before understanding how they do it.* The reader should not be overly concerned if he or she does *not* understand all the details of all programs. A mind stretched never goes back to its former shape; seeing the product may help us understand the process. The purpose of Part B is to show further possibilities and to arouse an interest in the further study of programming.

Programming is becoming theater (Alan Kay, 1984). The "theatrical context," as Kay calls it, is created by expert programmers through the development of programming languages that fit the human way of doing things. Then the user is able to be a director of the theatrical context. It is the user who "programs" using "toolkits" provided in the language. The design of good toolkits adheres to human intellect and intuition; that which facilitates learning, memory, and creative application.

It is in this light that we look at three commonly used languages, Pascal, BASIC, and LOGO. Only to some extent do they fullfill the "toolkit" concept and fit the human way of doing things. There is little else we can expect. We might not be using any of these languages in a decade from now. Or, they may have changed so dramatically over the next ten years as to be unrecognizable.

The proliferation of computer languages and language dialects—Tesler (1984) estimates anywhere from several hundred to over two thousand—attest to the effort being expended to tap the computer's capabilities. But only a dozen or so are in widespread use, including our selected trio. Each language has its own distinctive grammar and syntax, and its own way of doing things. In principle most computational and display tasks could be accomplished with any of the languages, but the programs would look different. Moreover, as we shall see, some tasks are easier in some languages than in others. The great diversity of programming languages is evidence of the great diversity of needs not met by any one. There is no such thing as the *best* programming language; it depends upon the purpose, as it may in natural languages. Tesler quotes Charles V of France: "I speak Spanish to God, Italian to women, French to men and German to my horse." A programming language too must be chosen for its capabilities and intended purpose.

Programmers are interested in processing; users are interested in output. This difference in focus leads to some interesting anomolies. For example, within these languages, no or limited procedures are provided for saving, storing, modifying, or transferring the *graphics output* produced by a BASIC, Pascal, or LOGO program on the Apple Macintosh (most likely this holds true for these languages on any machine). However, many facilities exist within these languages for saving, storing, editing, and transferring *program listings* that produce the graphics output. It is possible to transfer produced graphics using cut-and-paste capabilities on a *systems* level to a word processing document, or to a paint or computer aided drafting file.

---

* The author wishes to thank John DeSilva and Michael Nash for their valuable assistance developing a number of the programs in this chapter.

13.2 PROGRAM DEVELOPMENT

Programming is problem solving; and there are proven steps that have evolved that we should follow in developing a program. *A program is a set of instructions written in a particular language for performing some specified task, or solving some particular problem.* In graphics it might be a paint or drafting program, written by a highly skilled programmer, that allows those of us who do not know how to program to solve the problem of drawing images using a computer. However, there are times when we might wish to program a graphic using a particular language (see Exhibit 13.2 and related comments in the text).

When we first learn to program the problems we are capable of solving are simple: draw a circle, draw a series of shapes, repeat some pattern, choose to draw one image when certain conditions exist, and another when other conditions exist, and so forth. *A series of steps to solve a problem is called an algorithm.* The algorithm, or several algorithms, are represented in the program instructions or code. That is, using a given computer language, the lines of code or statements represent the algorithm. An algorithm does not leave any step out. Our solution to a problem cannot be phrased in terms such as, " I have this gut feeling that the answer is . . . " That will not do, because the computer cannot follow "gut feelings." The problem must be analyzed, each logical step specified, and then represented accurately in the program code written.

It has been discovered that there are three basic processes, or building blocks, we are able to use in programming that allow us to write workable and structured programs. They are *sequence, repetition,* and *selection,* and they are illustrated in flow-chart form in Exhibit 13.1.

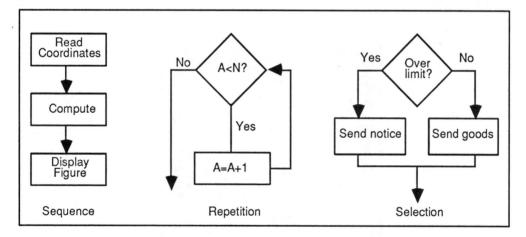

Exhibit 13.1: Program building blocks

The flow of execution of the instructions in a program is sequential unless another instruction or control statement indicates otherwise. For example, an instruction may call for the *repeat execution* of the same series of instructions, called *a loop.* Or an instruction may call for different sets of instructions to be executed depending on given conditions. This calls into play the *decision-making* capabilities of the computer. We shall see examples of sequence, repetition, and selection in the programs in this chapter.

A fourth building block needs to be mentioned, namely, the *subroutine*. A subroutine is a program that does a particular job that can be called by another program. Subroutines are very important; they are created only once, defined only once, and stored in only one place, but they can be used in many places. When we discuss *graphics toolboxes* later in this chapter, the toolboxes contain graphics subroutines that perform various tasks that we do not have to program, for example, draw a circle, or draw a rectangle. Using subroutine names in our main program, we are able to call subroutines from our library, or toolbox, of subroutines. Flow of execution is transferred temporarily to the subroutine called, and then control is returned to the main program.

13.3 LEARNING TO PROGRAM

There is one way to learn to program, and that is to program. It is a skill that cannot be acquired only by reading about it. Becoming a good programmer, as in other professions, takes time, effort, and interest. What can we reasonably expect to cover in one chapter? We can provide a "taste" in the form of a smorgasbord of sample graphics programs in a limited number of languages, and invite the reader to copy them into a computer, modify, and play with them. Play and imitation are powerful means for the initial learning in many disciplines. More formal study can be undertaken following aroused interest.

Further, we can explore when to use a programming approach to generating graphics and when to use interactive tools. In the first case, the generation of the graphic is under the program and the computer's control; in the latter it is under the user's control. A simple example will clarify the point being made. Consider the graphic in Exhibit 13.2.

Exhibit 13.2: Graphics we would want a program to generate

Under no circumstances would we want to draw the figure in Exhibit 13.2, or figures like it, using some paint or CAD system. The design is obviously based upon the repeated generation of a square, with the parameters that control the size and rotation of the square, changed with each repetition. The proper approach is to write a computer program that precisely controls the production of the squares and the final graphic. By comparison, entering numeric data to some program which in turn generates a business chart, an engineering diagram, or a freehand sketch, would be a painful way of interfacing with the computer and the wrong metaphor completely. In this case we require an intimate and interactive dialogue with the system in real time.*

13.4 PASCAL, BASIC, AND LOGO

Pascal, BASIC, and LOGO are high level languages (HLLs) as discussed in Chapter 2; high level because they contain some similarity to English and, therefore, by comparison with lower level languages closer to the machine language of the computer, are easier to understand.

Pascal is the most structured language of all three—some people feel it is positively bureaucratic in its demands—and is used extensively to teach programming and good structured programming practices on the university level. This makes Pascal programs harder to write but easier to read.

BASIC is unstructured and is the most widely used language on microcomputers. BASIC contains more "slack" than Pascal, making it initially easier to learn to write programs. But those programs, unless well documented, will be harder to understand later on. This makes BASIC programs easier to write but harder to read.

LOGO is initially the easiest to learn, the most graphics oriented, and is used primarily in secondary schools to teach children to program. But once we have gone past the initial stage, LOGO is *not* simple to use. In fact, there are many variations of all three languages, and all three languages in different dialects are capable of handling challenging tasks. When one has progressed past the initiation stage, *none* of the languages are trivial to learn to use to do nontrivial tasks.

Our coverage of these three languages will take place with different graphics output, in which the three languages are used to develop programs to produce the output. The programs include

1. The drawing of a simple shape
2. Using the shape to generate other graphics
3. A randomly generated mathematical function used as the basis for "found" art
4. Fractal geometry, the laws inherent in the apparent chaos of nature, used
    to generate a fantasy figure

In the first set of programs used in **Part A** of this chapter we draw different varieties of circles, and then we use the circle to generate cones. In the second set of programs used in **Part B,** the sine curve is used to generate weaving patterns, and finally, through the use of fractals, we produce a stylized "dragon." It is expected that the reader, with minimal study of the program listings and, if possible, entry of the programs into a computer, will have little difficulty understanding the programs in Part A. The programs in Part B are more challenging, and the listings are given for those with a greater interest in programming. However, we can all enter them into a computer and see what they do. All programs become more understandable when we see them in action. A reference table to the programs and exhibits in this chapter is provided in Exhibit 13.3.

---

* Without necessarily understanding the following code, we can certainly tell that it is *not* the way we should be required to instruct the computer to generate line charts: **XSPACE=200/NDPTS**, for spacing between data points; **YSCALE = (50-170/maximum-value y data point)**, for maximum data point and location of x-axis; and so forth (Quoted by permission: Artwick, 1984).

	Pascal	BASIC	LOGO
Purpose	Program numbers in chapter		
Simple figure shapes: a play on circles	1, 2, 3, 6	7	4, 5
Repeat simple shapes through loop procedures: a play on cones	9	8	10
Mathematics and aesthetics; curves, random numbers & creative "accidents"	12	11	not included
Fantasy and fractals: creating "dragons"	13	not included; no recursion in BASIC	14

Exhibit 13.3: Programs used to demonstrate languages

13.5 A SIMPLE SHAPE

All three programs can easily generate simple two-dimensional shapes, but, as we shall see, they sometimes do it differently, and the graphics output sometimes looks different. LOGO in the version used here, namely *ExperLogo* by ExperTelligence (Santa Barbara, CA) for the Macintosh, is also capable of generating 3D graphics, a capability not present in Pascal or BASIC. Here we show the generation of different circle figures. In Exhibit 13.4 is a simple circle figure generated by Pascal Program 1.

```
Program 1 (Pascal)
program Circle1;
   var
   x, y : integer;
begin
   x:= 50;
   y:= 50;
   Frameoval (x, y, x + 60, y + 60);
end.
```

Var stands for variables, which must be declared in Pascal at the beginning of the program. The only two used here are the coordinate points "x" and "y." Following the **begin** statement,

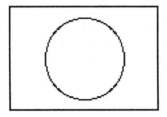

Exhibit 13.4: Circle generated by Pascal program 1

which marks the actual beginning of the program, the initial values of "x" and "y" are set to 50. If "x" and "y" were *not* set to some value greater than 0, the circle would appear crammed in the upper left corner of the graphics window. The values 0, 0 define this corner point of the window. In this program we do not actually need to define the initial "x" location because it is defined in the **for-do** statement. But, it is easier to read the program when both points are defined together as shown.

In Pascal, a circle is defined using Cartesian coordinates, that is, as an oval drawn within some defined rectangle, with equal extension on both the x and y axes, which makes the rectangle a square and the oval a circle. In this case, it is a rectangle 60 pixels wide and 60 pixels deep as shown in the **Frameoval** line. The reader may note that this program only uses sequence as the basic building block.

We can add one line to this program and produce a "fancy" circle as shown in Exhibit 13.5. The new listing is in Pascal Program 2.

```
Program 2 (Pascal)
program Circle2;
    var
    x, y : integer;
begin
    x := 50;
    y := 50;
for x := 50 to 65 do
Frameoval(y, x, y + 60, x + 60);
end.
```

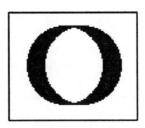

Exhibit 13.5: Circle generated by Pascal programs 2 and 3

Pascal program 2 draws the circle 16 times for 16 different values of the coordinate "x." This is controlled by the **for do** statement. Therefore, this program illustrates two basic building blocks: sequence, and repetition or looping. We can further modify this first program and gain more control over what is produced. Consider Pascal Program 3 as follows:

Program 3 (Pascal)
```
program Circle3;
   var
   x, y : integer;
begin
   y := 50;
   x := 50;
   while x < 65 do
 begin
     Frameoval(y, x, y + 60, x + 60);
    x := x + 1;
  end;
end.
```

The listing for Pascal Program 3 also produces the figure shown in Exhibit 13.5. But, if we vary the value added to x in the "x:=x+1" line to 2, 3, and 4, respectively, we obtain the images shown in Exhibit 13.6.

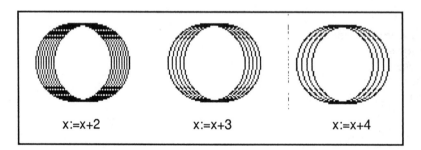

x:=x+2   x:=x+3   x:=x+4

Exhibit 13.6: Circles change in appearance with a change in the value added to "x" in program 3

Therefore, by varying the initial values of "x" and "y," we vary the location of the graphic; by changing the number in the **while-do** statement, we vary the number of repetitions; by varying the numbers in the **Frameoval** statement, we vary the size (and shape); and by changing the size of the step in the amount added to "x" we change the appearance of the circle from black to a series of concentric circles.These are a very few of the simple manipulations possible that can lead to dramatic changes in the appearance of the graphic. The object can be readily repeated in different places, varied in size, a different shape used, the texture (and the color in color systems) changed, and so forth, all with very few lines of code.

In the next program listing we show a LOGO program that produces a circle. It is a very simple program: one line.

Program 4 (LOGO)
Repeat 180[**forward** 1 **right** 2]

The manner in which LOGO produces a circle is very different from Pascal. In two-dimensional graphics in LOGO one defines a circle as a series of short lines joined together at a small angle to each other, or forward 1, right 2. (In 3D graphics it is defined as a line on a sphere.) We can fancy up the circle by coding the LOGO program shown in the next listing as follows:

Program 5 (LOGO)
Pensize 20 2
Penpat: gray
Repeat 180[**forward** 1 **right** 2]
  Pensize 2 2
  Penpat: black
Repeat 180[**forward** 1 **right** 2]

This produces the graphic shown in Exhibit 13.7.

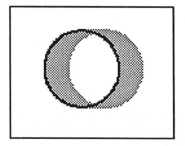

Exhibit 13.7: Circle generated by LOGO program 5

The graphic in Exhibit 13.7 looks different from those produced by the Pascal program because it is generated in an entirely different manner. A pen size and shade were specified in the LOGO program and then the circle was drawn using the pen defined. In Pascal we can also specify a pen size and shade, but it comes out different still! The listing in Pascal Program 6 produces the graphic in Exhibit 13.8.

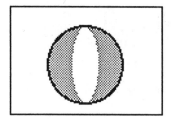

Exhibit 13.8: Circle generated by Pascal program 6

```
Program 6 (Pascal)
program Circle4;
   var
   x, y : integer;
begin
  x := 50;
  y := 50;
   PenSize(20, 2);
   PenPat(gray);
   Frameoval(y, x, y + 60, x + 60);
   PenSize(2, 2);
   PenPat(black);
   Frameoval(y, x, y + 60, x + 60);
end.
```

All the differences are attributable to how the programmers who produce the languages define the different operations in the different languages. Even the simple procedure of drawing a circle can be defined in different ways: short lines joined together, and a circle within a defined rectangle. BASIC defines a circle in a third familiar way: it uses polar coordinates, or defines a center point and a radius, as shown in the BASIC Program 7.

```
Program 7 (BASIC)
CIRCLE (70, 70), 50
```

The center is defined by the coordinates 70, 70, and the radius in pixels by the number 50. As we shall see in the next series of programs, namely the generation of cones based on the repeat drawing of circles, the difference between Cartesian and polar coordinates determines how easily we can draw a graphic in different languages.

13.6 REPEATING A SIMPLE SHAPE

In Exhibit 13.9 we show the result of the BASIC Program 8 listing.

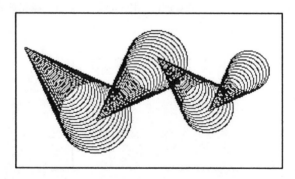

Exhibit 13.9: Cones generated by BASIC program 8

Program 8 (BASIC)
```
REM  Play on Cones
LET X=30
LET Y=40

FOR RADIUS=1 TO 35
    CIRCLE (X,Y), RADIUS
    LET X=X+2: LET Y=Y+2
NEXT RADIUS

FOR RADIUS=1 TO 30
    CIRCLE (X,Y),RADIUS
    LET X=X+2: LET Y=Y-2
NEXT RADIUS

FOR RADIUS=1 TO 25
    CIRCLE (X,Y),RADIUS
    LET X=X+2: LET Y=Y+2
NEXT RADIUS

FOR RADIUS=1 TO 20
    CIRCLE (X,Y),RADIUS
    LET X=X+2: LET Y=Y-2
NEXT RADIUS
```

The initial values of "X" and "Y" determine where the first cone starts; the FOR-TO statements determine the number of circles and the depth or size of each cone; and the LET statements change the location of the radii each time circles are produced.

Let us take a look at how a similar program might look in Pascal as shown in Pascal Program 9. Program 9 produces the two cones shown in Exhibit 13.10.

Program 9 (Pascal)
```
Program Play_Cone;
   var
   i, j, x : integer;
begin
   for i := 1 to 40 do
   Frameoval(i, i, 3 * i, 3 * i);
   j := 80;
   x := 1;
   for i := 80 to 150 do
   begin
     Frameoval(j, i, j + x, i + x);
     x := x + 1;
     j := j - 1;
   end;
end.
```

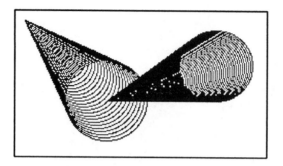

Exhibit 13.10: Cones generated by Pascal program 9

13.7 CARTESIAN AND POLAR COORDINATES

Pascal Program 9 produces two cones which are *not* at right angles to each other. Why? The answer lies in the difference between the Cartesian coordinates used in the Pascal program, and the polar coordinates used in the BASIC program. The diagram in Exhibit 13.11 helps explain why.

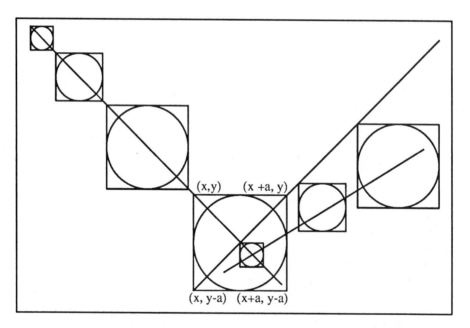

Exhibit 13.11: Cartesian and polar coordinates plot shapes differently

Exhibit 13.11 shows that in Cartesian coordinates the circle is described as an oval drawn within some defined rectangular frame with certain defined coordinates. When the oval is descending it is drawn at the same angle as the first oval defined in the BASIC program where the circles in the cone are defined by their center points and their radii. That is because the angle of a line joining the upper left corner points of the rectangles is parallel to a line joining the center points of the circles. But, when the cone is drawn upward in the Pascal program, this relationship no longer holds; a line joining the upper left corners of the rectangles is no longer parallel to a line joining the centers of the circles. This simple illustration shows that the drawing of certain figures in one set of coordinates is not necessarily easy in another set, and programming languages differ in the coordinates they use. A routine can be written that translates between Cartesian and polar coordinates. But, by this point things are no longer straightforward, and programs are getting more complicated and longer. Our purpose here is to point out the differences.*

A similar situation exists with LOGO program 10 as follows:

Program 10 (LOGO)

```
TO CIRCLE:THELIST          (Subroutine used later)
FRAMEOVAL:THELIST
END

TO DO_CONE :A1 :A2         (Entered by user with parameters)
MAKE A3 2                  (Initial values of A3 and A4)
MAKE A4 2

REPEAT 30 [ MAKE ALIST LPUT :A1 []     (Builds list)
            MAKE ALIST LPUT :A2 :ALIST
            MAKE ALIST LPUT :A3 :ALIST
            MAKE ALIST LPUT :A4 :ALIST

CIRCLE :ALIST              (Uses subroutine)
MAKE A1 :A1 + 1            (Increments values of A1, A2, A3, & A4)
MAKE A2 :A2 + 1
MAKE A3 :A3 + 4
MAKE A4 :A4 + 4]
END
```

In the LOGO program, circles and ovals are also defined using Cartesian coordinates. The above program makes a cone of 30 circles, and the location and size of the circles vary according to how A1 and A2 (location) and A3 and A4 (the size) are defined. The location may be defined as "0 0." In that case the cone begins in the center of the screen, the "0 0" location in LOGO, unlike in Pascal and BASIC, where "0 0" is defined as the uppermost left-hand corner of the screen. The circles increase in size by 4 pixels (see the last two statements before the final END).

---

* In addition, in the Pascal Cone program we had to "tinker around" to find the center point to begin the second cone. In the BASIC program, because polar coordinates are being used, one is already at the center point when the second, third, and fourth cones are generated.

PART B

The reader is reminded that here in part B the purpose of the text and the programs is to provide further examples of computer-generated graphics. The mathematics may not be understood by the reader in all of its detail. However, this does not prevent the reader from entering these programs and seeing the results; or learning to change parameters, that is, different values in the programs, and seeing how such changes affect output.

13.8 MATHEMATICS AND AESTHETICS

We now look at the use of the simple sine curve as the basis for creating weaving patterns. The discussion and programs in this section orginate with a program created by Daniel Cooper (1984) called Sinescape. Cooper's original program in BASIC is reproduced with minor changes in Program 11. The original program was written in Applesoft BASIC on the Apple IIe and included commands that controlled color. The program listed here is in MicroSoft BASIC on the Apple Macintosh, and includes no color commands because the Apple Macintosh has no color.

```
Program 11 (BASIC)
10 REM
15 REM      Based on Sinescape
20 REM      by Daniel Cooper
25 REM        (C) 1984
26 REM
27 REM Changes random numbers
30 RANDOMIZE TIMER
31 REM Start of curve phase
35 A = INT(RND(1)*200)
40 REM Frequency of curve
45 N=INT(RND(1)*58)+20
50 REM Axis location
55 Z=INT(RND(1)*92)+50
60 REM Height limit from axis
65 ZF=Z: IF Z > 96 THEN ZF=96 - (Z-96)
70 REM Curve height or amplitude
75 W=INT(RND(1)*ZF)
80 IF W<10 THEN W=10
85 REM Density of shade
90 G=INT(RND(1)*4)+1
95 REM Plotting routine
100 FOR X=0 TO 512 STEP G
105 REM Compute Y
110 Y=SIN ((X+A)/N)*W+Z
115 REM Draw vertical line
120 LINE (X,Z)-(X,Y)
125 NEXT X
130 REM Begin again
135 GOTO 35
```

The definition of the different variables in Program 11 are illustrated in Exhibit 13.12.

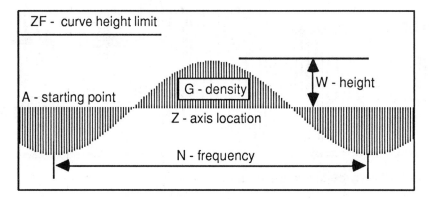

Exhibit 13.12: Variables used in Sinescape programs 11 and 12

Cooper's program runs in a continuous loop; the program will continually draw sine curves of varying phases, or lengths between peaks, of different heights, of changing location of axes, and of different densities or fill, until terminated at the keyboard by the operator. Two of an innumerable number of possible patterns are given in Exhibits 13.13 and 13.14 produced, as we shall discuss, in a slightly different manner.

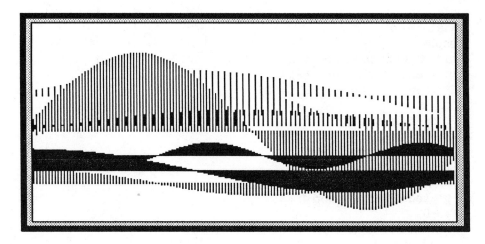

Exhibit 13.13: Sinescape based on 7 iterations

Cooper (1984) writes, "You have to watch, wait, and freeze the process at a moment when its form is most beautiful or right to you" And, "...Random numbers for the variables in the curves is an important part of the artistic conception. This element lets happy accidents occur, things that you or I might not have consciously chosen because of habits in our usual ideas of balance or texture."

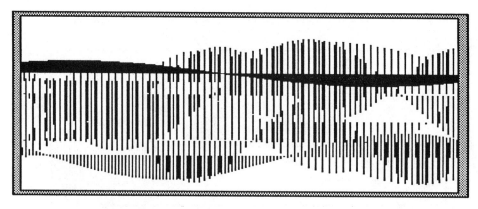

Exhibit 13.14: Sinescape based on 10 iterations

In order to explore another factor, namely the number of curves drawn, the Sinescape is programmed in Pascal in Program 12, but in a slightly modified form.

```
Program 12 (Pascal)
Program Sinscape7;
  var
  a, n, z, zf, w, g, x, y, c : integer;
begin
  c := 0;
  while c < 7 do
    begin
     a := abs(Random) mod 200;
     n := ( abs(Random) mod 58) + 20;
     z := ( abs(Random) mod 92) + 50;
     zf := z;
      if z > 96 then
     zf := 96 - (z - 96);
     w := abs(Random) mod zf;
      if w < 10 then
     w := 10;
     g := ( abs(Random) mod 4) + 1;
     x := 0;
       while x < 512 do
         begin
         y := Round(sin((x + a) / n) * w + z);
         drawline(x, z, x, y);
          x := x + g;
        end;
        c := c + 1;
    end;
end.
```

An additional variable, "c" for "counter," has been added, first initialized to zero, then incremented at the end of the loop by one, until the value in the first while-do statement is false, thus terminating the program run. This is how Exhibits 13.13 and 13.14 were produced; the first with seven iterations and the second with ten. It removes the watching, waiting, and freezing Cooper writes about, and the choice of what appeals waits until one sees the final graphic produced. The point here, however, is to demonstrate differences in programming, not aesthetic approaches.

The reader may also note that the manner in which BASIC and Pascal compute random numbers is different, thus leading to differences in how the line statements computing random values appear in the above programs. In BASIC, "RND" for "randomize" produces some random number between 0 and 1.0. Thus line 45, **N=INT(RND(1)*58)+20**, in the BASIC program produces a random integer number between 20 and 78.

In the Pascal program, **n:= (abs(Random) mod 58)+20;**, performs the same function. "Random" in Pascal is a function that returns a random integer number between -32768 and 32767. The "abs" command for "absolute" eliminates all negative numbers. The "mod" for "modulas" means "divide the random number by 58 and then use the remainder in the calculation." This, of course, very simply and cleverly ensures that the result never exceeds 78 or drops below 20. Thus, we obtain the same result using different approaches in the two languages. If the reader has access to a computer, he or she may wish to enter the above programs and systematically vary the parameters and observe the changes that occur.

13.9 FRACTALS AND FANTASY

A recent mathematical theory is based on the part being the whole, namely, the fractal geometry of Benoit B. Mandelbrot (1983). In fractal geometry ("fractal" for fractional dimension) each sub-part of a structure is similar to every other part, but the whole is as diverse as nature. Using the laws of fractal geometry, computer programs are able to simulate the appearance of mountains, plants, snowflakes, and shore lines with amazing reality. The apparent chaos of nature is lawful.

Fractals are constructed by repeatedly applying a set of rules to a given shape. Each fractal grows in generations from a seed called an initiator. Each generation is the product of the previous generation, n-1. The rule or set of rules used to transform a given fractal from its initiator to each succeeding generation is called the generator.

Recursion—or a function that calls itself—is used in fractal programs. The classic example of a recursive function is factorial n, defined as the product of the integers from 1 to n, or:

$$F(n)=n*F(n-1).$$

For example, with n=6 , F(6)=6*F(5), or F(6)=6*5*F(4), and so on. Notice we keep calling, or using, the factorial function in the next step of calculation.

The next program, Pascal Program 13, was written by Matthew Zeidenberg (1985) to produce stylized images of "dragons." The figures produced, based on different numbers of repeated calls, are shown in Exhibits 13.15 through 13.18. Not until we get to 12 repetitions or more do the "dragons" start to emerge. With 15 repetitions the dragon's "eyes" begin to appear!

Program 13 (Pascal)
by Zeidenberg (1985)
program Dragon;
  const

      {***Center point of Dragon***}

  xorig = 250;
  yorig = 180;
  scaling = 100;

  var
  x1, y1, x2, y2, x3, y3, n: **integer**;

      {***Procedure to create nth generation given three points for the initiator***}

  procedure dragonr (x1, y1, x2, y2, x3, y3, n: **integer**);

  var
  x4, y4, x5, y5, ydiff, xdiff : **integer**;

begin

      {***If n=1 then draw the seed curve or line***}

  if (n = 1) **then**
  begin
    drawline(x1, y1, x2, y2);
    drawline(x2, y2, x3, y3);
  end

      {***Otherwise construct the next generation***}

  else
  begin

      {***Calculate the next generation points***}

    x4 := ((x1 + x3) div 2);
    y4 := ((y1 + y3) div 2);
    x5 := x3 + (x2 - x4);
    y5 := y3 + (y2 - Y4);

      {***Recursive calls to dragonr to create
          succeeding generations***}

```
      dragonr(x2, y2, x4, y4, x1, y1, n - 1);
      dragonr(x2, y2, x5, y5, x3, y3, n - 1);
    end;
  end;
```

{***Draw text window, prompt for n, and display drawing window***}

```
  procedure init (var n: integer);
    var
     drawwin : rect;
    begin
      hideall;
      showtext;
      write(' input order of curve ');
      readln(n);
      hideall;
      drawwin.top := 40;
      drawwin.left := 0;
      drawwin.right := 512;
      drawwin.bottom := 512;
      setdrawingrect(drawwin);
      showdrawing;
    end;
```

{***Main program to draw dragon***}

```
  begin
    init(n);
    x1 := xorig + scaling;
    y1 := yorig;
    x2 := xorig;
    y2 := yorig - scaling;
    x3 := xorig - scaling;
    y3 := yorig;
```

{***Call dragonr to create nth generation***}

```
  dragonr(x1, y1, x2, y2, x3, y3, n);
  SaveDrawing('file name');

end.
```

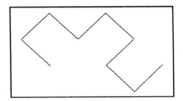

Exhibit 13.15: Fractal dragon with 3 iterations

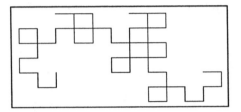

Exhibit 13.16: Fractal dragon with 6 iterations

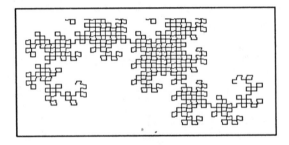

Exhibit 13.17: Fractal dragon with 10 iterations

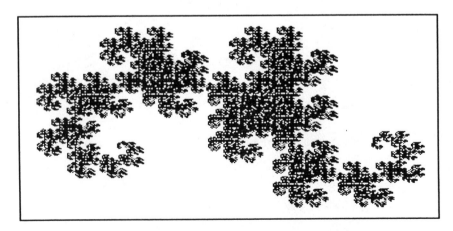

Exhibit 13.18: Fractal dragon with 15 iterations

The same output is produced by LOGO program 14 as follows:

Program 14 (LOGO)

```
TO DRAGON :x1 :y1 :x2 :y2 :x3 :y3 :n
   LOCAL x4
   LOCAL y4
   LOCAL x5
   LOCAL y5

  IF (:n = 1)

   [ MOVETO :x1 :Y1
     LINETO :x2 :y2
     MOVETO :x2 :y2
     LINETO :x3 :y3
   ]

  IF (:n > 1)

   [ MAKE x4 ROUND ((:x1 + :x3) / 2)
     MAKE y4 ROUND ((:y1 + :y3) / 2)
     MAKE x5 :x3 + (:x2 - :x4)
     MAKE y5 :y3 + (:y2 - :y4)
     dragon :x2 :y2 :x4 :y4 :x1 :y1 (:n - 1)
     dragon :x2 :y2 :x5 :y5 :x3 :y3 (:n - 1)
   ]

END

MAKE n 12
MAKE xorig 10
MAKE yorig 15
MAKE scaling 100
MAKE a (:xorig + :scaling)
MAKE b :yorig
MAKE c :xorig
MAKE d (:yorig - :scaling)
MAKE e (:xorig - :scaling)
MAKE f :yorig
CLEARSCREEN
dragon :a :b :c :d :e :f :n
```

The LOGO program looks very different, but it produces the same output. By changing the n in the 12th line from the bottom, now set to 12 as follows: **MAKE** n 12, the number of recursions changes.

13.10 MAKING PROGRAMS UNDERSTANDABLE

There are some general practices applicable with any language that make programming a more useful, communicative, and pleasurable process. They are listed in Exhibit 13.19.

---

1. Give the program a meaningful name or title, and, if necessary, describe the purpose of the program.
2. Annotate the program. Make remarks throughout the program to make the program more understandable, and document *as* you code because you are less likely to do so *after* you code.
3. Choose variable names that communicate their meaning. Unnecessary obscurity is caused by the poor choice of variable names. If a number is a radius then use "R," "rad," or "radius" as the variable name, not "N," "number," or "count."
4. Write the program so that the structure of what is going on is apparent. With BASIC programs, for example, where the language does not demand structure, we must provide structure in a disciplined manner.
5. Leave white space or blank lines between different program sections, for example, input or read, process or calculate, and print or display.
6. Indent loops. When there is some repeat process, set it off by indenting the group of lines of the program that make up the loop.
7. Use flow charts where appropriate. Flow charts should be used judiciously because they take time to draw. However, the graphics capabilities of small computers should encourage more creative flow charting.
8. Make the output understandable. This means labeling it to identify what different values mean, or the relevance of given graphics.
9. When programming on the Macintosh, a number of helpful structuring and debugging devices are available including:

   √ Reserved language words are automatically displayed in bold type.
   √ In Pascal, the loops and so forth are automatically indented.
   √ When an error occurs, an arrow points to the offending program statement, and an error message is displayed on the top in a separate window. In Pascal, the error message is accompanied by a picture of a "Bug"!
   √ When the first syntactic error occurs, a finger appears and points to the offending line statement.

Exhibit 13.19: Some general programming practices

13.11 TOOLBOXES

As stated earlier, the three languages discussed fulfill the toolkit concept and the human way of doing things to some extent only. They are not, however, devoid of these qualities. In fact, it is the access provided to various graphics toolboxes on various systems that gives the languages so much graphics power. Very often the graphics capabilities are in the toolbox, not in the language.

The language, however, must provide access to the toolbox. Therefore, graphics can be added by either writing graphics procedures in the language, or by obtaining a graphics package, or toolbox, of callable routines.

Some examples of different toolboxes include

IBM PC:
Halographics
GKS (which also defines the Graphics Kernal System standard)
GEM (which is a graphic, or icon, and window user-interface, *and* a toolbox)
Turbo-Graphix (which works with Turbo-Pascal)
Apple Macintosh: *Quickdraw* in ROM (Read Only Memory)
Amiga: Graphics and Animation custom chips (processors)

The hardware processors developed for graphics, and the software toolboxes developed to work with those processors, give rise to the problems of standards, compatibility, and transportability. Work performed on one system may not be available to other systems. Graphics standards are discussed in Appendix D.

In a highly graphic environment, languages take on more capabilities. For example, it is often possible to program mouse-controlled input and output, drop-down menus, and dialog boxes, as well as access the graphics routines. The graphics routines include selection of various text font faces and sizes; pen and line drawing routines; varieties of patterns for pens; routines to draw rectangles, ovals, arcs, and polygons; routines to fill shapes with various patterns or colors; and routines to hide, display, and vary the appearance of the cursor.

The concept of the toolbox will expand. It is, in fact, inhuman to expect humans to generate lengthy complex programs free of errors. Toolboxes will emerge whereby the computer will be instructed to generate program code that will be devoid of errors. Will we still need to know anything? Yes, most certainly. How to solve problems, meet needs, and reach goals will remain a human preoccupation. And, how to use the computer to accomplish such things will remain a human responsibility. The electric drill and power saw, automated tools of woodworking, do not guarantee that the carpenter will use them appropriately or well. They could provide the means to rapidly make a mess of things! But, in the hands of a skilled person, they create a powerful synergy. Further, the more persons who know how to use the tools directly, the greater the potential benefits. With computer systems and programming languages, we have only just begun to tap the immense possibilities.

14

Programming with Graphics

14.1 INTRODUCTION

In this chapter we discuss the use of graphics-based languages to program; the reverse, if you will, of using traditional programming languages to generate graphics.

Programming is an esoteric and abstract skill where one must learn to use a language which, no matter how much it might be claimed to resemble English, seems closer to a computer than to the human mind. Good programmers are rare, not because most people are unable to think logically or produce algorithms to solve problems, but because programming languages themselves are not particularly easy to learn to use.

In response to this problem some researchers and developers are creating graphics programming languages. Because images are used to represent program processes, the abstract becomes more concrete, and direct control over computer functioning is placed in the hands of more people, and more people become programmers.

Two systems are described in this chapter. The first is Odesta's databased information management and decision support system, *Helix*. The second, *Prograph,* is under development at the Technical University of Nova Scotia, Halifax, Nova Scotia, under the direction of Dr. Tomasz Pietrzykowski and his associate, Dr. Phillip Cox.

Odesta Helix, which is available for use on the Apple Macintosh, is not a complete programming language in a traditional sense, providing all the freedom—and all the work—that such languages provide. It has some faults and limitations, but it is a remarkable effort and a highly usable product.

14.2 REVIEW OF DATABASE

It is necessary to have some understanding of the basic concepts of database in order to use *Helix*, or any database management system. Although there are various types of database, namely, hierarchical, network, relational, and mixtures of these, we shall only consider *relational databases*. Relational databases are the most prominent form of database, and they are easy to understand.

A database management system (DBMS) is a computerized record–keeping system, an electronic filing cabinet, able to manipulate and display information in a manner that would be quite impossible with a manual system. In a relational database, data storage is in the form of tables. An example for information on wines is shown in Exhibit 14.1.

Note that there is only one value listed in each record for each data item or field; there is no space provided for repeated entries. Therefore, the table is a flat table usually referred to as a *flat file*. In many instances not providing for repeating groups makes complete sense; there is only one value that can exist. For example, all of the data items in our wine database can have only one value. If we had added "supplier" as a heading in the table, this data item could possess a number of entries. This is handled in a relational DBMS by simply setting up an independent table or file of the repeating group and relating the two tables or relations by some field containing common information.

14.2-1 File- or applications-oriented systems

A problem is created when data are stored in separate files related to some given application program only. Data and processing redundancy, inflexibility, difficulty in maintenance, and little

Table, relation, or file

BIN	WINE	PRODUCER	YEAR	BOTTLES	READY
1	Chardonnay	Grand Pre	84	12	86
2	Chardonnay	Buena Vista	79	1	88
3	Chardonnay	Louis Martini	79	5	87
6	Jo. Reisling	Jekel Vineyard	77	24	89
11	Fume Blanc	Buena Vista	79	20	86
14	Cab. Sauvgn.	Robt. Mondavi	77	24	87
25	Cab. Sauvgn.	Mirassou	78	8	89
34	Pinot Noir	Mirassou	81	12	90

Record   Data items or fields

Exhibit 14.1: Information on wines in the form of a table

or no support for rapid applications program development will occur. It is flogging a dead horse to attempt to make a grand case for database over file management systems; there is no case for applications-oriented file systems except in simple situations. Many filing problems for a small business enterprise, or for the individual professional or executive, can often be handled by a file management system, but one is still better off having access to a system with relational database capabilities. Exhibit 14.2 shows a diagram of the general situation in a file- or applications-oriented system.

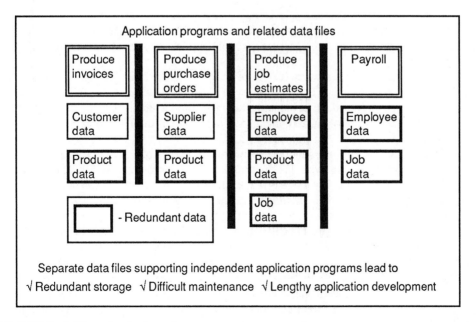

Exhibit 14.2: A file-oriented system

14.2-2 Database- and subject-oriented systems

The same applications as in Exhibit 14.2 are shown in a database environment in Exhibit 14.3.

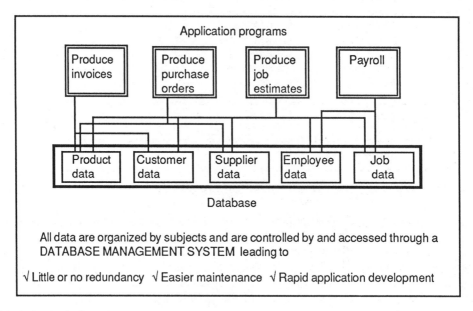

Exhibit 14.3: A database-oriented system

With a database, the same data are used for all applications. Therefore, there is minimal redundancy, greater flexibility, and more support for rapid applications development by both end users and programmers.

A database management system is a piece of software for managing the database. DBMSs possess different characteristics, capabilities, even styles as if tailored for different users. Some capabilities enhance the productivity of programmers (applications may be developed without concern for how the data are organized; the DBMS takes care of that), and other capabilities are for the end users.

The capabilities for end users include software that allows one to query, or ask questions of, the database ("How many employees in department A make more than $123,000 per annum?" The DBMS answers: None.) But query languages ask questions in different ways: some through a query command language that resembles a structured English; some through the use of menus, tables, forms, or icons that provide choices, and some through the use of ordinary English in the form of requests like the above. The latter depends upon Artificial Intelligence (AI) built into the system and is the easiest to use. The menu, table, form, or icon approaches are the next most congenial, and command languages can sometimes be quite complicated. However, as Date (1983) points out, command languages will use on the order of eight lines of code and perform what would take on the order of eight pages of code if the same request had to be programmed in COBOL.

Other associated programs include form, report, graphics, and application generators, which allow the end user to generate programs independently of programmers.

An introduction to data modeling, the process whereby we model the database required based on needs, and prototyping, the process whereby we approximate the desired end system, is provided in *Systems Analysis and Design: Alternative Structured Approaches* (Marshall, 1986).

14.3 HELIX

Helix, like many other DBMS systems, attempts to place the tools for data management in the hands of the user, and decrease reliance on the computer specialist. But *how* Helix approaches and accomplishes this task is quite different. Helix uses graphics or icons to establish the database and represent processing. Many processing capabilities that would normally require a programmer can be accomplished independently by the user.

However, some effort must be made to learn Helix. It is not, at first, particularly easy to use. Some of the difficulties come from poor, but not critical, design choices in regard to the human interface; some from the lack of knowledge users might have solving problems with computers.

Although Helix makes abstract processes more concrete and visible through the use of icons, this does not in any way eliminate the task of creating well-designed databases that are accurately modeled to meet all user needs. Further, the database must be implemented properly to make optimal use of computer resources in the system being used.

14.3-1 Helix in Application

Helix opens on the Macintosh with the window shown in Exhibit 14.4.

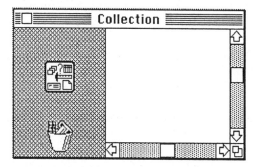

Exhibit 14.4: The first *Helix* window

The dark area can be considered a toolbox. There are only two tools displayed at this level: an icon which represents the tool for creating a file or a relation, and a wastebasket for getting rid of an unwanted file or relation. One drags the image of the create icon into the white work area to the right, as shown in Exhibit 14.5. The icon is now automatically labeled "Relation." By dragging the create icon a number of times into the white work-space area, we can have more than one "Relation," or as many relations as required in a given application. The relations are then renamed by the user as shown in Exhibit 14.6 with the same subject names as portrayed in Exhibit 14.3.

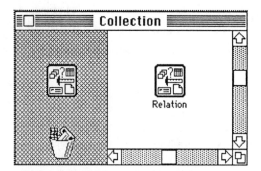

Exhibit 14.5: A single relation is initiated

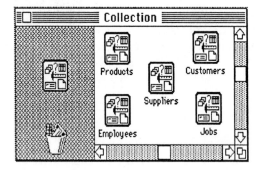

Exhibit 14.6: Many relations labeled with their subject content

Exhibits 14.7 and 14.8 show relations for a library system and a quilt business, respectively, provided by Helix. These applications are not trivial, and the Exhibits display how the "Relation" icons may be labeled in other applications. We will use a simpler example to demonstrate the further use of Helix.

Helix allows us to obtain help at any time. More important, Helix allows us to create our own custom help screens, as shown in Exhibit 14.9. Exhibit 14.9 shows that Helix sometimes uses unfamiliar terms; a *collection* for a database, a *relation* for a file (familiar to computer specialists but not most users), and so forth. This may delay initial learning.

14.3-2 A survey example

Let us assume we need to survey food prices on a periodic basis at different store locations. We wish to determine and compare the average and variability of consumer food costs. Let us begin to create a database and information system to support this need. We create a relation, or file, as shown in Exhibit 14.10. When we click twice on the "Product Prices" icon, a new toolbox and work area appear, shown in Exhibit 14.11.

Exhibit 14.7: A library database

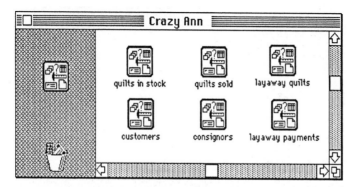

Exhibit 14.8: A database to support a quilt business

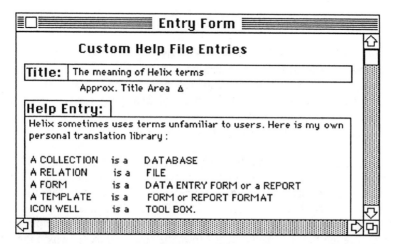

Exhibit 14.9: Custom help screen created by the user

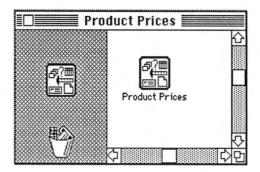

Exhibit 14.10: Initiating a file of information on product prices

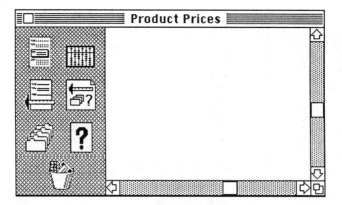

Exhibit 14.11: The icon tools used to create relations

Six new tools are displayed. Reading from left to right and top to bottom they are

- an icon used for creating fields in files or relations
- an abacus icon used for specifying processing
- a template icon used for creating forms and reports
- a forms and reports icon used for entering data and displaying results
- an index icon used to create indexes
- a query icon used to create selected queries of the database

All these functions are created by dragging the icon into the work area. In Exhibit 14.12 all the icons created and named in our example system are shown for tracking consumer product prices. If we click twice on the "Price Entry Design" icon, we see a template used to design the price entry screen. This is shown in Exhibit 14.13. The details for creating this screen are not shown. The larger letters in the boxes on the left of the work area are the prompts, and the smaller labels on the right are the fields of data dragged from the new toolbox shown on the far left, where fields of data are listed rather than portrayed in icon form.

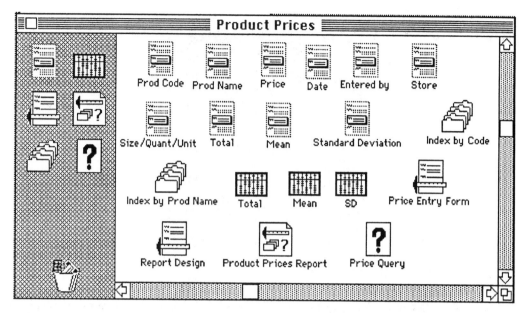

Exhibit 14.12: The icons representing the product prices relation or file

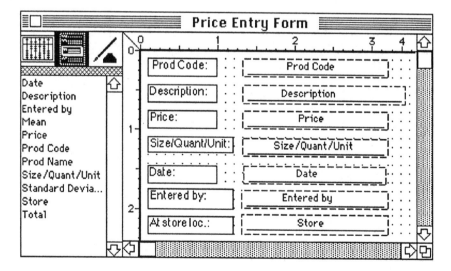

Exhibit 14.13: The template used to create the data entry screen

We can index our data for more rapid retrieval. The telephone directory indexes information by city and last name. This allows for more efficient retrieval. In a similar but automated fashion, indexes to databases perform the same basic function. Exhibit 14.14 shows the window for creating indexes.

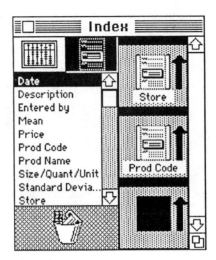

Exhibit 14.14: The indexing screen

The data in this relation is indexed first by store and then within each store by product code. The up arrow means that the indexing is either in alphabetical order A to Z, or numeric order 1, 2, 3. If the arrow was clicked to show down, then the ordering would be in reverse order, that is, Z to A, and back to 1. Exhibit 14.15 shows the data entry screen with an item entered.

Product Prices	
Prod Code:	D128
Description:	Homogenized Milk
Price:	$2.50
Size/Quant/Unit:	gallon
Date:	11/6/86
Entered by:	GRM
At store loc.:	A

Exhibit 14.15: The data entry screen

In order to summarize our data, we need to sum the prices across all items for each store and then take the average of that sum. In order to evaluate the variability in prices between stores and/or at different times, we compute the standard deviation of scores from the average. Exhibit 14.16 shows the abacus icon one would select from the toolbox to compute averages.

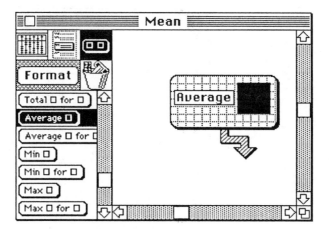

Exhibit 14.16: The abacus screen used to specify processing

We indicate the operand by dragging it from the toolbox into the black box of the operator, as shown in Exhibit 14.17. In this case, the operand is price.

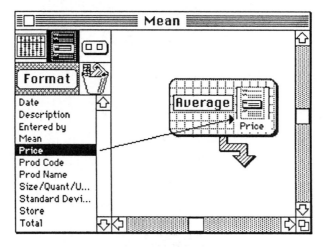

Exhibit 14.17: The operand entered from the toolbox

The tiles, as they are called, are provided by Helix for performing a great variety of functions which can be used in many combinations. They constitute the heart of the graphics programming language of Helix and are shown in Exhibit 14.18.

The tiles used to compute the standard deviation, defined as

$$SD = (\sqrt{\Sigma X^2 - (\Sigma X)^2/N})/N$$

are shown in Exhibit 14.19. The computation of this formula demonstrates nine of the over eighty tile functions available.

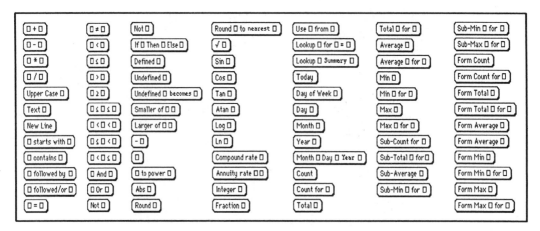

Exhibit 14.18: Computation tiles

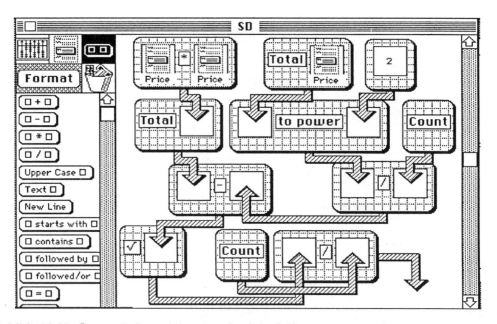

Exhibit 14.19: Computation of the standard deviation

Exhibit 14.20 shows a selection window for this application. We have two templates, one for data entry and the other for reports. We click or choose the report design as shown by the dark bar, and we can then choose to index the report. The resulting output is shown in Exhibit 14.21.

We establish a query by dragging the query icon into the work space. When we click on the query icon itself, the screen in Exhibit 14.22 is displayed. Let us assume we wish to select records for report that fall into the dairy category. We have coded products with a "D" for dairy, or a "P" for produce, and so on. We click the "Product Code" field and the screen in Exhibit 14.23 appears.

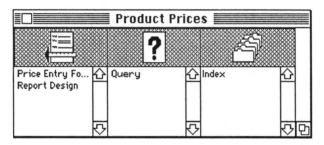

Exhibit 14.20: A selection window for creating reports

Average and Variation of Cost of Food Products: Store A. December, 1986		
Total: 16.35	Mean: 2.04	SD: .43
Prod Code:	**Description:**	**Price:**
D128	Homogenized Milk	$2.50
D213	Cottage Cheese	$1.25
M012	Calves Liver	$1.35
P008	Beets	$1.50
P123	Lettuce	$1.25
P213	Spinach	$1.25
P451	Potatoes	$2.25
P905	Carrots	$5.00

Exhibit 14.21: Report selected by store and ordered by product code

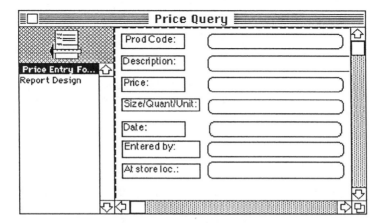

Exhibit 14.22: The screen for specifying queries of the database

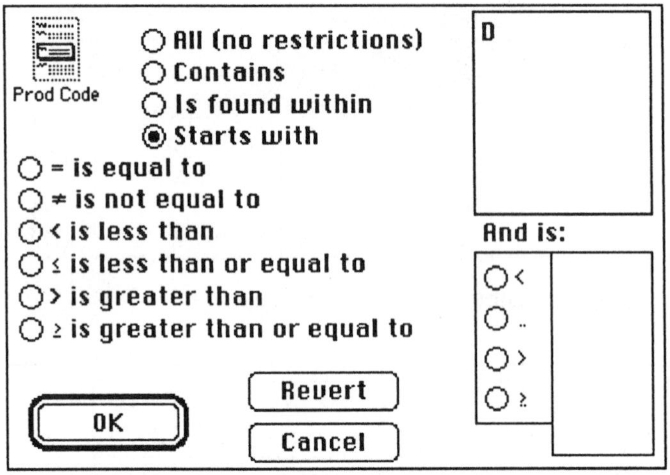

Exhibit 14.23: Menu showing selection of records of product codes beginning with "D"

We choose "starts with" and enter a "D," click on the "OK" button and return to the former window. It has "Prod Code" highlighted in the field, which means we are using that field to select records. Exhibit 14.24 displays the resulting report now showing only the dairy products surveyed.

Average and Variation of Cost of Food Products: Store A. December, 1986		
Total: 16.35	Mean: 2.04	SD: .43
Prod Code:	Description:	Price:
D128	Homogenized Milk	$2.50
D213	Cottage Cheese	$1.25

Exhibit 14.24: Report on dairy products only (The total, mean, and standard deviation are for *all* products. Helix could have been readily programmed to display these values for dairy products only.)

14.3-3 Some comments

In Helix, to enter a record, update records, and scan through records during data entry, one needs to use the keyboard, the mouse, and a pull-down menu. This is *not* the best use of the Macintosh interface. A button to scan through a file, or use of the slide bar would have been preferable. Each time the menu is pulled down, it hides the record being viewed.

Helix suffers from poorly conceived icons. They do not immediately communicate the meaning of the function they represent; for example, an icon of a pen and ink bottle is used to represent the designing of forms. However, to most people, this icon communicates a writing function, not forms design. Icons should communicate immediately. If they are too cluttered, then we try to "read" them and the immediate impact of communication is lost. This interferes in the early stages of learning, the most critical stages, when the user is likely to reject the product because he or she cannot understand it.

The design of icons is not trivial and should not be undertaken lightly. Their design is based on the science of *Semiotics*, that is, the science of signs (Marcus, 1983). Signs or icons may vary from the very representational (brush and paper to represent a "paint" program) to the very abstract but conventional symbol (red stop sign). But in all cases icons must immediately communicate what they represent. Some examples of well-designed icons are given in Exhibit 14.25 where the visual appearance is appealing and simple, and the related meaning obvious.

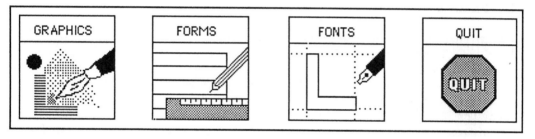

Exhibit 14.25: Well-designed icons (Marcus, 1983)

Familiar references are sometimes not used in Helix. The manual, for example, gives no reference to "Reports." The same template icon is used for designing data entry forms and information reports. One thinks of forms as an input process and reports as an output process, and differentiating the two in the basic design of Helix would have been helpful.

There are some built-in functions, called summary tiles, such as count, total, average, minimum, and maximum, but the user cannot create his or her own functions or macros. This latter capability would amplify the power of the system.

Time or date tagging does not appear to be possible, unless entered manually. The current date is displayed on a record, but does *not* get entered and, therefore, the record is not actually time tagged. The next time one views the record, a new current date appears.

In Helix one cannot have branched "wires." That is, it is not possible to send the same data item, computed or retrieved, to different places in a process. This could become a serious limitation in more complex applications.

However, Helix performs many things extremely well. For example, Helix will automatically download current work in volatile memory to permanent storage on magnetic disk if no activity occurs for some given period of time, and the time period is under the user's control. This is a valuable safeguard against loss of data.

Another aspect of Helix—and very much to the credit of the designers—is that it assumes users are intelligent. Helix does not hold things up or lose work because of gaps in information or the logic of the system during the time the user is creating an application. For example, it is possible to design a form before defining all the fields that will be entered into that form. But, one can choose "save anyway" and then define additional fields required later.

Helix possesses good error capture capabilities. It will not allow for illogical operations when using the calculate tiles. It also possesses flexible report options, but it takes some time to discover how to access and use them. Helix is excellent for prototyping.

We have reviewed Helix rather thoroughly because it is a new concept, one with promise, and a great effort in the proper direction. One might question whether such a complete return to icons, including the determining of all processing, is wise. Languages and mathematics evolved to solve communication problems. Is it easier to program in icons? For initial understanding and for limited functions, probably yes. For long complicated programming, most likely not. But only further empirical study will tell. No one knows.

14.4 PROGRAPH

For years programmers have been using Third Generation High Level Languages (HLLs), like COBOL, FORTRAN, Pascal, and BASIC. In order to get a picture of what was going on in the line-by-line sequence of instructions—or to communicate that information to someone else—the programmer might use *flow charts to graphically represent program logic*. But many programmers do not like flow charts; they are tedious to draw. Frederick Brooks, considered the "father of the IBM System/360," writes (Brooks, 1974), "The flow chart is a most thoroughly oversold piece of program documentation....The detailed blow-by-blow chart is an obsolete nuisance." And why? Because the flow chart is the visual *documentation* of a written program; the flow chart itself does nothing in relation to instructing the computer to perform some task. The actual program consists of lines of code, originating in the early days on paper and then transferred to punched cards. Later the coding using traditional languages took place using an editor or a word processor on *non*graphics systems. Moving from punched cards to interactive editors speeds up the process of program generation, but our thinking remains linear; we still think of programs as lines of instructions to be written one after the other.

Here we discuss a visual programming system called *Prograph*, a product developed by Dr. Tomasz Pietrzykowski and Dr. Phillip Cox of the Technical University of Nova Scotia, and principals in the company responsible for its development, Gunakara Sun Systems Limited (Halifax, Nova Scotia). A version of Prograph has been developed for the Apple Macintosh. It should be no surprise that visual programming is available on the Macintosh and not on the IBM PC; without graphics capabilities—icons, pull-down menus, graphics toolbox—visual programming would be much more difficult—or impossible—to develop. When MicroSoft Windows or another graphics interface becomes dominant on the IBM PC, then visual programming will appear for the IBM PC.

Programming in Prograph is also pictorial. The Prograph, the equivalent of a program, is a set of diagrams called frames. Pietrzykowski writes, "The Prograph combines the clarity and simplicity of data flow and data modeling diagrams with the power and compactness of such languages as LISP [the foundation of LOGO] and APL." (Private communication to author, 1986) Prograph represents the state-of-the-art in visual programming. There are two fundamental concepts which are in conflict in traditional languages: expressive power and compactness or clarity. These are harmoniously combined in Prograph.

Prograph is free of variables, variable declarations, and the linear production of code as required by most present-day high level languages. Wires represent variables, but they do not need to be identified or declared. Wires at the top of a frame are input, and at the bottom, output. A Prograph consists of a collection of frames. Frames are connected, as are the icons representing different functions within frames. Some frames are complex and consist of a number of connected compartments, and represent control structures, as found in other languages; for example, IF-THEN-ELSE, WHILE-DO, FORALL, SELECT, and so forth. An example Prograph is shown in Exhibit 14.26 to demonstrate some of the language's capabilities.

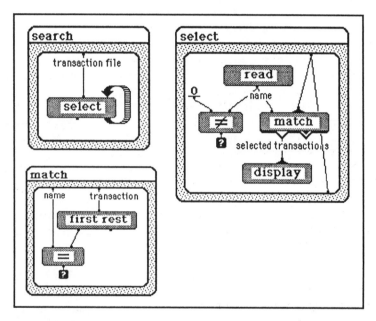

Exhibit 14.26: A Prograph

This Prograph searches a master file of transactions to find every transaction involving a particular product, the name of which is supplied by the user. The selected transactions are displayed and the process is repeated for different user-supplied transaction names until the name given is *0*. The definition *search* supplies the master file to the operation *select,* which is repeated as indicated by the loop icon. In the definition of *select* a name is read from the user's input terminal by the *read* operation, and supplied to the ≠ operation which compares it with *0*. If it is not *0* the rest of the definition is executed, and the whole process is repeated. If it is *0,* the loop terminates. The *match* operation is marked as a partition, indicated by the two special output terminals: white and black. This means that the operation is applied to each item in the master file, and the list of items which pass the test applied by *match* are directed through the left white terminal to the *display* operation. The definition *match* inputs a transaction to the operation *first rest*, which sends the *first* field of the transaction, where its name is stored, to its left output and the remaining fields in the transaction to the right. The name input by the user is then compared with this first field.

The Prograph in Exhibit 14.26 can perform a task which in languages like COBOL would require many lines or pages of complicated code. These simple but expressive pictures are easy to construct using the Prograph editor; the Prograph in Exhibit 14.26 required only 17 keystrokes and 58 mouse clicks. The Prograph editor is constructed in such a way that no name typed during the building of a Prograph file need be typed more than once. It also detects syntactical errors during the editing process.

An advanced feature of the Prograph development environment is that the process of building a Prograph can be concurrently accompanied by the process of executing it. Once an operation has been drawn and named it can be immediately executed. The execution is illustrated on the screen so the user may follow its progress and interrupt it at any time. Furthermore, during such an interruption the user may inquire about any past partial results, may modify any values in the procedure currently being executed, and even make modifications to this procedure. Upon instruction from the user, the system will resume execution, but will reexecute only those parts of the current procedure that have been affected by such changes. These features provide an excellent environment for rapid development and testing of complex Prographs.

Although the development environment allows for the rapid development and debugging of solutions to complex problems, it is not economical to run fully debugged Prographs in such a mode. The Prograph system, therefore, also provides an efficient optimizing compiler that produces directly executable machine language files for fast execution.

The strengths of Prograph are its simplicity, ease of use, syntactic and semantic error capture, the ability to test partially completed Prographs, process lists and graphical data, and design, query, and update database. Semantic error capture is possible because the user may interrupt execution at any time, and request partial results, if necessary correct the prograph, and then resume execution. Other programming languages do not allow for this type of interactive "debugging"; they require the development and running of tracing procedures, and reediting after the tracing is complete.

Prograph is particularly suitable for parallel processing. This is clearly visible in the general format of the Prograph. The reader will have to imagine a large number of frames connected by wires representing a large program, or Prograph. It is easier to see patterns and follow the logic of a process when the process is diagrammed, than when it is in the form of lines of programming code contained in many pages.

14.5 CONCLUSION

Both Helix and Prograph represent a unique use of computer graphics. One is available now with surprising power; the other is in a stage of development with great promise. Comparing the two systems is of minimal value; their purposes are quite different. The major difference is the potential flexibility and power of Prograph; its intent is to be a complete programming language, where the user, for example, would model and design the database and how it works. Helix is already established in this regard; it is already a database system. Prograph allows for database development, but is not set up as such. Prograph is being designed to function on the Apple Macintosh, but also on systems with parallel processing capabilities, systems that are not readily available at present. Helix does not have such ambitions. Both represent a new wave, a powerful approach to solving problems and instructing computers: the use of pictures. Truly, a picture will be worth a thousand words—in this case many thousands of lines of code.

Visual programming had to wait for the low cost graphics computer to arrive. In visual programming, the graphics interface to the computer allows us to draw an image—something like a flow chart—of what we want, and once the image is complete the computer is instructed; *the picture is the program*. Visual programming will revolutionize programming and the availability of programming, and it will also change the way we think, or how we imagine solutions to problems. Visual programming will arouse our perceptual brains; our right hemispheres. Further, as we progress to the use of parallel process computers, linear programming will be impossibly complex; we will literally not be able to see what we are doing. But if we can draw a map, a diagram, or a chart that is a representation of the parallel processing itself, then we will be able to visualize what we want, and express it in the visual language available.

The use of graphics or icons, however, does *not* guarantee that systems will optimize human-system performance. Careful attention must be paid to factors that influence both learning *and* retention. If we learn a system but then, with disuse, forget how to use it, there is a problem. It is the proper, and balanced, use of graphics that is required; only study and experience will tell us what that proper and balanced use is.

15

Needs Analysis and Systems Development

15.1 INTRODUCTION

Humans and computers complement each other well; the inherent weaknesses in one are the strengths of the other. Humans are slow, possess poor memories, are highly innovative, and a complex mixture of the intellectual and the emotional. Computers are fast, possess excellent memories, but are not terribly clever, and lack flexibility and intention. Computers are good at providing content; people are good at providing context. We can respond intuitively, and the response can be correct, but we are hard pressed to figure out how we did it. Computers are not capable of such responses. One major purpose of systems analysis is to determine what work is appropriate for computers to perform that acts in support of the higher levels of human functioning. Exhibit 15.1 diagrams the relationships we are discussing, provided by W.L. "Scot" Gardiner, a colleague at the GAMMA Institute (Montreal, Quebec).

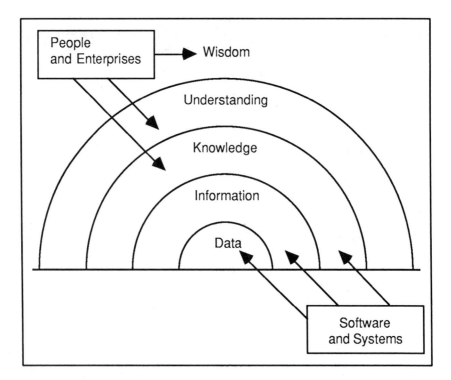

Exhibit 15.1: Computers provide content; people provide context
(Courtesy of Dr. W. L. Gardiner, GAMMA Institute, Montreal, Quebec)

Exhibit 15.1 redefines, in some sense, what it is to be human by defining what computers can or should do. It is inhuman to assign data, information—and sometimes knowledge—storage, organization, and selected retrieval to humans. We are simply not good at it. (Conversely, it is unthinkable to expect understanding and wisdom to be reflected in a computer's response.) Graphics facilitates our responsibility to provide context.

Graphics helps create knowledge, which is data transformed into information and turned into something useful. For example, diagrams have been used for millenia in all cultures to represent higher realms of human thought, feeling, expression, relationship, and action.

This chapter has four goals: one, to illustrate the importance and the stages of systems analysis and development and how we might think about the process; two, to outline the steps to follow in selecting or developing a graphics computer system; three, to provide some examples of the use of graphics in systems analysis itself; and, four, to provide a method and a set of criteria for evaluating and comparing graphics software, systems, and components.

15.2 PURPOSE OF ANALYSIS

Systems analysis consists of the detailed identification of user and enterprise needs, problems, and goals. The latter serve as the basis for the specifications of a system. The specifications that are the result of analysis determine systems design, development, or selection. The purpose of analysis is to ensure that the software and systems serve the users and the enterprise, not the reverse. The relationship of enterprise to systems is diagrammed in Exhibit 15.2.

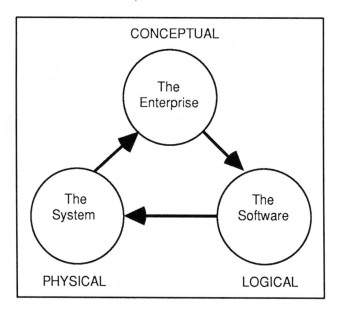

Exhibit 15.2: The model conceived on the enterprise level determines the logic implemented in the software to drive the physical system established to serve the enterprise

Exhibit 15.2 illustrates that the model conceived on the enterprise level determines the logic of the software implemented on the selected hardware. The latter then support the enterprise. The model conceived on the enterprise level determines the logic of the software, which in turn drives the system in support of the enterprise goals and needs.

Quite obviously, the output of the system is of prime importance. Exhibits 15.3 and 15.4 illustrate this fact and the requirement that *analysis and design take place in the reverse order of use*. That is, we define the outputs we need, and the form we need them in, to help solve our problems, meet our needs, and reach our goals. Then the outputs become the basis for the specifications for the rest of the system.

Exhibit 15.3: Output required specifies system

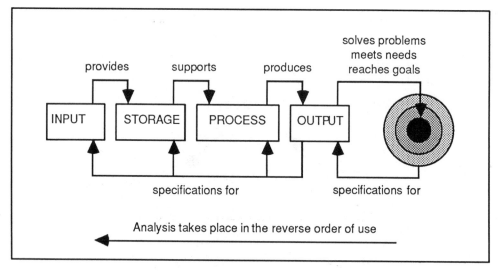

Exhibit 15.4: The order of analysis; the order of use

The analysis must also specify what form the outputs need to take, for whom, by when, and where. The analysis must determine what data need to be stored and processed to provide the outputs required. For example, the storage requirements may involve the design of a text and graphics database, and the design will require the *modeling* of how the text and graphics need to be stored and accessed so as to serve all user requirements effectively. An engineering or design company with a number of engineers, designers, and/or illustrators requiring access to the same information, would want to pay close attention to the design of a text and graphics database. The *same* set of text and graphics data and application software should support *all* users, thus providing minimal redundancy of the data and consistency in processing.* A key factor is that users must be involved in the data modeling; they are the "experts" on information needs and required access.

In this regard an interesting approach is offered by *Reflex For The Mac*, a database management system from Borland International (Scotts Valley, CA). The defining of files, fields of data within files, and the relation of files to other files in the database is graphic; once the data model diagram is complete, then the database has been defined and is ready for use. Exhibit 15.5 illustrates this fact using a system for attorney time and billing as an example.**

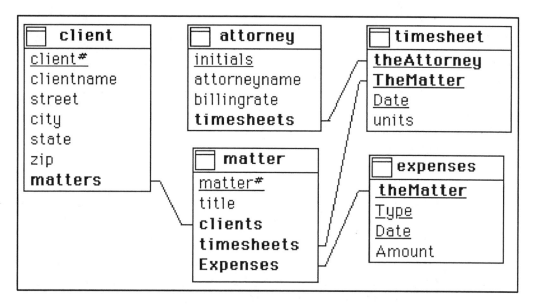

Exhibit 15.5: A graphics approach to defining relational database
(Courtesy of Borland International)

15.3 STAGES OF ANALYSIS

Large systems—the only kind that existed in the early days—require many man-years to develop, and the analyst's prime role is to translate user needs into system specifications for programmers to develop application programs to meet needs. The analyst in this capacity acts as a communication link, a technological "anthropologist" who understands the language of two "native" groups who need to communicate with each other but do not understand each other. Users know and speak the language of the enterprise and its problems, needs, and goals, and systems designers and programmers know and speak the language of computer technology and programming. The analyst

---

* General descriptions of the analysis and design process involved in data modeling for database is discussed elsewhere (Martin, 1982; Marshall, 1986).
** Reflex is impressively intuitive. The author was able to modify an existing database, add a relation, link the created relation to other relations, and specify indexes (underlined), without referencing the user's manual at all.

is supposed to speak *both*; sometimes things get lost in translation. The analyst in this traditional role is the manager of the system's development life cycle illustrated in Exhibit 15.6.

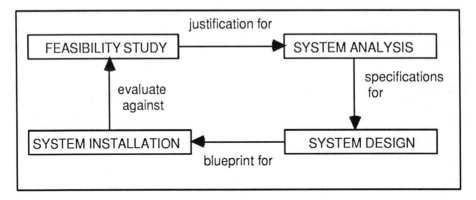

Exhibit 15.6: Traditional systems development cycle

As the reader might imagine, this process takes time, is expensive, and voraciously consumes human and other resources. With large system installation the formal stages are necessary. Even with large systems, however, automation of the tools of analysis, high user involvement, and user generated applications are possible and lead to superior systems installed at lower costs requiring less in the way of maintenance and support.

With small systems alternate systems development approaches need to be considered. Systems analysis and design is no less important with small systems; a $25,000 mistake for a small enterprise may be more damaging than a $250,000 mistake for a large enterprise.

The traditional cycle needs to be expanded. The analyst has a broader range of responsibilities, beyond translating user needs to programmers. They include educating users in the many possible uses of computers, establishing support from top management, selecting the appropriate systems development approach, establishing means for the rapid and smooth integration of the computer system into the user's operation, and training users in direct interactive use.

There are more development options than the traditional option of programming all that is required. In fact, with graphics systems it is highly unlikely that structured analysis and design to support custom programming would be the option of choice; the development time and the cost of graphics systems is too high. An alternate development cycle is suggested in Exhibit 15.7 and expanded upon in Exhibit 15.8. We shall briefly discuss each stage summarized in Exhibit 15.8.

15.3-1 Educate users

Client and user education is the first stage required. If possible, that education should be hands-on. Education should not be confused with training. Training follows systems installation; education precedes everything. Otherwise a "catch 22" situation is created; the user knows he needs something but does not know how to ask the right questions to find out. Executives and managers require education on the impact of computer systems on their enterprise, as well as the applications possible. All potential users require education on the use of applications related to jobs.

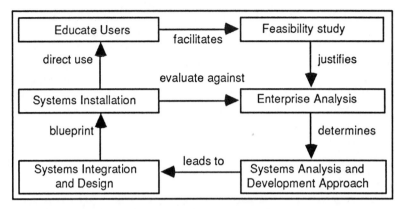

Exhibit 15.7: An expanded systems development cycle

CYCLE	ACTIVITIES
Educate Users	√ Evaluate attitudes √ Provide an overview of applications and related software √ Provide an overview of systems √ Make computer resources visible √ Provide hands-on experience
Feasibility Study	√ Corporate or enterprise feasibility? √ Economic feasibility? √ Technical feasibility? √ Estimate benefits and costs

Enterprise Analysis	√ Identify problems, needs, and goals
	√ Identify critical success factors
	√ Relate functional areas of enterprise
	  to database and computer applications
	  required

Systems Analysis and Development	√ Select a systems development approach
	  • Produce RFP for turnkey system
	  • Assemble from "off-the-shelf"
	  • Use existing graphics routines
	  • Program graphics routines
	  • Use a combination of the above

Systems Integration and/or Design	√ Evaluate and select software and systems √ If design, then use tools of structured analysis and design
Systems Installation	√ Evaluate and select vendors √ Establish installation timetable √ Train users √ Monitor and evaluate operation √ Establish support

Exhibit 15.8: Systems development cycle and related activities

Stories abound of perfectly sound systems scuttled because the human aspects were ignored. Attitudes to technology need to be dealt with early. Will engineers embrace or resist CAD? Will artists or designers consider the use of computers as antiaesthetic or threatening? We fear the unknown; familiarity breeds less fear. The task is to make computers familiar.

Planning must be top-down and design must be bottom-up. Or, executives must agree on and support the installation, and the installation must serve all parties in the enterprise, not only those at the top. In this regard, it is wise to provide clients and users with an overview of possible applications and application software. Users cannot be assumed to know the many applications possible. The very purpose of this text is to provide an image of computer graphics possibilities. Users need to know, at first in overview form, the specific functions performed by specific classes of software. Then, as discussed and charted at the end of this chapter, those functions need to be specified in more detail.

Users need to know, again in overview form, what computer graphics systems are available, including personal computers, enhanced personal computers, computer graphics workstations, network systems, and graphics systems functioning in large mainframe environments. They need to know the general differences in capabilities between these classes of systems, how they overlap in capabilities, and their relative strengths, weaknesses, and cost. For example, personal computers enhanced with high-resolution graphics cards and related graphics software selected and integrated by the user, and costing in the vicinity of $15,000, can provide a viable alternative to the turnkey graphics workstation, selected and integrated by computer professionals for a specific industry (engineering, publishing), and costing in the vicinity of $50,000. Specific technical capabilities of enhanced microcomputers may match turnkey systems. For example, the resolutions of enhanced personal computers equal, and sometimes exceed, 1,024 by 1,024 pixels, with many color options. However, integration and system function as a whole may still remain problematic. Total integrated systems for specific purposes may be well worth the extra cost in comparison to a system assembled by the user from different components of software and hardware. Then again, it may not. It is the function of analysis to determine feasible systems.

15.3-2 Feasibility study

The purpose of the feasibility study is to determine the *organizational, economic,* and *technical feasibilities* of a computer system. Does automation fit the enterprise's functioning, is it cost effective, and can what needs to be done be accomplished by available technology? All three types of feasibility must be demonstrated. Consider the understandable high resistance to computer aided drafting and design (CADD) by those who earn their living drafting. One draftsman might replace three, and the impact on the institution and people must be considered. Further, there are drawbacks to CADD. The graphic subroutines are developed by persons other than the engineer and the subroutines are used over and over again in different circumstances. There is no thought involved, and the impact could be deadening to subtle differences. The computer is less intelligent and the engineer must not be swayed by efficiency in favor of effectiveness of the final design and its rendition. Dr. G. Daniel Theophilus, Director of the School of Engineering at Acadia University, to whom the author owes the above discussion, is concerned that unless one is careful, a loss in depth perception occurs with computer aided design systems, unless the system is very sophisticated and expensive. For example, in mechanical drawing and engineering, parts may not be rendered in three dimensions and fitted together as well with a CADD system as they can by a skilled draftsperson. Some combination of CADD and manual drafting and engineering may be superior to either one alone. But this must be perceived and planned on an enterprise level before the economic and technical benefits can be realized.

15.3-3 Enterprise analysis

The needs, goals, and problems are identified in detail. Two useful approaches are described in more detail in Marshall (1986). The first is to ask people in the enterprise what they find irritating, a block to their work, difficult to find or produce, and so forth. That is, ask them what is wrong rather than ask them how they think they might use a computer system. If users do not know what a computer system is they will not know how they might use it. But, we all know how to complain, and we should take advantage of this human capability to find out how we might best use computers. This process helps identify *what* to automate.

The second approach is to perform a matrix analysis in which one coordinate of the matrix names the major resources of an enterprise (including people, money, materials), energy, and information, and the other coordinate names the actions possible in relation to those resources, namely, acquire, distribute, change, conserve, produce, move, and monitor. The analysis consists of managers and staff brainstorming on ways computers might serve at the intersection of any two of the above. This process helps identify *where* to automate. Exhibit 15.9 provides an example.

CHARTER:	*Does the enterprise change?*				No
PLANNING PROCESS: *Does the planning process change?*					Yes
RESOURCES:	People	Money	Materials	Energy	Information
ACTION:					
Acquire:	?		Yes		Yes
Distribute:	Yes	Yes	Yes		Yes
Change:	Yes				Yes
Conserve:	?	Yes	Yes	Yes	Yes
Produce:	!		?		Yes
Move:	Yes	Yes	Yes		Yes
Monitor:	Yes	Yes	Yes	Yes	Yes

Exhibit 15.9: Matrix analysis to initiate thought on the use of computers in an enterprise

The executives and managers of an enterprise need to identify its *Critical Success Factors*. These are factors which if not performed satisfactorily will seriously threaten the operation's survival and success. There are usually three to six of them.* In a commercial audio-visual media production house they might include *client satisfaction, media quality, production speed,* and *cost control*. Further, these critical success factors may then be related to automation; that is, how might computers facilitate the performance of these factors?

Another phase of analysis on the enterprise level is to relate the functional areas of an enterprise—planning, administration, management, production, distribution, publicity, marketing, personnel, education, and training—whatever those areas happen to be, to the major functional systems of a computer system. For example, in relation to graphics another matrix analysis is possible, where one axis lists all the possible computer graphics applications, from presentation graphics to CAD, and the other lists the functional areas of the enterprise. This form of matrix analysis could of course be conducted with many classes of computer applications—data processing, numeric control, computer aided learning, knowledge and decision support systems, robotics—and the functional areas of an enterprise. Elsewhere (Marshall, 1986), application of this type of matrix analysis was conducted relating the major capabilities of computers to the major problems of mankind. A similar approach could be fruitfully taken with enterprise needs.

In essence, each functional area of an enterprise sometimes needs the same and sometimes needs different bodies of information, in different forms, and at different times, and a coherent system is required based on those disparate but overlapping needs. For example, in-house publishing is becoming a highly feasible alternative because of low-cost graphic systems and laser printing. Which of the above named enterprise areas could use such capabilities, and what data stored in some database of text and images could effectively support an in-house publishing effort? Other aspects of a system, including data processing, would be analyzed in a similar fashion. Methods for modeling the data and the processing required have emerged and are discussed by various authors in texts on analysis and design. Martin and McClure (1985) provide an extensive tutorial on systems analysis and design diagramming techniques, and Marshall (1986) describes approaches in the form of plans, charts, work sheets, and diagramming techniques suitable for small systems installations.

15.3-4 Systems analysis and development approach

Selection of a systems development approach is related to the economics, the style, and the needs of an enterprise, as well as the availability of systems. There are four basic systems development options. From the viewpoint of computer graphics they include

- The acquisition of a turnkey system
- The assembly of a system from "off-the-shelf" application graphics software and hardware
- In-house application development using some programming language that works with an existing library of graphics procedures
- Custom programming of graphics routines

A fifth option is some combination of the above four.

---

* Critical success factors are discussed in greater length in Martin (1982) and Marshall (1986).

Turnkey graphics computer workstations are a highly viable alternative. Graphics workstations tailored to the needs of a specific class of end-users are available: systems for engineering, architecture, product design, media production, and publishing. Applications do not require a knowledge of programming, but often include sophisticated graphics command languages familiar to a given profession. Turnkey systems are usually more expensive because they are tailored. When a company is well established, where budget is not a critical factor, when installation needs to be rapid and well supported, and no on-site computer expertise exists, when personnel neither have the time nor the interest in programming or establishing operation, then a turnkey system should be considered.

One prepares a Request for Proposal (RFP) in which detailed requirements are provided possible vendors, but no specifications are made as to how those requirements should be met. Then the vendor responses are evaluated and a selection made. The process should be guided by a well-informed consultant. A poor choice is expensive in many ways.

If an enterprise is not well established, funds are limited, installation does not have to take place rapidly, and there exists an interest in being involved in the system's integration and installation, then a turnkey system is a less viable choice. But the next two development options, namely to assemble a system from off-the-shelf software and hardware, and/or to develop graphics applications through some programming language and a related library of graphics routines, increase in attractiveness. There are many graphics application programs and graphics computer systems configurations from which to choose. The choice is made difficult by the sheer number. Some objective evaluation method that takes into consideration both system features and user needs is required. The method acts as a Decision Support System (DSS), and a form for evaluating and comparing graphics software and systems is introduced as a conclusion to this chapter.

Languages on graphics computer systems usually operate with access to libraries of graphic routines already available. It is not necessary to code the graphic routines oneself. For example, on the Macintosh there exists a graphics toolbox called *QuickDraw* that is accessed by Pascal, BASIC, LOGO, C, in fact, all the languages available for the Apple Macintosh. Similarly, there are graphics toolboxes available for the IBM PC, including the *Graphical Kernal System (GKS)* which is available from IBM and conforms to the standard by the same name, and *Halographics*. Further, there are a number of libraries of graphics routines that are specific to given industries and applications *(smARTWORK* on the IBM PC for electrical or electronic schematics). The existence of the toolbox saves many hours of programming time, and may provide, when the toolbox is well integrated into the physical system, capabilities that would be difficult or time consuming for the individual programmer to create through a given programming language.

Sometimes, however, for economic, technical, or pedagogic reasons, custom programming of graphics routines will be undertaken. Custom programming, and possibly the other systems development approaches, may involve the use of the tools of structured analysis, structured design, and data modeling. A good number of the tools used consist of graphics diagrams. The diagrams allow for more accurate specifications and improved communication between clients and system designers and programmers. By analogy, when we look at the blueprints of a house we are having built, we see our dream home. The architect does not see our dream home; he or she sees the technical specifications for a building. Similarly, when clients look at the structured diagrams of a system they see a model of their business or enterprise. The systems analyst, designer, or programmer sees the technical specifications for a computer system.

We briefly introduce one structured analysis tool here: the data flow diagram (DFD). The DFD is a widely used analysis tool; sometimes too widely misused. Further, we will discuss three systems that automate the analysis process that include, as part of their capabilities, the generation and documentation of data flow diagrams.The first is *Excelerator* from Intech (Cambridge, MA); the second is *DFD Draw* from McDonnell Douglas Automation Company (Saint Louis, MO); and the third is a system developed by the author and a senior student, Mr. Paul Hibbitts, using *Filevision* on the Apple Macintosh, and called *InfoImage. Excelerator* and *DFD Draw* function on an IBM PC XT.

The purpose of data flow diagrams is to show an overall picture of a system, the logic of its major components, and the automation boundaries, that is, what part of an enterprise should be automated and what part not. Data flow diagrams show *in overall form* where data and information come from, where they go, how they are stored, and how they are processed. "In overall form" should be emphasized; DFDs are not good at showing the detail of processing, the structure of data storage, the output, or the form of output required. The symbols used in DFDs are diagrammed in Exhibit 15.10.

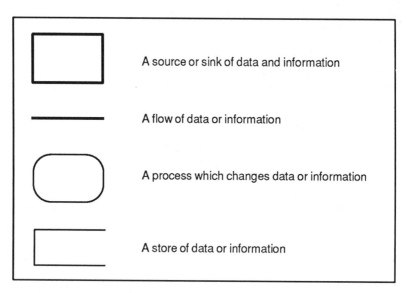

Exhibit 15.10: Symbols used in data flow diagrams (DFDs)

The DFD shown in Exhibit 15.11 was produced using *DFD Draw* on an IBM PC and a Hewlett Packard desk plotter. It shows part of an inventory control system. *DFD Draw* contains a template of the symbols used to produce DFDs. Under direct user control, the symbols are displayed on a screen, moved, placed, connected, enlarged, and reduced. These capabilities reduce editing and maintenance, lead to more accurate diagrams, and save time and money.

Exhibit 15.12 shows the overall structure of the *Excelerator* system used in systems analysis and design. Exhibit 15.12 shows that the *Excelerator* produces and integrates the documents and diagrams needed to specify a computer system. All the data and information parts of a system, from the smallest element of data to the largest database, are defined in a document called a *data dictionary,* which forms part of the system narrative. Data flow diagrams diagram data processing and data models diagram data structure. Screen and report specifications define output and input. The final document produced by *Excelerator* is a complete set of system specifications.

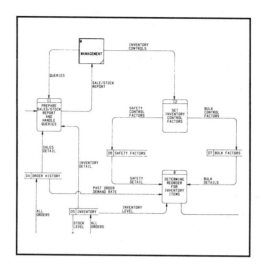

Exhibit 15.11: DFD produced using *DFD Draw* (Copyright © 1984 by McDonnell Douglas Corporation)

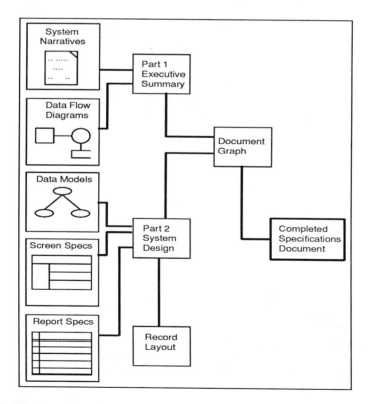

Exhibit 15.12: The *Excelerator* analysis and design system (Courtesy of Index Technology Corp.)

InfoImage on the Apple Macintosh takes advantage of the visual database capabilities of *Filevision*. DFDs are invariably developed in nested stages; that is, the *parent* diagram is an overview picture of the whole operation. Then a *child* DFD is a more detailed blow-up of a process within the parent diagram. The ability to link images in *Filevision* lends itself well to this kind of application. Exhibit 15.13 diagrams the basic design of *InfoImage*, and Exhibits 15.14 and 15.15 show a parent DFD and a child DFD, respectively. The reader should note that the child DFD is an expansion of the processing involved in process 3, *enter patient file details*, in the parent DFD.

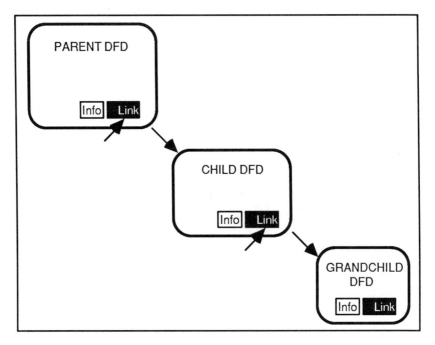

Exhibit 15.13: Overall design of *InfoImage*

In addition, the data records available in *Filevision,* which can be associated to different components of a diagram, allow the user to record information on data storage (database), processing, movement of data (data flows), and sources and sinks (where data originate and terminate). An example is shown in Exhibit 15.16. The total data maintained on a design becomes the data dictionary, the documentation that allows for consistency in design and use.

InfoImage based on *Filevision* and an Apple Macintosh is surprisingly effective at low cost. It cannot match, however, the capabilities of *Excelerator*. But then its cost, considering both hardware and software, is approximately one fifth the cost of an IBM PC XT based *Excelerator* system.

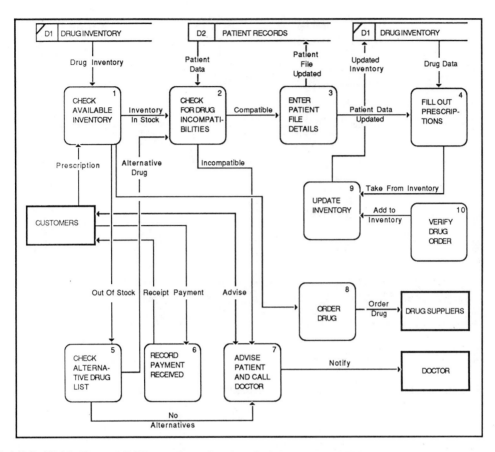

Exhibit 15.14: Parent DFD produced using *InfoImage* and *Filevision*

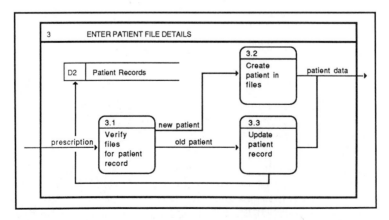

Exhibit 15.15: Child DFD produced using *InfoImage* and *Filevision*

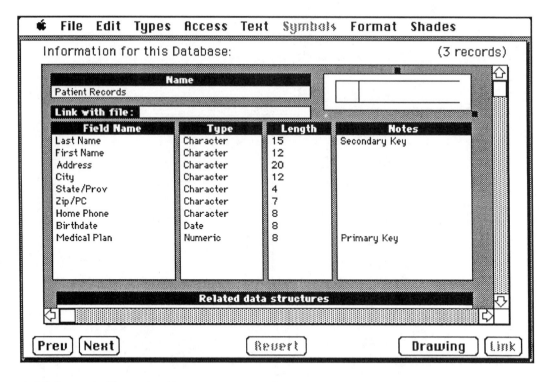

Exhibit 15.16: Record in data dictionary produced using *InfoImage* and *Filevision*

15.3-5 Systems Integration and/or Design

Systems design consists of translating specifications into a functioning system including

- personnel
- procedures
- hardware
- software
- data

As Kroenke (1984) points out, *these five components make up a complete functioning system*. Further, *software is to data as procedures are to personnel*. The point is that a perfectly designed system, without good procedures for use, and an adequately trained staff, will be an imperfectly applied system.

The *system block diagram* often used by graphics system vendors to show the overall design structure of a system. Exhibit 15.17 shows a block diagram for the *Sun-2/160 Color SunStation* from Sun Microsystems, Inc.(Mountainview, CA). The block diagram is easy to follow. A bus is a cable for connecting components. We see that the Sunstation can connect to an *Ethernet* coaxial cable-based network of systems. This allows for the sharing of different resources, such as high

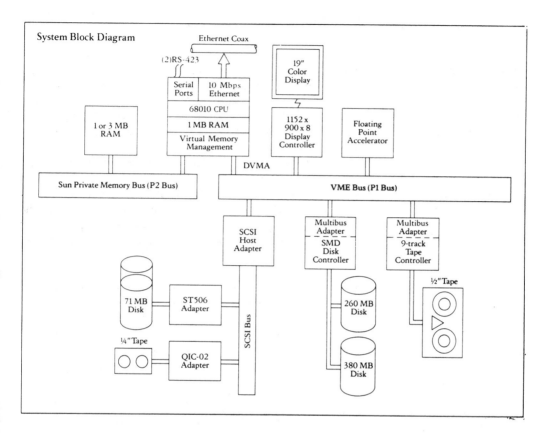

Exhibit 15.17: System block diagram of the Sun Color Workstation
(Courtesy of Sun Microsystems)

quality printers and high volume auxiliary storage. It possesses a RAM memory of 1 to 3 mega-bytes, high resolution color display, and a variety of auxiliary storage and back-up choices in the form of disks and tapes. The block diagram helps communicate a lot of technical information.

15.3-6 Systems installation

Finally, the system is installed in various controlled stages, operating procedures are established, and the system evaluated against the requirements and specifications determined in earlier stages. Operation of the new system should take place in parallel to previous manual or automated systems until its trustworthiness is well established. Marshall (1986) describes the steps and criteria for vendor selection, system installation, user training, and system's operation and support.

15.4 EVALUATING GRAPHICS SYSTEMS

Systems software and hardware need to be evaluated, compared, and selected objectively. If we are foolish we will choose a system by name (a poor guide indeed); on the recommendation of a friend or colleague (we justify our choices *after* we make them to make ourselves feel good that we chose so wisely!); the advice of vendors (biased); individual reviews (helpful but tending to get "trendy"); demonstration (good idea but time consuming, and should follow some narrowing down process); and the advice of consultants (expensive, we should prepare for them, and not leave ourselves at their mercy since they do not know our needs or enterprise like we do).

We discuss graphics system evaluation and selection in relation to the key features or criteria for comparing graphics systems. An automated system, E-CHART, is in development. Manual charts are presented here. Like a navigation system, finding and selecting an appropriate graphics computer system must be based on two sets of information; the *features of systems*, and the *importance of those features to a given user or class of users*. These are the "longtitude" and "latitude" in the "Sea of Systems," diagrammed in lighthearted but accurate fashion in Exhibit 15.18.

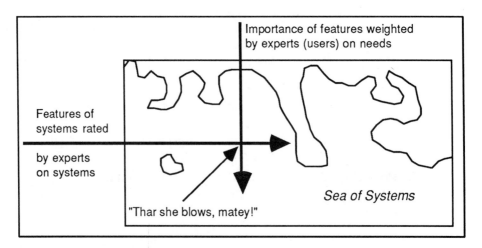

Exhibit 15.18: The necessary coordinates for safely navigating in the Sea of Systems

There are three sets of features or criteria: *critical, general,* and *specific*. Critical features are those that must be present for the system to be worthwhile considering, either from a technical or an application point of view. General features are those applicable to any component, software or hardware, and include features that contribute to ease of use, reliability, service and support, and the availability of related products in the industry in support of the system, for example, application software. Specific features are those specific to a given class of graphics products (screen resolution and display monitors; rotation and perspective and CAD software).

The charts provide a simple means to record the ratings of the features of graphics systems, software, and components, and further a means to add weightings reflecting the importance of those features for given enterprises or users. In rating features, those with knowledge of graphics systems, software, and components are the experts. In assigning weights, those with knowledge of enterprise functioning—the users—are the experts.

It is important to use the charts properly, otherwise an immense amount of unnecessary work is involved. *First,* find all critical features. *Next,* evaluate graphics systems or software under consideration on *critical features only.* One may find that this process is sufficient to make a clear decision. If not, then use additional features—those less critical but still important—to make a decision. One should *not* have to use *all* the features given in the charts to make a decision.

A simple rating scheme is to use numbers from 0 through 5 to reflect the lack of, the presence, or the superiority of a feature in a given system. The same numbering scheme can be used to reflect the importance of the feature, or a simpler set of numbers, namely **0** for not important at all, **.5** for some importance, and **1** for important. In a manual system, the latter weightings reduce the arithmetic involved. When the ratings and the weights are multiplied, the results summed across all features, and an average taken, then the resulting number is an index of relevant capability. Divide this number into the cost of a product and we have a performance cost index; that is, the cost of each unit of performance of a given system. An example is shown in Exhibit 15.19 using only a sample of possible features.

Evaluation Chart: Product "X"

Feature*	R.	W.	Result	Feature	R.	W.	Result
Oper. Sys.	5	2	10	*Reliability*	4	5	20
Ease of use	3	5	15	*Service/support*	2	5	10
Resolution	5	5	25	Industry support	3	3	9
Suitable naive user	5	4	20	Windows	3	3	9
Suitable expert user	3	2	6	Multi-user	0	1	0
Data capture	4	5	20	*Edit control*	3	5	15
Copy features	4	4	16	Erase features	4	4	16
Color features	0	5	0	*Text capabilities*	5	5	25
Animation	1	2	2	3D features	1	2	2
Scale functions	1	4	8	*Paint functions*	5	5	25
	TOTAL:		122		TOTAL:		129

Performance Index= Sum (Rating x Weight) / Number of Features = 12.55
Cost Performance Index = Cost / Performance Index **
Cost Performance Index = $125 / 12.55 = $ 9.96

---

* The critical features, as indicated by the high weights given to those features, are in **bold italic**. The product is assumed to cost $125.

** We have computed the Cost Performance Index using *all* the above features and weighted ratings. However, it is correct to *first consider only the highly weighted* (**bold italic**) *features.*

Exhibit 15.19: An example of E-CHART

The *Performance Index* is the cost of a product divided by the sum of all weighted ratings. There-fore, the *lower* the obtained amount the *less* one is paying for *more* performance; that is the *higher* the value.

The E-CHARTS are in Appendix E, and are organized as follows:

- The name of the type of graphics software or hardware being evaluated.
- The evaluation criteria.
- Blank spaces for entering additional criteria.
- Space for entering both ratings: "R" stands for the rating of a system on a feature, and "W" stands for the weight given to reflect the importance of a feature.

In addition, a blank chart is provided that allows the reader to create his or her own charts for evaluating and comparing other graphics systems, software, and peripherals (plotters, printers).

16

Future Capabilities and Impacts

16.1 INTRODUCTION

The purpose here is to describe the leading-edge capabilities and impacts of computer graphics and related technologies; and to discuss the capabilities and impacts within the framework of *key areas*, rather than listing specific changes in computer graphics capabilities alone. The latter are somewhat obvious: friendly machines, with more flexible software, on more powerful hardware, possessing higher resolutions, more color, 3D capabilities, animation, and intelligence; with many choices of single user, multiuser, or networked systems, better integrated, and at lower prices.

The key areas of computer graphics impact are

√ General impact on how we think and create
√ Improved connection between humans and computers
√ Increased connection of systems
√ Development of the universal workstation, personally configured
√ Use in decision support, early warning, and expert systems
√ Movement from database to knowledge-base systems
√ Development of construction kits for instructing the computer
√ Applications in personal and in-house publishing

The chapter concludes with a discussion of how the new graphics systems provide a common development environment for cooperation between education, research, and private enterprise; considering that graphics is a universal language, it may help create the bridges.

16.2 GENERAL IMPACT ON HOW WE THINK AND CREATE

The general impact of computer graphics is to arouse the visual mind; to awaken the right hemisphere of the brain. Exhibit 16.1 portrays how information might be stored in the brain; in the left hemisphere by the word, and in the right by the image. Each stores and conveys a different meaning.

Words can be very colorful and graphic through cultural use. Consider the word, *Bull!* The image of the animal might come to mind, but it is doubtful. Images work differently; they make patterns and relationships more obvious. We see relations not readily seen in text or linear lists. Images can show the big picture, the detail, and the relationship between the two. They make concrete what is abstract; they reveal and mirror. For many of us, an inability to draw denies us the opportunity to convey to others the pictures we have in our minds. Easy-to-use graphics computer systems help transcend this barrier.

16.2-1 The visual proverb

Benzon (1985) discusses the concept of the visual proverb which, like a verbal proverb, instructs and guides. For example, the pyramid shown in Exhibit 16.2 has been used by this author in many different contexts to introduce and bring home the importance of accurate information as a necessary but not sufficient requirement for communication and consensus, which in turn is necessary but not sufficient for successful and appropriate action. The pyramid and added text act as a visual proverb.

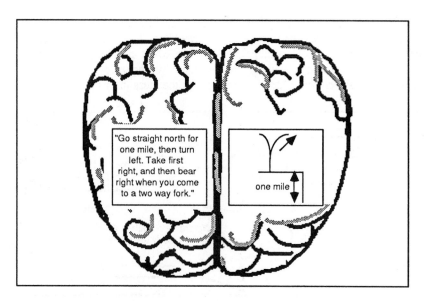

Exhibit 16.1: The left verbal and the right visual sides of the brain

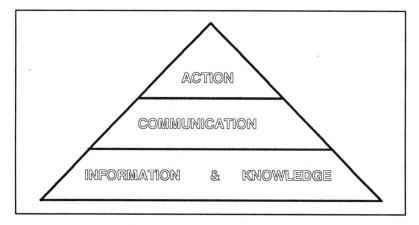

Exhibit 16.2: A visual proverb

16.2-2 Informal mind-mapping

Most of us are left-brain dominated, that is, verbal, linear, and analytic, and we tend to organize our ideas in a similar fashion: lists with an occasional word underlined or capitalized. Rodger W. Sperry, the scientist responsible for making many discoveries regarding left and right brain functioning, went so far as to say that modern society discriminated against the right hemisphere. But we are capable of receiving and recording ideas with images; that is, using our right hemispheres, which are image, spatial, wholistic, and pattern oriented.

Graphics may be used to express *formal* relations, organization, and structure; and *informally* to organize, structure, remember, and create. The formal uses are innumerable. The informal use is known as *mind-mapping*, and workshops are available where people are taught to create mind-maps; that is, to use their whole brain to arouse creativity and memory. Exhibit 16.3 shows a mind-map drawn using *MacDraw* which relates some of the ideas in this chapter.

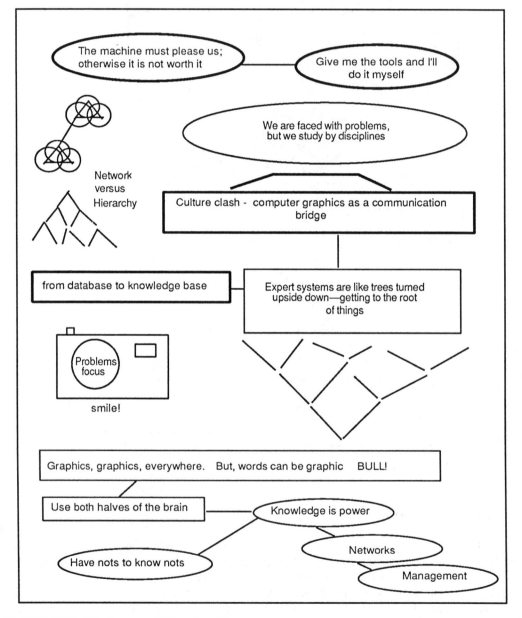

Exhibit 16.3: Mind-map of Chapter 16

16.2-3 Formal mind-mapping

Flow diagrams, ven diagrams, hierarchy charts, trees, and networks can serve informal idea organization, retention, and transmission, and more formal expression of relations. This author often turns to the ven diagram to express organization and division of labor, rather than to a hierarchy chart. The ven diagram suggests a network form of management versus the more traditional hierarchical form. An example is given in Exhibit 16.4.

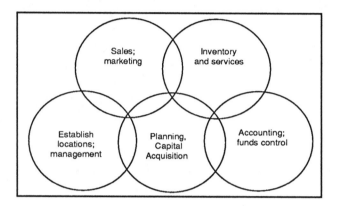

Exhibit 16.4: The ven diagram used as an organization map

Another example, the network shown in Exhibit 16.5, portrays the frequency of association between various members of different enterprises. This process, called *Link Analysis,* is used by law enforcement agencies to identify criminal activities and organizations.

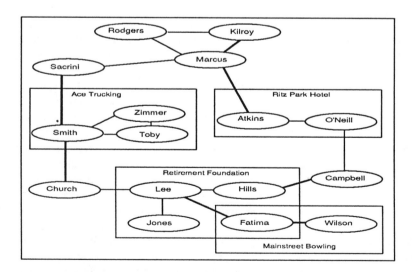

Exhibit 16.5: Link analysis of criminal and legitimate associations (Based on a diagram from Kantowitz and Sorkin, 1983)

The family tree in Exhibit 16.6 conveys in a glance who begat whom, and with whom, associations far less obvious in the list of statements shown in the same exhibit.

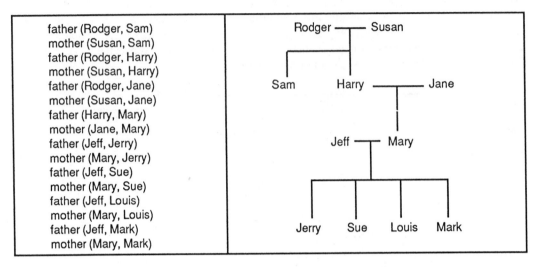

father (Rodger, Sam)
mother (Susan, Sam)
father (Rodger, Harry)
mother (Susan, Harry)
father (Rodger, Jane)
mother (Susan, Jane)
father (Harry, Mary)
mother (Jane, Mary)
father (Jeff, Jerry)
mother (Mary, Jerry)
father (Jeff, Sue)
mother (Mary, Sue)
father (Jeff, Louis)
mother (Mary, Louis)
father (Jeff, Mark)
mother (Mary, Mark)

Exhibit 16.6: A family tree is easier to read when diagrammed

The statements are given in a notation used in logic which reads as follows: "father (Rodger, Sam)," meaning, "Rodger is the father of Sam." This same notation is used in the computer language PROLOG, introduced briefly in Chapter 2, to express relations. PROLOG is used to develop *knowledge bases (KBs)* in support of expert systems. The KBs are developed and organized in a manner very similar to the family tree shown, but larger and more complex. The information in the KB may be supplied by many people expert in a given area—medicine, law, auto repair, computer configurations, oil explorations—and the KB can be queried for answers to relevant questions. The simple family tree in Exhibit 16.6 tells us that Jerry, Sue, Louis, and Mark are siblings, facts generated when one plots parenthood. More on KBs, expert systems, and the use of graphics is presented later in this chapter.

A program called *Barriers and Bridges*, developed by the author and colleagues, evaluates the communication between members of the same management unit, task force, sports team, or family, or any small identifiable group. One part of the program asks group members to evaluate the *actual* communication and the *preferred* communication they experience with each other member of the same group. The program then portrays the actual and preferred communication in a network. An example is shown in Exhibit 16.7. The networks make visible the communication "space" of the group. For example, it would appear that in relation to each other, both Sam and Susan want the same thing; a less intimate connection. Do Sam and Susan know this? Diagrams like the one shown in Exhibit 16.7 help pinpoint group dynamics and facilitate communication. The task is to use our whole brain, and the graphics quality of present-day computer supports whole-brain functioning; the various examples are a few of many possible applications.

In previous cultures where oratory was a principal means of influence, rather than TV, radio, newspapers, and computers, memory was critical. The orator would map a route through the temple, associating each location with an image and the content of his speech. "Friends, Romans,

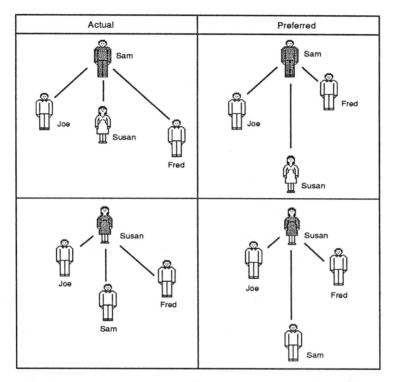

Exhibit 16.7: Networks uses to make the communication space visible
(based on a program called *BARRIERS and BRIDGES* by G. R. Marshall & Associates)

Countrymen, lend me your ears. The evil that men do ..." As Benzon points out, Marc Antony might have associated a bunch of ears with the first location for the first line, a skull with the second location for the second line, and so forth. Memory, however, may still remain important in this age of multimedia.; there are many occasions when we are required to think on our feet; thinking wholistically—visually as well as verbally—should facilitate spontaneous creativity.

16.3 THE HUMAN-COMPUTER CONNECTION

The connection between humans and computers will get closer and more convivial, with more forms of input and output available. For example, a low cost and efficient method of encoding data on paper has been discovered—and is now available—that promises to further improve the distribution of information, including computer programs, text, images, and sounds. Strips of code called *Softstrip*, that look like condensed bar codes, are imprinted on paper. The strips contain the encoded information, and are read with a low cost Softstrip Reader. The distribution of application or demonstration software is accomplished by encoding the object code in the Softstrip. The strip could be included in a journal or magazine. Using the reader, programs, texts, graphics, and sounds can be readily transferred to other auxiliary storage (floppy and hard disks), *without a single keystroke*. Very friendly.

16.3-1 More intuitive and interactive interfaces

The principal means by which humans communicate is speech. We talk to each other, usually accompanied by gestures and postures, delays and grunts, foot shuffles and grins; a complexity of communication that computers may never understand, or certainly not for a long time. Firstly, there is the problem of information capture, and secondly, the larger problem of information interpretation. But voice input is now a firm reality, and a realistic alternative. It is being used by shop foremen making on-site verbal note of manufacturing operations; designers making input for CAD; secretaries inputting commands for document handling; and by executives selecting different operations.

Pointing and dragging with a mouse is usually superior to keyboarding for controlling the cursor, making selections, moving objects, and opening disks and files. But many, including executives, older persons, and those with certain handicaps, may not interact with computers very much until they can talk to them.

The great challenge for computer science is to make computers usable by everyone. Computers, long viewed as a dehumanizing force, will become *the most powerful means for personal creative expression and communication ever known* (Joel Birnbaum, 1985; italics are the authors).

The great challenge for those who wish to apply computers is to familiarize themselves as much as possible with the powerful and positive capabilities of computers, know how to analyze and understand problems, needs and goals, and apply the power of computers appropriately. There is much to be learned here, quite independently of the technical details of computer operation and programming. Knowledge of the tools and what they can do changes how we perceive problems, and that in turn can change how we solve them. We are in the third stage of penetration of computer technology into our world.

16.3-2 The Evolutionary Stages of Technologies

Four stages of technological penetration into a society as identified by Joel Birnbaum are

Stage 1: Experimental rarity
Stage 2: Exotic tool or toy
Stage 3: Well known but used by only a small portion of the populace
Stage 4: The technology has become an integral part of daily life

We are presently in the third stage, and will enter the fourth stage within ten years; or, as Birnbaum puts it, computers will finally be "domesticated."

There are examples of the four stages of development in all technologies. Consider television. Three decades ago we would be invited to a neighbor's house to "watch television"; we watched the screen—the content was immaterial. Or, we huddled as a group, rain or shine, cold or dry, with noses pressed to the store window, to watch very small, poor quality, flickering black-and-white images of Howdy Doody and Milton Berle. Television was in its third stage. No one today invites neighbors to watch TV; videotapes, maybe. But when this author lets it be known that he has a desktop computer-based publishing system at home, people are interested in visiting. Third stage.

The computer graphics discussed in this text is part of the domestication process. Birnbaum quotes R. M. Pirzig, author of *Zen and the Art of Motorcycle Maintenance* as follows, "The test of the machine is the satisfaction it gives you. There isn't any other test. If the machine produces tranquility, it's right. If it disturbs you, it's wrong until either the machine or your mind is changed."

It is the human resource that must be optimized; not just cost/performance. What should we look for? Systems that optimize the human resource as they hide the system's complexity, by offering a rich, powerful, but simple to use, set of functions. The computer specialist's task becomes harder as the end-user's task gets easier. More transparent complexity is more difficult to program; the user will only experience the computer's beautiful face.*

16.3-3 The universal graphics workstation

Graphics, database, publishing, analysis and decision support, and artificial intelligence all exist on a desktop system. Further, the system can be selectively or personally configured to fit the individual using it—truly the universal workstation. Further, we might work interactively all day with the station, and at night it might be performing other tasks: sending and accepting data and information to and from other stations, recording and producing images on different media, and so forth.

A survey entitled "Micros at Work" conducted by *High Technology* (1985), of small computer applications in business, technical, manufacturing, professional, educational, and consumer areas, showed that users are able to

√ produce complex graphics in black and white or color on various media
√ design and use database management systems
√ access very large databanks of information
√ receive and send information to and from other systems
√ work either at home or at the office
√ produce their own newsletters and newspapers
√ make complex decisions with documented support
√ design machines, houses, and toys, in 3D and color
√ produce animated presentations
√ plot and chart natural and manmade phenomena
√ manufacture and maintain products
√ test engines
√ provide brokerage advice and track investments
√ provide legal aid and track cases
√ keep medical records orderly
√ educate and train
√ automate solar energy and other services in a home
√ play games, some of a serious nature

---

* As Birnbaum notes, interactive software is hot and dynamic. By contrast television, literature, and hi-fi are passive, cool, static, and one-way media. Hot software draws us into the computer environment; we are all potential hackers. As my colleague, Scot Gardiner, points out, a motto for the present Information Revolution could be: *No Impression Without Expression.*

Further, all the above are accomplished by end-users *without the benefit of a computer specialist,* on personal workstations designed to use computer graphics extensively. At present, however, *these users constitute a small proportion of our populace.*

16.3-4 Distributed systems connecting personal workstations

As connectivity increases, complexity increases; graphics will help create and maintain friendly user interfaces. Further, the networks will distribute graphics of many varieties, allowing people remote from each other to communicate and work together in ways that are presently denied.

As Leonard Kleinrock (1985) points out, "nature has been extremely successful in implementing distributed systems that are far more clever and impressive than any computer machine humans have devised. The point is that we do not understand very much about distributed systems, and we need to establish a foundation of knowledge in order to develop and plan systems that meet needs and function optimally."

However, complex computer network systems do exist. Like a multitude of overlapping spiderwebs, networks of all varieties cover the planet. On a large scale, there are telecommunication systems supported by telephone, radio signal, and satellite. On a small scale, on site at different facilities, we find computer time-sharing systems, networked microcomputers, PBX systems, video systems, FAX machines, and some few integrated office systems. These systems are mostly incompatible with each other.

Incompatibility is the price we pay for free enterprise. Will systems become compatible? Yes, compatibility is a necessity. At some point we will see the emergence of an *information utility,* analogous to electricity, our energy utility. We will connect by simply plugging in.

"What is needed is a standard digital communication service to connect the many user devices with one another across the room or across the world," states Kleinrock. A standard is being explored called the ISDN (Integrated Services Digital Network) which, by the end of this decade, may lead to the massive connectivity necessary if we are to derive the full benefits from distributed systems. The nodes of these networks will consist of personal workstations, and the systems that connect the nodes will be supported by parallel architecture computers providing massive computational power. The software on the personal workstations will increase and improve, and the information access and communication capabilities will also increase. Kleinrock says we could suffer from *feature shock,* simply too much to choose from; it might lead people to shut down and shut out.

16.4 GROUP DECISION SUPPORT SYSTEMS

Group decision support systems (GDSSs) are applicable in all areas of an enterprise, but are likely to be used initially for planning and management; computer graphics will play an important part. Alan Paller (1985) writes, "Nearly every large company knows that computer graphics can be a powerful competitive tool in research, marketing, planning, engineering, data processing and financial management."

In large measure we can expect to see a greater use of graphics in management. Management will become more visual (more visionary?), and ideas will be shared graphically. The coupling of video, computers, computer graphics, and telecommunications capabilities provide the required technology for GDSSs. Decisions in business are often made collectively. The diagram in Exhibit 16.8 suggests four different configurations for a group decision support system.

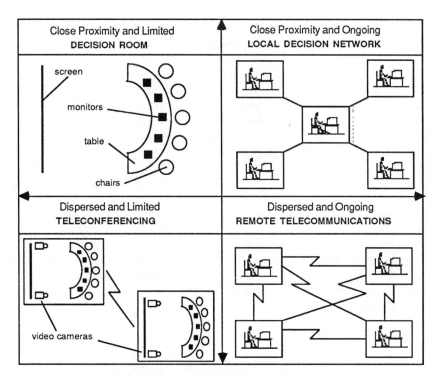

Exhibit 16.8: Support systems for making group decisions (Based on a diagram by DeSanctis and Gallupe, 1985)

The sharing of accurate and current information in a form that allows for rapid understanding and consensus is the guiding motive. The arrows in Exhibit 16.8 suggest that one configuration is not necessarily chosen over another, but there is a gradation of selection possible; a given location might include elements of all four, depending on needs.

Individual decision support software has existed for a number of years. They include the ubiquitous ESSs and DBMSs of great variety. But, to break a complex decision into its component parts, weigh the probabilities of different events, and track the consequences of choices, ESSs and DBMSs are not adequate for this kind of analysis. Specialized DSS software exists for this purpose, including *Decision Analyst, Lightyear, Expert Choice,* and *DecisionMap* (a listing of products of this type is provided in Appendix C).

16.4-1 Early warning systems

GDSSs are closely related to Early Warning Systems (EWSs); systems that continuously update sensitive data (costs, sales, margins), change a library of graphics charts and tables of that data, and allow the executive and manager to display the charts and tables on demand. These charts are a continuous barometer of changes in the enterprise, and may thus act as a signal, or an early warning.

EWSs are *push-button graphics management systems for executives.* Previous graphics packages served those who need and create charts. Executives do not create charts; their assistants do. But executives need information and want it graphically. Following display, the charts or tables may be selected for production in an overhead, slide, or paper form, also at the push of a button.

EWSs currently exist on mainframe or minicomputers. The trend is towards mainframe use, because most corporate data is located on mainframes, many people need to share the information, and mainframes offer the combination of data, graphics, software, storage, and networking required for these types of systems in large enterprises. High quality slides or charts are then produced using mainframe graphics, or dedicated graphics workstations. However, high quality color graphics are becoming available on microcomputers (*Lumena* from Time Arts, Inc., Santa Rosa, CA). But systems are still expensive; when fully configured, around $50,000. The point is that there is nothing in present-day technology that prevents EWSs on a smaller scale being developed solely within the framework of networked microcomputers. Lower cost microcomputer-based systems, with less costly graphics capabilities, can act as graphics terminals to a mainframe, or be linked in a network to a graphics workstation, as well as function as a stand-alone system. Programs like Lotus 1-2-3, Symphony, Framework, Jazz, or Excel, on the microcomputer, can provide the spreadsheet data, convert the data to a chart, allow for preview, and may then send instructions to the mainframe or graphics workstation to produce the high quality slide or chart. Critical features are ease of use, speed, shared resources, and the software required to support communication and data and image transfer.

16.4-2 Negative rebound?

The implementation of visual early warning systems, an approach used in the military for many years, might be a portent of a near future with some definite negative possibilities: commercial warfare with automated weapons, a shootout across mainstreet America, a business enterprise "starwars," with everything more finely tuned, high strung, and fragile, demanding quicker responses and better decisions.

More information and knowledge delivered under pressure may not necessarily lead to more understanding and wiser actions. The answer is to slow down but, once on a roll, that may not be possible. Whether positive or negative—and surely a combination of both—this technology cannot be ignored. Ignoring these trends will mean less access to accurate information, decreased communication, and less responsive and appropriate action; or, in business terms, decreased profits or going out of business. On the positive side, these comprehensive systems may force us to consider the larger human, social, and environmental impacts of our actions (see Exhibit 15.1).

16.5 ARTIFICIAL INTELLIGENCE AND COMPUTER GRAPHICS

Interactive systems are becoming intelligent systems; that is, systems that not only provide a friendly interface but also augment the interface in intelligent ways: a CAD system that checks for design constraints, a robot simulator that assists in avoiding collisions between industrial robots, other equipment, and parts in production, and a slide-making system that automatically selects and produces appropriate business chart layouts.

AI and Computer Graphics have been used together in the past, especially in the area of image processing and robotics. The information captured and analyzed by one—the image processing system—determines the behavior and monitors the internal state of the other—the robot. Newer applications relate to providing a graphics user shell or interface to expert systems.

16.5-1 Expert or knowledge-based systems

Imagine having, not one or two, but many experts at your elbow when you were solving different problems: the best three or four dozen auto mechanics when working on your car, the best medical diagnosticians when feeling ill with a given set of symptoms, the most knowledgeable cooks on food preparation and the use of spices when faced with the making of a formal dinner, and so on. Essentially, that is what expert or knowledge-based systems provide us.

Expert or knowledge-based systems solve problems in given domains based on an extensive body of knowledge about a specific problem area called the knowledge base (KB). Typical domains include medicine, geological exploration, agriculture, computer configuration, insurance, law, and automechanics. Forsyth (1984) writes, "This knowledge-based approach to systems design represents an evolutionary change with revolutionary consequences; for it replaces the software tradition of Data + Algorithm = Program (see Chapter 13) with a new architecture centered around a 'knowledge base' and an 'inference machine,' so that now, Knowledge + Inference = System, which is clearly similar, but different enough to have profound consequences." An expert system contains the components diagrammed in Exhibit 16.9.

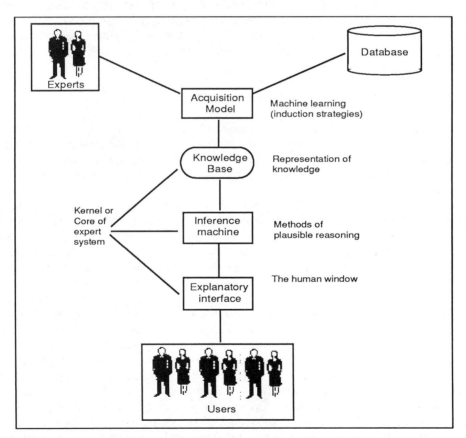

Exhibit 16.9: An expert system (Based on a diagram by R. Forsyth, *Expert Systems: Principles and Case Studies*, New York, NY: Chapman and Hall, 1984.)

The KB is a set of facts and rules built up from the input of experts in a given area. Facts are short-term information that may change rapidly; rules are longer term information that may be used to generate new facts. The KB is established so that it serves multiple uses: make decisions, construct explanations, create tutorials. The inference engine contains methods of reasoning known as *backward chaining* and *forward chaining*. Simply put, forward chaining is reasoning from facts to hypotheses, and backward chaining, the search for facts to prove or disprove hypotheses. The system will contain a means for offering explanations, justifying conclusions, and giving probabilities representing the system's confidence that indeed given facts and rules are true. A shell acts as an interface for the user to the system. The shell includes an interaction manager, a knowledge acquisition system, a KB debugger, a KB editor, and an explanation generator (Forsyth, 1984; Badler and Finin, 1985).

Doctors, for example, in practice or in training, may ask a medical expert system and knowledge base for a probable diagnosis based on a set of symptoms presented by the patient (severe headache, nausea, stiff neck, etc.). The expert system may be established to respond with several possibilities, with related probabilities presented to the inquiring physician in the form of a tree. The tree shows a taxonomy of disorders and symptoms differentiated by the expert system (meningitis, chronic, acute, viral, etc.) A complete audit of rules used, facts or disorders believed to have been identified, and associated probabilities is maintained. The graphic tree makes the knowledge more understandable and credible. All expert systems, whether based on the input of experts, or able to learn and build up facts themselves, work this way; graphics help users understand and work with the knowledge base.

16.5-2 Data processing to knowledge engineering

In a recent subscription invitation to a new journal called *EXPERT*, devoted to the presentation of findings on expert systems, the headline to the invitation read, "In the sixties and seventies we processed data: today, we engineer knowledge." Knowledge engineering is another name for the development of knowledge base and expert systems. An example problem will provide an image of developments in this area.

There are some problems in computer aided design and manufacturing (CAD/CAM) that are not suitably supported by traditional database systems used to manage business data. The relational database, for example, provides only for a single construct or form of relation, namely entities (customers, vendors) described by certain attributes (names, addresses, balances). But the representation of the design, manufacture, sale, and service of a product requires more constructs or forms. For example, in a system called *SAM*, for Semantic Association Model, seven forms of relation are defined (S. Y. W. Su, "Modeling Integrated Manufacturing Data with SAM," *IEEE Computer*, 19, 1, January, 1986; © 1986 IEEE). *SAM* is designed to support CAD/ CAM operations including product definition, design, manufacture, distribution, and so forth. In design and manufacturing temporal and positional relationships are of equal importance to procedural or entity relationships. The seven relations include those based on membership or *homogeneity* (all parts; all positions), *aggregation* (attributes or characteristics of an object or event), *interaction* (actions or relationships between different entities), *generalization* (two entities that are members of a more general class or set), *composition* (parts which compose a given entity), *cross-product* (a grouping of some type whose occurrence is defined as the cross-product of its component types; for example, a part category being defined by technical group, part type, and manufacturer), and *summarization* associations (defining entities statistically, as in back-order counts and in-stock counts). The last two relations are often used together in statistical databases. Very complex data relationships can be defined, and the seven association types help the database users, adminstrators, and designers to categorize and represent the properties of entities. A knowledge base is more intelligent than a database, and users do not have to do as much through their applications programs. Computer graphics play a key part, because images are efficient at representing, symbolizing, and transmitting knowledge. Images act as a powerful means for guiding analysis, design, cooperation, consensus, and action.

16.5-3 When should an expert system be considered?

The problems faced determine the type of system required. Forsyth offers the table shown in Exhibit 16.10 as a guide.

Suitable versus	Unsuitable
Diagnostic	**Calculative**
No established theory	**Magic formula exists**
Human expertise scarce	**Human experts are two-a-penny**
Data is 'noisy'	**Facts are known precisely**

Exhibit 16.10: Features that affect suitability of using a knowledge base approach (Based on R. Forsyth, *Expert Systems: Principles and Case Studies*, New York, NY: Chapman and Hall, 1984)

Topics like tax law, motor repair, weather forecasting, and most branches of medicine, contain too many variables for a complete and consistent theory; we depend on the knowledge and intuition of the experienced and the expert. These are areas that lend themselves well to the use of expert systems. The case examples below are expert knowledge-based systems designed for different purposes, and all involve the use of computer graphics in some capacity. Some are in operation and others are experimental systems.

16.5-4 Instructional design

APEX (Automated Pictorial EXplanations) is a system that generates instructional pictures (how to use a piece of equipment) based on the description of a set of physical objects, the actions that are required, and a user's knowledge of the objects and setting (Feiner, 1985). *APEX* automatically determines good graphic descriptions—objects to be shown, distinguishing objects from each other, level of detail required, how to portray an action—of required actions. These are tasks that we would definitely call intelligent and expect a human to determine. An example is shown in Exhibit 16.11. The view, the detail, and the arrow used to show movement required are all determined and rendered automatically; that is the point.

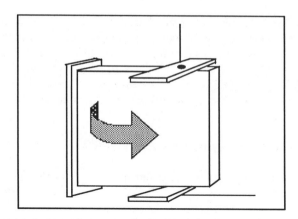

Exhibit 16.11: Image generated by *APEX* instructing user to rotate panel back to its original position (Redrawn in MacDraw from a diagram by Feiner, 1985; © 1985 IEEE)

16.5-5 Interface design

SAGE (*Sensitivity Analysis Graphic InterfacE*) is a system for building graphics interfaces for a wide class of sensitivity analysis models (Clemons and Greenfield, 1985). Sensitivity analysis is used by decision makers to determine the effects of making changes and what subsequent actions to take. The decision maker, besides making a choice, needs to determine the robustness—the stability and safety—of a choice. In sensitivity analysis the user makes changes to a model and conducts a simulation. A system should allow for rapid evaluation of the results. Graphics facilitate rapid presentation of the effects of model changes. The overall design of SAGE is shown in Exhibit 16.12.

Clemons and Greenfield use the example of a vehicle routing problem to demonstrate how SAGE works. Vehicles deliver goods daily to customers based on orders received. Each order occupies a given portion of a vehicle's total capacity, and must be delivered within a specified time. The goal is to determine a set of delivery routes that are as economical as possible. All of the pertinent information—customer hours, time windows for deliveries, truck capacities occupied, potential routes, total truck loads, truck sizes required—are shown graphically. For example, different trucks and vans are represented and displayed during simulation in varying sizes and colors (for low capacity, display a van; for high capacity, display an 18 wheeler; if capacity is close to being exceeded, display vehicle in red; if it exceeds capacity, display vehicle overturned). The SAGE system combines features of modeling, simulation, expert, decision support, and construction kit systems. The set-up and operation of SAGE is under the control of the end-user.

16.5-6 Document design

Since few of us are experts on graphics design, knowledge-based document design systems have been created: chartbooks, layout intelligence, and color selection (Harris, 1985). *Chartbooks* are predesigned graphics. Charts are designed by professionals and users select a format; the computer looks up the relevant data, and creates a chart according to the template in the chartbook. Many

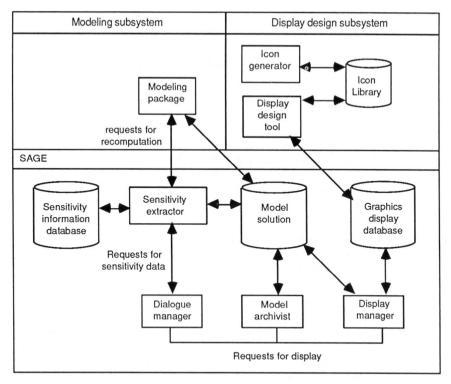

Exhibit 16.12: The components of SAGE and two subsystems for modeling and display design (From Clemons and Greenfield; © 1985 IEEE)

stand-alone presentation graphics systems will default to a given format, font, ratio between axes, and so forth; CHART discussed in Chapter 6 contains a chartbook. *Layout intelligence* relies on a database of facts on chart formatting; how big to make charts to fit overhead transparencies, the length-width ratios of 35mm slides, or the sizes required for quarter, half, or full page publication, and so forth. The system provides the answers automatically. Some graphics computer systems offer thousands of colors. The question remains: what colors go well together? A *color palette selection system* solves this problem for the user, and the "smart" system chooses combinations. The user may ask for a "look," like "spring" or "winter," and the palette selects an appropriate and pleasing set of colors.

16.5-7 Document update

Documents, for example, manuals, are often written by several persons (Harris, 1985). When updates occur in one section, there may exist ripple effects throughout the manual calling for changes in other places. A database could keep track of all the topics, subtopics, key words, illustrations, and pictures in a manual. A knowledge base and expert system could do more. It could keep track of both format and context, and make context and design decisions automatically, including the placement and the sizing of illustrations, the selection of fonts, the tracking of related costs, and making decisions on the basis of optimal cost.

16.5-8 Regional advertising

National magazines publish different editions of their magazines directed to different regional locations (Harris, 1985). The reason is to allow regional advertisers to publish ads with targeted markets at lower costs. At present, human experts determine the number of pages that must be made over. The aim is to keep page changes and prepress page remakes to a minimum because of the related expense. The present capabilities of AI would allow a computer to automatically place regional ads and recompose the pages.

Newspaper production faces a somewhat different set of problems, but again expert technical knowledge can be built into expert systems that will allow for more rapid, less costly, and better designed pages. In fact, it might be possible to collect the expert knowledge of those who get the newspaper out, build an expert system, distribute that knowledge, and base future newspaper production on that knowledge.

16.5-9 Presentation graphics, DSS, and EWS

We are experiencing a massive growth in the use of presentation graphics. It is estimated that more than 100 million presentation images were created using personal computers in 1985. Of those, approximately two thirds were created using plotters, and the majority of the balance with dot matrix printers; a small percentage—about five percent—were created by a laser printer, or as slides and photographs. There will be a shift over the next few years to the use of the latter because of high quality at low cost. Using an outside graphics service might lead to a cost per slide of $50 to $70; now these costs can be reduced by a factor of ten.

A creative approach to presentation is taken in *Atlas* for the IBM PC and *MacMap* for the Apple Macintosh (both by Strategic Locations Planning (SLP), San Jose, CA). Data produced using an ESS or DBMS are projected onto maps and users may call up the data for projection. Examples include demographic, census, sales, and stock information. These developments dovetail with the design and use of decision support (DSS) and early warning systems (EWS).

We will also see an increase in the integration of computer graphics with other images produced using video and film. Still and animated sequences, interspersed with appropriate text in a variety of fonts and faces, will be stored on video discs possessing encyclopedic storage capacities, and attached to desktop computer workstations. The selection of sequences for viewing will be under interactive user control; the learning machine finally comes of age.

16.6 MEDIA BYPASS

Bypassing is the creation of resources normally provided by an outside service. Common examples—especially in larger companies—are private telephone networks, heating systems, and transportation systems; services we normally expect to receive from some large public provider. Bypassing also occurs on a smaller and more personal level, and one major and new bypass recently created by the technology is personal or in-house publishing and media production.

Slides can now be created at a price affordable to small companies. The technological break-through responsible is a device called a digital film recorder costing between $10,000 and $30,000. Connected to a computer, the digital film recorder allows for the rapid and economical production of high resolution slides in many colors. Slide-making service bureaus will switch to automation, but much of the slide making will move in-house; another bypass.

Billions are spent on typesetting, line art, plate making, and printing to publish documents. Until 1985, automation played a part in phototypesetting and photocomposition, but small in comparison to near-future involvement. Photocomposers that produce high quality camera-ready copy of text in various fonts, illustrations, and pictures, cost in excess of a quarter million dollars. Now it is possible to duplicate a goodly number of these same capabilities, using a system that costs between $10,000 and $100,000.

Another technological breakthough is responsible: the laser printer. Laser printers in the next few years will appear with more fonts, improved graphics handling, typeset quality, higher capacities, and at lower prices. The laser printer now produces acceptable quality documents, but below typeset quality. Further, improved page layout software for combining text, line work, and images, and improved font handling software for controlling the appearance of print, leading (the space betweeen lines of print), and kerning (the space between letters) will be available on small computers and bypass publishing will increase.

Acceptable, though not high resolution quality, color production graphics are now available at low costs, using color ink-jet and thermal color printers; soon color laser printers will be available, but at high costs.

16.7 CONSTRUCTION KITS

Kits in the form of construction sets exist for computers; they are used to instruct the computer without having to write any programming code. Use of kits include

√ Designing houses
√ Drawing schematics
√ Developing animated sequences
√ Constructing fonts
√ Simulating production
√ Performing cash management
√ Constructing pinball games
√ Composing and playing music
√ Teaching programming skills by manipulating a robot in an environment

How do the kits work? We are provided with the components of some domain of exploration, for example, notes, rests, keys, and staff in music, and by pointing and dragging with some hand-held device we place the components onto the electronic page or into the work area in order to compose, create sheet music, or play the music through the computer. None of this involves writing a line of programming code. We can expect the use and sophistication of kits to increase, and to appear in many areas. Many of the applications discussed in this text are kits including paint, CAD, project management, and graphics programming languages. Kits are designed for all classes of users; beginners to expert programmers.

16.8 CONCLUSION

Discovery disrupts patterns, and some discoveries disrupt patterns more than other discoveries (Kettle, 1985). The discoveries and inventions related to low-cost but powerful graphics computer systems—primitive today—are beginning to change the mode and quality of how we communicate. Computer graphics, because it is so closely related to designing better connections between man and machine, will be a major part of the technology used to help solve the problems that the technology was responsible for creating. Consider the major trends in society and business identified by John Naisbitt and his group of researchers in *The Year Ahead—1986: Ten Powerful Trends Shaping Your Life* (Warner Books, New York, NY, 1985), trends that are likely to continue:

√ Movement from hierarchical to network management
√ Pressing need for management retraining
√ Selective labor shortages by geographic location and occupation
√ The increased use of computers in education and training
√ The use of bypassing to provide services (phone, travel)

In all of these areas we can see and envision computer graphics applications; the mapping of management networks to better track communication and decision making; the use of computer graphics in computer aided learning for more rapid retraining of managers; similar use of graphics to help train people and reduce selective labor shortages; use of graphics displays to show the location of job opportunities and related information; more computers and computer graphics in education in general and actually performing, rather than supporting, instruction—with instructors becoming guides, lights, and sources of inspiration rather than information; and, as already discussed, bypassing, a form of self-reliance, that appears most notably in the area of computer aided publishing and media production.

"The annual output of information now exactly equals the value of all the goods we produce," writes John Kettle (1985). This means that we have come to a turning point in the movement from the industrial to the information age; information is of definite value, or, as is often quoted in AI circles, knowledge is power. Small computers, if taken advantage of, will advance the process and help avoid the creation of another major minority to join the existing "have-nots," namely, the "know-nots."

16.8-1 Stronger and wider bridges

There is a great pressure and need for cooperation among education, research, and business. It is necessary for the leading edge of research to meet the cutting edge of application, as Roland W. Schmitt, Senior Vice-President of corporate R & D for General Electric puts it (Schmitt, 1985). We have not paid enough attention to creating bridges among people teaching, researching, and doing. There is a gap between the generation and the application of knowledge, and a gap in the education of those who will join the labor force following their schooling. Educators need to study and do research in order to do, not merely to know. Further, industry must support research, because in order to do, time must be spent on knowing; it is a two-way street. The use of computers and computer graphics especially, may be a powerful bridge, a common development environment, where the interactive and intelligent systems used when learning are, in fact, the same systems as used when working.

As Schmitt correctly observes, there are difficulties realizing such a goal. The problem-solving culture of business and industry comes up against the discipline or content-oriented culture of the university; generalists come up against specialists.

But problems dictate solutions, not disciplines; they transcend disciplines. Schmitt calls attention to the late George Low, president of Rensselaer Polytechnic Institute, and a pioneer of the Engineering Research Center concept, a concept that could be followed in other fields. Schmitt writes of Low as follows, "To train engineers, he believed it wasn't enough just to put them to work in the classroom and the laboratory. They also had to experience the frustration and the excitement of putting advanced technology to work. In a program at RPI involving composite materials, for example, the students conceived of a product concept—a glider made of new composites—and immersed themselves in all the difficulties involved in getting a product out the door. As the final exam, they were required to test-fly the glider themselves!"

Graphics-based computer systems allow for the kind of training Schmitt is referencing and Low performed. It is no longer necessary to spend many months or years learning how to use the tools of computer technology; we can direct our attention to the problems and apply the tools. Education and training can be problem-oriented, calling upon the content of disciplines within the focusing light of problems, through access to workstations and the guidance of inspired teachers. This form of education is parallel to a new form of emerging management: managers as guides rather than bosses. Teachers become managers and managers become teachers, facilitated by direct student and employee access to knowledge-based networked graphics computer systems.

Bibliography

Armstrong, W. P., and **R. P. Burton.** "Perception Cues for N Dimensions," *Computer Graphics World,* 8, 3, March 1985.

Artwick, Bruce A. *Applied Concepts in Microcomputer Graphics.* Englewood Cliffs, NJ: Prentice-Hall, Inc., 1984.

Badler, Norman I., and **Timothy W. Finin.** "Computer Graphics and Expert Systems," *IEEE Computer Graphics and Applications,* 5, 11, November 1985 (© 1985 IEEE).

Benzon, Bill. "The Visual Mind and The Macintosh," *Byte,* 10, 1, January 1985.

Birnbaum, Joel S. "Toward the Domestication of Microelectronics," *IEEE Computer,* 18, 11, November 1985 (© 1985 IEEE).

Bishop, Jack. "Technical and Business Graphics on the IBM PC," *Byte Guide to the IBM PC,* Fall, 1984.

Blackwell, Gerry. "Videotext and the Office," *InfoAge,* 4, 4, April 1985.

Brooks, Frederick P. *The Mythical Man-Month.* Menlo Park, CA: Addison-Wesley Publishing Co., Inc., 1974.

Christopher, Tom. "The Digitizing Camera Picture," *PC Magazine,* 3,12, June 26, 1984.

Clemons, Eric K., and **Arnold J. Greenfield.** "The SAGE System Architecture: A System for the Rapid Development of Graphics Interfaces for Decision Support," *IEEE Computer Graphics and Applications,* 5, 11, November 1985 (© 1985 IEEE).

Coleman, Terry, and **Skip Powers.** "The Xtar Graphics Microprocessor," *Byte,* 9, 12, November 1984.

Cooper, D. "Computer Landscapes," *Byte,* 9, 10, September 1984.

Corr, Robert. "More than Pretty Pictures," *PC Magazine,* 4, 2, January 8, 1985.

Cortes, Camila C. "Computer Aided Design Trend in the 80's," in *Computer Graphics: Theory and Applications,* ed. Tosiyasu L. Kunii. New York: Springer-Verlag, 1983.

Crider, Bill. "Presentation graphics alternatives," *PCWORLD,* 2, 8, August 1984.

———————— · "Every Word a Key," *MacWorld,* 2, 10, October 1985.

Danish, Adel. "Touch pads provide easy user interface with use of customer overlays," *Computer Technology Review,* 5, 1, Winter 1984.

Date, C. J. *Database: A Primer,* Menlo Park, CA: Addison-Wesley Publishing Co., Inc., 1983.

DeSanctis, G., and **B. Gallupe.** "Group Decision Support System: A New Frontier," *DATA BASE,* 16, 2, February 1985.

DiCocco, John. "PC Graphics: The Art of Persuasion," *Business Computing,* 11, 10, October 1984.

Fastook, James L., and **Terence Hughes.** "When Ice Sheets Collapse," *IBM Perspectives in Computing,* 2, 1, March 1982.

Feiner, Steven. "APEX: An Experiment in the Automated Creation of Pictorial Explanations," *IEEE Computer Graphics and Applications,* 5, 11, November 1985 (© 1985 IEEE).

Foley, James D., and **Andries Van Dam.** *Fundamentals of Interactive Computer Graphics.* Menlo Park, CA: Addison-Wesley Publishing Co., Inc., 1982.

Forsyth, Richard. *Expert Systems: Principles and Case Studies.* New York: Chapman and Hall, 1984.

Francis, Ely. *Using Charts to Improve Profits.* Englewood Cliffs, NJ: Prentice-Hall, Inc., 1962.

Gardiner, W. Lambert. "On the Need for Planners to See Things Whole," *Canadian Associations,* November 1985.

Gibson, Steve. "Bottles Full of Nothing," *InfoWorld,* 6, 24, June 11, 1984a.

——————— · "Colors of the Rainbow," *InfoWorld,* 6, 25, June 18, 1984b.

Giesecke, F. E., A. Mitchell, H. C. Spencer, I. L. Hill, R. O. Loving, and, **J. T. Dygdon.** *Engineering Graphics with Computer Graphics* (3rd ed.). New York: Macmillan Publishing Co., 1985.

Groover, Mikell P., and Emory W. Zimmers, Jr. *CAD/CAM Computer Aided Design and Manufacturing.* Englewood Cliffs, NJ: Prentice-Hall, Inc., 1984.

Harris, Barry. "The Role of Artificial Intelligence in Computer Aided Printing and Publishing," *The Communicator,* XXIX, 1, First Quarter, 1985.

Harris, Dennis. *Computer Graphics and Applications.* New York: Chapman and Hall, 1984.

High Technology Editorial Staff. "Micros at Work," *High Technology,* 5, 11, November 1985.

Howitt, Doran. "The New Look of Presentations," *InfoWorld,* 6, 52, December 24, 1984.

Hutzel, Ingeborg. "Computer Graphics in Broadcasting," *Computer Graphics World,* 8, 4, April 1985a.

——————— · "Trends in PC Paint System Development," *Computer Graphics World,* 8, 3, March 1985b.

Jankel, Annabel, and Rocky Morton. *Creative Computer Graphics.* New York: Cambridge University Press, 1984.

Jarett, Irwin M., and **Howard W. Johnson.** "Using Computer Generated Graphics to Present Financial Statements," in *Computer Graphics: Theory and Applications,* ed. Tosiyasu L. Kunii. New York: Springer-Verlag, 1983.

Jones, Jim. "Choosing an Electronic Publishing System," *Canadian Data Systems,* 17, 12, December 1985.

Kantowitz, Barry H., and **Robert D. Sorkin.** *Human Factors: Understanding People-System Relationships.* New York: John Wiley & Sons, 1983.

Karplus, W. L. "The Spectrum of Mathematical Models," *IBM Perspectives in Computing,* 3, 2, May 1983.

Kay, Alan. "Computer Software," *Scientific American,* 251, 3, September 1984.

Kettle, John. "Sneaking a Peek at the Future," *The Globe and Mail,* Friday, October 4, 1985.

Kleinrock, Leonard. "Distributed Systems," *COMPUTER,* 18, 11, November 1985 (© 1985 IEEE).

Koff, Richard M. *Using Small Computers to Make Your Business Strategy Work.* New York: John Wiley & Sons, 1984.

Kroenke, David M. *Business Computer Systems: An Introduction* (2nd ed.). Santa Cruz, CA: Mitchell Publishing, Inc., 1984.

Krouse, J. K. "Engineering Without Paper," *High Technology,* 6, 3, March 1986.

Kuklinski, Theodore T. "A Case for Digitizer Tablets," *Computer Graphics World,* 8, 5, May 1985.

Lambert, Steve. *Presentation Graphics on the Apple Macintosh.* Bellevue, WA: MicroSoft Press, 1984.

Lambert, Steve. "The Graphic Gallery," *PC World,* 2, 12, December 1984 .

Lu, Cary. *The Apple Macintosh Book.* Bellevue, WA: MicroSoft Press, 1984.

MacLeod, Douglas. "The Graphic Frontier," *InfoAge,* 4, 2, February 1985.

Mandelbrot, Benoit. *The Fractal Geometry of Nature.* San Francisco: W. H. Freeman and Company, 1982.

Marcus, Aaron. "Graphic Design for Computing Graphics," in *Computer Graphics Theory and Application,* ed. Tosiyasu L. Kunii. New York: Springer-Verlag, 1983.

Marshall, G. R. "Word Processing: Teaching Approaches," *Computers in Education,* October 1984.

—————————— · *Systems Analysis and Design: Alternative Structured Approaches.* Englewood Cliffs, NJ: Prentice-Hall, Inc., 1986.

Martin, James. *Application Development Without Programmers.* Englewood Cliffs, NJ: Prentice-Hall, Inc., 1982.

Martin, James, and **Carma McClure.** *Diagramming Techniques for Analysts and Programmers.* Englewood Cliffs, NJ: Prentice-Hall, Inc., 1984.

Martin, Janette. "Dynamic Design," *PC World,* 3, 6, June 1985.

McCandless, Keith. "A Moving Pixel Show," *MacWorld,* 2, 11, November 1985.

McGeever, Christine. "The Mac Makes a Hit Comic," *InfoWorld,* 7, 14, April 8, 1985.

McGrath, Nigel. "Computer Graphics Push the 3D Limits," *Canadian Data Systems,* 18, 4, April, 1986.

McMahan, Mike. "TI's Mike McMahan Discusses Speech Technology," *Personal Computing,* 8, 1, January 1984.

Miastkowski, Stan. "MicroSoft Flight Simulator," *Byte,* 9, 3, March 1984.

Mufti, Aftab A. *Elementary Computer Graphics.* Reston, VA: Reston Publishing Company, Inc., 1983.

Naisbitt, John. *Megatrends: Ten New Directions Transforming Our Lives.* New York: Warner Books, 1982.

Naisbitt, John, and **the Naisbitt Group.** *The Year Ahead—1986: Ten Powerful Trends Shaping Your Life.* New York: Warner Books, 1985.

Noma, T., and **T. L. Kunii.** "ANIMENGINE: An Engineering Animation System," *IEEE Computer Graphics and Applications,* 5, 10, October 1985 (© 1985 IEEE).

O'Connor, Rory. "Laser Printing's Myth: Prettier Is Better," *InfoWorld,* 7, 21, May 27, 1985.

Paller, Alan. "Trends Shaping Business Graphics, " *Canadian Data Systems,* 17, 12, December 1985.

Prueitt, Melvin L. *Art and the Computer.* New York: McGraw-Hill Book Co., 1984.

Rock, Irving. *Perception.* New York: Scientific American, Inc., 1984.

Schmitt, Roland W. "Engineering Research and International Competitiveness," *High Technology,* 5, 11, November 1985.

Shaffer, Richard. "Now the 'New' Commodore," *Personal Computing,* 9, 8, August 1985.

Shea, Tom. "Order out of Chaos," *InfoWorld,* 6, 15, April 9, 1984.

Sørenson, Peter. "Fractals," *Byte,* 9, 9, September 1984.

Spielman, Howard A. "Computer Graphics for Management: Prerequisites for an Effective Introduction," in *Computer Graphics: Theory and Applications,* ed. Tosiyasu Kunii. New York: Springer-Verlag, 1983.

Sprague, Richard. "The Language that Talks to Your Printer," *MacWorld,* 2, 2, February 1985.

Stover, Richard. *An Analysis of CAD/CAM Applications with an Introduction to CIM.* Englewood Cliffs, NJ: Prentice-Hall, Inc., 1984.

Strawhorn, John K. "Future Methods and Techniques," in *The Future of the Printed Word,* ed. Philip Hill. Westport, CT: Greenwood Press, 1980.

Strehlo, Kevin. "When the Objective Is Efficient Project Management," *Personal Computing,* 8, 1, January 1984.

Tesler, Lawrence G. "Programming Languages," *Scientific American,* 251, 3, September 1984.

Tucker, Jonathan B. "Visual Simulation Takes Flight," *High Technology,* 4, 12, December 1984.

Zeidenberg, Mathew. "Snowflakes and Dragons," *MacWorld,* 2, 8, August 1985.

Texts used as general references for the history chart in Exhibit 1.7 in Chapter 1.

Freiberger, Paul, and **Michael Swaine.** *Fire in the Valley: The Making of the Personal Computer.* Berkeley, CA: Osborne/McGraw-Hill, 1984.

Goldstine, Herman H. *The Computer: From Pascal to Von Neumann.* Princeton, NJ: Princeton University Press, 1972.

Grun, Bernard. *The Timetables of History.* New York: Simon & Schuster, 1982.

APPENDIX A

CHAPTER QUESTIONS and EXERCISES

CHAPTER 1 QUESTIONS and EXERCISES

1. Locate computer graphics applications or research in one or more of the following areas (or other areas of your choice): Business, Architecture, Education, Art, Engineering, Science.

2. Locate some enterprises in your area presently using computer graphics in their activities. Visit one or more of them. Describe, point by point, how they are using computer graphics. Try to obtain sample outputs for viewing by others.

3. Name five computer graphics applications that are used to help an enterprise function.

4. Name three key developments that allowed users access to low cost professional quality computer graphics, formerly available only to those with access to expensive systems.

5. How can passive graphics be contrasted to interactive graphics?

6. Fill in three predictions for the next few years in computer graphics and related areas, in the blank spaces provided at the end of the history chart in Exhibit 1.7. At the end of the semester review your predictions.

CHAPTER 2 QUESTIONS and EXERCISES

1. Name and describe briefly the three components which diagram *any* computer system. Give two examples demonstrating application *not* given in the text.

2. Name three of the four major areas we must remain aware of in order to understand computer design, application, and impact.

3. What are the three major forms of processing? Describe and give an example of each.

4. New technology changes perception. What does this mean? Describe in your own words. How might computer graphics change our perception? Describe briefly.

5. "Man is nothing but an information processing machine." Do you agree or disagree with this statement? Explain your answer briefly.

CHAPTER 2 QUESTIONS and EXERCISES (Continued)

6. What are input and output devices? Name three of each.

7. A computer system is more than a computer. Name seven components of a computer system. You may describe more than one in a major category (software, hardware).

8. What differentiates a nongraphics from a graphics computer system? Name and describe three major differences.

9. Define BIT, BYTE, BITMAPPED, SCREEN RESOLUTION, ASCII CODE.

10. With 5 wires we can transmit _____ different _____ bit messages. Fill in the blanks.

11. What is a pixel?

12. Define MODELESS OPERATION, OPEN ARCHITECTURE, CLOSED ARCHITECTURE. Which of the above is closely related and why?

13. Define MEMORY, AUXILIARY STORAGE, RAM and ROM.

14. Name and describe briefly three different forms of auxiliary storage.

15. Define TRACKS and SECTORS.

16. Define and describe briefly the CPU and the operating system. What are their major respective functions?

17. CPUs can be compared on five different variables. Name and describe three.

18. Unaddressable memory is useless memory. What does this mean?

19. Name and describe briefly, and in proper order, the five generations of programming languages described in the text.

20. Software is organized hierarchically. Draw a diagram showing that organization.

CHAPTER 3 QUESTIONS and EXERCISES

1. Four different modes of operation of graphics systems are described in the text. Describe the two most used today.

2. What differentiates graphics systems? Name and describe four major factors.

3. Different graphics systems were described in the text. Name and describe three.

CHAPTER 3 QUESTIONS and EXERCISES (Continued)

4. Is it possible to enhance a microcomputer so that it can perform as a graphics workstation? Describe and give an example.

5. What is a network? Define and draw three major configurations or topologies.

6. How would you compare the IBM PC and the Apple Macintosh systems? Describe five features that differentiate them.

7. Visit two local computer stores, armed with a short checklist of factors on which graphics systems can be compared. Choose computer stores that carry different equipment. Select at least two systems with software and do an initial comparison. Later, in Chapter 15, we will refine this process.

CHAPTER 4 QUESTIONS and EXERCISES

1. Define ERGONOMICS, SEMIOTICS, SYNTACTICS, SEMANTICS, PRAGMATICS.

2. For the purposes of discussion we grouped languages into four major categories. What are they, and which one communicates to the widest audience?

3. Name and describe the use of four data capture devices.

4. When would you use voice entry? Give an example.

5. We cannot expect that any more input devices will be devised beyond the many now in existence. Do you agree with this statement? Justify your answer.

CHAPTER 5 QUESTIONS and EXERCISES

1. What is the most important part of a system? Why?

2. What are the different classes of output devices? Is it possible for them to be intelligent? If yes, what does that accomplish?

3. Describe vector and raster displays. Name two advantages and disadvantages of each.

4. Why are color displays a "kludge"? The answer is related to the workings of an RGB monitor.

5. White is the presence of all colors. How do we know this?

6. Name five factors that influence the perception of depth.

CHAPTER 5 QUESTIONS and EXERCISES (Continued)

7. What are three principles of form perception?

8. Are the factors described in questions 6 and 7 used in computer graphics? If, yes, describe two applications where this is the case.

9. Name three hard copy output devices. When would you use one over the other? Describe.

10. What impact will the improvements in output devices have on our communication with each other using computers? Describe point by point, and briefly.

CHAPTER 6 QUESTIONS and EXERCISES

1. Define the different purposes of presentation and analytic graphics.

2. We named four objectives of presentation graphics. Name and describe three of them.

3. We presented a taxonomy of business graphics. Business graphics fell into two major groups, and presentation graphics also fell into two major groups. Name and describe each of the four groups briefly.

4. Draw a chart with all of its major components, and label the chart to identify the components.

5. We named eight principles of making good graphics presentations. Name and describe five.

6. We named eleven pitfalls to avoid in making graphics presentations. Name and describe six.

7. We named and illustrated eleven different types of presentation charts. Name and draw a rough sketch of six.

8. Briefly state when and how you might use each of the presentation charts identified in question 7.

9. Define CAL. Is the development of CAL materials more demanding than developing a lecture? Explain your answer.

10. Visit a local computer store or two and ask to see a demonstration of some presentation graphics systems. What control do they offer you?

11. Here is a set of data: Sales volumes (in thousands by territories): A - 1,500; B - 3,500; C - 3,000; D - 4,000; E - 7,600. Select two appropriate chart methods for presenting these data in graphic form and create two complete charts.

CHAPTER 7 QUESTIONS and EXERCISES

1. Define four uses of the electronic spreadsheet.

2. Here are some data on stock shares held, and the price of each share. You wish to compute the total value for each stock, and the grand total of your holdings. Use an available spreadsheet, and then turn the result into an appropriate chart showing the value of each stock held.

ABC Co. 100 shares - $15; The Famous XYZ Co. 500 - $5.78; Acme Ltd. 1,250 - $1.25; ZZZ Ltd. - 2,000 - $1.50.

3. Taking the above figures in question 2, you want your stock to at least increase in value at the rate of inflation over the next five years. Let us assume the inflation rate is 9%, and you will choose to sell the stock if it does not *at least* increase this amount each year. Using an electronic spreadsheet, compute what the bottom-line must be for each stock held. Further, turn the results into an appropriate chart.

4. Compute and diagram a price sensitivity curve based on the following data: sales of widgets at a price of $10 are 400, and sales at a price of $20 are 100. The cost to make each widget is $2. Fixed overhead costs are $1,000. Use the formulas and methods on pages 163 and 164 of the text to complete the assignment.

5. Obtain (or make up) some income and expense data in order to construct a *Profit Projections Report* similar to the report shown in Exhibit 7.14 on page 165. Use the blank work sheets provided at the end of this Appendix. From these data take *one* break-even figure (number to sell in order to break even, total income per week, or month, to break even), and compute the figure manually (if your instructor provides you with the formulas and methods), and on computer (if a system and appropriate software are available).

6. Obtain the income statement and balance sheet from two businesses, with each in a different country. Select two businesses that are in the same enterprise. Plot their respective income statements and balance sheet statements in the manner described in the text on page 167 through 169. How do they compare graphically? What is obvious in the graphics image that is not obvious in the tables?

7. What capabilities do integrated systems offer? If you have access to an integrated system, design a one-page memo that contains text, data, and graphics, along the lines of the example contained in the text (page 172), and use the integrated system to produce the memo. Did the system allow you to create the memo with ease? Did you encounter any places where you could envision how the system might work better? Did the system allow you to write macros?

8. Define and describe DYNAMIC ANALYSIS.

9. Define and describe the two major categories, or purposes, of statistical analysis.

CHAPTER 7 QUESTIONS and EXERCISES (Continued)

10. What is covariation? Give an example of how we might use it.

11. Sketch, or use a computer to generate, scattergrams that represents zero, perfect positive, and perfect negative correlation. What **r** values are these? Label the scattergrams.

12. Do correlations imply causality? Explain your answer.

CHAPTER 8 QUESTIONS and EXERCISES

1. Define and give an example of MODELS and SIMULATIONS.

2. What is the relationship among models, simulations, and reality? Define and/or illustrate.

3. In your field of study describe three examples of models and simulations in the form of input of data or conditions to the model or system, and the resulting output (similar to the examples shown on page 183).

4. On pages 184 through 194 we defined models in a number of different ways. Again, using your own field of study, select five of those definitions and give an example for each.

5. Why are mathematical models less likely to be reflective of reality in the areas of economics, social action, and politics? Does this mean we should not use mathematical models in these areas? Explain your answer.

6. Select a familiar daily activity. Draw a flow diagram of that activity, similar to the one shown on page 187. Remember to not overlook any possible sequences, loops, or decisions. (We will encounter these terms again when we discuss programming in Chapter 13. You may be surprised at how complex a simple activity turns out to be when we diagram it. This should give you a hint as to the complexity and cleverness of the brain and mind, and the difficulty encountered when programming computers.)

7. As stated on page 188, entities are composite, not monolithic. Select some entity in your field of study and diagram its composition.

8. Again, using your field of study, select a natural phenomenon, model it, and either run or predict the results of a simulation.

9. We defined network models as a part of operations research. What kinds of problems in your field of study would lend themselves to the kind of analysis provided by networks? Define and describe briefly.

10. Can you think of two or three conceptual models in your field of study? What is their purpose?

CHAPTER 8 QUESTIONS and EXERCISES (Continued)

11. Describe three functions of models.

12. Problems call for different approaches. They are called *analysis, synthesis,* and *control.* Define these terms.

13. Since computers are so fast and can remember more than we can, they are bound to be more accurate in their predictions. Do you agree? Explain, and provide examples in support of your answer.

14. What is CGI? Name four applications.

15. Define POLYGONS, RAY TRACING, FRACTALS.

16. In the text we named nine different reasons for using business simulations on computer. Name and describe five.

CHAPTER 9 QUESTIONS and EXERCISES

1. Define CAD, CAM, CAE.

2. Name four application areas for CAD, CAM, CAE.

3. CAD, CAM, and CAE are beyond the resources of small companies and individuals. Do you agree? Explain your answer.

4. Describe four major differences between CAD and paint systems.

5. What are the benefits of CAD? Name five.

6. We defined five different levels of CAD capabilities. Name and describe four of them.

7. We described the variables that influence ease of visualization. The *least* effective was a wire frame rendition from an orthographic view. What are the other views and what view is the best? (See Exhibit 9.11, page 223.)

8. Why is hidden line removal and surface texturing important in solids modeling? Explain.

9. Define RUBBERBANDING, MIRRORING, SNAP, ZOOM, PAN, FILLETS.

10. We can create a drawing on computer in different ways: draw each dot or pixel, or enter mathematical formulas, or geometric data, and let the computer generate the image. When would you use each of these two approaches? Describe and give examples.

CHAPTER 9 QUESTIONS and EXERCISES (Continued)

11. We describe an application of CAD to the study of populations and families. Can you think of applications of a similar nature to your own family, to your neighborhood, to other aspects of community life (for example, resources—Buckminster Fuller taught us to make our resources visible by mapping them; this gives us the bigger picture, and shows the relationships between things). Describe and, if possible, do it.

12. Describe five CAD or paint applications in your field of study.

CHAPTER 10 QUESTIONS and EXERCISES

1. There are three different ways graphics may be used with files or databases of information. Name them.

2. Of the three ways graphics may be used with databases of information, describe briefly the most powerful way.

3. Are automated databases always superior? Explain and provide an example illustrating your answer.

4. Select a problem in your field of study that would lend itself to the use of a graphics-oriented information manager like *Filevision*. Describe and illustrate with sketches, or drawings on computer, how you would set up and link the graphics and information files.

5. Describe three applications for the use of graphics as a data type.

CHAPTER 11 QUESTIONS and EXERCISES

1. Define GANTT CHART, CPM, PERT, TASKS, MILESTONES, NETWORK DIAGRAM, CRITICAL PATH.

2. Select some familiar process that involves a sequence of tasks. For example, in preparing for a trip, returning to school, or getting a new job, there are a number of possible required tasks: close house, say goodbye, check out car, pick up airline tickets, buy travel checks, buy clothes, and so forth. Using this type of example, set up a Gantt Chart, network diagram, tasks, milestones, critical path, and task assignments, as illustrated in the chapter. If possible, use a computerized system.

3. Define RESOURCE, DURATION, EARLIEST START, EARLIEST FINISH, LATEST START, LATEST FINISH.

4. We can take a top-down approach to project management. What does this mean?

CHAPTER 11 QUESTIONS and EXERCISES (Continued)

5. What are a Task Gantt Chart and a Resource Gantt Chart? Describe.

6. What is the difference between a project manager and an electronic spreadsheet? We describe in this chapter that they each function in a manner *opposite* to each other. How? Can you think of other software that function in a similar opposite manner? Name and describe briefly.

7. Define PROJECT CALENDAR, TASK DEFINITION, TASK SEQUENCE, COST DEFINITION, PROJECT MONITORING, PROJECT TRACKING.

8. We describe ten guidelines to using project managers. Name five.

9. What does the future of project management involve? Describe briefly.

CHAPTER 12 QUESTIONS and EXERCISES

1. There are four basic stages in producing a book. What are they? Name and describe briefly.

2. Desktop computer-based publishing systems threaten to eliminate traditional publishing. Do you agree or disagree? Explain your answer.

3. What are the traditional responsibilities of an author? Where does the author traditionally have no or very little influence?

4. Why do we use the metaphors of director and producer to describe the new roles of author and publisher brought about by computer aided publishing? Describe briefly.

5. On page 282 the traditional publishing cycle is described. It would have been good if we had drawn a flow diagram to illustrate the steps. Sketch, or use a computer graphics system, to generate a flow diagram based on the information provided on page 282.

6. Describe the author support functions now available with desktop publishing.

7. Describe the production functions now available with desktop publishing.

8. With desktop systems, authors do not write articles and books as such; they generate databases of text and graphics information from which articles, books, and so forth are extracted. What do you think of this? What impacts will this have? (Some authors have reacted very negatively to this idea. Are they justifiably concerned?)

9. Using your own field of study, show the setup of a database with at least two relations or files that would act in support of your work and writing.

CHAPTER 12 QUESTIONS and EXERCISES (Continued)

10. How would you use systems like *Factfinder* and *ThinkTank* in your work and study? Describe two applications.

11. Sketch or illustrate, using pencil or pen, some small diagram or design. Keep track of time, number of redrawings, and level of satisfaction with your production. Now take the same task and repeat it using a paint program on a computer. Keep track of the same variables. What was your experience? Repeat the same procedure in the reverse order (paint program used first) with another similar sketch or illustration.

12. Consider the use of icons. Using your own field of study, make up three or four icons that you feel would communicate effectively to fellow students, teachers, and colleagues. Test them out. Redesign them and test again. (Hint: Describe the objectives of communication for each icon very precisely before proceeding. For example, an image of a man riding a bicycle could be used to convey different messages: use bicycle path, bicycle for health, no bicycles allowed, and so forth.)

13. Define FONT, FACE, ASCENT, DESCENT, BASELINE, KERNING, LEADING, SPLINES, BITMAPPED FONTS.

14. What are the major differences between low- and high-end desktop publishing systems? Name and describe five.

15. Name seven applications for desktop publishing.

CHAPTER 13 QUESTIONS and EXERCISES

1. What are the basic building blocks of programs? (Are they familiar? Go back and look at question 5 in Chapter 8.)

2. What is a subroutine? Describe briefly.

The following simple programming exercises are offered in case the course instructor wishes to further introduce programming. However, in order to perform even these simple exercises, the instructor will have to provide additional information on the specific language and system being used.

3. Using the language available to you, write a program to
   Draw an ellipse.
   Draw a rectangle.
   Draw several ellipses or rectangles rotated by equal degrees around some defined point.

4. Write a program that draws an image of a house with four windows. (You might try drawing the windows using a subroutine to draw each window.)

CHAPTER 13 QUESTIONS and EXERCISES (Continued)

5. As a further enhancement to the house, add lines of instructions to the program to shade or color the roof, walls, windows, and doors, with a different shade or color for each.

6. Enter any of the programs provided in the chapter, and play with the parameters.

CHAPTER 14 QUESTIONS and EXERCISES

1. Define DATABASE, FILE, FIELD, RELATION, TABLE, DATA ITEM, RECORD.

2. Illustrate with a sketch, and describe three differences between file and database management systems.

3. Describe two applications in your area of study that would lend themselves to a database application.

4. Although most readers may not have access to *Helix*, using the exhibits provided on page 340 of the text as a reference, select some formulas used in your field of study (they need not be particularly complex), and see how they might be expressed in the iconic language of *Helix*.

5. What are the aims of *Prograph*? Describe point by point.

6. *Helix* is not really a graphics programming language, but *Prograph* is. What might we mean by this?

7. The use of graphics, since visuals communicate more clearly, just about guarantees that the languages that use graphics will be easier to learn, remember, and use. Do you agree? Explain your answer.

CHAPTER 15 QUESTIONS and EXERCISES

1. Computers provide content; people provide context. Explain.

2. What are the purposes of systems analysis? Describe point by point.

3. The order of analysis takes place in the reverse order of use. Explain.

4. Define the traditional systems development cycle. You may use a diagram.

5. Define the expanded systems development cycle suggested in the text. You may use a diagram.

CHAPTER 15 QUESTIONS and EXERCISES (Continued)

6. What are four of the five suggested activites involved in educating users? Describe and justify them. Why are they important, and why is it important to start the systems development cycle with them?

7. Apply matrix analysis to a situation in your field of study with which you are familiar.

8. Make a list of things you find irritating, difficult to find, difficult to do, and so forth, in your work or study. Then, based on this list, think of how you might use a computer system, and more specifically a graphics computer system, to alleviate some of that irritation. Compare your findings to the findings of others. Do certain commonalities emerge? What would such commonalities suggest?

9. There are five suggested approaches to systems development identified in the text. Name and describe three, and identify in your answer when you would use one approach over another.

10. Define DFDs. What do they do? Draw an illustration of a simple DFD showing the major components, and label the components appropriately.

11. What are the five major components that make up a total computer system? Draw a diagram of your own choosing that illustrates the relationship between all five components. (Hint: think of the hardware as being a communication link or path.).

12. When choosing a system we could rely on a number of different sources of information (or *mis*information). Name three approaches that are *not* particularly wise to follow when selecting a system.

13. In evaluating systems we need two sets of important information on the features that systems might possess. What are those two sets of information? (We likened them to navigation coordinates.)

14. Features or criteria are of three different types. Name them. Which one should you use *first* in evaluating systems? Explain why.

CHAPTER 16 QUESTIONS and EXERCISES

1. We identified eight major areas of impact of computer graphics. Name five.

2. What is a visual proverb? Make one up. Test it out. Does it work? What is the purpose of a proverb?

3. You have a presentation, paper, or lecture to prepare. Make a list of possible topics, ideas, thoughts, inspirations, etc. Underline the key thoughts. Now perform the same task using a mind-map. Does the mind-mapping process arouse anything different? If, yes, what?

CHAPTER 16 QUESTIONS and EXERCISES (Continued)

4. Select two of the *formal* mind-mapping techniques given in the text, and apply them to a problem in your field of study.

5. Four stages of technological evolution were described. Name and describe them briefly. Use an example.

6. What do we mean by the universal graphics workstation?

7. What is a group decision support system? How would graphics be used in such a system?

8. What is an early warning system (EWS)? How would graphics be used?

9. We describe a possible negative rebound in using automated EWSs. Describe and offer an opinion.

10. We are moving from data processing to knowledge engineering. What does this mean, and how are expert systems related?

11. When is it appropriate to use an expert system approach to a given problem? Name four.

12. We described a few applications of expert systems involving graphics. Scan them, and describe a possible application in your field of study.

13. What is *bypassing?* What is *media bypassing?*

14. What are *construction kits?* Name five applications for construction kits.

15. Discovery disrupts patterns. What does this mean? How would this process relate to education, to your field of study, to your work? How might computer graphics assist in softening the disruption? (This question is purposely broad in order to challenge you to think carefully of positive possibilities and negative impacts.)

PROFIT PROJECTIONS WORKSHEET

Enterprise Qty
12 months

Your Name
Your Business Name

Income Sources	Rate ... per month	Price per ...	------Income------ per month total
Sales	_____ _____		_____ _____

Variable Expenses	Rate ... per month	Cost per ...	------Expense---- per month total
Cost of Goods	_____ _____		_____ _____
Freight	_____ _____		_____ _____
Selling expense	_____ _____		_____ _____
Commissions	_____ _____		_____ _____

Fixed Expenses	------Expense------ per month total
Payroll	_____ _____
Payroll taxes	_____ _____
Advertising	_____ _____
Office supplies	_____ _____
Depreciation	_____ _____
Repairs	_____ _____
Interest expens	_____ _____
Rent	_____ _____
Utilities	_____ _____
Insurance	_____ _____
Misc. expenses	_____ _____

APPENDIX B

STUDENT QUESTIONNAIRE

Course Title: _____   Instructor: _____

Student Name: _____   Student No.: _____

Students enter this course with varied areas and levels of knowledge. It will help if I have some idea of what they are. Please answer the following questions. *Please Print Clearly.*

1. What is your major course of study?   Business: _____

                                                   Computer Science: _____

                                                   Other: _____

2. What *business courses* have you taken?

Course Number   *Course Title*

_____

_____

_____

_____

_____

3. What *computer science courses* have you taken?

Course Number   *Course Title*

_____

_____

_____

_____

4. What *graphics or graphics-related courses* have you taken?

Course Number   *Course Title*

_____

_____

_____

_____

5. Please check which concepts and tools you are familiar with and the level of your familiarity. "High" means you are able to use the concept or tool with skill and confidence. Please check in the appropriate column to indicate level of knowledge.

Concept/Tool	√	None	Low	Medium	High
microcomputers. If yes, which one(s):					
how a computer works					
presentation graphics					
analytic graphics					
statistics					
simulation					
modeling					
computer aided design					
paint programs					
database					
project management					
GANTT charts					
CPM/PERT					
publishing					
systems analysis and design					
electronic spreadsheet					
programming. If yes, what languages:					

6. What do you wish to learn from this course? *Describe briefly, point by point.*

_____

_____

_____

_____

_____

_____

_____

_____

_____

_____

APPENDIX C

REFERENCE LIST OF SYSTEMS AND SOFTWARE

The list of products included in Appendix C are those discussed in the text, plus others of interest. A perusal of the index will indicate which products are discussed. The product listing is organized by software and hardware for the Apple Macintosh and the IBM PC family. Products are listed according to the category to which they belong. Some graphics workstations are also listed.

Not all software listed is graphics software; a larger context is required. Graphics software works in conjunction with other applications. The choice of categories to list and the choice of names for categories are somewhat arbitrary. We have attempted to follow the lead provided by other compendiums and overviews, including special report issues from *BYTE* (McGraw-Hill, Inc., Peterborough, NH), *Computer Technology Review* (West World Productions, Inc., Los Angeles, CA), *IEEE Software* (IEEE Computer Society, New York, NY), *IEEE Computer Graphics* (IEEE Computer Society, New York, NY), *InfoWorld* (CW Communications Inc., Framingham, MA), *Macintosh Buyer's Guide* (Redgate Publishing Company, Vero Beach, FL), *New in Computing Magazine and Buyer's Guide* (Computer Education Services of America, Inc., Milwaukee, WI), *PC Magazine* (Ziff-Davis Publishing, New York, NY), and *PCWorld* (PC World Communications, Inc., San Francisco, CA).

In order to provide as much useful information in the least amount of space, each listing provides the name of the product, the publisher, and the city and state, or province, of the publisher. From this the reader may readily obtain additional information on any set of products. However, the listing is not meant to be complete; it is a sample of an expanding number of offerings.

SOFTWARE—Apple Macintosh

Communications

Product	Publisher	City and State
Dow Jones Straight Talk	Dow Jones & Company, Inc.	Princeton, NJ
MacLink	Dataviz Inc.	Norwalk, CT
MacNAPLPS (emulation)	Electrohome	Kitchener, ONT
MacTerminal	Apple Computer, Inc.	Cupertino, CA
PC to MAC and BACK (Also IBM)	Dilithium Press	Beaverton, OR
SideKick	Borland International, Inc.	Scotts Valley, CA

Database/File Management

1st Base	Desktop Software, Inc.	Princeton, NJ
Pusiness Filevision	Telos Software	Santa Monica, CA
Filemaker	Forethought, Inc.	Mountain View, CA
Interlace	Singular Software, Inc.	San Jose, CA
MacLion	Computer Software Designs	Anaheim, CA
MSFile	MicroSoft Corporation	Bellevue, WA
Odesta Helix 2.0	Odesta	Northbrook, IL
Omnis 3	Blyth Software, Inc.	San Mateo, CA
OverVUE 2.0	Provue Development Corp.	Huntington Beach, CA

Database/File Management (special applications)

Art Manager	MicroSoft Corporation	Bellevue, WA
AUTOREF (bibliography)	Scilab, Inc.	Guilderland, NY
Factfinder	Forethought, Inc.	Mountain View, CA
PictureBase	Symmetry Corp.	Mesa, AR
Professional Bibliographic System	Personal Bibliographic Soft.	Ann Arbor, MI

Decision Support Systems/Expert Systems

DecisionMap	Softstyle, Inc.	Honolulu, HI
Document Modeler	The Model Office Company	Toronto, ONT
ods/CONSULTANT	Organization Develop. Soft.	Des Plaines, IL
ods/People Management	Organization Develop. Soft.	Des Plaines, IL
Macsmarts	Cognition Technology Corp.	Cambridge, MA
MindSight	Execucom Systems Corp.	Austin, TX
Nexpert	Neuron Data Corp.	Palo Alto, CA

Education/Training

ChipWits (programming)	BrainPower, Inc.	Calabasas, CA
Entrepreneur (simulation)	MicroSoft Corporation	Bellevue, WA
LightSource (authoring)	Computer Learning Systems	Concord, MA
MacTag (track grades)	Paragon Courseware	Del Mar, CA
MacType (typing)	Palantir Software	Houston, TX
Notes (for Jazz and Excel)	Layered, Inc.	Boston, MA
The Master (BASIC)	Orion Training Systems	Dallastown, PA
Typing Tutor (typing)	Paragon Courseware	Del Mar, CA
Wormstat (statistics)	Small Business Computers	Amherst, NH

Fonts and Font makers

Fluent Fonts	Casady Company	Carmel, CA
Fontagenix	Devonian International Soft.	Montclair, CA
Laserfonts Library	Century Software	Los Angeles, CA
LaserWorks	E.D.O. Communications	West Hartford, CT
Mac the Knife	Miles Computing, Inc.	Van Nuys, CA
Professional Fonts	Kensington Microware	New York, NY
Professional Headlines	Kensington Microware	New York, NY
Techfonts	Paragon Software	Del Mar, CA

Graphics—Animation

MacFats Storyboarder	American Intelliware Corp.	Marina Del Rey, CA
Slide Show Magician	Magnum Software	Chatsworth, CA
VideoWorks	Hayden Software	Lowell, MA

Graphics—Computer Aided Design

Draft Math	DM Systems	Bay Shore, NY
Easy 3D	Enabling Technologies	Honolulu, HI
EZ-Draft	Bridgeport Machines	Willow Grove, PA
MacDraft	Innovative Data Design, Inc.	Consord, CA
MacDraw	Apple Computer, Inc.	Cupertino, CA
MacPerspective	B. Knick Drafting	Melbourne, FL
MacSurf (Marine design)	Graphic Magic Pty. Ltd.	Cottesloe, W. Australia
Minicad 3D-Designer	Diehl Graphsoft, Inc.	Ellicott City, MD

Graphics—Paint

Art Grabber with Body Shop	Hayden Software	Lowell, MA
ClickArt Effects	Sheharazam	Milwaukee, WI
Fullpaint	Ann Arbor Software Inc.	Ann Arbor, MI
MacPaint	Apple Computer, Inc.	Cupertino, CA
Make-a-Mug	Shaherazam	Milwaukee, WI
QuickPaint	Enterset, Inc.	San Francisco, CA

Graphics—Presentation

Cricket Graph	Cricket Software	Philadelphia, PA
MacAtlas	Micro;Maps	Morristown, NJ
MacMap	Strategic Location Planning	San Jose, CA
MSChart	MicroSoft Corporation	Bellevue, WA

Graphics—Libraries

500 Menu Patterns	Fingertip Software	Long Beach, CA
Accessory Pak 1	Shaherazam	Milwaukee, WI
Art Portfolio	Axlon Inc.	Sunnyvale, CA
ClickArt	T/Maker Company	Mountain View, CA
DaVinci Building Blocks	Hayden Software	Lowell, MA
DaVinci Buildings	Hayden Software	Lowell, MA
DaVinci Commercial Interiors	Hayden Software	Lowell, MA
DaVinci Interiors	Hayden Software	Lowell, MA
DaVinci Landscapes	Hayden Software	Lowell, MA
Mac the Knife	Miles Computing, Inc.	Van Nuys, CA
MacAccessories Accents	Kensington Microware	New York, NY
MacArt for Business	Wiley Professional Software	New York, NY
MacArt Library	CompuCRAFT	Englewood, CO
MacBits	MacPoint Publications	Chicago, IL
MacPublishing Designs	Boston Software Publishers	Boston, MA
McPic!	Magnum Software	Chatsworth, CA
Q-Art	Queue, Inc.	Bridgeport, CN
SmArtmouse	Pleasant Graphics Ware	Pleasant Hill, OR
The Card Shoppe	Axlon Inc.	Sunnyvale, CA
The Mac Art Dept.	Simon and Schuster	New York, NY

Idea Processors

Calliope	Innovision	Los Altos, CA
ThinkTank	Living Videotext	Mountain View, CA

Integrated Software

Ensemble	Hayden Software	Lowell, MA
Excel	MicroSoft Corporation	Bellevue, WA
Genesis	Boston Software Publishers	Boston, MA
Jazz	Lotus Development Corp.	Cambridge, MA

Programming

ExperLisp	ExperTelligence Inc.	Santa Barbara, CA
ExperLogo	ExperTelligence Inc.	Santa Barbara, CA
MSBASIC	MicroSoft Corporation	Bellevue, WA
MSPascal	MicroSoft Corporation	Bellevue, WA
Prolog II	Avenue Software, Inc.	Terminus, QUE

Project Management

MacProject	Apple Computer, Inc.	Cupertino, CA
MicroPlanner	Micro Planner Software	San Francisco, CA
Project Modeler	The Model Office Company	Toronto, ONT

Publishing

Glue (graphics transfer)	Solutions Inc.	Montpelier, VT
MacPublisher	Boston Software Publishers	Boston, MA
PageMaker	Aldus Corporation	Seattle, WA
ReadySetGo	Manhattan Graphics	New York, NY
DisplayAd Makeup System	Digital Technology Int'l.	Orem, UT

Spreadsheet, Templates, and Analysis Software

ClickOn	T/Maker Graphics	Mountain View, CA
Financial Analysis	RealData, Inc.	Southport, CN
Multiplan	MicroSoft Corporation	Bellevue, WA
Overture	Brainstorm Development	Austin, TX
Profit Planning	Softouch Software, Inc.	Lake Oswego, OR
Profit Projections/Breakeven	Harris Technical Systems	Lincoln, NE
Supercrunch	Paladin Software Corp.	San Jose, CA

Statistics and Numerical Analysis

Mac Stat Pak	Scientific MicroPrograms	Raleigh, NC
PowerMath	BrainPower, Inc.	Calabasas, CA
StatView	BrainPower, Inc.	Calabasas, CA
TK! Solver	Software Arts, Inc.	Wellesley, MA

Utilities

Automac (macro)	Genesis Micro Software	Bellevue, WA
Copy II MAC	Central Point Software	Portland, OR
MacPlot (for plotter)	Microspot	Maidstone, Kent, England
Paint Cutter	Silicon Beach Software	San Diego, CA
Sidekick (desktop)	Borland International	Scotts Valley, CA
Work n' Print (buffer)	Assimilation, Inc.	Los Gatos, CA

Word Processing

1st Merge (with 1st Base)	Desktop Software	Princeton, NJ
Hayden Speller	Hayden Software Company	Lowell, MA
MacIndex	Boston Software Publishers	Boston, MA
Mac Spell Right	Assimilation, Inc.	Cupertino, CA
MacWrite	Apple Computer, Inc.	Cupertino, CA
QuickWord	Enterset, Inc.	San Francisco, CA
Word	MicroSoft Corporation	Bellevue, WA

HARDWARE—Macintosh

Drives—Disk

10 to 80 MB drives	Lodown	Pleasanton, CA
Apple Unidisk 3.5 (800K)	Apple Computer, Inc.	Cupertino, CA
Apple Hard Disk 20	Apple Computer, Inc.	Cupertino, CA
Bernoulli Box	Iomega Corp.	Roy, UT
Corvus OmniDrive (45MB)	Corvus Systems, Inc.	San Jose, CA
Dataframe	Supermac	Mountain View, CA
MacBottom	Personal Computer Periph.	Tampa, FL
MacDrive	Tecmar, Inc.	Solon, OH
MacNifty Personal	MacNifty	Minneapolis, MN
Superdrive 20	Supermac	Mountain View, CA
HyerDrive	General Computer	Cambridge, MA
HD-20	MD-Ideas Inc.	Foster City, CA
HD-30	MD-Ideas Inc.	Foster City, CA
Superdrive 20	Supermac Technology	Mountain View, CA

Drives—Tape

10 or 60 MB cassette	MD-Ideas Inc.	Foster City, CA
20 MB digital cassette	Lodown	Pleasanton, CA
60 MB 1/4" tape	Lodown	Pleasanton, CA

Input Devices

KAT (touch tablet)	Koala Technologies Corp.	San Jose, CA
Image Blue (optical scanner)	Image Communications, Inc.	Greenwich, CN
Image Scanner	Microtek	Gardena, CA
Macintizer	GTCO Corp.	Rockville, MD
MacTablet (graphics tablet)	Summagraphics Corp.	Fairfield, CN
Mac Turbo Touch (trackball)	Assimilation, Inc.	Los Gatos, CA
Omni-Reader (character reader)	Oberon International	Irving, TX
Thunderscan (digitizing scan)	Thunderware, Inc.	Orinda, CA
View Control System (visual)	Personics Corp.	Concord, MA

Memory expansion

MacBoard	VOAD Systems	Los Angeles, CA
MacMemory Megabyte	MacMemory Electronics	Mountain View, CA
Meg and Meg-d	Supermac Technology	Mountain View, CA
MegaMac and MegaRAM	MicroGraphic Images Corp.	Woodland Hills, CA
Enhance	Supermac Technology	Mountain View, CA
512 and 1MB upgrade	MassTech Development	Groton, MA
512 upgrade	FutureVest	New York, NY
The MAX	MacMemory, Inc.	Mountain View, CA

Monitors

The Big Mac (23 inch)	Professional Data Systems	Mill Valley, CA
MacMonitor (19 inch)	Contrex International	Newport Beach, CA
Project-a-Mac	Professional Data Systems	Mill Valley, CA

Networks

3Server (Also for IBM PC)	3Com Corp	Mountain View, CA
Blue Mac!	Cogitate, Inc.	Southfield, MI
Mac File Server	Infotek, Inc.*	Patchogue, NY

* Infotek produces other hardware products including ports, printers, memory boards, and disk drives.

Video Outputs

CineMac	MicroGraphic Images Corp.	Woodland Hills, CA
Composite Video Adaptor	Mentauris Technologies	San Marcos, TX
MacVid	Infotek, Inc.	Patchogue, NY

SOFTWARE—IBM PC family of computers and look-alikes

The amount of software and hardware for the IBM PC family of computers is very large. In some categories the following list is a small sample of what is available. The reader is advised to scan various periodicals (*BYTE, PC Magazine, PCWorld*).

Communications

Crosstalk	Microstuf, Inc.	Roswell, GA
BARR/HASP	BARR Systems, Inc.	Raleigh, NC
Mirror	Softklone	Tallahassee, FL
Move-it Version 4	Woolf Software Systems	Canoga Park, CA
Lanlink	Software link	Atlanta, GA
PFS:Access Communications	Software Publishing Corp.	Mountain View, CA

Database/File Management

DataFlex	Data Access Corporation	Miami, FL
dBASE III	Ashton-Tate	Culver City, CA
Formula II	Lifeboat Associates	New York, NY
Knowledgeman	Micro Data Base Systems, Inc.	Lafayette, IN
PC/Focus	Information Builders, Inc.	New York, NY
Personal Pearl	Pearlsoft, Inc.	Wilsonville, OR
Rbase 5000	Microrim	Bellevue, WA
XDB	Software Systems Technology	College Park, MD

Database/File Management (Special applications)

pcEXPRESS	Information Resources, Inc.	Waltham, MA
Photobase	Chorus Data Systems, Inc.	Merrimack, NH
Picturepower	Pictureware Inc.	Bala Cynwyd, PA

Decision Support Systems/Expert Systems

Arborist	Texas Instruments, Inc.	Austin, TX
Automated Reasoning Tool	Inference Corp.	Los Angeles, CA
Decision Aide	Kepner-Tregoe, Inc.	Princeton, NJ
Decision Analyst	Executive Software Inc.	Dover, DE
Deja vu	Kingsley & Associates	San Francisco, CA
Expert Choice	Decision Support Software	McLean, VA
GURU	MDBS	Lafayette, IN
Lightyear	Lightyear	Santa Clara, CA
MicroFCS	EPS, Inc.	Windham, NH
Trouble Shooter	Kepner-Tregoe, Inc.	Princeton, NJ

Education/Training

ATI series	ATI	Los Angeles, CA
Automentor	Software Recording Corp.	Dallas, TX
CRS Trainer 4000	Computer Systems Research	Avon, CT
Demo Program	Software Garden Inc.	West Newton, MA
Interactive Instruction Authoring	IBM Corporation	Boca Raton, FL
The Intro Series	Comprehensive Software	Redondo Beach, CA
The Professor	Individual Software, Inc.	Foster City, CA
Thoughtware	Thoughtware, Inc.	Coconut Grove, FL
Typing Instructor	Individual Software, Inc.	Foster City, CA

Fonts and Font makers

Font Editor and Fonts	VS Software	Little Rock, AR
Fancy Font	Softcraft, Inc.	Madison, WI
Fontrix	Data Transforms Inc.	Denver, CO
Lasersoft	Business Systems Int'l.	Canoga Park, CA
LaserType	SoftLab	St. George, UT
Poems Font Editor	Poems	Thousand Oaks, CA

Graphics—Analytic and Presentation

35MM Express	Treck Photographic	Toronto, ONT
Atlas Mapping Software	Strategic Locations Planning	San Jose, CA
BPS Business Graphics	Business & Prof'l. Software	Cambridge, MA
ChartMaster	Decision Resources	Westport, CN
Chartstar	Micro Pro	San Rafael, CA
Charts Unlimited	Graphware	Middleton, ONT
Energraphics	Enertronics Research, Inc.	St. Louis, MO

Graphics—Analytic and Presentation (continued)

Executive Picture Show	PCsoftware	San Diego, CA
Execuvision	Prentice-Hall, Inc.	Englewood Cliffs, NJ
Freelance	Graphic Communications	Waltham, MA
GRAFPLUS	Jewell Technologies, Inc.	Seattle, WA
GRAPHER	Golden Software	Golden, CO
Graphwriter	Graphic Communications	Waltham, MA
Grafix Partner	Brightbill-Roberts & Company	Syracuse, NY
GRAFPLUS	Jewell Technologies Inc.	Seattle, WA
Graftalk	Redding Group Inc.	Ridgefield, CN
GDSS	Data Business Vision, Inc.	San Diego, CA
GraffHopper	Data Business Vision, Inc.	San Diego, CA
Fast Graphs 2.0	Innovative Software, Inc.	Overland Park, KS
Freeform and Highlight	Artech Software, Inc.	Reston, VA
Freelance (Works with Lotus 1-2-3)	Graphics Communication, Inc.	Waltham, MA
Harvard Presentation Graphics	Software Publishing	Mountain View, CA
Image Management System	Electronic Cottage	San Francisco, CA
Monografx (needs no board)	Analytics International	Arlington, MA
MSChart	MicroSoft Corporation	Bellevue, WA
R-Graph	Fox and Geller, Inc.	Elmwood Park, NJ
SignMaster	Decision Resources	Westport, CN
Samna Decision Graphics	Samna Corp.	Atlanta, GA
Sound Presentations	Communication Dynamics, Inc.	Wilsonville, OR
Syon	Stella Systems Corp.	Cupertino, CA

Graphics Animation

PC Storyboard	IBM Corporation	Menlo Park, CA
PicturePak	Marketing Graphics, Inc.	Richmond, VA
ScreenPLAY	Frontier Software, Inc.	West Allis, WI

Also see **Graphics Workstations** at the end of this appendix.

Graphics—Computer Aided Design

AutoCAD	Autodesk Inc.	San Jose, CA
Computer Aided Production (CAP)	Innovative Computer Aided Tech.	Lawndale, CA
Design Board Illustrator	Mega Cadd	Seattle, WA
Generic Cadd	Generic Software Inc.	Bellevue, WA
In-A-Vision (under Windows)	Micrografx	Richardson, TX
ProDesign II	American Small Business	Pryor, OK
VersaCAD ADVANCED	T & W Systems	Huntington Beach, CA

Also see **Graphics Workstations** at the end of this appendix.

Graphics—Paint

4 Point Graphics (also animation)	International Microcomputer	San Rafael, CA
ARTPAK	Palsoftware Corp.	Los Angeles, CA
Dr. Halo	Lifeboat Associates	New York, NY
Imigit	Chorus Data Systems, Inc.	Merrimack, NH
Island Graphics (true color)	Island Graphics	Sausalito, CA
Lenipen	Computerized Technologies	Hillside, NJ
Lumena (high end system)	Time Arts, Inc.	Santa Rosa, CA
Mouse Systems Paint Program	Mouse Systems	Santa Clara, CA
Paintbrush 400 (for Color 400 card)	Sigma Designs	San Jose, CA
Paint by PC	Vetrix Corp.*	Greensboro, NC
Picture Painter	Penguin Software	Geneva, IL
PC Crayon	PCsoftware	San Diego, CA
PC Draw	Micrografx	Richardson, TX
PC Paintbrush	ZSoft Corporation	Marietta, GA

* Vetrix Corp. also supplies graphics boards and monitors.

Idea Processors

MaxThink	MaxThink Inc.	Piedmont, CA
ThinkTank	Living Videotext	Palo Alto, CA
Ready! (memory resident)	Living Videotext	Palo Alto, CA
THOR	Fastware, Inc.	East Orange, NJ

Integrated Software

Aura	Softrend, Inc.	Salem, NH
Enable	Software Group	Ballston Lake, NY
Electric Desk	Alpha Software Corp.	Burlington, MA
Framework	Ashton-Tate	Culver City, CA
Goldengate	Cullinet PC Software	Westwood, MA
IBM Assistant Series	IBM Corporation	Boca Raton, FL
Integrated-7	Mosaic Software Inc.	Cambridge, MA
Miracle	Micro-Systems Software, Inc.	Boca Raton, FL
Open Access	Software Products Int'l.	San Diego, CA
Lotus 1-2-3	Lotus Corporation	Cambridge, MA
PFS Series	Software Publishing Corp.	Mountain View, CA
Reflex	Analytica Corp.	Fremont, CA
Smart Software System	Innovative Software	Overland Park, KS
Symphony	Lotus Corporation	Cambridge, MA
T/Maker Integrated Software	T/Maker Company	Mountain View, CA

Programming

Halo (graphics toolbox)	Media Cybernetics	Takoma Park, MD
Logo (DR)	Digital Research Corporation	Pacific Grove, CA
Logo (IBM)	IBM Corporation	Boca Raton, FL
Logo (PC)	Harvard Associates	Somerville, MA
Logo (Waterloo)	Waterloo Microsystems Inc.	Waterloo, ONT
MSBASIC	MicroSoft Corporation	Bellevue, WA
MS Pascal	MicroSoft Corporation	Bellevue, WA
Turbo Pascal	Borland International	Scotts Valley, CA
Turbo-graphix (graphics toolbox)	Borland International	Scotts Valley, CA

Project Management

Advanced Project 6	SoftCorp, Inc.	Clearwater, FL
Harvard Project Manager	Harvard Software, Inc.	Harvard, MA
MicroGANTT	Earth Data Corp.	Richmond, CA
Milestone	Digital Marketing Corp.	Walnut Creek, CA
Pertmaster	Westminster Software, Inc.	Menlo Park, CA
Pathfinder	Garland Publishing	New York, NY
Planning Pro	Kepner-Trego, Inc.	Princeton, NJ
Plantrax	Omicron Software	Atlanta, GA
PMS-II	North America Mica, Inc.	San Diego, CA
Primavera Project Planner	Primavera Systems, Inc.	Bala Cynwyd, PA
Project Control System	ETI	Lansing, MI
Project Scheduler Network	Scitor Corporation	Sunnyvale, CA
Qwiknet	Project Software & Develop.	Cambridge, MA
RMS-II	North America Mica, Inc.	San Diego, CA
Super Project	Sorcim/IUS Micro Software	San Jose, CA
Task Monitor	Monitor Software	Los Altos, CA
VisiSchedule	VisiCorp	San Jose, CA

Publishing

Clickart Personal Publisher	T/Maker Company	Mountain View, CA
Do-It	Studio Software Corp.	Irvine, CA
Magna-Type	Magna Computer Systems	Sherman Oaks, CA
PC Publisher	Bestinfo Inc.	Springfield, PA
Printrix	Data Transforms	Denver, CO
ScenicWriter	ScenicSoft, Inc.	Edmonds, WA
Superpage	Bestinfo	Ridley Park, CA
Ventura Publisher	Ventura Software Inc.	Morgan Hill, CA
XyWrite II+	XyQuest Inc.	Bedford, MA

Also see **Graphics Workstations** at the end of this appendix.

Spreadsheets, Templates, and Analysis Software

Forecast Plus	Walonick Associates	Minneapolis, MN
Multiplan	MicroSoft Corporation	Bellevue, WA
OZ (financial modeling)	Fox and Geller	Elmwood Park, NJ
SuperCalc	Sorcim Corporation	San Jose, CA

Statistics and Numerical Analysis

Dataplot	U.S. Dept. of Commerce	Springfield, VA
Exec*U*Stat	Exec*U*Stat Inc.	Princeton, NJ
Research	Economics Software Inc.	Eugene, OR
SPSS/PC	SPSS Inc.	Chicago, IL
Statistics Software for Micros	Kern International	Duxbury, MA
StatPac	Walonick Associates	Minneapolis, MN
SmartForecasts	Smart Software, Inc.	Belmont, MA
STATGRAF	Village Information Co. Inc.	New York, NY
STATPLAN	The Futures Group, Inc.	Glastonbury, CN

Systems Development

Structured Development System	ETI	Lansing, MI
The Excelerator	Intech	Cambridge, MA
ProKit*Analyst 2.0	McDonnell Douglas	St. Louis, MO

User Interface and Applications Integrators

DESQ	Quarterdeck Software	Santa Monica, CA
GEM	Digital Research Inc.	Monterey, CA
TopView	IBM Corporation	Boca Raton, FL
Windows	MicroSoft Corporation	Bellevue, WA

Utilities

Copy II PC	Central Point Software	Portland, OR
EZ-DOS Utility	Software Company	Bedford, TX
GSS*CGI (device indep. interface)	GSS	Wilsonville, OR
Key One (macro)	National Software Associates	The Colony, TX
Norton Utilities (highly regarded)	Peter Norton	Santa Monica, CA
Padlock	Glenco Engineering	Arlington Heights, IL
XenoCopy (disk format conversion)	SofTech Microsystems	San Diego, CA

Word Processing

Multimate	Multimate International Corp.	East Hartford, CT
OfficeWriter	Office Solutions, Inc.	Madison, WI
PFS:Write	Software Publishing Corporation	Mountain View, CA
Perfect Writer	Thorn EMI Computer Software	Costa Mesa, CA
Samna Word III	Samna	Atlanta, GA
Word	MicroSoft Corporation	Bellevue, WA
WordPerfect	Satellite Software Int'l.	Orem, UT
WordStar	Micropro International Corp.	San Rafael, CA

HARDWARE—IBM PC family of computers

Drives—Disks and Tapes

There are a great variety of offerings, as independent devices attached to an IBM, or as parts of an IBM PC look-alike computer. The reader is advised to scan some periodicals. Here are four disk drives for under $1,000 reviewed and compared in "Special IBM Issue," *BYTE*, 10, no.11 (Fall, 1985), 203-208.

Megaflight 100 (10MB)	Kamerman Labs Inc.	Beaverton, OR
Rodime (10MB)	Micro Design International, Inc.	Winter Park, FL
Syquest (30MB)	Micro Design International, Inc.	Winter Park, FL
The Sider (10MB)	First Class Peripherals	Carson City, NV

Graphics Controller Boards

See Appendix D for a discussion of graphics standards, graphics controller boards, and the variety of resolutions and color capabilities available. The following are a sample from over 60 graphics controller boards available.

Color 400	Sigma Designs	San Jose, CA
EGA	IBM Corp	Boca Raton, FL
Edge	Everex	Fremont, CA
Hercules	Hercules	San Jose, CA
Paradise Autoswitch EGA Card	Paradise Systems Inc.	Brisbane, CA
Preview	AST	Irvine, CA
Quad EGA+	Quadram Corp.	Norcross, GA
Revolution	Number Nine	Cambridge, MA
Spectrum	Genoa Systems Corp.	San Jose, CA
Tecmar	Tecmar, Inc.	Cleveland, OH
Ultra-Res	C.S.D. Inc.	Sudbury, MA
VEGA	Video-7	Milpitas, CA

Input Devices

ATT Truevision Image Capture	AT&T	Indianapolis, IN
Capture (image digitizer board)	Genoa Systems	San Jose, CA
Datacopy Model 700 Scanner	Datacopy Corp.	Mountain View, CA
Image Blue (optical scanner)	Image Communications, Inc.	Greenwich, CN
Image Scanner	Microtek	Gardena, CA
Introvoice V	The Voice Connection	Irvine, CA
Jet Scanner	Datacopy Corp.	Mountain View, CA
PC-Eye Video Capture	Chorus Data Systems, Inc.*	Merrimack, NH
Softstrip Computer Readable Print	Cauzin Systems, Inc.	Waterbury, CT
Summasketch drawing tablet	ZSoft Corp.	Marietta, GA

* Chorus Data Systems provides a wide variety of graphics software, digitizers, cameras, monitors, and telecommunications systems.

Memory expansion

Many offerings; often available with graphics board.

Monitors

Nanao Monitors	Nanao USA Corp.	Foster City, CA
Princeton Monitors	Princeton Graphics Systems	Princeton, NJ
WY-700 (15"; 1280 by 800)	Wyse Technology	San Jose, CA

Networks

Many offerings; no standards.

Presentation Graphics

Color Video Imager	Eastman Kodak Company	Rochester, NY
Polaroid Palette	Polaroid Corporation	Cambridge, MA
VideoShow (video generator)	General Parametrics Corp.	Berkeley, CA
Robotic Plotter *	Penman Products Corporation	Richardson, TX
Samurai Image Processor	Image Resource Corporation	Westlake Village, CA

* Low cost three pen color robot plotter—a fascinating product!

PRINTERS

Laser

Corona Laser Printer	Corona Data Systems, Inc.	Thousand Oaks, CA
Lasergrafix 800 Printer	Quality Micro Systems	Mobile, AL
LaserWriter	Apple Computer, Inc.	Cupertino, CA
HP Laserjet	Hewlett-Packard Company	Palo Alto, CA
QMS KISS	Quality Micro Systems	Mobile, AL

WORKSTATIONS

The following are a very few of the many workstations available. The list includes basic units used by producers of turnkey systems to develop computer aided design, publishing, TV production, and advertiser animation systems, as well as a small selection of turnkey systems. Systems range in price from a base of approximately ten thousand to many thousands of dollars.

Basic Units

Apollo	Apollo Computer Inc.	Chelmsford, MA
CDP 4000 Series	Computervision	Bedford, MA
Graphics Workstations	Evans and Sutherland Corp.	Salt Lake City, UT
IBM RT PC	IBM Corporation	Boca Raton, FL
MicroVAX II	Digital Equipment Corp.	Maynard, MA
PERQ Graphics Workstation	PERQ Systems Corporation	Pittsburgh, PA
Sun Workstation	Sun Microsystems	Mountain View, CA
Tektronix Stations	Tektronix, Inc.	Beaverton, OR

Turnkey Systems

Advanced Personal Station (CAD)	Auto-Trol Technology Corp.	Denver, CO
Alias/1 3D	Alias Research Inc.	Toronto, ON
Aurora 75 (color 3D animation)	Aurora Systems	San Francisco, CA
Bravo! (CAD)	Applicon, Inc.	Burlington, MA
Documenter (publishing)	Xerox Corp.	El Segundo, CA
Inovion Personal Graphics System	Inovion	Layton, UT
Interleaf (publishing)	Interleaf, Inc.	Cambridge, MA
Kodak Image Mgmt. System(KIMS)	Eastman Kodak Company	Rochester, NY
Olivetti FileNet Sys. (image proc.)	Olivetti Canada Ltd.	Markham, ON
PictureMaker (color 3D animation)	Cubicomp Inc.	Berkeley, CA
Power Station (publishing)	Corel System Corporation	Toronto, ONT
TGV Vitesse (publishing)	Commercial Scientific Corp.	Palo Alto, CA

APPENDIX D

GRAPHICS STANDARDS*

There is a strong trend for all microcomputers to be graphics-based. Earlier microcomputers only supported text and largely ignored graphics. On graphics-based computers, text is simply treated as another form of graphics.

On the Macintosh, there is a built-in program in read only memory (ROM), called Quick-Draw, to which all Macintosh applications must send instructions in order for images and text to be displayed. Because all programs share this common set of instructions they can easily share pictures and text. Thus, the user of the Apple Macintosh experiences an integration and unformity of operation because of the standard demanded by the existence of QuickDraw in memory.

On the IBM PC, however, there are no provisions for graphics. There is, therefore, no standard. If graphics are desired, then a graphics board must be added to the basic IBM PC system. Further, all applications for the IBM PC specify graphics format differently. This makes the sharing of images more difficult or impossible.

IBM has a strong influence in the industry; what IBM decides to produce and support determines a strong trend, not necessarily a standard. IBM has produced a board called the *Enhanced Graphics Adapter (EGA)*. However, there are a number of other graphics boards for the IBM PC family of computers which function differently from the EGA board. An application program must be written to function on a given board in order for it to work on a system that contains that board. Therefore, if there are several boards currently in prominent use, a software developer must write a different graphics board driver for each board with which they want their software to function.

There are ways around this dilemma. One approach is for the industry to decide on a graphics standard; that is, *a uniform way of specifying pictures and text*. Then each graphics board would use this standard, and software compatibility and a uniform interface for users (so that skills learned with one application would transfer to other applications) would emerge. This has not happened as yet in the IBM PC environment.

Another approach is for manufacturers to produce graphics boards that emulate, and even switch automatically between, different graphics modes. For example, the *Autoswitch EGA Card* from Paradise Systems Inc. (South San Francisco, CA) emulates the IBM's Enhanced Graphics Adapter (EGA) and several other adapters, including IBM's Monochrome Display Adapter, IBM's Color Graphics Adapter, Hercules Computer Technology's Monochrome Controller, and Plantronics' 16-color graphics board. The *Autoswitch EGA Card* automatically senses when a program is attempting to use another mode other than the one currently in use.

For the end-user, the above means that a watchful eye must be kept on whether incompatibilities will develop as new applications are acquired. Manufacturers of boards and publishers of software will, of course, attempt to make all software work on all boards. This may not be possible, and it will be up to the user to protect his or her own interests.

---

* The information in this appendix is taken primarily from an article by Cary Lu, "Micros Get Graphic," *High Technology*, 6, 3, March, 1986. Lu's discussion is much more extensive.

APPENDIX E

CHARTS FOR EVALUATING GRAPHICS SYSTEMS

See Chapter 15, pages 366 through 368, for detailed instructions on the use of the charts. Each of the charts that follow are organized as follows:

- The name of the type of graphics software or hardware being evaluated
- The evaluation criteria
- Blank spaces for entering additional criteria
- Space for entering both ratings: **R** stands for the rating of a system on a feature, and **W** stands for the weight given to reflect the importance of a feature

In addition, a blank chart is provided for the reader to design his or her own charts for evaluating and comparing other graphics software or hardware *not* covered by the charts provided.

Instructions

1. Place the *highest weighting* being used next to all features that are critical. Use critical features or criteria *only* to initially evaluate and compare software and hardware. Only progress to the use of additional features if a decision cannot be made based on critical criteria.

2. *Rate* software or hardware on the critical criteria.

3. Multiply ratings by weightings, sum, and divide total by the number of critical features.

4. Divide cost of software or hardware by the result obtained in step 3.

Chart E1: General Features

Feature	R.	W.	Result	Feature	R.	W.	Result
Oper. Sys.	—	—	—	**Reliability**	—	—	—
UNIX	—	—	—	Error checking	—	—	—
MSDOS	—	—	—	Error capture	—	—	—
Macintosh	—	—	—	Error recovery	—	—	—
CP/M	—	—	—	Error messages	—	—	—
Other:_____	—	—	—	Response time	—	—	—
Other:_____	—	—	—	Release number	—	—	—
Other:_____	—	—	—	Age of release	—	—	—
Ease of use	—	—	—	**Service/Support**	—	—	—
Manuals	—	—	—	Available locally	—	—	—
Documentation	—	—	—	Technical support	—	—	—
Sign and start	—	—	—	Speed of response	—	—	—
Demo	—	—	—	Hot line	—	—	—
Card reference	—	—	—	Low cost upgrade	—	—	—
On-line tutorial	—	—	—	Support on mods.	—	—	—
Clarity of dialogue	—	—	—	Warranty/guarantee	—	—	—
Escape from menus	—	—	—	Extended license	—	—	—
Plain English	—	—	—	Vendor reputation	—	—	—
Undo facility	—	—	—	Years in trade	—	—	—
Link to other appl.	—	—	—	User ratings	—	—	—
Window mgt.	—	—	—	**Industry Support**	—	—	—
Cursor control	—	—	—	Compatibility	—	—	—
Training to use	—	—	—	Expandability	—	—	—
Training to profic.	—	—	—	Transportability	—	—	—
Easy to remember	—	—	—	No. of installations	—	—	—
Suitable naive user	—	—	—	**Oper. Features**	—	—	—
Suitable expert user	—	—	—	Multi-user	—	—	—
Copy protected	—	—	—	Security	—	—	—
Response speed	—	—	—	Hard disk compat.	—	—	—
Search/sort speed	—	—	—	Auto backup	—	—	—
_____	—	—	—	_____	—	—	—
_____	—	—	—	_____	—	—	—
_____	—	—	—	_____	—	—	—
_____	—	—	—	_____	—	—	—
_____	—	—	—	_____	—	—	—

TOTAL: ____   TOTAL: ____

Performance Index= Sum (Rating x Weight) / Number of Features   = _____

Cost Performance Index = Cost / Performance Index   = _____

Chart E2: Presentation Graphics

Feature	R.	W.	Result	Feature	R.	W.	Result
Editing	___	___	___	Font choices	___	___	___
Moving	___	___	___	Font size choices	___	___	___
Centering	___	___	___	Multiple axes	___	___	___
Sizing	___	___	___	Multiple on page	___	___	___
Speed	___	___	___	Chart format options	___	___	___
Integration	___	___	___	Combine charts	___	___	___
Orientation of text	___	___	___	Customize charts	___	___	___
Slide presentation	___	___	___	Predefined charts	___	___	___
Float labels/legends	___	___	___	Flexibility	___	___	___
Stack/rotate legends	___	___	___	Quality	___	___	___
Line size	___	___	___	Freehand	___	___	___
Memory required	___	___	___	Plotter support	___	___	___
Pies	___	___	___	Histograms	___	___	___
proportional	___	___	___	Input support	___	___	___
exploded	___	___	___	Printer support	___	___	___
Bars	___	___	___	Line charts	___	___	___
stacked	___	___	___	line plot	___	___	___
clustered	___	___	___	scatter plot	___	___	___
vertical	___	___	___	curve fitting	___	___	___
horizontal	___	___	___	statistical	___	___	___
3D	___	___	___	log	___	___	___
Data other programs	___	___	___	Fill-in (patterns)	___	___	___
Fill-in (color)	___	___	___	Animation effects	___	___	___
Step and repeat	___	___	___	Rotation capabil.	___	___	___
_____	___	___	___	_____	___	___	___
_____	___	___	___	_____	___	___	___
_____	___	___	___	_____	___	___	___
_____	___	___	___	_____	___	___	___
_____	___	___	___	_____	___	___	___
_____	___	___	___	_____	___	___	___
	TOTAL:	___			TOTAL:	___	

Performance Index= Sum (Rating x Weight) / Number of Features   = _____

Cost Performance Index = Cost / Performance Index   = _____

Chart E3: Computer Aided Design (CAD)

Feature	R.	W.	Result	Feature	R.	W.	Result
Major capabilities							
2D drafting	___	___	___	3D drafting	___	___	___
3D Wire frame	___	___	___	Solids modeling	___	___	___
Contour maps	___	___	___	Surface plots	___	___	___
Full perspect. view	___	___	___	Full rotate capabil.	___	___	___
Number of vectors	___	___	___	Complexity capab.	___	___	___
Rubber banding	___	___	___	Layer handling	___	___	___
DBMS	___	___	___	Text management	___	___	___
Graphics com. def.	___	___	___	List generation	___	___	___
_____	___	___	___	_____	___	___	___
_____	___	___	___	_____	___	___	___
Data entry							
Absolute coord.	___	___	___	Line types	___	___	___
Relative coord.	___	___	___	Line weights	___	___	___
Polar coord.	___	___	___	Help commands	___	___	___
Freehand	___	___	___	Text styles	___	___	___
Color	___	___	___	Arcs-2 pts.	___	___	___
Arcs-2 pt. & center	___	___	___	Arcs-angle specif.	___	___	___
Circle-rad. & center	___	___	___	Circle-diameter	___	___	___
Circle-3 pts.	___	___	___	Ellipse	___	___	___
Bezier curves	___	___	___	Curve smoothing	___	___	___
Fill irregular shape	___	___	___	Fill with color	___	___	___
Crosshatch	___	___	___	User-defined hatch	___	___	___
_____	___	___	___	_____	___	___	___
_____	___	___	___	_____	___	___	___
Edit Control							
Cursor style change	___	___	___	Coordinate dial	___	___	___
Status on screen	___	___	___	Status of item	___	___	___
Ability to pan	___	___	___	Zoom by scaling	___	___	___
Zoom by window	___	___	___	Move item	___	___	___
Move group of items	___	___	___	Move by window	___	___	___
Move between layers	___	___	___	Move and rotate	___	___	___
Move and scale	___	___	___	_____	___	___	___
_____	___	___	___	_____	___	___	___
_____	___	___	___	_____	___	___	___
		TOTAL:	___			TOTAL:	___

Performance Index= Sum (Rating x Weight) / Number of Features   = _____

Cost Performance Index = Cost / Performance Index   = _____

Chart E3 Computer Aided Design (CAD) (Continued)

Feature	R.	W.	Result	Feature	R.	W.	Result
Copy Features							
Copy item	___	___	___	Copy group of items	___	___	___
Copy from disk	___	___	___	Copy by window	___	___	___
Window to disk	___	___	___	Between layers	___	___	___
Copy and rotate	___	___	___	Copy and scale	___	___	___
_____	___	___	___	_____	___	___	___
_____	___	___	___	_____	___	___	___
Erase Features							
Erase item	___	___	___	Erase group of items	___	___	___
Erase by window	___	___	___	Erase a layer	___	___	___
Erase a shape	___	___	___	Erase previous	___	___	___
Erase beyond prev.	___	___	___	Restore last	___	___	___
Restore beyond last	___	___	___				
_____	___	___	___	_____	___	___	___
_____	___	___	___	_____	___	___	___
Partial Deletes							
Lines	___	___	___	Arcs	___	___	___
Circles	___	___	___	Ellipses	___	___	___
Trapezoids	___	___	___	Solids	___	___	___
Irregular shapes	___	___	___	Groups or blocks	___	___	___
Multiple layers	___	___	___	Multiple colors	___	___	___
_____	___	___	___	_____	___	___	___
_____	___	___	___	_____	___	___	___
Text Capabilities							
Number of fonts	___	___	___	User-definable fonts	___	___	___
Width scaling	___	___	___	Height scaling	___	___	___
Rotation	___	___	___	Center justify	___	___	___
Word processor	___	___	___	_____	___	___	___
_____	___	___	___	_____	___	___	___
_____	___	___	___	_____	___	___	___
		TOTAL:	___			TOTAL:	___

Performance Index= Sum (Rating x Weight) / Number of Features   = _____

Cost Performance Index = Cost / Performance Index   = _____

Chart E3 Computer Aided Design (CAD) (Continued)

Feature	R.	W.	Result	Feature	R.	W.	Result
Other functions							
Explode	___	___	___	Quick save to disk	___	___	___
Autosave	___	___	___	Autosave user-def.	___	___	___
Graphic libraries	___	___	___	Merge with drawing	___	___	___
Merge exploded	___	___	___	Merge/scale/rotate	___	___	___
Autodimensioning	___	___	___	Angular dimension.	___	___	___
Dimen. switching	___	___	___	Variables dimen.	___	___	___
Dimen. leaders	___	___	___	Center mark dimen.	___	___	___
Diameter dimen.	___	___	___	Radius dimen.	___	___	___
Blocks	___	___	___	Nested blocks	___	___	___
Grid user-defined	___	___	___	Multiple X & Y scales	___	___	___
Snap to grid	___	___	___	Mixed color in layer	___	___	___
Object snap	___	___	___	Snap by endpoint	___	___	___
Snap by midpoint	___	___	___	Snap by node	___	___	___
Snap by quadrant	___	___	___	Snap by intersection	___	___	___
Snap by insert	___	___	___	Snap by perpendic.	___	___	___
Snap by tangent	___	___	___	Snap by nearest	___	___	___
Def. attrib. of layers	___	___	___	Regen. active layer	___	___	___
Plot active layer	___	___	___	Save active layer	___	___	___
Unlimited layers	___	___	___	Fillets	___	___	___
Menu on screen	___	___	___	Menu for editor	___	___	___
Menu for I/O	___	___	___	Menu user-defined	___	___	___
Macro commands	___	___	___	Icon Interface	___	___	___
Shape dragging	___	___	___	Named views	___	___	___
Rotate grid/snap/axis	___	___	___	Isometric planes	___	___	___
Attribute assignment	___	___	___	Attribute editing	___	___	___
Attrib. extract to DB	___	___	___	Attrib.extract to ESS	___	___	___
Extract to post-proc.	___	___	___	Mirroring	___	___	___
CAM utilities	___	___	___	CAE utilities	___	___	___
Math calculations							
Engineering	___	___	___	Architectural	___	___	___
Precision	___	___	___	Scale choices	___	___	___
Distance	___	___	___	Area	___	___	___
Irregular area	___	___	___	Volume	___	___	___
Angle	___	___	___	Dimensions	___	___	___
Diagr. from data	___	___	___	_____	___	___	___

TOTAL: ____   TOTAL: ____

Performance Index= Sum (Rating x Weight) / Number of Features   = _____

Cost Performance Index = Cost / Performance Index   = _____

Chart E4 Paint Programs

Feature	R.	W.	Result	Feature	R.	W.	Result
Input device support	___	___	___	Output dev. support	___	___	___
Colors	___	___	___	Command menu	___	___	___
Color mixing	___	___	___	Color blending	___	___	___
3D	___	___	___	Windows	___	___	___
Variety brushes	___	___	___	Custom brushes	___	___	___
Variety sprays	___	___	___	Custom sprays	___	___	___
Patterns	___	___	___	Custom patterns	___	___	___
Shades	___	___	___	Tints	___	___	___
Line variation	___	___	___	Shape variation	___	___	___
Rotation	___	___	___	Animation	___	___	___
Realtime playback	___	___	___	In-betweening	___	___	___
Cell animation	___	___	___	Spin rotations	___	___	___
Color cycling	___	___	___	Perspective	___	___	___
Fonts variety	___	___	___	Shape construction	___	___	___
Size variation	___	___	___	Zoom	___	___	___
Pixel touchup	___	___	___	Move	___	___	___
Copy	___	___	___	Erase	___	___	___
Fill	___	___	___	Lasso	___	___	___
Overlay	___	___	___	Mirroring	___	___	___
Undo	___	___	___	Negative imaging	___	___	___
Scaling	___	___	___	Panning	___	___	___
Translating	___	___	___	Stenciling	___	___	___
Anti-aliasing	___	___	___	Speed	___	___	___
Broadcast quality	___	___	___	Videotext capab.	___	___	___
Video prod. capab.	___	___	___	Weathergraph. cap.	___	___	___
_____	___	___	___	_____	___	___	___
_____	___	___	___	_____	___	___	___
_____	___	___	___	_____	___	___	___
_____	___	___	___	_____	___	___	___
	TOTAL:	___			TOTAL:	___	

Performance Index= Sum (Rating x Weight) / Number of Features   = _____

Cost Performance Index = Cost / Performance Index   = _____

Chart E5 Graphics Terminal or Workstation

Feature	R.	W.	Result	Feature	R.	W.	Result
Main processor	___	___	___	Graphics display	___	___	___
Graphics processor	___	___	___	Graphics buffer	___	___	___
Resolution	___	___	___	Input device support	___	___	___
Variable resolution	___	___	___	Accuracy of device	___	___	___
Bits per pixel	___	___	___	Point/select ability	___	___	___
Color palette	___	___	___	Image size	___	___	___
Screen size	___	___	___	Output device supp.	___	___	___
Screen orientation	___	___	___	Accuracy of device	___	___	___
Display speed	___	___	___	Output speed	___	___	___
Retrace speed	___	___	___	Output color options	___	___	___
RAM size	___	___	___	Ergonomics	___	___	___
Hard disk size	___	___	___	Integration	___	___	___
Floppy disk size	___	___	___	Flexibility	___	___	___
ROM primitives	___	___	___	Back-up	___	___	___
Quality slide gener.	___	___	___	Other film formats	___	___	___
Video presentation	___	___	___	Camera res.(option)	___	___	___
Hard copy options	___	___	___	_____	___	___	___
_____	___	___	___	_____	___	___	___
_____	___	___	___	_____	___	___	___
_____	___	___	___	_____	___	___	___
_____	___	___	___	_____	___	___	___
_____	___	___	___	_____	___	___	___
_____	___	___	___	_____	___	___	___
_____	___	___	___				

TOTAL: ____   TOTAL: ____

Performance Index= Sum (Rating x Weight) / Number of Features   = _____

Cost Performance Index = Cost / Performance Index   = _____

Chart E6 Application/Product: _____

Feature	R.	W.	Result	Feature	R.	W.	Result

TOTAL: ____   TOTAL: ____

Performance Index= Sum (Rating x Weight) / Number of Features   = _____

Cost Performance Index = Cost / Performance Index   = _____

Author Index

Subject Index

Product Index